THE ROUTLEDGE

CRITICAL DICTIONARY

OF

Feminism and Postfeminism

THE ROUTLEDGE

CRITICAL
DICTIONARY

OF

Feminism and
Postfeminism

Edited by
Sarah Gamble

Routledge
New York

The Routledge critical
dictionary of feminism and

Published in the United States of America in 2000 by
Routledge
29 West 35th Street
New York, NY 10001

Originally published in Great Britain in 1999 by
Icon Books Ltd.
Grange Road
Duxford
Cambridge CB2 4QF

Library of Congress Cataloging-in-Publication Data

The Routledge critical dictionary of feminism and postfeminism / edited by
Sarah Gamble.
        p. cm. — (The Routledge critical dictionary series)
Includes index.
ISBN 0-415-92518-5 (paper: alk. paper)
1. Feminism—Dictionaries. I. Gamble, Sarah. II. Series.
HQ1115 .R68 2000
305.42'03—dc21   99-054689

CONTENTS

v

CONTENTS

EDITOR'S INTRODUCTION

THE CONTROVERSIES OF FEMINISM

It would not be overstating the case to say that feminism has been one of the most far-reaching movements this century, whose influence has been felt in every area of social, political and cultural life worldwide. Indeed, feminism has achieved the dubious distinction of becoming an utterly familiar part of our cultural landscape. We all know, or think we know, what feminism means, and we all, to a greater or lesser extent, pay it lip-service. Yet for most people, it appears, feminism remains something 'out there' rather than an internalised, actualised belief; a view promoted by a number of recent highly publicised surveys, which appear to show that few women are now willing to explicitly identify themselves as feminist.

However, that is not to say that all the goals feminism has set itself have been achieved, since the changes it has set in motion may be as much defensive as accommodating, with male institutions striving to protect cherished areas of privilege and superiority. So although, as the very existence of this dictionary proves, feminism is a theory (or set of theories), something capable of being studied and debated on an academic level, it is simultaneously a movement which retains a commitment to change the real world outside the universities.

But what, exactly, is feminism? A general definition might state that it is the belief that women, purely and simply because they are women, are treated inequitably within a society which is organised to prioritise male viewpoints and concerns. Within this patriarchal paradigm, women become everything men are not (or do not want to be seen to be): where men are regarded as strong, women are weak; where men are rational, they are emotional; where men are active, they are passive; and so on. Under this rationale, which aligns them everywhere with negativity, women are denied equal access to the world of public concerns as well as of cultural representation. Put simply, feminism seeks to change this situation.

The Routledge Critical Dictionary of Feminism and Postfeminism cannot lay claim to the distinction of being the first dictionary of feminism to be published. However, it appears at an apposite moment, a period in which 'feminism' is becoming an increasingly contested term. This is something this volume is intended to highlight, as indicated by the inclusion of the controversial term 'postfeminism' in its title. The introduction of the word 'postfeminism' into the popular lexicon has been taken to imply that we have somehow moved beyond the need for feminist activism, hence its linkage to the work of a disparate group of British and American writers, such as Naomi Wolf, Rene Denfeld and Natasha Walter, who argue in support of a change in the feminist agenda. Consequently it has come under extensive attack by feminists who still adhere to the tenets of the second wave as a betrayal of more than a century of feminist activism. Whether or not this is the case, the 'traditional' feminist versus the 'post' feminist debate is vociferous and ongoing, its fires stoked, no doubt, by a media only too willing to capitalise on the opportunity to portray it as a break in the massed ranks of the 'sisterhood'.

What this dictionary is intended to illustrate, however, is that feminism has always been a dynamic and multifaceted movement. Although, as has already been stated, it can very generally be categorised as the struggle to increase women's access to equality in a male-dominated culture, there has never been a universally agreed agenda for feminism. Exactly what 'equality' for women entails, the means by which it is to be achieved, even the exact nature of the obstacles it faces, are all disputed issues. To read feminism's history, therefore, is to uncover a record of debates, schisms and differing viewpoints and, approached in this way, the postfeminist debate merely dramatises a situation which has always, in fact, held true for feminism, a movement which thrives on diversity. So, to read postfeminism as indicating that the feminist movement has fragmented beyond the point of no return could be a misinterpretation, since it may constitute nothing more than the latest divergence in the constantly shifting parameters of feminist thought. Additionally, what can be termed 'postfeminism' has followed the example set by theoretical second wave feminism in negotiating fruitful relationships with postmodernism, drawing on theories of difference, identity and deconstruction in order to interrogate the ways in which the category 'woman' is constructed.

STRUCTURE AND SCOPE OF THE VOLUME

The Routledge Critical Dictionary of Feminism and Postfeminism goes beyond the scope of a simple dictionary in its inclusion of essays alongside lists of definitions of names and terms, thus enabling the areas covered by this volume to be elaborated on in greater depth and detail than would ordinarily be the case. These essays form Part I of the book, and they have been collected and arranged with two aims in mind.

Firstly, the four essays with which the book opens, when read together, give an overview of the development of feminist thought in Great Britain and America. Although feminism is conventionally dated from the inception of the first wave in the nineteenth century, this study looks further back in order to demonstrate that women were expressing views we would now identify as 'feminist' long before the development of a discourse of liberation. The essay on 'Early Feminism' is followed by essays on 'First Wave Feminism' and 'Second Wave Feminism', which introduce the reader to these crucial periods in the formation of the feminism we know today. This historical section is brought up-to-date with the inclusion of an introduction to the postfeminist debate, and the diverse ways in which this most recent offshoot of the feminist movement is being regarded.

Although the trajectory traced in this section of the volume is chronological, in that it begins in the seventeenth century and ends in the late twentieth century, the reader must not be tempted to thus conclude that each phase in the feminist agenda can be assigned a date on which it officially ended. It is certainly the case that each movement can be defined through reference to certain key historical moments or movements – for example, the impetus for the first wave can be traced back to the eighteenth-century Enlightenment project, while the advent of the second wave is indebted to the rise in political and student activism across Europe and America in the 1960s. However, any consideration of the history of the feminist movement must conclude that one feminist wave never retreats entirely in the face of the one that follows it. Thus, in the early decades of the twentieth century, the emphasis on social and political emancipation that was the essence of first wave feminism coexisted alongside a desire (expressed, for example, by female modernist writers such as Virginia Woolf and Dorothy Richardson) to define a 'feminine' identity and discourse: an impulse which was to become a central concern of certain sectors of second wave feminism. Similarly, although some postfeminists would claim otherwise, agendas and attitudes born out of the second wave remain of immediate concern to many women, with the result that it is difficult to treat postfeminism – also sometimes referred to as feminism's 'third wave' – from earlier manifestations of feminism.

Secondly, the essays that follow examine the impact of the theories and ideas that have come out of the feminist movement on various areas of culture, such as literature, philosophy, film and religion. Mindful of the fact that feminism is not just a European or American phenomenon, an essay on 'Feminism and the Developing World' has also been included in order to give the reader some idea of the controversies and liberating possibilities evoked in the translation of feminism into a non-Western context.

Together, these essays define the perimeters of this dictionary, which concentrates on the influence of feminism on cultural theory. The political and sociological areas of the feminist debate are not addressed in detail, as, for the most part, they lie outside the scope of this publication. However, there is no definitive cut-off point, and the reader will find some names and terms associated with sociology and politics included here, indicative of the way in which different areas of feminist thought interlink in productive ways.

Part II takes the form of a dictionary, which gives the reader information regarding many of feminism's most prominent thinkers, activists, performers and writers, as well as the names of figures who, while not feminists themselves, have informed the feminist theoretical debate, such as Sigmund Freud, Jacques Lacan and Michel Foucault. Definitions are also provided of key terms and concepts within feminist discourse, particularly those which, because of their links with psychoanalytic, poststructuralist and deconstructive theory, may be particularly baffling to the general reader.

It is also important to emphasise that, particularly where the essays are concerned, no editorial attempt has been made to 'iron out' differences between contributors, which has allowed points of difference to emerge which illustrate the diversity that is a characteristic of the movement itself.

How to Use This Book

The material contained within this dictionary can be accessed in several ways. The self-explanatory nature of the titles of the essays in Part I, and the alphabetical arrangement of Part II, make it easy to 'dip into' in order to find an isolated fact or concept. However, the names and terms included in Part II are highlighted wherever else they appear in the text, thus facilitating a progressive process of reading, which will enable a fuller picture to be assembled from separate, but interlocking, pieces of information.

For example, if you want to know more about cyberfeminism, you might begin with the dictionary definition, where certain names and terms are highlighted to indicate that they exist as separate entries. Supposing you decide to follow up the entry on Donna **Haraway**, you would find a brief summary of her career, publications and influential theories, again with certain names and terms highlighted – **cyborg, postmodern, nature, culture, technological, 'other'** – which you could follow up if you so chose. In this way, you would build up a picture of feminist views on technology, which might eventually lead you to read the more detailed essay 'Women and New Technologies' in Part I. It is up to you to decide how far you wish to go!

CONTRIBUTORS

The contributors to *The Routledge Critical Dictionary of Feminism and Postfeminism* are drawn from a number of different academic disciplines, thus allowing the range of feminism's influence on many different areas of thought to be fully represented. They are, in alphabetical order: Pamela Sue Anderson, Joanne Benford, Fiona Carson, Peter Dempsey, Natalie Fenton, Sarah Gamble, John Gange, Mel Gibson, Janet Hand, Stephanie Hodgson-Wright, Alison Jasper, Janis Jeffries, Alka Kurian, George Larke, Jill LeBihan, Jill Marshall, Andrea Peterson, Sophia Phoca, Danielle Ramsey, Valerie Sanders, John Storey, Mary M. Talbot, Sue Thornham, Liza Tsaliki, Angie Werndley, Rosie White and Alison Younger.

I
FEMINISM: ITS HISTORY AND CULTURAL CONTEXT

1

EARLY FEMINISM

STEPHANIE HODGSON-WRIGHT

INTRODUCTION

In Early Modern England **feminist** activity took a different form from
the feminist movement of the twentieth century. Indeed, the issue of
whether or not the efforts made by women for better treatment at the
hands of men in this period can really be called 'feminism' at all is still
being debated. However, our own century has shown, and is still showing, us the massive variety of ways in which feminist thought, writing and
action can manifest itself. The twentieth century began with the
suffragettes fighting for the right to vote, and at its close we see the **Spice
Girls** in bra tops asserting **'girl power'**. The late twentieth-century
media has room for both Germaine **Greer** and Julie **Burchill**, whose
discussion on BBC Radio 4's *Woman's Hour* (February 1999) highlighted that differences in **class**, **education**, opportunities and generation will shape different kinds of feminisms. If feminism solidified into
a political movement in the 1960s and 1970s, the millennium sees it
diversifying again. In the light of this, when we look backwards into the
history of women's struggle against **oppression**, we are able to identify
instances of resistance which we can legitimately identify as feminist in
nature, without judging those instances unfavourably against the organised feminism of the twentieth century. For the purposes of this essay,
'feminism' will be defined as any attempt to contend with **patriarchy** in
its many manifestations between 1550–1700. Chris Weedon's definition
of patriarchy in *Feminist Practice and Poststructuralist Theory* (1987) will
be employed here:

> The term 'patriarchal' refers to power relations in which women's inter-
> ests are subordinated to the interests of men. These power relations take
> on many forms, from the sexual division of labour and the social organ-
> isation of procreation to the internalised norms of femininity by which we
> live. Patriarchal power rests on social meaning given to biological sexual
> difference.

3

Taken together, the two definitions may appear to cover a great deal of ground. This might be the case if they were applied to the twentieth century. But the period 1550–1700 saw no legislated improvement in the position of women. At the end of the period, as at the beginning, women did not have any formal rights in local or national government, including the right to vote. Although conditions for the education of women largely improved from 1550–1700, women were barred from receiving a university education and the concomitant benefits. Having said that, the vast majority of the population, male and female, had no voting rights, and but little access to education and legal representation. It is certainly not true to say that all men were more empowered than all women. Yet, whilst the aristocratic lady might enjoy more socio-economic power than a male apprentice, she enjoyed less than a man of equivalent rank, just as the male apprentice enjoyed more power than a woman of a similar social standing. Women had no recourse to law for equality of pay and conditions, and married women had no legal independence from their husbands.

This latter condition was exacerbated by the fact that it was very difficult for women to achieve economic independence, and so **marriage** was one of the few ways in which women could secure their future. Unless exceptional circumstances prevailed, upon marriage, all property that belonged to the wife, and all property that she subsequently received, automatically became her husband's. The financial arrangements of a marriage throughout the period were, largely, this: a wife would bring a 'dowry' with her, which was as substantial an amount of property (money, valuables, land) as she and her family could put together. In return for this dowry, the husband provided the wife with a 'jointure', the purpose of which was to maintain her for the rest of her life. Where the wife predeceased the husband, this merely meant keeping her in food, shelter and clothing, the scale of which was determined by the means and disposition of the husband. Where the husband predeceased the wife, the 'jointure' was usually expressed as a lifetime's interest in a property, so that the widow would have the means and a place to live. Childbearing was a major part of the wife's role, be it to provide male heirs to her husband's lands and titles or to provide a source of labour. However, women had no rights over their children; the bringing up, education and disposal in marriage were entirely the preserve of the father. In the eyes of the law, they belonged to their fathers, and where parents fell out or separated (divorce was not possible for most people), the father could prevent the mother having any contact with her children.

The 'feminism' engendered under such circumstances was inevitably one which had to change attitudes before it sought to change conditions. Most feminist writers of the period sought to challenge the prevailing idea that women were an inferior branch of the human race, tainted by Eve's transgression in the Garden of Eden (Genesis 3) with fewer capabilities than men for moral behaviour and rational thought. The events of the period 1550–1700 presented women with grounds upon which to challenge the inevitability of patriarchal authority. The long and successful reign of Elizabeth I (1558–1603) and the cultural influences of powerful women such as Anna of Denmark (queen to James VI and I), the Countess of Bedford, the Countess of Pembroke and Henrietta Maria (queen to Charles I) demonstrated that, given the right opportunities, women could flourish in politics and the arts. The Civil War and Interregnum (1642–60), and the Glorious Revolution (1688) showed that the supreme patriarchal power of the King could be successfully contested by his male and female subjects. After the Restoration of Charles II in 1660, the rise of the professional woman in the arts as performer, dramatist and poet gave both an effective channel to express feminist ideas and a practical vehicle for giving the lie to notions of women's inferiority.

The rest of this chapter deals with three arenas, conceptual and actual, in which feminist thought and activity could be seen to be taking place. The first section deals with a particular strategy to combat the negative view of women drawn from Judeo-Christian writing. The second section looks at the ways in which women began to argue that their 'inferiority' was culturally imposed rather than naturally derived, and proposed methods for alleviating their position. The third section looks at early forms of or proposals for 'separatism', emphasising the benefits of female support networks, and takes into account the ways in which women writers, in the later part of the century, supported each other in print and in practice.

REVISIONISM

One of the first things any group seeking public recognition will do is try to create a sense of its history; indeed, to own and determine that history. Classical philosophy, the Scriptures and the early Church all pronounced upon women, in almost exclusively **masculine** voices. Aristotelian philosophy deemed women to be 'inferior men', and this was corroborated by the interpretation of the creation of Eve as 'posterior et inferior' (last and lesser). Later, in Medieval Europe, the *Querelle des Femmes* developed; this was a literary debate in which male writers attacked and defended women. The humanist philosophers of the Renaissance generally put forward enlightened views of women, especially with regard to their education, yet with the caveat that educated women should confine their learning to the private, domestic sphere. In his *Education of a Christian Woman* (trans. Richard Hyrde, 1540) the humanist Juan Luis Vives wrote:

> [I]t neither becometh a woman to rule a school, nor to live among men, or speak abroad, and shake off her demureness and honesty, either altogether or else a great part: which if she be good, it were better to be at home within and unknown to other folks. And in company to hold her tongue demurely. And let few see her, and none at all hear her. . . . For Adam was the first made, and after Eve, and Adam was not betrayed, the woman was betrayed into the breach of the commandment. Therefore because a woman is a frail thing, and of weak discretion, and that may lightly be deceived: which thing our first mother Eve sheweth, whom the devil caught with a light argument. Therefore a woman should not teach, lest when she hath taken a false opinion and believe of anything, she spread it into the hearers[.]

Here, Vives refers to the book of Genesis in the Old Testament and St. Paul's Epistles in the New Testament to support his recommendations.

It was not until the later sixteenth century in England that women entered the debate in their own voices. In an age when the ideal of female behaviour was 'chaste, silent and obedient', the very act of a woman publishing, or publicly pronouncing her own polemic, constituted a challenge to patriarchal authority and can therefore be identified as 'feminist'. The early polemicists returned to the very sources used to justify the oppression of women. When Jane Anger wrote the first piece of feminist polemic in English, *Her Protection for Women* (1589), she put an entirely different gloss upon Genesis:

> The creation of man and woman at the first, he being formed . . . of dross and filthy clay, did so remain until God saw that in him his workmanship was good, and therefore by the transformation of the dust which was loathsome unto flesh it became purified. Then lacking a help for him, God, making woman of man's flesh that she might be purer than he, doth evidently show how far we women are more excellent than men.

Anger here refutes the notion of 'posterior et inferior', using the

6

progression of God's creation to point out that logically, Eve is last and *best*. Several other writers are anxious to recover Eve from taking all the blame for the fall of humankind, for this interpretation underpinned the negative view of women. Rachel Speght in *A Muzzle for Melastomus* (1617) argued that if women are the weaker sex, then Eve cannot take full responsibility for the fall, because the stronger Adam should have prevented her:

> Satan first assailed the woman, because where the hedge is lowest, most easy it is to get over, and she being the weaker vessel was with more facility to be seduced. Like as a crystal glass sooner receives a crack than a strong stone pot. Yet we shall find the offence of Adam and Eve almost to parallel: for as an ambitious desire of being made like unto God was the motive which caused her to eat, so likewise was it his. . . . And if Adam has not approved of that deed which Eve had done, and been willing to tread the steps which she had gone, he being her head would have reproved her, and have made the commandment a bit to restrain him from breaking his master's injunction.

Speght and other writers such as Aemilia (Bassano) Lanyer *in Salve Deus Rex Judaeorum* (1611), Esther Sowernam in *Ester Hath Hang'd Haman* (1617), Margaret (Fell) Fox in *Women's Speaking Justified* (1667) and Sarah (Fyge) Egerton in *The Female Advocate* (1686) offer reinterpretations of Genesis chapter 3 which demonstrate that Adam was as much to blame as Eve, if not more so, and that God recognised this by tempering Eve's punishment with mercy in that she should be the mother of the human race, and that one of her descendants would be the mother of Christ.

During the Civil War and Interregnum (1642–60), the emergence of radical religious sects created a window of opportunity for women preachers and prophesiers. The stress put upon the equality of souls before God by groups such as the Quakers and the Fifth Monarchists facilitated public proclamations upon religious and political issues by women such as Elizabeth Poole and Anna Trapnel. Once the precedent had been set, it was difficult to insist upon women relinquishing preaching and prophesying when the Monarchy was restored in 1660. Furthermore, the execution of Charles I in 1649, followed by the ultimate failure of the Republic, demonstrated that patriarchal rule was not an unassailable monolith, but an imperfect structure, subject to assault and defeat. Margaret Fox drew on the Scriptures in order to justify women's continuing right to speak and publish on matters of religion:

> [T]he Lord is pleased, when he mentions his Church, to call her by the name of Woman, by his Prophets, saying, "I have called thee as a Woman forsaken, and grieved in spirit, and as a wife of youth," [Isaiah 54]. . . . And David, when he was speaking of Christ and his Church, he saith, "The Kings Daughter is all glorious within, her clothing is of wrought gold; she shall be brought unto the King; with gladness and rejoycing shall they be brought; they shall enter into the Kings Pallace." [Psalms 45] . . . And John, when he saw the wonder that was in Heaven, he saw "a woman clothed with the Sun, and the Moon under her feet, and upon her head a Crown of twelve Stars" [Revelations 12]. . . . Thus much may prove that the Church of Christ is a woman, and those that speak against the woman's speaking, speak against the Church of Christ, and the Seed of the woman, which Seed is Christ; that is to say, Those that speak against the Power of the Lord, and the Spirit of the Lord speaking in a woman, simply by reason of her sex, or because she is a Woman, not regarding the Seed, and Spirit, and Power that speaks in her; such speak against Christ, and his Church, and are of the Seed of the Serpent, wherein lodgeth the enmity.

Women writers could also make use of the Scriptures, to provide precedents and role models. The Old Testament characters of Sarah, Rebecca, Esther, the Apocrypha character Susannah, together with New Testament characters such as Elizabeth, the Virgin Mary and Mary Magdalen, were frequently cited as a means of counterbalancing less positive characters from the Bible, such as Delilah and Jezebel, to destabilise the argument that women were naturally sinful and weak. Strong and virtuous women from Classical **mythology**, ancient Greek and Roman history, and recent European history were also cited, including Queen Elizabeth I, who provided an ideal exemplar for many women writers.

MATERIAL REALITIES

Whilst writing about women in the Scriptures and in European history pointed the way towards a revision of attitudes towards women at a very general level, women also tried to change ideas at a much more mundane level. Didactic writing by men about wifely behaviour constantly cited the writings of St. Paul to justify the complete subjection of wives to their husbands. For example, the following verses from his epistles to the Corinthians and Ephesians:

> Let your women keep silence in the churches; for it is not permitted unto them to speak; but they are commanded to be under obedience, as also saith the law.

8

And if they will learn any thing, let them ask their husbands at home: for it is a shame for women to speak in the church. [1 Corinthians 14:34–5]

Wives, submit yourselves unto your own husbands, as unto the Lord.

For the husband is the head of the wife, even as Christ is the head of the church: and he is the saviour of the body.

Therefore as the church is subject unto Christ, so let the wives be to their own husbands in every thing. [Ephesians 5:22–4]

However, the official 'Homily on Matrimony', first published in *Certain Sermons and Homilies* (1547), stressed mutual respect between husbands and wives, and demanded that, notwithstanding their position as the 'weaker vessel', wives should be treated well by their husbands.

St. Peter giveth this precept, saying; you husbands deal with your wives according to knowledge, giving honour to the wife as unto the weaker vessel, and as unto them that are heirs also of the grace of life, that your prayers be not hindered [1 Peter 3]. This precept doth particularly pertain to the husband. For he ought to be the leader and auctor of love, in cherishing and increasing concord, which then shall take place if he will use measurableness and not tyranny and if he yield some things to the woman.

Excessive severity by husbands was frowned upon, and the Protestant ideal of marriage stressed mutuality and cooperation between husband and wife. Addressing themselves to their immediate social context, women writers elaborated on these ideas to advocate a more empowered position for wives. More than one writer reminds the reader that God created Eve from Adam's side (as opposed to his head or foot), signifying that she should be his equal (as opposed to his ruler or servant). Furthermore, Rachel Speght says

The other end for which woman was made was to be a companion and helper for man and if she must be a helper, and but a helper, then are those husbands to be blamed which lay the whole burthen of domestical affairs and maintenance on the shoulders of their wives. For, as yoke-fellows they are to sustain part of each other's cares, griefs, and calamities. But as if two oxen be put in one yoke, the one being bigger than the other, the greater bears most weight, so the husband being the stronger vessel is to bear a greater burthen than his wife.

To counterbalance the material fact that they had no legal powers over their own children, some women emphasised the nurturing role of the

9

mother, especially as moral instructor and initial educator of her children. For example, Constantia Munda dedicates *The Worming of a Mad Dog* (1617) to her mother, the Lady Prudentia Munda:

> As first your pains in bearing me was such
> A benefit beyond requital that 'twere much
> To think what pangs of sorrow you sustained
> In childbirth, when mine infancy obtained
> The vital drawing in of air, so your love
> Mingled with care hath shown itself above
> The ordinary course of Nature. Seeing you still
> Are in perpetual Labor with me even until
> The second birth of education perfect me . . .
>   . . . Thus I pay
> My debt by taking up at interest, and lay
> To pawn that which I borrow of you: so
> The more I give, I take; I pay, I owe.
> Yet lest you think I forfeit shall my bond,
> I here present you with my writing hand.

Other women, such as Elizabeth Grymeston in *Miscellanea, Meditations, Memoratives* (1604) and Elizabeth Joceline in *The Mother's Legacie to her Unborn Child* (1624) used their role as mothers to justify the act of writing and publishing their work. Dorothy Leigh in *The Mother's Blessing* (1616) writes

> But lest you should marvel, my children, why I do not, according to the usual custom of women, exhort you by word and admonitions rather than by writing . . . know therefore that it was the motherly affection that I bear unto you all which made me now (as it often hath heretofore) forget myself in regard of you. Neither care I what you or any shall think of me if among many words I may write but one sentence which may make you labour for the spiritual food of the soul, which must be gathered every day out of the word, as the children of Israel gathered manna in the wilderness.

Whilst on the one hand women wrote to advocate a better deal within the institution for which most of them were destined, i.e., marriage, motherhood and the attendant domestic duties, others complained of the fact that these duties compromised their intellectual development. In 1656, Mary Oxlie wrote these telling lines (prefixed to an edition of William Drummond's *Poems*) which, whilst on one level appears to be defeatist, on another points out that if a woman is intellectually inferior to a man, it is because she is denied the same opportunities:

I Never rested on the Muses bed,
Nor dipped my Quill in the Thessalian Fountain,
My rustic Muse was rudely fostered,
And flies too low to reach the double mountain.
Then do not sparks with your bright suns compare,
Perfection in a Woman's work is rare;
From an untroubled mind should Verses flow;
My discontents makes mine too muddy show;
And hoarse encumbrances of houshold care
Where these remain, the Muses ne're repair.

Oxlie makes the important point that women's inferiority, rather than being natural, is culturally imposed. The evidence that women could, under the right circumstances, reach the same levels of intellectual development as men, had been in existence for many years. Certain women of the aristocracy and gentry classes stood as exemplars of female achievement in the sixteenth century, including Jane (Fitzalan) Lumley, Jane (Grey) Dudley, Margaret (More) Roper, Elizabeth (Tanfield) Cary and Queen Elizabeth I. By the end of the seventeenth century, some of them became part of the feminist historical narrative, for instance being cited by Bathsua (Pell) Makin as historical exemplars in *An Essay to Revive the Antient Education of Gentlewomen* (1673). In this, Makin develops Oxlie's argument:

> Custom, when it is inveterate, hath a mighty influence: it hath the force of Nature itself. The Barbarous custom to breed Women low, is grown general amongst us, and hath prevailed so far, that it is verily believed (especially amongst a sort of debauched Sots) that Women are not endued with Reason, as Men; nor capable of improvement by Education, as they are. It is looked upon as a monstrous thing, to pretend the contrary.

> . . . I verily think, Women were formerly Educated in the knowledge of Arts and Tongues, and by their Education, many did rise to a great height in Learning. Were Women thus Educated now, I am confident the advantage would be very great. . . .

> Were a competent number of Schools erected to Educate Ladies ingenuously, methinks I see how asham'd Men would be of their Ignorance, and how industrious the next Generation would be to wipe off their Reproach.

Makin's justification of the education of women also has a practical purpose: a postscript to her tract advertises her own school for gentlewomen at Tottenham-high-cross.

COMMUNITIES OF WOMEN

One of the crucial features in feminist activity is that women come together as women in order to provide mutual support against patriarchal oppression. In the Early Modern period, this occurred on a textual level and also in a practical fashion. Perhaps the earliest example of a woman creating an exclusively female community in a text is Aemilia Lanyer's *Salve Deus Rex Judaeorum*. This publication is a collection of poems and two pieces of prose which are addressed exclusively to women. The largest poem of the collection, which bears its title, is a feminist revisionist version of key events from the Scriptures, centring upon the crucifixion of Christ. Women, including Pilate's wife, are characterised as the virtuous onlookers who do not collude in his execution, whereas the men are cast as the Christ-killers. The other poems in the collection are exclusively addressed to royal and aristocratic women, although there are two addressed 'To all virtuous ladies in general' and 'To the virtuous reader'. The latter is also clearly directed to women:

> I have written this small volume, or little book, for the general use of all virtuous Ladies and Gentlewomen of this kingdom; and in commendation of some particular persons of our own sex. . . . And this have I done, to make known to the world, that all women deserve not to be blamed. . . . [I]t pleased our Lord and Saviour Jesus Christ, without the assistance of man, being free from original sin and all other sins, from the time of his conception, till the hour of his death, to be begotten of a woman, born of a woman, nourished of a woman, obedient to a woman; and that he healed woman, pardoned women, comforted women, yea . . . after his resurrection, appeared first to a woman, sent a woman to declare his most glorious resurrection to the rest of his Disciples. Many other examples I could allege of diverse faithful and virtuous women, who have in all ages not only been Confessors, but also endured most cruel martyrdom for their faith in Jesus Christ. All which is sufficient to enforce all good Christians and honourable minded men to speak reverently of our sex[.]

In *Renaissance Women* (1994), Diane Purkiss suggests that in her collection, Lanyer creates an 'interpretive community of female virtue . . . bringing together the power of women as readers in order to register and display that power'.

Women poets in the later half of the seventeenth century, including Katherine Philips, Aphra Behn and Anne Finch, took up the subject of female friendship, and wrote in passionate terms about their relationships with other women. For example, Katherine Philips describes her friend Mary Awbrey thus:

> Soul of my soul, my joy, my crown, my friend,
> A name which all the rest doth comprehend;
> How happy are we now, whose souls are grown,
> By an incomparable mixture, one:
> Whose well-acquainted minds are now as near
> As love, or vows, or friendship can endear?
> I have no thought but what's to thee reveal'd.
> Nor thou desire that is from me conceal'd.

The extent to which we can identify either a separatist agenda or a lesbian eroticism in such poetry is still a matter for critical debate; nevertheless, there is a clear sense in which these friendships demonstrate the endurance of significant emotional, spiritual and intellectual bonds outside of marriage. The sense of woman-identification is very strong, and marks a radical shift away from the male lover/poet and mistress/muse dynamic that characterised much of the poetry written about women in the earlier part of the period.

The real possibility of women living separate lives was limited by opportunity. In the early 17th century the English Catholic reformer Mary Ward created a radical new religious order on the continent, namely the Institute of the Blessed **Virgin Mary**. This was non-monastic, and non-cloistered, with the devotees being active in their local community and teaching in the public schools set up alongside its religious houses. The schools offered a rare opportunity for English girls to receive a free education. Whilst the option of retiring to a convent was available only at great personal cost, and was therefore impossible for most women, some writers used the model of the convent in their writing to make feminist statements about the lived experience of women in a patriarchal society. Mary Astell in *A Serious Proposal to the Ladies* (1694) reiterates the notion that women are only intellectually inferior if bred to be so. As a remedy, she recommends a kind of religious retreat for women, where they can be spiritually and intellectually nourished:

> You are therefore Ladies, invited into a place where you shall suffer no other confinement, but to be kept out of the road of sin: You shall not be depriv'd of your Grandeur but only exchange the vain Pomps and Pageantry of the world, empty Titles and Forms of State, for the true and solid Greatness of being able to despise them.

Margaret Cavendish's play *The Convent of Pleasure* (1668) reworks the convent into a secular institution in which women can indulge in sensual and intellectual pleasures, safe from the company of men. Throughout the play the convent is assailed by men, but those who attempt to get in by force are unsuccessful. The successful assailant is a **cross-dressed** Prince, with whom the heroine, Lady Happy, falls in love whilst believing him to be a woman. Perhaps the message of the play is that only a man prepared to acknowledge his feminine side, and live with women on their terms, however briefly, is an acceptable husband.

Towards the end of the seventeenth century, as women writers increasingly competed with (largely hostile) men in the professional literary arena, the public expression of mutual support and admiration amongst women writers became a key strategy. The exemplars of Katherine Philips (Orinda) and Aphra Behn (Astrea) who achieved outstanding intellectual and commercial success were constantly cited, particularly after their deaths (in 1664 and 1689 respectively). This facilitated the construction of a female literary tradition/community into which women writers could insert themselves and their writing. Writing for the public stage was particularly perilous for women, who had much to fear from the mainly chauvinistic male wits in the playhouse audience. Aphra Behn was the only woman who achieved any sustained success in this arena during the 1670s and 1680s, and as such is rightly hailed as a feminist heroine. After her death in 1689, no female playwrights emerged for seven years, but in 1696 they did so with a vengeance. Three women, Delariviere Manley, Mary Pix and Catherine Trotter, all had plays premiered in the public theatre in that year, and sought to support each other in their attempts to gain acceptance and recognition as professional playwrights. Mary Pix places Delariviere Manley in a tradition harking back to Ancient Greece, describing her as 'Like Sappho Charming, like Afra Eloquent, / Like Chaste Orinda, sweetly Innocent'. Manley herself wrote a verse for the first edition of Trotter's tragedy, *Agnes de Castro* (1696):

> Orinda, and the Fair Astrea gone,
> Not one was found to fill the Vacant Throne:
> Aspiring Man had quite regain'd the Sway,
> Again had Taught us humbly to Obey:
> Till you (Natures third start, in favour of our Kind)
> With stronger Arms, their Empire have disjoin'd,
> And snatched a Laurel which they thought their Prize,
> Thus Conqu'ror, with your Wit, as with your Eyes.
> Fired by the bold Example, I would try

To turn our Sexes weaker Destiny.
O! How I long in the Poetic Race,
To loose the Reins, and give their Glory Chase:
For thus Encourag'd, and thus led by you,
Methinks we might more Crowns than theirs Subdue.

Here, Trotter is hailed as the natural successor to Katherine Philips and Aphra Behn, and also the role model for other writers, including Manley herself. The poem has a crusading quality, a sense that women playwrights are not breaking new ground, but reclaiming ground that is rightfully theirs. Within a year of their premieres Manley, Pix and Trotter were cruelly satirised in a play called *The Female Wits*. Despite the unpleasant nature of this play, it is a sure testimony to the fact that this community of women was making its presence felt in one of the country's most crucial cultural arenas.

The increasing number of literary voices making feminist statements by the end of the seventeenth century did not, however, affect the legal and constitutional position of women; their overall material and economic conditions had not improved much either. Mary Astell in *Some Reflections upon Marriage* (1700), uses the recent erosion of the power of the monarch, by the Civil War and Glorious Revolution, to point out that half the nation is still subject to tyranny:

> [I]f absolute Sovereignty be not necessary in a State, how comes it to be so in a Family? Or if in a Family why not in a State; since no Reason can be alleged for the one that will not hold more strongly for the other? If the Authority of the Husband, so far as it extends, is sacred and inalienable, why not that of the Prince? . . . is it not then partial in Men to the last Degree, to contend for, and practise that Arbitrary Dominion in their Families, which they abhor and exclaim against in the State? . . . If all Men are born Free, how is it that all Women are born Slaves?

The 'feminism' of the period 1550–1700 fought its battles in cultural and social arenas. However, the change in attitudes that they helped to shape was crucial in laying the foundations for more radical changes in the centuries to come. It is hard to imagine how the **suffragettes** could have argued that women should have the vote, because of their naturally moralistic, civilising influence, without the precedents set by the women writers dealt with here.

2

FIRST WAVE FEMINISM

VALERIE SANDERS

Modern feminism begins with Mary **Wollstonecraft**'s *Vindication of the Rights of Woman* (1792) – though the extent to which the book was initially ignored and its author vilified is often forgotten. Its argument, too, tends to be less memorable than the colourful details of Wollstonecraft's life and her personal significance as an icon of the women's movement. Everyone recalls her anguished search for love and economic survival, her unsuccessful liaison with Gilbert Imlay, her suicide attempts, marriage (against their principles) with William Godwin, and protracted death after a botched childbirth in 1797; fewer, perhaps, remember what she actually said about the difficulties women faced in late eighteenth-century society. Yet the connection between her life and her writing is vital, as it was to be for most of the women whose contribution to the development of feminism is discussed in this section. Nineteenth-century feminism evolved very much as a response to the specific difficulties individual women encountered in their lives: hence the emergence of 'key personalities', and a series of campaigns to achieve clearly defined ends. By the end of the century, major reforms had been accomplished, but the terms **'feminist'** and 'feminism' had only just begun to be used. This seems emblematic of the discontinuous, sometimes hesitant and inconsistent pattern that campaigners for women's rights established in the period under review.

THEORISTS

Wollstonecraft's *Vindication* emerged from the social and political turbulence caused by the French Revolution. Although there had been other proto-feminist treatises, such as Mary Astell's *A Serious Proposal to the Ladies* (1694), Wollstonecraft's was the first to issue an outspoken rallying cry to middle-**class** women, especially mothers, as major influences on society. Her emphasis was on the need to make women rational: 'till women are more rationally educated,' she argued, 'the

16

progress of human virtue and improvement in knowledge must receive continual checks.' Far from portraying women as superior to men, Wollstonecraft wanted to raise their overall moral and intellectual stature to make them into more rational citizens. For the most part, she did not envisage their leaving the **domestic** sphere; nor did she ask for anything as radical as the vote. 'The ideal woman pictured in the *Vindication*,' suggests Miriam Kramnick, one of its recent editors, 'is active and intelligent, blending civic and familial responsibilities, freed from drudgery and debasing frugality.' Wollstonecraft is therefore mainly concerned with the way society constructs **femininity**, especially through its inadequate, misdirected **education** of young girls. Having worked as a governess, and with sisters who ran a school, she stressed the importance of early moral and intellectual influences. Although she accepted that most middle-class women would marry and remain at home, she wanted girls' education to prepare them for the possibility of economic independence, to give them freedom and dignity, rather than the ability to fascinate potential husbands. Wollstonecraft's avowed aim in her 'Introduction' is to 'show that elegance is inferior to virtue', and the 'first object of laudable ambition is to obtain a character as a human being, regardless of the distinction of sex'. She saw women as degraded by the flirtatious and chivalrous behaviour of their male companions, but the reader who expects the *Vindication* to announce a programme of sweeping practical reform will be disappointed. The book essentially calls for a revolution in manners. It does, however, make a case for state-run, co-educational day schools, so that girls and boys might both benefit from being taught alongside one another. Wollstonecraft's hope was that much of what was false and damaging about the relationship of men and women would thus be eradicated at an early stage. Towards the end of her argument, she hints that women might in future train as doctors, pursue business, or study politics; there is even a tantalising suggestion that 'women ought to have representatives, instead of being arbitrarily governed without any direct share allowed them in the deliberations of government'; but this gesture towards participation in the country's legislature remains undeveloped.

The initially enthusiastic reception of Wollstonecraft's work was blighted – ironically – by her husband's *Memoirs* (1798) of her life. Once readers knew the details of her 'immoral' personal life, they rejected what she had to say in the *Vindication*, which subsequently went out of print until 1844. Few Victorians mention being favourably influenced by her, and many regarded her as a dire warning against uncontrolled emotionalism. Far from inspiring a feminist trend, the *Vindication* was followed largely by a period of reaction, dominated by writers of advice manuals and conduct books, such as Hannah More's writings on female education, and Mrs Sarah Ellis's immensely successful *Women of England* (1839), which was followed by *The Mothers of England* (1842) and *The Daughters of England* (1843). Aimed at the middle classes, these books were designed to inspirit women with a sense of mission (it was no coincidence that Ellis's husband was a missionary) which combined patriotism with dedication to their families. It was at this time that the notion of 'separate spheres' gained common currency: the idea that the man exposed himself to the temptations of the market-place, while the woman stayed at home and preserved a place of peace and purity for her **family**. Considerable doubt has now been cast over the literal existence of 'separate spheres' – it certainly meant nothing to the working-class wives who needed paid employment in order to feed their children, nor to many middle-class single women who had to work – but as an ideal, it held considerable appeal in the wake of the Evangelical revival dating from the late eighteenth century, and the effects of the Industrial Revolution. The invention of machinery for spinning and weaving in particular removed traditional women's occupations from the home and took them into the factories, creating a newly gentrified middle class without anything very pressing to do during the day. Mrs Ellis's conduct books appeared at just the right moment to give these women a sense of their own importance as moral influences. She famously described women as 'relative creatures', meaning that they had no significance as isolated beings: it was their connection to parents, husbands and children that gave them a role in society. Similar manuals were written by Mrs John Sandford, and Sarah Lewis, whose *Woman's Mission* (1848) caught the mood of the times and became a bestseller.

While the period from Mary Wollstonecraft's death until Caroline Norton's child custody campaign of 1839 can been characterised as reactionary, it was not without feminist activity. The best-known feminist text of this time was William Thompson's *Appeal of One-Half of the Human Race, Women, against the Pretensions of the Other Half, Men* (1825), which apart from holding the record for the longest title, rebutted the contempt for women expressed by James Mill's 'Essay on Government' (1821) to which it was a reply. Whereas Mill maintained that neither women nor the working classes needed to be enfranchised, because their interests were already being taken care of, Thompson argued that it was wrong even to regard women themselves as a cohesive group. Dividing them into three separate categories – wives, adult daughters living with their fathers, and women with neither husbands

18

nor fathers – he drew attention to the different problems faced by all three. Thompson was thus one of the first to recognise that even women whom society treated as fortunate and settled were privately suffering from unacknowledged needs and repressive treatment from men. His work particularly emphasises the differing and often conflicting needs of men and women, husbands and wives, fathers and daughters: an injustice that was further publicised by campaigners later in the century.

The next significant stage of the debate about women's rights occurred in the 1860s, in the polemical opposition of John Ruskin (1819–1900) and John Stuart **Mill** (1806–73). 'In Mill one encounters the realism of sexual politics, in Ruskin its romance and the benign aspect of its myth,' Kate **Millett** argues in her analysis of the debate in *Sexual Politics* (1969). In fact both men approached the 'woman question' from distinctly peculiar and idiosyncratic standpoints, their totally opposed attitudes emphasising the profound disunity of so-called 'Victorian' thinking about women's rights in Victoria's heyday, and the unrepresentative nature of its chief exponents. Ruskin's thinking in his lecture 'Of Queens' Gardens', originally delivered at Manchester Town Hall to a mixed audience and reprinted in *Sesame and Lilies* (1865), upholds the 'separate spheres' philosophy popularized by Mrs Ellis, and, as Kate Millett suggests, romanticises it into a male fantasy of a medieval walled garden enclosing a pure and queenly guardian of the home. Designating the man as 'the doer, the creator, the discoverer', Ruskin saw the woman's great function as 'Praise: she enters into no contest, but infallibly adjudges the crown of contest', – as in a medieval tournament, from which Ruskin derived his imagery. Notoriously, Ruskin's own marriage to Euphemia Gray had been a disastrous failure: their marriage was annulled in 1854 on grounds of non-consummation, and Ruskin fell in love with Rose La Touche, a nine-year-old girl whom he was teaching to draw. His lecture was full of sentimental pictures of medieval Lady Bountifuls tending the fallen 'feeble florets' (his phrase for prostitutes) outside their garden walls, and while he urged parents to educate their daughters thoroughly, he assumed the majority would be helpmeets to their husbands: 'All such knowledge should be given her as may enable her to understand, and even to aid, the work of men.'

Mill's treatise, *The Subjection of Women* (1869), was published only a few years after Ruskin's, but seems to belong to a different century. Mill's experience of women was perhaps as odd as Ruskin's. Having fallen in love with a married woman, Harriet **Taylor**, Mill waited patiently for many years until her husband died, and then married her in 1851: the year in which she published her 'Enfranchisement of Women', which attacked the notion that all women should be treated as potential mothers, and argued for an expansion of employment opportunities. By the time Harriet Mill died in 1858, her husband had absorbed many of her ideas and dedicated himself to publicising them. Where Ruskin's writing is emotional, Mill's is wholly rational. He concentrates on the way society has traditionally **oppressed** women and treated them as slaves: an analogy he makes at intervals throughout the book. For this he blames the 'legal subordination of one sex to the other', which he sees as being wrong in itself and 'one of the chief hindrances to human improvement'. The legal subordination, he argues, is based on nothing more than the fact that men are physically stronger, which Mill proves to be an absurd reason for wanting to give one group of people power over another. One of his most important arguments is that the true nature and capability of women must remain unknown in the highly artificial conditions in which modern societies were living. 'What is now called the nature of women is an eminently artificial thing,' Mill insists. Throughout his essay he suggests that the legal relations of the sexes have corrupted their nature, and caused the faults of each to be exaggerated. The only way in which this can be corrected is through the equality of rights: 'the only school of genuine moral sentiment is society between equals.' Much of Mill's language was too tough and uncompromising to win him widespread understanding and support at the time, while modern commentators regard his interests as too narrow: he says nothing about the plight of single women, for example, and assumes, like Ruskin, that most women will marry. His efforts seem more intently focused on improving the status quo, rather than suggesting any radical departure from it.

ACTIVISTS

The specific injustices faced by mothers in unhappy marriages were highlighted in 1839 by the Caroline Norton case, which was the first major controversy to begin the long process of undermining the total legal unity of husband and wife. In the early nineteenth century the status of a married woman was still that of *femme covert*, as defined in Sir William Blackstone's *Commentary on the Laws of England* (1765). This stated that by **marriage**, 'the very being or legal existence of a woman is suspended, or at least it is incorporated or consolidated into that of the husband, under whose wing, protection and cover she performs everything'. When Caroline Norton's husband, George, abducted their three sons in 1836, and tried to sue her for divorce by bringing a charge of 'criminal conversation' against Lord Melbourne, she researched the legal position for herself, and with the help of a young Whig barrister, Thomas Talfourd, a sergeant-at-law, wrote a pamphlet attacking the existing law on the custody of children. While Talfourd fought for an Infant Custody Bill in Parliament, Caroline Norton wrote a second pamphlet, *A Plain Letter to the Lord Chancellor on the Infant Custody Bill* (1839) (written under the male pseudonym of Pearce Stevenson), again attacking the anomalies in the law which deprived an innocent woman of her legitimate children. The result of their combined efforts was the Infant Custody Act (1839) which permitted separated wives of 'good character', against whom adultery had not been proven, to have custody of any children under seven (with the Lord Chancellor's approval), and access to their older children. This was a limited victory for Caroline Norton, whose children by this time had been removed to Scotland and were beyond the Lord Chancellor's jurisdiction; but the Act still implied that the father was the natural or usual guardian of the children. It was not until 1873 that mothers were given custody of children up to the age of sixteen, and not till 1973 that mothers were given exactly the same legal authority over their children as fathers.

Nor were all Caroline Norton's personal legal difficulties resolved by the legislation of 1839. All the time she had been separated from her husband she had been supporting herself by writing, but according to the married women's property laws of the time, her earnings legally belonged to her husband. When he stopped paying her an annual income from a Trust Fund established for herself and her sons, the Nortons were back in court, this time locked in a dispute leading to married women's property reform. Although Norton never saw herself as a feminist, her research on women's legal position resulted in her *English Laws for Women in the Nineteenth Century* (1854), the same year that Barbara Leigh-Smith **Bodichon** produced her *Brief Summary in Plain Language of the Most Important Laws of England Concerning Women.* After 25,000 women had signed a petition in favour of married women's property ownership (1856), limited legal rights were introduced by the Matrimonial Causes Act of 1857. There were to be eighteen more acts concerned with married women's property by 1882, of which the most significant was the 1870 Act. This allowed married women to keep their earnings, and to inherit personal property, with everything else going to their husband. In reality, many Victorian families had sidestepped these restrictions by setting up trust funds when their daughters married, so as to safeguard a certain amount of money or property from husbands in case of need.

The 1857 Matrimonial Causes Act was mainly concerned with divorce – again highlighted by the Norton case. In 1853, Caroline Norton had written a *Letter to the Queen on Lord Chancellor Cranworth's Marriage and Divorce Bill*, arguing that husbands and wives should be subject to the same standards of behaviour in marriage, though in fact divorce, before 1857, was complicated and expensive for anyone to obtain, as it required a separate Act of Parliament. In Dickens's *Hard Times* (1854), for example, divorce is out of the question for the downtrodden worker Stephen Blackpool, although his wife is an alcoholic: as his employer Mr Bounderby tells him unsympathetically:

> 'Why, you'd have to go to Doctors' Commons with a suit, and you'd have to go to a court of Common Law with a suit, and you'd have to go to the House of Lords with a suit, and you'd have to get an Act of Parliament to enable you to marry again, and it would cost you (if it was a case of very plain-sailing), I suppose from a thousand to fifteen hundred pound.' (*Hard Times*, Book I, Ch. 11)

Although this picture is exaggerated, divorce was undoubtedly cumbersome and expensive; moreover, access was unequal for husbands and wives. The situation as it stood was that a husband could sue his wife for divorce on grounds of adultery, whereas a wife had to prove incest or bigamy in addition to adultery. The 1857 Act transferred jurisdiction for divorce to the law courts, and improved the position of women by adding cruelty and desertion to the list of aggravating circumstances justifying divorce. For women, therefore, the Act retained the principle of inequality with men, while recognising a fuller range of injustices in their position. Like many nineteenth-century political reforms, it began a process of gradual change: it did not cause a feminist stampede to the divorce courts.

THE 1850s: DECADE OF ACTIVISM

The 1850s generally saw a major resurgence of feminist activity, and was perhaps the most important decade of the nineteenth century for Victorian women. The two Norton cases helped air long-standing concerns about the legal position of married women, while the growing numbers of single middle-class women looking for economic independence as an alternative to marriage drew attention to their limited employment options. Partly through personal networking, and partly through the eruption of individual crises and the discovery of individual

needs, a series of important legislative and social changes were introduced over the next decades.

Instrumental in effecting the change of attitude behind these reforms
was the so-called 'Langham Place' circle: a group of middle-class, activist
women who discussed and published their views about women, and met
(from 1857) at 19 Langham Place in London. The most famous members of this group were Barbara Leigh Smith (later Bodichon), author of
Women and Work (1856) and Bessie Rayner Parkes, author of *Remarks
on the Education of Girls* (1854). Together they established their own
publication, *The English Woman's Journal* (1858–64), later renamed
The Englishwoman's Review, and a Society for the Promoting of the
Employment of Women (1859).

Most of their work was geared towards providing women with alternatives to marriage and motherhood, and quickly demonstrated the
interrelatedness of the various problems they were trying to tackle.
Women found it hard to get work, partly because few openings other
than teaching were available; at the same time, women's education
prepared them badly even for teaching, and not at all for anything else.
A key development was the revelation of the 1851 Census that about
30% of English women between twenty and forty were unmarried, and
therefore likely to be facing economic hardship. 'One great corresponding cry rises from the suffering multitude of women saying, "We
want work,"' Barbara Bodichon claimed in *Women and Work*; while
Harriet Martineau in 'Female Industry', an important article in the
Edinburgh Review (1859) argued that far more professions should be
opened up to middle-class women prevented by false notions of gentility
from becoming economically independent. Their greatest challenge was
to oppose the notion that a 'lady', by definition, was not supposed to
work, and that marriage was the true vocation of women otherwise
considered 'redundant': a term popularized by W. R. Greg in his
Edinburgh Review article of 1862, 'Why are Women Redundant?'.
Greg's proposed remedy was to ship 500,000 women off to the colonies
to marry, thus relieving the glut at home.

American Feminism

In America, feminist **activism** started slightly earlier with the **Seneca
Falls** Convention of 1848, a meeting attended by 300 people (including
40 men) to demand an end to all discrimination based on sex. Feminism
had been developing slowly over the preceding decades, as it had in
Britain, though in connection with temperance and anti-slavery

23

activism. The issue of women's rights emerged inevitably alongside debate about the rights of black slaves, though not all abolitionists were feminists. Indeed, women delegates were excluded from the World Anti-Slavery Convention held in London in 1840, and many male abolitionists feared that feminist activism within their movement would detract from the main issue of racial equality. Elizabeth Cady **Stanton** (1815–1902), with Lucretia Mott the main instigator of Seneca Falls, used the 1776 Declaration of Independence as a model for the Declaration of Sentiments issued by the Convention. Working closely with Susan B. **Anthony** (1820–1906), a former temperance crusader, Cady Stanton became the most important of the American feminists campaigning for modification of the divorce laws, married women's property rights, and the vote; while key theorists were Sarah Grimké (*Letters on the Equality of the Sexes*, 1838) and Margaret Fuller (*Woman in the Nineteenth Century*, 1845). The most significant difference between Britain and America, in terms of first wave feminist development, however, was that in America, different state legislatures passed reform measures independently of the central government. Hence the women of Wyoming and Utah had the vote in 1869 and 1870 respectively, whereas women in the northern states remained unenfranchised until 1920. Once activated, American feminist campaigns proceeded at different rates around the country towards reforms similar to those in Britain.

EDUCATION AND EMPLOYMENT

Employment reformers, meanwhile, had to tackle a mindset that resisted the notion of middle-class women working for a living (though it had long since accepted the notion of working-class women doing so), and was concerned that women might oust men from hitherto unchallenged professions. Initially, therefore, women's employment opportunities developed in areas that were seen as an extension of their 'natural' sphere as mothers and carers: teaching, philanthropy, nursing, workhouse visiting, and work on school boards. Teaching became more professionalised as more girls were educated at school rather than by governesses at home. The Governesses' Benevolent Institution, founded in 1843, recognised that the governess was a 'needy *lady*' (Lady Eastlake in the *Edinburgh Review*, 1848), whose old age and periods of unemployment must be provided for. The new women's colleges, Queen's in Harley Street (1848) (designed particularly for governesses), and Bedford College, London, in offering 'lectures to ladies', began the process of bringing girls' education closer to the standard of boys'.

Although the Cambridge Local examinations were opened to girls in 1863, the Taunton Commission of 1865–8 found that girls' schools were in a wholly inadequate state: 'the general deficiency of girls' education can be stated with absolute confidence.' Once secondary education for girls had been placed on a more professional footing, the demand for higher education was likely to follow; and if the 1850s was the decade for marriage reform, the 1860s and 70s became, largely through the efforts of Emily Davies (1830–1922) a time of education reform. In 1869, the first College for Women was established experimentally at Hitchin, on the way to Cambridge: as Girton College (1873), it was swiftly followed by Newnham (1875) in Cambridge, and Lady Margaret Hall (1878) and Somerville College (1879) in Oxford, but it was still many years before women were accepted into the two ancient universities on exactly the same terms as men. It was not till 1948 that women at Cambridge were awarded degrees fully equal to men's, and Girton and Newnham were adopted as colleges of the University.

The admission of women to medical schools was another aspect of university reform and another stage in the erosion of long-standing prejudices against allowing women into a hitherto male monopoly. Women who managed to qualify as doctors, such as Elizabeth Blackwell (1821–1910) and Elizabeth Garrett Anderson (1836–1917), did so abroad; while Sophia Jex-Blake (1840–1912) opened her own medical school, the London School of Medicine for Women, in 1874. By 1880 women could obtain a medical education and practise in Britain, but objections continued on the grounds of impropriety. Florence **Nightingale**'s nursing reforms, meanwhile, had done much to raise the professionalism of nursing, though she was otherwise disengaged from the feminist movement, and had a poor view of women's disinterestedness and reliability.

Other important gains for women were the new opportunities in public and clerical work. Clerical work was a major area of expansion in the 1860s, especially in government departments such as the post office; while local government positions became accessible to women in the same period. Emily Davies and Elizabeth Garrett Anderson were both elected to London school boards in 1870, and Emmeline **Pankhurst** gained much of her political experience from her work as a Poor Law Guardian in the 1890s. Although women's work of this kind was unpaid, it gave them valuable insight into committee work and their first opportunity to speak in public. The campaign for the vote was accelerated by the increasing confidence and experience of its leaders, as was the extended opposition to the Contagious Diseases Acts in the 1860s.

THE DOUBLE STANDARD AND WOMEN'S CIVIL LIBERTIES

The Contagious Diseases Acts of 1864, 1866, and 1869, in authorising the intimate examination of any woman suspected of being a prostitute in a garrison town, were an attempt to fight the spread of syphilis in the army, but were seen as an infringement of women's civil rights. Any woman caught with the disease could be sent to a 'Lock' hospital to be forcibly cured; those who refused examination could be imprisoned and put to hard labour. As legislation, the Contagious Diseases Acts clearly perpetuated the 'double standard' of sexual morality, regulating the women's behaviour and apportioning the moral blame to them, rather than to the soldiers who used prostitutes in the first place. For many Victorian middle-class women it was difficult even to talk about such matters in public. Those who did, such as Josephine **Butler** (1828–1906), swallowed their embarrassment and became effective campaigners against state-regulated prostitution, succeeding in having the Acts repealed in 1886.

THE VOTE

Within a matter of thirty years, Victorian women had shown how effectively they could mobilise to campaign for specific reforms in the areas of matrimonial law, property ownership, child custody rights, work and educational opportunities, and government regulation of sexual morality. It may therefore seem surprising that the one reform with which we tend to associate modern feminism – votes for women – was one of the last major campaigns to be launched, and remained unachieved at the end of the nineteenth century. The issue of women's suffrage was raised from the 1830s onwards, and more frequently from the 1860s. In 1867, John Stuart Mill was the first MP to propose giving women the vote, but his proposal in the House of Commons was defeated by 196 votes to 73. Pressure intensified in the 1880s and 90s, in conjunction with a more urgent debate about the role of women: it was in 1895 that the term 'feminist' was first used, in the *Athenaeum*, a year after the popular novelist Sarah Grand had coined the phrase '**New Woman**' to describe the new generation of women who sought independence and refused the traditional confines of marriage. As sexual roles for men as well as women came under intense critical scrutiny, the **suffragettes** fought hard to give married and single women a stake in the country's political process. Becoming militant in 1905, the suffragists were divided among themselves and alienated a cross-section of women who formed anti-suffrage groups to fight the National Union of Women's Suffrage Societies (1894) and the Women's Social and Political Union (1903). While it may seem extraordinary that women would oppose the enfranchisement of their own sex, many argued that women's interests were already being well represented by men, and that the vote would be especially awkward for married women who might vote in opposition to their husbands. When the vote was finally won in 1918, it was offered to women over thirty; it was not until 1928 that women were enfranchised on the same terms as men. The remains of a 'separate spheres' philosophy therefore persisted well into the twentieth century: a deep-rooted belief remaining that most 'normal' women lived quiet lives at home with their husbands and children. As it was, the outbreak of war in 1914 both put a stop to the militant suffrage campaign, and released women into new areas of work, especially nursing, to support the war effort. By the time the war was over, women's participation in public events had come about by historical accident, and the new challenge was to educate them for active and responsible citizenship. Developments slowed down again until the next major outbreak of feminism in the 1970s.

Conclusion

Victorian feminism is a difficult concept to analyse. On the one hand, some of the greatest reforms of women's social and legal position before those of the late twentieth century occurred in a few decades of the nineteenth century; on the other, many of those women who were active campaigners – Caroline Norton, Florence Nightingale, Emily Davies, and Barbara Bodichon – were ambivalent about the extent of their own feminism, and over-anxious to distance themselves from unconventional lifestyles and behaviour. Moreover, they seemed concerned mainly with the plight of intelligent middle-class single women. Their commitment to respectability gave them something of a timorous or half-hearted allegiance to a more wide-ranging kind of feminism; in any case, their contribution to the feminist cause was often narrowly specialised as they concentrated on a particular campaign – whether for women's colleges at Cambridge or child custody rights – to the exclusion of others, and many still relied on men to help them with the legal or parliamentary part of their activism. For some, however, it was impossible to avoid being drawn into a wider examination of women's rights, as happened with Caroline Norton and Harriet Martineau, for example, and by the end of the century, most of the major journals were carrying heated debates about the unsatisfied needs of the modern woman. Beginning initially with spasmodic bursts of activism, first wave feminism gathered pace through the work of specific individuals working for specific ends, until the momentum of events made concern for women's full participation in social and political life a matter of public interest across the whole political spectrum. This in itself was no mean achievement.

3

SECOND WAVE FEMINISM

SUE THORNHAM

The fact is that to women born after 1920, feminism was dead history. It ended as a vital movement in America with the winning of that final right: the vote. (Betty **Friedan**, *The Feminine Mystique* (1965))

This book is part of the second feminist wave.
(Germaine **Greer**, *The Female Eunuch* (1971))

For Betty Friedan, writing *The Feminine Mystique* in 1963, feminism was dead. For those who followed her analysis of the 'problem that has no name' by taking up the challenge of naming and defining women's **oppression**, the relationship of this emerging 'new feminism of women's liberation' to the 'old feminism of **equal rights**' was more complex. Most initially preferred to draw a line between the two, arguing like Sheila Rowbotham that whilst 'women's liberation does have strands of the older equal-rights feminism, . . . it is something more': it is the product of a changed social and political context and possesses a sharper and far more **radical feminist** consciousness (*Woman's Consciousness, Man's World* (1973)). Whilst 'old feminism' was individualist and reformist, they argued, 'women's liberation' was collective and revolutionary. Others, however, chose to assimilate the two, reclaiming as the **first wave** of 'the most important revolution in history' earlier **feminist** writing and **activism**. Temporarily halted by a fifty-year counter-offensive, the 'onslaught' of feminism was now resurgent; it could, in Kate **Millett**'s words, 'at last accomplish its aim of freeing half the race from its immemorial subordination' (*Sexual Politics* (1970)).

FOUNDING MOMENTS

This divergence of views in the early 1970s signals both the complex origins of **second wave** feminism and its internal divisions. In America two major strands can be distinguished. Following the impact of *The*

Feminine Mystique, Betty Friedan had herself founded NOW (**National Organization for Women**) in 1966. Formed as a direct result of the failure of America's Equal Employment Opportunity Commission (EEOC) to take seriously the issue of sex **discrimination**, NOW's aims lay very much within a liberal Equal Rights tradition. It sought 'to bring women into full participation in the mainstream of American society now, assuming all the privileges and responsibilities thereof in truly equal partnership with men'. Its Board members included two former EEOC commissioners and three trade union representatives, and in its first conference, in October 1967, it formally adopted a Bill of Rights for women.

In contrast, the origins of the **Women's Liberation** Movement in America lay in the civil rights, anti-Vietnam War and student movements of the 1960s. As participants within these various left-wing movements, women found, in Juliet **Mitchell**'s words, 'the attitude of the oppressor within the minds of the oppressed' (*Woman's Estate* (1971)), an attitude most famously expressed in Stokeley Carmichael's 1964 comment that 'the only position for women in SNCC (Student Non-violent Coordinating Committee) is prone'. 'Movement women' began to defect to a range of localised, non-hierarchical women's liberation groups. Unlike NOW, these groups had no national organisation; instead they drew on the infrastructure of the radical community, the underground press, and the free universities. In a speech given at the Free University in New York City in February 1968, Anne Koedt describes this development:

> Within the last year many radical women's groups have sprung up throughout the country. This was caused by the fact that movement women found themselves playing secondary roles on every level – be it in terms of leadership, or simply in terms of being listened to. . . . As these problems began being discussed, it became clear that what had at first been assumed to be a personal problem was in fact a social and political one. . . . And the deeper we analyzed the problem and realized that all women suffer from this kind of oppression, the more we realized that the problem was not just confined to movement women. (*Radical Feminism* (1973))

What Koedt is describing here is the process of '**consciousness-raising**' – the move to transform what is experienced as personal into analysis in political terms, with the accompanying recognition that 'the personal *is* political', that male power is exercised and reinforced through 'personal' institutions such as **marriage**, child-rearing and sexual practices. Commitment to a female revolution in consciousness via the process of consciousness-raising became a defining characteristic of women's liberation groups. The same impetus underlay the first major public action of the Women's Liberation movement, the demonstration in September 1968 against the Miss America **beauty contest**. For the demonstration's organisers, the contestants epitomised 'the role all women are forced to play in this society, one way or another: apolitical, unoffending, passive, delicate (but delighted by drudgery) *things*' (Robin Morgan, *The Word of a Woman* (1993)). Among the demonstrators' actions was the creation of a 'Freedom Trash Can' into which were thrown 'objects of female torture' such as dishcloths, high heels, bras and girdles – and the media myth of 'bra-burning' was born.

In Britain, the context in which 'second wave' feminism emerged was somewhat different. Here, too, the 1960s saw the appearance of Equal Rights groups, but these were identified not with an organisation of professional women, but with the industrial militancy of working-class women like the sewing machinists at Fords in Dagenham, who in 1968 went on strike for equal pay. In Britain, too, there were American women working against the Vietnam War, and this provided another strand. The biggest impetus, however, came from women active in radical left-wing politics, and this gave the British Women's Liberation Movement, in common with its European counterparts, a Marxist-socialist inflection rather different from the liberal or radical feminism dominant in the USA. Nevertheless, feminists in Britain followed their American counterparts in demonstrating against the 1970 Miss World competition in London, and in February 1970 the first national Women's Liberation conference was held at Ruskin College, Oxford, with over 500 participants. Twenty years later Juliet Mitchell could reflect that, despite the different strands making up the movement, 'In 1970, at Ruskin, we felt we had one goal, we were unified. . . . [We] could have one feminism. One "women's liberation"' (in Michelene Wandor, *Once a Feminist: Stories of a Generation* (1990)). The four demands formulated by the conference, for equal pay, equal education and opportunity, 24-hour nurseries, and free **contraception** and **abortion** on demand, signal again the double focus which marked second wave feminism: on women as an oppressed *social* group and on the female *body* with its need for sexual autonomy as a primary site of that oppression.

Feminism, then, sought both to voice (in Friedan's terms, to *name*) women's immediate and subjective experience and to formulate a political agenda and vision. To connect the two, what was needed was a new **language** of *theory* that would encompass both. As Sheila

31

Rowbotham argued in *Woman's Consciousness*, 'Ultimately a revolutionary group has to break the hold of the dominant group over theory. . . . We can't just occupy existing words, we have to change the meanings of words even before we take them over.' Before turning to these theoretical writings, however, I should like to return to the issue of internal divisions which lay beneath this quest for unity.

DIVERGING VIEWS

In the USA, according to Juliet Mitchell in 1971, 'The Black Movement was probably the greatest single inspiration to the growth of Women's Liberation.' Moreover, black women, disillusioned by the **sexism** of the 1960s Black Movement, were active in the formation of the first radical feminist groups. In 1969 Cellestine Ware was a co-founder of the New York Radical Feminists along with Shulamith **Firestone** and Anne Koedt; in 1970 'A Historical and Critical Essay for Black Women', written by Patricia Haden, Donna Middleton and Patricia Robinson, appeared in Leslie Tanner's *Voices from Women's Liberation*; and in the same year Frances Beale's 'Double Jeopardy' was published in Robin Morgan's *Sisterhood is Powerful.* The latter, which described the double burden of race and **gender** that black women confronted, became the most anthologised essay in the early years of women's liberation publications. Nevertheless, in it Beale clearly distinguishes what she calls black women's 'life-and-death struggle' for total emancipation from the 'basically middle-class' *white* women's liberation movement, arguing that until the latter adopted an anti-imperialist and anti-**racist** stance it could have 'absolutely nothing' in common with the black woman's struggle. Thus although the 1973 manifesto of the National Black Feminist Organization maintained that it was the 'distorted male-dominated **media** image' of the Women's Liberation Movement which was responsible for its characterisation as white and middle-class, black women were on the whole sceptical about a movement which claimed '**sisterhood**' but in which they had to struggle for visibility. In 1989 Angela **Davis**, interviewed for *Feminist Review*, concluded that the 'overwhelming majority of black women' had felt no connection with the 1970s feminist movement.

In Britain, the most prominent social division centred on **class** rather than race. 'When we planned the Ruskin conference,' writes Sheila Rowbotham in *Once a Feminist*, 'I wanted working-class women to come. They didn't, really.' Despite the claims of the Women's Liberation Movement to speak for all women, 'we knew there was a gap between our grievances and those of working-class women'. Despite the militancy of **working-class** women in the late 1960s, then, they, like Black women, remained largely outside the Women's Liberation Groups and Workshops.

The position of lesbian women within 1970s feminism was also a contested one. Like black women, lesbian women were active within radical feminism from its beginnings. Moreover, radical feminists recognised the pathologising function of the label 'lesbian' in the sexual policing of *all* women: 'the final warning', as Anne Koedt put it, 'that you are about to leave the Territory of Womanhood altogether'. In 'The Woman Identified Woman' (1970), the group Radicalesbians argued that 'A lesbian is the rage of all women condensed to the point of explosion. She is the woman who, often beginning at an extremely early age, acts in accordance with her inner compulsion to be a more complete and freer human being than her society . . . cares to allow her.' Defined in this way, lesbianism becomes synonymous with women's liberation: a solution to the problems of sexual relationships with men, the logical conclusion of a politics of the personal. Nevertheless, the relationship was an uneasy one. Anne Koedt's 1971 response to the Radicalesbians rejects the argument that 'feminism is the theory; lesbianism the practice', arguing that such a view produces its own unacceptable policing of sexual desire. Her counter-argument that lesbianism is merely 'a small part' of feminism's total fight against the 'sex role system', however, renders invisible the specific oppressions of lesbian women just as the 'double jeopardy' of black women was masked within a feminist 'sisterhood' articulated largely by white, middle-class, heterosexual women. Increasingly, then, the charges of racism and **heterosexism** were levelled within feminism itself.

As a conscious political movement which sought to unite women through a sense of a shared oppression – however differently articulated – manifest at the level of the personal and subjective as well as the social, second wave feminism was characterised as much by the search for an over-arching theory as it was by activist struggles. The two, indeed, were interdependent. Shulamith Firestone's *The Dialectic of Sex* (1970), for example, was the culmination of a period of sustained feminist activism in which, following her disenchantment with the American New Left, she co-founded the earliest women's liberation collective in Chicago and then the New York Radical Feminists. Other feminist theorists have described the way in which feminist activism 'opened a space' for them to rediscover themselves as women and thence to theorise that **identity** and its possible transformation.

FEMINIST THEORY

1970 is the year which marks an explosion of feminist theoretical writing. Kate Millett's *Sexual Politics*, Shulamith Firestone's *The Dialectic of Sex* and Robin Morgan's edited collection *Sisterhood is Powerful* were all published in the USA, and in Britain Germaine Greer's *The Female Eunuch* and Eva **Figes'** *Patriarchal Attitudes* appeared. But to understand this wave of theoretical writing, we have to go back a little further, to Simone de **Beauvoir's** *The Second Sex* (1949), for it is de Beauvoir's account of the cultural construction of woman as *Other* which laid the foundations for much of the theoretical work of the 1970s. 'One is not born, but rather becomes, a woman,' she writes. 'No biological, psychological, or economic fate determines the figure that the human female presents in society; it is civilization as a whole that produces this creature, intermediate between male and eunuch, which is described as **feminine**.' The category of the *Other*, she argues, is fundamental in the formation of all human subjectivity, since our sense of Self can be produced only in opposition to something which is not-self. But men have claimed the category of Self or Subject exclusively for themselves, and relegated woman to the status of eternal *Other*. The category 'woman' has thus no substance, being merely a projection of male fantasies (the 'myth of the eternal feminine') and fears. But since all cultural representations of the world presently available to us – whether in **myth**, religion, literature or popular culture – are the work of men, women too have internalised these definitions and learned to 'dream through the dreams of men'. Indeed, a 'true woman' is *required* to accept herself as *Other* for man: she must 'make herself object . . . renounce her autonomy'.

In her analysis of how woman *became* the *Other*, de Beauvoir considers the explanations of biologists, Freudian psychoanalysts, and Marxists. All three, she argues, are unacceptably determinist. Biological science reduces to a matter of physiology, **psychoanalysis** to a matter of unconscious drives, and Marxism to a matter of economics a subordination which is in fact socially and culturally produced. As such, it is capable of being changed *if* women can grasp the subjecthood they have been so far denied. De Beauvoir's conclusion, then, is a mixture of optimism and exhortation. Economic self-interest, she writes, has led men to give partial social and economic **emancipation** to women. Women must now seize this opportunity to achieve complete economic and social equality. This done, an 'inner metamorphosis' will follow. Woman will exist for herself: she will be a Subject as man is a Subject, an *Other* for him only so far as he is for her.

USA

De Beauvoir's argument that the key to women's oppression lay in their cultural construction as *Other* was taken up with varying degrees of theoretical sophistication by second wave feminist theorists. Betty Friedan's *The Feminine Mystique* (1963), which has been seen as heralding feminism's second wave, also calls for a 'drastic reshaping of the cultural image of femininity that will permit women to reach maturity, identity, completeness of self'. Friedan's book, based on the results of a questionnaire she circulated among her former Smith College classmates in 1957, fifteen years after their graduation, set out to analyse the profound but apparently unnameable dissatisfaction felt by these educated American housewives. She identifies the cause as the 'feminine mystique':

> The feminine mystique says that the highest value and the only commitment for women is the fulfilment of their own femininity. . . . It says that this femininity is so mysterious and intuitive and close to the creation and origin of life that man-made science may never be able to understand it. . . . The mistake, says the mystique, the root of women's troubles in the past is that women envied men, women tried to be like men, instead of accepting their own nature, which can find fulfilment only in sexual passivity, male domination, and nurturing maternal love.

In bringing to public visibility the widespread frustration felt by her contemporaries, Friedan is a key contributor to the emphasis on consciousness-raising within second wave feminism. Her book had a huge impact not least because she, unlike De Beauvoir, wrote not just about but *from* the personal and everyday experience of women. But it drew back from the radical conclusions which her analysis suggests. In the description above, the 'feminine mystique' seems curiously free-floating: it 'arises', it 'spreads', it 'speaks', but it is not *authored*. There is an absence of any analysis which would locate its origins in oppressive power structures. For Friedan, the solutions can be found within existing social structures. Since American society already espouses the goal of individual fulfilment, all that is needed for the release of women's potential is their admission into full participation in that society. Friedan's proposal is for a national programme of education for women which will lead to fulfilling 'work' – though not necessarily, she adds, to paid jobs. The ensuing changes will be liberating for both sexes. No great social upheaval will be necessary – not, at least, in America.

One of the most troubling aspects of both De Beauvoir's and Friedan's accounts is a tendency to blame women themselves for their position, an effect of the focus of both writers on individual self-transformation as the way forward. Despite its contribution to consciousness-raising, therefore, *The Feminine Mystique* is rooted firmly within a **liberal feminist** tradition; its goals stretch only to equality of opportunity for women within the public sphere. In her later book, *The Second Stage* (1981), Friedan was to go much further in seeking to 'protect' the sphere of 'the **family**' and the personal from the inroads of feminist analysis, protesting that the 'feminine mystique' had now been replaced by an equally pernicious 'feminist mystique'.

In contrast, both Kate Millett's *Sexual Politics* and Shulamith Firestone's *The Dialectic of Sex* (both 1970) were hugely ambitious theoretical works that emerged from the radical feminist movement. Millett's book popularised both the phrase '**sexual politics**' and the broadening of the term 'patriarchy' beyond its original definition as the rule of a dominant elder male within a traditional kinship structure, to mean the institutionalised oppression of all women by all men. Patriarchy, argues Millett, is a *political* institution, and sex a 'status category with political implications'. Moreover, patriarchy is the *primary* form of human oppression, without whose elimination other forms of oppression – racial, political or economic – will continue. Patriarchal domination is maintained principally, though not exclusively, through *ideological* control:

> One is forced to conclude that sexual politics, while connected to economics and other tangibles of social organization, is, like racism, or certain aspects of caste, primarily an **ideology**, a way of life, with influence over every other psychological and emotional facet of existence. It has created, therefore, a psychic structure, deeply embedded in our past, capable of intensification or attenuation, but one which, as yet, no people have succeeded in eliminating.

Like De Beauvoir, then, Millett argues that women have internalised the ideology of femininity, and with it their inferior status. In instances of failure of ideological control, however, patriarchy will also, in common with other 'total ideologies' like racism or colonialism, call on force. Such force may be institutional, from legal penalties for women's adultery to the lack of abortion rights, but it may equally be enacted in the sphere of the personal: in **rape** or its cultural equivalent, **pornography**.

This emphasis on the cultural and ideological as the primary means through which patriarchy maintains its 'merciless, total, and seemingly irrefutable control' finds its strongest expression in Millett's scathing critique of the work of novelists D.H. Lawrence, Henry Miller and Norman Mailer. Insisting that their work be read *ideologically* – as a **discourse** which speaks from and for their social and cultural positioning within patriarchy – Millett inaugurates a mode of feminist analysis which was to produce a distinctive body of critical writing about literature, film, and popular culture. She also gives a distinctive, and distinctively *angry*, voice to such criticism. Unlike de Beauvoir and Friedan, Millett does not cite women's complicity as a factor in their continued oppression. For her, patriarchal ideology is a matter of false representations politically deployed against women, who are its victims. Women's apparent complicity can be explained by their status as 'a dependency class' who 'like all persons in their situation (slaves are a classic example here) . . . identify their own survival with the prosperity of those who feed them. The hope of seeking liberating radical solutions of their own seems too remote for the majority to dare contemplate and remains so until consciousness on the subject is raised'. Millett's own polemic is clearly designed to bring about such consciousness-raising, and although her work can be criticised for its sweeping generalisations and lack of theoretical complexity, her account of patriarchy as a system of institutionalised oppression maintained by ideological means was crucial in the development of feminist thinking.

Shulamith Firestone's *The Dialectic of Sex* is an equally uncompromising view of patriarchal history. Like Millett, she argues that women's oppression is 'the oldest, most rigid class/caste system in existence'. Pre-dating oppression based on race or economic class, it is founded on 'the natural reproductive difference between the sexes' which led to a sexual division of labour and the construction of a class/caste system based on biological difference. Women's liberation, therefore – following the Marxist model which Firestone employs – requires 'the revolt of the underclass (women) and the seizure of control of *reproduction*'. Firestone's vision of a feminist Utopia is one in which **reproductive technology** will have removed the tyranny of sexual division based on biology. With such a removal will come the collapse of those social and cultural structures – the family, cultural myths of **romance, marriage** and motherhood – which have provided the ideological support for this sexual division.

All of these theorists, whether emerging from a liberal feminist or a radical feminist tradition, together with other representatives of early second wave feminism such as Germaine Greer (*The Female Eunuch* (1970)) and Eva Figes (*Patriarchal Attitudes* (1970)), have in common a view of culture as *political,* its images, meanings, representations working to define and control women. They also share an approach which combines an attempt to situate cultural representations in their wider social and economic context with a broad historical and cultural sweep which emphasises, sometimes at the expense of a flattening out of historical and cultural differences, the all-pervasiveness of patriarchal structures. But between liberal feminists, who see change as possible within current socio-political structures, and radical feminists who argue that nothing short of revolution will effect such change, there are also major theoretical differences. In Britain, however, the major theoretical developments lay in neither of these two directions, but within two further strands of feminist thinking which emerged during the early 1970s: **socialist feminism** and psychoanalytic feminism.

BRITAIN

In 1966 Juliet Mitchell's essay 'Women: the Longest Revolution' appeared in *New Left Review*. Pre-dating by some two years both Mitchell's own feminist activism and the founding of Britain's first women's liberation groups, the essay was a response to the publication in 1961 of *The Long Revolution* by Marxist critic Raymond Williams. Williams had argued that the 'long revolution' through which we are living has three aspects: the 'democratic revolution', the ' industrial revolution', and the revolutionary expansion of communication technologies. To understand this 'long revolution', however, we must see these strands not as separate but as profoundly interactive, producing a 'deeper cultural revolution' which 'is a large part of our most significant living experience, and is being interpreted and indeed fought out, in very complex ways, in the world of art and ideas'. Mitchell's essay is a response to Williams' complete silence on the subject of women in his 'inclusive' analysis, but it also draws on his methodological emphasis on the complex 'overdetermination' of any revolutionary change.

In both this essay and her 1971 book *Woman's Estate*, then, Mitchell attacks Marxism's failure to offer any materialist analysis of women's oppression: Marxist/socialist theory, she argues, sees women's liberation as merely an adjunct to class analysis. But she also critiques what she sees as the over-simplistic and transhistorical accounts of 'patriarchy' offered by radical feminists like Kate Millett and Shulamith Firestone. Like them, she sees women's oppression as operating largely through ideology, an ideology manifest in the 'psychology of femininity' and lived out in women's roles within the 'personal' sphere of sexuality and the family. But women's oppression takes place always in *specific* historical circumstances: its analysis requires both a radical feminist consciousness *and* the tools of historical materialism. It is the product of four distinct but overlapping ('overdetermining') structures: those of production, reproduction, sexuality and the socialisation of children. Transformation of all four structures must be achieved if the movement towards women's liberation is to succeed. Transformation in only one – as, for example, in the 'wave of sexual liberalization' of the sixties – may simply open the way to a shift in the form of women's oppression – in this case to women's *increased* sexual objectification.

A similar analysis was offered by Sheila Rowbotham in *Woman's Consciousness, Man's World* published in 1973. Like Juliet Mitchell, Rowbotham was active in the organisation of the 1970 Women's Liberation Conference at Ruskin College, coming to feminist activism from an involvement in Marxist politics. She too argues for both a revolution in consciousness and a historical analysis of women's oppression within capitalism. Women, she argues, have to struggle for control over both production and reproduction. What is vital therefore is the emergence of a movement of *working-class* women, since their experience 'spans production and reproduction, class exploitation and sex oppression'. But Rowbotham also draws substantially on earlier writers like Simone de Beauvoir and Virginia **Woolf** to argue that what is required is a revolution within language and culture as well as material structures. Socialist feminists must seek to transform 'the inner world' of bodily experience, psychological colonisation and cultural silencing, as well as the outer world of material social conditions.

It was this 'dual structure' of oppression identified by both Rowbotham and Mitchell which led Juliet Mitchell towards an engagement with psychoanalytic theory and thus into conflict with the dominant view of psychoanalysis within early second wave feminism. Kate Millett, Shulamith Firestone, Germaine Greer and Eva Figes all identified Freudian psychoanalysis, with its accounts of '**penis envy**' and feminine passivity, as a key agent in the 'counterrevolution' against first wave feminism. Yet the theories of ideology on which Millett in particular drew in her explanation of the power of patriarchy, depend on some notion of unconscious processes if they are to have any force. What feminist theory needed was an explanation of the processes through which our sexed identities are acquired and maintained which would both account for the strength and ubiquity of these identities *and* see them as culturally constructed and thus open to change. It was this which Juliet Mitchell saw psychoanalysis as offering. Her account of psychoanalysis as the theorisation of how human beings learn to occupy – but also resist – their ideologically-given roles as men or women within patriarchy was taken up not only by theorists interested in the construction of gendered identity, but also by those seeking to explore how forms of popular culture – films, magazines and popular fiction – construct feminine identities. But it has also been much contested. Mitchell's use of psychoanalysis, it is argued, denies the *material* basis of women's oppression and undermines feminism as a political struggle founded on the status of women as a distinctive *social* group. To locate the source of women's oppression within unconscious processes, after all, renders that oppression just as inaccessible to conscious change, and just as impervious to political struggle, as it is if we locate it within *biological* differences.

FRANCE

A similar charge has been made against the feminist theory which developed in France during the 1970s. As in the USA, **French feminism** emerged out of the politicised climate which followed a period of student unrest, though it differed in sharing with its British counterparts a **Marxist** inflection. The Paris student revolt of May 1968 which threatened to topple the government had led, as in America, to disillusionment amongst the women students who found themselves performing traditional 'feminine' services for their male comrades, and in the summer of 1968 the first women's groups were formed. Like the American Women's Liberation Movement, the French **MLF** (*Mouvement de Libération des Femmes*) distinguished itself from earlier reformist groups. Simone de Beauvoir, for example, who in *The Second Sex* had not identified herself as a feminist, now did so, arguing that 'the new feminism is radical' (Toril **Moi**, *Sexual/Textual Politics*, 1985). From its beginnings, however, French feminist theory was distinguished from its American counterparts in one major respect: its use of psychoanalytic theory as an explanatory tool. Whereas Kate Millett denounced **Freud** as a key agent of patriarchy, French theorists Luce **Irigaray**, Hélène **Cixous** and Julia **Kristeva** followed de Beauvoir's analysis of woman's construction as the '**Other**' by seeking to explore the ways in which **language** and **culture** construct sexual **difference**, and to do this they drew on the work of the French psychoanalytic theorist Jacques **Lacan**.

Lacan had described the infant's entry into culture as occurring through, firstly, its identification with its own mirror-image and consequent sense of possessing an independent identity, and, secondly, its entry into the **'Symbolic Order'** via the acquisition of language. The Symbolic Order, argues Lacan, is patriarchal, constructing meaning through sets of binary oppositions – for example, man/woman, mind/nature, activity/passivity – in which the 'male' term is always privileged. It is the **Law of the Father**, and its privileged signifier is the **Phallus**. It is opposed to the realm of the Imaginary, the world of the first mother-child relationship in which the child acquires, through seeing its reflection, a sense of itself as a separate being. It is this view of sexual difference as constructed in and by language which was to influence the development of French feminist theory. In their various ways, Irigaray, Cixous and Kristeva sought to establish a female identity, language and writing which would subvert and/or deconstruct the **phallocentricity** of the Symbolic Order. In so doing, they opened up for feminist investigation questions about the relationship between **desire** and language and about the constructedness of identity, and their work was taken up by **Anglo-American** feminist theorists in literary, cultural and film studies in the 1980s. But they were also challenged by materialist feminists who insisted on the social and economic roots of women's oppression. In locating the source – and the solution – of women's oppression within language, it is argued, French feminist theory, like other forms of feminism which draw on psychoanalysis, undermines a feminist political struggle which must be based on a shared social identity and shared social and political goals.

Looking Back

Rosi **Braidotti** has commented that much of the feminist theory written during the early years of second wave feminism seems to be 'written in the simple future tense, expressing a deep sense of determination, of certainty about the course of history and the irresistible emancipation of women' (*Nomadic Subjects* (1994)). Yet if such writing seems often to be, as she says, 'half prophecy and half **utopia**', the apparent certainty was polemical, its purpose political. As one feminist theorist has written, 'Suddenly a perspective on the world had unfolded that gave women a position to speak from, and things that had to be said not from choice but from political necessity' (Laura **Mulvey**, *Visual and Other Pleasures* (1989)). But despite a unity around 'sisterhood' forged within activism, theoretical differences and political exclusions were always in evidence.

The last National Women's Liberation Conference in Britain was held in 1978, marked by a split between radical and socialist feminists, but clashing feminist political positions had been in evidence since 1974. The titles of the essay collections edited by Juliet Mitchell and Ann **Oakley** at ten-year intervals since 1976 give some sense of the cultural position of feminism since those early years. *The Rights and Wrongs of Women* of 1976 was followed by the far less certain but more theoretically assured *What Is Feminism?* of 1986, and by *Who's Afraid of Feminism? Seeing Through the Backlash* in 1997. During the thirty-year period since the beginnings of the 'second wave', feminism has acquired an academic voice both within and beyond **Women's Studies**, but as a political identity it has fractured along lines of multiple differences between women, and both young women and high-profile media women seem to believe that 'second wave feminism' has dissolved into '**post-feminism**'. In their latest collection, Mitchell and Oakley catalogue the depressing lack of change in women's position in the workplace since 1970 (in the UK women's earnings have remained at roughly two-thirds those of men), the very real gains in women's sexual and familial rights, and the ideological **backlash** which portrays feminism as at once *passé* and monstrously triumphant. If we look back at the four demands formulated by the Ruskin College conference in 1970, however – for equal pay, equal education and opportunity, 24-hour nurseries, and free contraception and abortion on demand – we find evidence of at best partial fulfilment. Looking back on that conference, one of its participants comments on the limitations of its political agenda, ' We were criticised for being all white and middle class: neither criticism was wholly true, but there was a real truth behind the criticism. As sisters we were too similar; or in stressing sisterhood and our common oppression and strengths as women, we repressed and ignored differences which should have been recognised.' This should not mean, however, an abandonment of the project of second wave feminism: 'The political – and personal – struggle now needs a larger, more diverse "we", who will combine in resistance to all the overlapping oppressions. I hope I'll go on being part of that.' (Michelene Wandor, *Once a Feminist*).

4

POSTFEMINISM

SARAH GAMBLE

Currently, feminism seems to be a term without any clear significance. The 'anything goes' approach to the definition of the word has rendered it practically meaningless.

(bell **hooks**, *Feminist Theory: From Margin to Center* (1984))

'**Postfeminism**' is a term that is very much in vogue these days. In the context of popular culture it's the **Spice Girls**, **Madonna** and the *Girlie Show:* women dressing like bimbos, yet claiming male privileges and attitudes. Meanwhile, those who wish to maintain an allegiance to more traditional forms of feminism circle around the neologism warily, unable to decide whether it represents a con trick engineered by the media or a valid movement. In books such as Tania **Modleski**'s *Feminism Without Women: Culture and Criticism in a 'Postfeminist' Age* (1991) and Imelda Whelehan's *Feminist Thought: From the Second Wave to 'Post-feminism'* (1995) the term is barricaded between inverted commas, thus keeping both author and reader at a properly sceptical distance.

Much of this distrust is to do with the fact that, outside of its infinitely flexible **media** definition, exactly what postfeminism constitutes – even whether it exists at all as a valid phenomenon – is a matter for frequently impassioned debate. As Vicki Coppock, Deena Haydon and Ingrid Richter put it in *The Illusions of 'Post-feminism'* (1995), 'post-feminism has never been defined. It remains the product of assumption.' It is a characteristic postfeminism shares with its semantic relative, **postmodernism**, which has been similarly described as 'an amorphous thing'.

Indeed, even the most cursory reading of texts tagged with the 'postfeminist' label reveals that there is little agreement among those with whom it is popularly associated as to a central canon or agenda. Very generally speaking, however, postfeminist debate tends to crystallise around issues of victimisation, autonomy and responsibility.

Because it is critical of any definition of women as victims who are unable to control their own lives, it is inclined to be unwilling to condemn **pornography** and to be sceptical of such phenomena as date-**rape**: because it is skewed in favour of liberal humanism, it embraces a flexible **ideology** which can be adapted to suit individual needs and desires. Finally, because it tends to be implicitly **heterosexist** in orientation, postfeminism commonly seeks to develop an agenda which can find a place for men, as lovers, husbands and fathers as well as friends.

The term 'postfeminism' itself originated from within the media in the early 1980s, and has always tended to be used in this context as indicative of joyous liberation from the ideological shackles of a hopelessly outdated **feminist** movement. This is the view which has reached the ninth edition of *The Concise Oxford Dictionary*, where 'postfeminism' is defined as 'of or relating to the ideas, attitudes, etc., which ignore or reject feminist ideas of the 1960s and subsequent decades'. However, those to whom the postfeminist label is most often attached by the media do not generally regard themselves as part of any kind of anti-feminist movement, as Justine Picardie's 1996 article for the *Independent on Sunday* on a TV show called *Pyjama Party* testifies:

> There has been much feverish talk in the press about these programmes ... do they represent the snarling face of the postfeminist babe – 'the new ladette' – or is this just a pre-feminist excuse for titillating the viewers with a great deal of cleavage? The girls on their way to *Pyjama Party* ... couldn't care less about this debate ('postfeminist what?' says one, while her friends look equally blank: 'never heard of it!').

The source of such confusion, for postfeminism as much as for postmodernism, is at least partially due to the semantic uncertainty generated by the prefix. Turning again to the *Concise Oxford Dictionary*, 'post' is defined as 'after in time or order', but not as denoting rejection. Yet many feminists argue strongly that postfeminism constitutes precisely that – a betrayal of a history of feminist struggle, and rejection of all it has gained. Tania Modleski's dismissal of postfeminist texts as 'texts that, in proclaiming or assuming the advent of postfeminism, are actually engaged in negating the critiques and undermining the goals of feminism – in effect delivering us back to a prefeminist world' is typical of such attacks.

The assertiveness of Modleski's rhetoric here makes the issue appear beyond dispute, but it is possible to argue that the prefix 'post' does not necessarily always direct us back the way we've come. Instead, its trajectory is bewilderingly uncertain, since while it can certainly be interpreted as suggestive of a relapse *back* to a former set of ideological beliefs, it can also be read as indicating the *continuation* of the originating term's aims and ideologies, albeit on a different level. This more positive interpretation is certainly, however, complicated in postfeminism's case, given that it lacks both an agreed-upon set of ideological assumptions and any prominent figureheads. This latter statement may seem rather odd, since postfeminism abounds in 'personalities' – glamorous Naomi **Wolf**; the swaggering self-publicist Camille **Paglia**; Rene **Denfeld**, the streetwise amateur boxer. It is telling, however, that most – if not all – of the women who are widely identified with postfeminism have not claimed the term for themselves, but had it applied to them by others; nor does a great deal of solidarity exist between them as a group.

POSTFEMINISM AND THE BACKLASH

The notion that postfeminism, to paraphrase Modleski's words quoted above, 'delivers us back' to some kind of prefeminist state is an argument frequently deployed by its critics. The most influential definition of postfeminism through reference to a rhetoric of relapse is Susan **Faludi**'s, who in *Backlash: The Undeclared War Against Women* (1991) portrays postfeminism as a devastating reaction against the ground gained by **second wave** feminism.

> Just when record numbers of younger women were supporting feminist goals in the mid-1980s (more of them, in fact, than older women) and a majority of all women were calling themselves feminists, the media declared that feminism was the flavour of the seventies and that 'post-feminism' was the new story – complete with a younger generation who supposedly reviled the women's movement.

For Faludi, postfeminism *is* the **backlash**, and its triumph lies in its ability to define itself as an ironic, pseudo-intellectual critique on the feminist movement, rather than an overtly hostile response to it. In a society which largely defines itself through media-inspired images, women are easily persuaded that feminism is unfashionable, *passé*, and therefore not worthy of serious consideration. 'We're all "post-feminist" now, they assert, meaning not that women have arrived at equal justice and moved beyond it, but simply that they themselves are beyond even pretending to care.'

While most critics date the inception of postfeminism from about the mid-1980s onwards, Faludi claims that 'postfeminist' sentiments appeared much earlier, 'not in the 1980s media, but in the 1920s press'. In her identification of it as merely the most recent label for a much older phenomenon – a knee-jerk reaction on the part of the mainstream in defence of the *status quo* – Faludi attempts to unmask postfeminism as a wolf in (albeit trendy) sheep's clothing.

The notion of backlash can, however, operate in the opposite direction. It's interesting to note that some of the women predominantly identified with postfeminism have themselves employed the backlash argument in attacks on second wave feminism. In *The Morning After: Sex, Fear and Feminism* (1993) Katie **Roiphe** turns the discourse of backlash upon its originators, claiming that

> feminists are closer to their backlash than they like to think. The image that emerges from feminist preoccupations with rape and sexual harassment is that of women as victims. . . . This image of a delicate woman bears a striking resemblance to that fifties ideal my mother and the other women of her generation fought so hard to get away from. They didn't like her passivity, her wide-eyed innocence. They didn't like the fact that she was perpetually offended by sexual innuendo. They didn't like her excessive need for protection. She represented personal, social, and psychological possibilities collapsed, and they worked and marched, shouted and wrote, to make her irrelevant for their daughters. But here she is again, with her pure intentions and her wide eyes. Only this time it is feminists themselves who are breathing new life into her.

Roiphe's text focuses on the phenomenon of sexual harassment on American campuses, and argues that feminist initiatives such as Take Back the Night are self-defeating; 'intended to celebrate and bolster women's strength, it seems instead to celebrate their vulnerability'.

That second wave feminism has fostered an inappropriate image of female victimisation is also the central claim of Rene Denfeld's *The New Victorians: A Young Woman's Challenge to the Old Feminist Order* (1995). Although the scope of Denfeld's argument is wider than Roiphe's, she nonetheless echoes Roiphe's claim that feminism has overrun the academy. In the process, it has become totalitarian and inflexible in its upholding of views that are reminiscent of those of an earlier age. And whereas Roiphe regards feminism as having lapsed into a view of women more appropriate to the 1950s, Denfeld looks even further back:

> In the name of feminism, these extremists have embarked on a moral and spiritual crusade that would take us back to a time worse than our

mother's day – back to the nineteenth-century values of sexual morality, spiritual purity, and political helplessness. Through a combination of influential voices and unquestioned causes, current feminism would create the very same morally pure yet helplessly martyred role that women suffered from a century ago.

For Denfeld, the term 'feminism' has come to stand for an extremist cabal which alienates a younger generation of women in its insistence on pursuing an agenda based on an unswerving belief in female victim-isation at the hands of an all-powerful **patriarchal** system, open hostility to heterosexual practices, and the embracing of New Age **goddess**-worship. In this way – in particular its valorisation of the figure of the female victim – feminism is becoming a spent force, since it has lost all credibility in the eyes of those whose real social and political inequality still needs to be addressed:

> While women move ahead in their lives – with the tenets of equality entrenched firmly in their hearts – the women's movement itself has stalled. Trapped in a stagnant, alienating ideology, the only thing most of the feminist movement is heading toward is complete irrelevance.

Both Roiphe's and Denfeld's analyses, however, encapsulate many of the problems raised by the postfeminist phenomenon. Caught up in the necessity to define exactly what it is they're reacting against, both books adopt a dangerously simplistic attitude towards feminism, portraying it as a didactic and monolithic structure bent only on stifling dissent. Denfeld's argument is particularly problematic in this respect, since her claim that second wave feminism has led to a replication of Victorian notions of femininity involves her in the dismissal of an entire history of female struggle from the first wave onwards. As Deborah L. Seigel has maintained in her essay 'Reading Between the Waves: Feminist Historiography in a "Postfeminist" Moment', such sweeping critiques do more harm than good, for although

> [d]issenting feminist voices participate in a much-needed intergener-ational conversation at the very moment in which feminist discourses within and outside the academy have taken a self-reflexive turn. . . . the authors' desires for mastery overwrite any attempt to keep a dialogue moving. . . . [in] their incorporation of a rhetoric of possession, in their masterful articulation of "good" feminism, and in their righteous condem-nation of "bad" feminism. (in Leslie Heywood and Jennifer Drake, eds., *Third Wave Agenda: Being Feminist, Doing Feminism* (1997))

Implicit in Seigel's statement is the fact that neither Roiphe nor Denfeld reject feminism altogether: indeed, both are extremely careful to display their feminist credentials. Denfeld defines herself as an 'equity feminist' who believes that 'women should have the same opportunities and rights as men', while Roiphe claims that feminism for her is 'something assumed, something deep in my foundations'. However, this merely serves to complicate the issue, since it locks feminists and postfeminists in dialectical opposition, with both parties attempting to lay claim to some kind of 'pure' or 'correct' version of feminism.

In her essay Seigel singles out one other writer for criticism on this score: Naomi Wolf. Wolf has become one of the most identifiable faces of postfeminism, and for many of its detractors represents the embodiment of a bias within postfeminism towards the young, white, liberal and media-attractive. Although she first came to public attention with *The Beauty Myth* (1990), which was basically a reiteration of the standard feminist argument that women were coerced by society into pursuing an unattainable aesthetic ideal of 'femininity', it was *Fire With Fire* (1993) which confirmed her identification with the postfeminist phenomenon.

In *Fire With Fire*, Wolf argues that feminism has for the most part failed to recognise, much less capitalise on, its gains. In portraying the late 1980s as a period in which fewer and fewer women were willing to identify themselves as 'feminist', and in her attribution of much of this failure to the backlash phenomenon, Wolf recalls the arguments of Faludi, Roiphe and Denfeld. But whereas Roiphe and Denfeld, to some extent at least, use backlash discourse in their own attacks on the feminist movement, thus defining it as an issue which sets women against women, Wolf can be aligned with Faludi in her viewing of the backlash as primarily a defensive manoeuvre on the part of the male-dominated establishment. If it can be seen as 'an eminently rational, if intolerable reaction to a massive and real threat', the backlash becomes a signifier of just how far the feminist movement has come.

Although not as openly hostile as either Denfeld or Roiphe, Wolf is certainly critical of feminism in this book. Rather than engaging in personal attacks on individuals, she lays much of the responsibility for feminism's image problem at the door of the popular media, who have mounted a campaign of 'lies, distortion and caricature' against the movement. Nevertheless, she doesn't absolve feminism of all responsibility, claiming that it is also 'bad habits in the movement itself' which have hindered its capability to counteract the damaging media stereotypes which many women are finding so alienating. The development of an 'ideological hardline' amongst some sections of feminism means, says Wolf, that

> the *definition of feminism* has become ideologically overloaded. Instead of offering a mighty Yes to all women's individual wishes to forge their own definition, it has been disastrously redefined *in the popular imagination* as a massive No to everything outside a narrow set of endorsements [my italics].

The above quotation is a telling summary of Wolf's agenda, for in its drawing of a distinction between feminism as an actual phenomenon and a 'definition' of feminism as it exists 'in the popular imagination', she exhibits a rather more subtle and self-conscious approach than that adopted by some of her postfeminist peers. It is one that enables her to at least partially evade the stark opposition between 'good' and 'bad' feminism, as according to her version of the argument, 'bad' feminism does not really exist in the sense that it is not an ideology being promoted by any particular individual or group. Instead, it is a media-orchestrated misunderstanding which women must surmount in order to embrace 'power feminism', the aims of which are equality, economic empowerment, and the confidence to act both collectively and individually to achieve such goals.

One of the most immediately attractive, yet also deeply problematic, aspects of *Fire With Fire* is how Wolf makes the attainment of such an objective appear a relatively simple matter. Her entire argument rests on the assumption that power is there for the taking – but is it, can it ever be, as easy as that? If one is a white, middle-class, educated and solvent American, perhaps; but what if you are black, or poor, or subject to an oppressive political, military or religious regime? These are things that Wolf tends not to consider, an omission which highlights the problems encountered when attempting to define postfeminism. While writers such as Roiphe and Denfeld mull over the mistakes of the past, Wolf represents an alternative approach, imagining a future which, though appealing, is also impossibly **utopian**. We have, therefore, arrived back at the tautology at the heart of postfeminism identified at the beginning of this chapter; namely that it is a phenomenon held in suspension between the opposing definitions indicative in its use of the prefix. Unsure as to whether to go forward or back, it remains a paper-bound ideology, more theoretical than actual.

POSTFEMINISM AND POSTMODERNISM

In fact, to accept the inherently theoretical nature of the postfeminist project perhaps offers the most convincing way in which the term can be used. In this context, postfeminism becomes a pluralistic epistemology dedicated to disrupting universalising patterns of thought, and thus capable of being aligned with **postmodernism**, **poststructuralism** and **postcolonialism**.

One example of this approach is provided by Ann Brooks in *Postfeminisms: Feminism, Cultural Theory and Cultural Forms* (1997). She argues that second wave feminism bases its claims on an appeal to 'the liberal humanism of enlightened modernity': for example, it assumes that a simple reversal of the hierarchical dualism of 'man/woman' will effect the liberation of the female half of the equation. A feminist approach indebted to postmodernist thought, however, will tend to question the ideological process by which 'man' and 'woman' are placed in separate, oppositional, categories, and may, indeed, seek to destabilise the notion of the autonomous subject (gendered or otherwise) altogether, thus rendering the development of any kind of overarching metatheory impossible.

According to Brooks, therefore, postfeminism replaces dualism with diversity, consensus with variety, and thus 'establish[es] a dynamic and vigorous area of intellectual debate, shaping the issues and intellectual climate that has characterised the move from modernity to postmodernity in the contemporary world'. Brooks's analysis does not mention Wolf, Roiphe, or any of the other women popularly defined as postfeminists within the media. Instead, she appropriates theorists such as Julia **Kristeva**, Hélène **Cixous**, Laura **Mulvey** and Judith **Butler** for postfeminism, claiming that such writers 'have assisted feminist debates by providing a conceptual repertoire centred on "deconstruction", "**difference**" and "**identity**".'

Interesting though Brooks's argument is, however, certain aspects of it are problematic, since in transforming postfeminism into another theoretical movement, she runs the risk of removing it from the 'real' world of political agency and social activism. Although she may maintain that postfeminism 'facilitates a broad-based, pluralistic conception of the application of feminism, and addresses the demands of marginalised, diasporic and colonised cultures for a non-hegemonic feminism capable of giving voice to local, indigenous and post-colonial feminisms', it remains difficult to see how these theoretical debates can be translated into concrete action. For some, indeed, her approach may bear out the claims of some of the popular postfeminists that the development of feminism as an academic discipline has limited its appeal outside the universities. Rene Denfeld, for example, accuses academic feminists of having 'climbed out on a limb of academic theory that is all but inaccessible to the uninitiated', while Naomi Wolf complains that it has adopted 'an exclusive and elaborate professional jargon' which amounts to no more than 'pig-Latin'.

POSTFEMINISM OR THIRD WAVE?

In 1970 Germaine **Greer** published *The Female Eunuch*, which become one of the founding texts of second wave feminism: 1999 has seen the publication of its sequel, *The Whole Woman*, a book which places Greer once again at centre stage in the feminist debate. In her introduction, Greer makes it quite clear she has written this book as a reaction against postfeminist ideology: 'The future is female, we are told. Feminism has served its purpose and should now eff off. Feminism was long hair, dungarees and dangling earrings; postfeminism was business suits, big hair and lipstick; post-postfeminism was ostentatious sluttishness and disorderly behaviour.' As Greer defines it, postfeminism is little more than a market-led phenomenon, for 'the most powerful entities on earth are not governments, but the multi-national corporations that see women as their territory'. Its assurance to women that they can 'have it all' – a career, motherhood, beauty, and a great sex life – actually only resituates them as consumers of pills, paint, potions, **cosmetic surgery**, **fashion**, and convenience foods. Greer also argues that the adoption of a postfeminist stance is a luxury in which the affluent western world can indulge only by ignoring the possibility that the exercising of one person's freedom may be directly linked to another's **oppression**. In such a situation, she asks, how can a woman believe that she has passed beyond feminism?

> If you believe, as I do, that to be a feminist is to understand that before you are of any race, nationality, religion, party or family, you are a woman, then the collapse in the prestige and economic power of the majority of women in the world as a direct consequence of western hegemony must concern you.

Whether one agrees with Greer or not – and her love of inflammatory rhetoric should not be forgotten – the publication of this book makes clear that the debate concerning the future of feminism is not over. Second wave feminism isn't dead, and a triumphant postfeminist world is still far from being imaginable, let alone a reality. While it is certainly true that feminism, like all other ideologies, must adapt to respond to the exigencies of a changing world – and any failure to address younger women must certainly be addressed – the postfeminist phenomenon, which was always primarily a media-led movement anyway, has reached an impasse out of which a coherent solution cannot be developed.

But perhaps there is another way for feminism to accommodate itself to changing times. Increasingly, feminists in their twenties and thirties are distancing themselves from the problematic politics of postfeminism by describing themselves as participating in a 'third wave'; a term in which the twin imperatives of continuity and change are neatly entwined. A number of third wave women's groups have sprung up in the US, including the Women's Action Coalition and Third Wave (founded by Rebecca Walker, daughter of the novelist Alice **Walker**). The editors of *Third Wave Agenda*, Leslie Heywood and Jennifer Drake, maintain that the primary difference between third wave and second wave feminism is that third wave feminists feel at ease with contradiction. Because they have been brought up within competing feminist structures, they accept pluralism as a given.

> We know that what oppresses me may not oppress you, that what oppresses you may be something I participate in, and that what oppresses me may be something you participate in. Even as different strands of feminism and activism sometimes directly contradict each other, they are all part of our third wave lives, our thinking, and our praxes: we are products of all the contradictory definitions of and differences within feminism, beasts of such a hybrid kind that perhaps we need a different name altogether.

Heywood and Drake make absolutely clear, however, that that 'different name' will not be postfeminism, which is something third wave feminists define as fundamentally conservative and reductive in its thought.

At the beginning of this chapter I traced postfeminism back to its origins in the eighties media, and have argued that it is through the media that it has, to a great extent, maintained its cultural presence. Intriguingly, the term 'third wave' was born at about the same time, but found its way to public notice by a rather different route. Heywood and Drake identify its moment of origin in 'critiques of the white women's movement that were initiated by women of color, as well from the many instances of coalition work undertaken by U.S. **third world** feminists'. It is this, they say, which has led to the third wave's innate acceptance of hybridity, its understanding that no account of oppression is true for all women in all situations all of the time. Moreover, its links with political activism should ensure that the third wave is more than just a theory, but an approach that will actively work against the social injustices which still form part of the everyday experience of many women.

It's no coincidence that one of the women predominantly identified with a feminist 'third wave' is the black theorist and writer bell hooks, whose work has persistently challenged white bourgeois women's unthinking assumption of an oppressed subject position. As early as 1984, hooks was arguing against a homogenised feminism which was seen 'as a lifestyle choice rather than a political commitment' – a statement which could be seen as a rather prescient description of popular postfeminism. Instead, she proposes a position from which feminism is 'advocated' rather than assumed.

> A phrase like 'I advocate' does not imply the kind of absolutism that is suggested by 'I am'. . . . It implies that a choice has been made, that commitment to feminism is an act of will. It does not suggest that by committing oneself to feminism, the possibility of supporting other political movements is negated.

It is this combination of commitment with flexibility which is now being claimed by the third wave.

CONCLUSION

In *Faces of Feminism* (1998) Sheila Tobias states that 'If feminism is going to survive the coming decades it has to be different.' The question is, what form, exactly, will this difference take? I don't think it is difficult to see the attractiveness of popular postfeminism. Its rejection of theoretical language ensures that it remains widely accessible, and its repudiation of victim status seeks to endow a sense of empowerment upon its readers. Nor do I think postfeminists are wholly misguided in focusing attention upon what feminism has already gained for women. But it's also easy to be too optimistic and to take one's own privileged position as representative, which can lead to the conclusion that the time for feminism is past, and that those who still cling to activist principles are deluded and fanatical.

Of course, this – or any – attempt to differentiate between third wave feminism and postfeminism may be achieving nothing more than a little juggling with semantics. Some will undoubtedly argue that, whatever the third wavers say, they're no more than a hipper, slicker branch of postfeminism. I would claim, however, that embracing the idea of a third wave may solve at least some of these problems this chapter has raised in connection with the postfeminist phenomenon. Mimicking the nomenclature of its predecessors, third wave feminism acknowledges that it stands on the shoulders of other, earlier, feminist movements, and so avoids the defensive relationship adopted by Roiphe, Denfeld and others. In tracing its origins back to the activism of the US immigrant community, it roots itself in a process of social and political endeavour that doesn't begin and end with the white middle classes, the point at which much of Wolf's analysis founders. Moreover, the third wave is not hostile to theory: on the contrary, it is clearly informed by such arguments as Gayatri **Spivak**'s notion of **subalternity**, as well as by the critiques of **gender** identity offered by Judith Butler, Hélène Cixous and others. Its desire to deconstruct **essentialist** assumptions concerning race and gender could therefore be considered as constituting an attempt to bridge the gap between theory and practice.

It may be, therefore, that third wave feminism is capable, as post-feminism is not, of describing a position from which past feminisms can be both celebrated and critiqued, and new strategies evolved. The state of economic, political and technological flux which characterises modernity presents opportunities and dangers for women which the feminists of the first and second wave could not have imagined. But whatever we call it, and whatever form it takes, it is essential that women continue to advance their cause into the next millennium. To refer back to the words of bell hooks quoted at the beginning of this chapter, the word 'feminism' must not become meaningless.

5

FEMINISM AND GENDER

SOPHIA PHOCA

Can men theorise feminism, can whites theorise racism, can the bourgeois theorise revolution, and so on. It is only when the former groups theorise that the situation is politically intolerable. Therefore it is crucial that the members of these groups are kept vigilant about their assigned subject positions.

> Gayatri Chakravorty Spivak, 'A Literary Representation of the
> Subaltern: A Woman's Text from the Third World', in
> *In Other Worlds: Essays in Cultural Politics* (1987)

In the above quotation, Gayatri Chakravorty **Spivak** invites men (amongst other culturally empowered groups) to keep vigilant about their hegemonic status when theorising **subaltern** identities. So, how do men theorise vigilantly?

Contemporary feminism has employed deconstructive strategies in order to destabilise a binary model inscribed in the masculine/feminine dyad. Instead, **feminists** have provocatively elaborated new frameworks in which to locate the gendered and sexual subject. These theorists have drawn from the **Derridean** model, which argues that binary structures will always privilege one of the binaries over the other: for example, male over female. Rather than trying to reverse this so that the **feminine** will be privileged over the **masculine**, as emancipatory feminism has striven to do, these feminists have attempted to destabilise the foundational structures on which binarism relies.

In the 1990s, three US academics, Judith **Butler**, Eve Kosofsky Sedgwick and Donna **Haraway** – who have now become feminist cult figures – have proposed some exciting and provocative ways of re-thinking gendered and sexual **subjectivity**. Butler introduces the idea that all **gender** and all sexual identities are performed, while Sedgwick offers us a range of new modes of classifying gender and sexuality. Haraway responds to **postmodern** technological developments by con-figuring the contemporary subject as a **cyborg** who is not locked into

55

organic gender identification. So if we are to accept the idea that the dualism between the masculine and feminine is no longer the reigning discourse in the construction of gender, it would seem that, regardless of their gender, both men and women can and should stay vigilant and participate in developing new ways of configuring the contemporary subject.

Emancipatory feminist theory took shape in the 1960s with the development of **women's studies**, where the questioning of gender-assigned subject positions began to be thoroughly investigated by exploring all aspects of gendered identities. Concomitantly, men's studies (or **masculinity studies**) emerged as a body of theory which began to consider masculine **identity** and sexuality. Although men's studies became established as an area of study in its own right by the 1980s, it did not develop as substantially as women's studies. However, like women's studies, men's studies encompasses a range of **ideological** positions which have taken identity as, variously, a biological, cultural, social and/or psychic construct. Feminism has been configured as an ideological category that promotes gender equality and **emancipation**. Although feminist concerns may be the province of both genders, historically women participated and invested in its discourses more prolifically than men. The issue of how men should participate in feminist discourses has been a contentious one. The key concern is that men will appropriate feminist **discourse** and paradoxically inscribe it with the same **phallocentric** strategies feminism has sought to challenge. So although the question 'what is masculinity?' is an important one, it was initially seen as an area which should be developed in men's studies.

Masculine sexuality became a key issue in gender studies in the 1980s, when feminism began to be theorised in **psychoanalytic** terms. The publication of Laura **Mulvey**'s seminal essay in 1975, 'Visual Pleasure and Narrative Cinema' (*Screen* (Autumn 1975) 16:3), was one of the most influential papers on sexual **difference** from a psychoanalytic point of view. She employed Lacanian psychoanalysis to analyse how the cinematic **gaze** is organised like a language, according to **patriarchal** codes and conventions, where masculinity is empowered through the act of looking, while femininity is disempowered by being reduced to passively being looked at ('to-be-looked-at-ness'). Mulvey argued that sexual difference controls how we view a film where the male subject lives out his fantasies and obsessions. The male gaze is constructed according to structures of control inscribed by sadistic voyeurism and/or fetishistic scopophilia (looking as a source of **pleasure**).

Mulvey's essay was important because it offered an analytical framework revealing the symbolic relations of power in patriarchal representation. Psychoanalysis provided a clear methodology to analyse the unconscious of patriarchal language. The problem was that Mulvey imposed masculinity as a point of view. So in 'Afterthoughts on "Visual Pleasure and Narrative Cinema" Inspired by King Vidor's *Duel in the Sun*' (*Framework* (Summer 1981) 15–17), she asks 'what about the women in the audience?'. In this paper, Mulvey proposes the idea of 'trans-sex identification', where the female viewer shifts between a feminine passive identification and masculine active identification. The former is social and inscribed in language, and the latter is psychoanalytic. According to **Freud**, femininity emerges out of a masculine period which is compulsory for both genders. As a result, in her early formative stages the girl experiences both masculine and feminine identification. Mulvey draws on Freud to resolve the dilemma of the female spectator's subject positioning. Therefore she proposes that if cinematic representation is seen as the *mise-en-scène* of desire, and the site of **fantasy**, it may offer the female spectator multiple subject positions, both male and female.

Mulvey's essays gave fresh impetus to the debate about the male gaze and voyeurism, masculinity, power and subordination. For example: how is the male body eroticised and presented as a voyeuristic fantasy for the female or the homoerotic gaze? How does male masochism operate? What is the configuration of power in a discourse on race and masculinity? In order to tackle these issues, writers turned to feminist theory. The cultural theorist Stephen Heath believes that 'Men have a necessary relationship to feminism – the point after all is that it should change them too' (Alice Jardine and Paul Smith, eds., *Men in Feminism*, 1987). In 1988 Rowena Chapman and Jonathan Rutherford argued that in the light of feminist theory, it was time to address issues concerning masculinity. In the introduction to their book *Male Order: Unwrapping Masculinity*, they write about

> The necessity for men to redefine masculinity, to imagine new forms of sexual and erotic expression, to produce a masculinity whose desire is no longer dependent on oppression, no longer policed by homophobia, and one that no longer resorts to violence and misogyny to maintain its sense of coherence.

Chapman and Rutherford highlight a paradox in contemporary thinking. On the one hand, feminists were drawing from the writing of male psychoanalytic and deconstructive theorists to challenge phallocentric configurations of gender identification and politics. On the other, male theorists were turning to feminist theorists to reconfigure patriarchal discourses on gender and identity. As a result the question emerged: do masculinity theorists necessarily need to draw on feminism in order to critique masculinity? This called into question the approach that feminist theory and masculinity theory are categorised as different bodies of thought, based on different ideological agendas. The notion of **essentialism** became a significant issue in this debate: that is, that gender is biologically determined, and therefore that men and women are fundamentally different.

In English a useful distinction emerged from the linguistic differentiation associated with the two adjectives for the terms 'men' and 'women'. One adjectival derivation – feminine/masculine – is used to refer to social, cultural or psychic constructions. The other – female/male – represents the biological aspects of gendered identities. This linguistic distinction is crucial in understanding the thinking behind essentialist and anti-essentialist discourses. Broadly, essentialist gender positioning is taken to imply that the identities of men and women are biologically fixed and determined. On the other hand, anti-essentialist thinking is predicated on the notion that patriarchy positions woman as **'other'**. She therefore signifies sexual difference, but this is not a fixed and stable identity.

The French writer Hélène **Cixous** famously challenged this simplistic binary approach, dismissing it for being reductive. Although a complex, controversial and divisive issue, pro- and anti-essentialist debates draw attention to the fact that gender politics is not only determined by issues of emancipation, but also how gender categories are configured, understood and represented.

When Spivak demands that men should be vigilant when theorising feminism, she also recognises that women stay vigilant. Women would find it intolerable if men were always to speak on their behalf. However, Spivak questions the assumption that a woman's identity means that she speaks for women from a position of 'knowledge'. She believes that all efforts to speak on behalf of a putative group will undermine the authenticity of that subject's voice.

> The position that only the subaltern can know the subaltern, only women can know women and so on, cannot be held as a theoretical presupposition either, for it predicates the possibility of knowledge on identity. Whatever the political necessity for holding the position, and whatever the advisability for attempting to 'identify' (with) the other as subject in order to know her, knowledge is made possible and sustained by irreducible difference, not identity.

Spivak argues that feminism has set itself up as a unitary body for political reasons; but she believes that women remain different. Equally, men should not be grouped under an umbrella term that fails to recognise the difference between men. Therefore, although an ontological construction of the gendered subject has been claimed for political reasons, the assumption of an essential identity consigns subjectivity to biological reductionism. This does not allow for non-binary difference. The notion of 'identity' is bound up in essentialist assumptions about the gendered subject, while 'irreducible difference' suggests that gender positioning can be inscribed in anti-essentialist configurations of gender.

While men are invited to keep vigilant by not making a hegemonic claim to speak on behalf of women, Spivak also says that women must not assume the right to speak on behalf of other women on the grounds of a shared or common identity. Following her logic, this means that men cannot claim to know and therefore speak for men. In this way, the categories 'women' and 'men' are troubled as subject positions. In short, although men should be vigilant about speaking on behalf of women, both men and women should be vigilant not to assume to necessarily 'know' or speak on behalf of any group which claims a shared gender identity.

Spivak proposes the Derridian idea that western philosophical discourse has constructed woman as a product of linguistic difference, according to a model of binary oppositionality. Spivak circumscribes essentialist gender politics by establishing a dialectical understanding of identity, where the subject is constructed through gender identification and **desire**. Masculinity is seen to stand in for a normative/dominant category. She argues that for deconstruction to become available to feminism, the category of 'woman' must not be taken as an object of analysis. Instead, she must be restored to the questioning subject, and ask 'what is man that his desire creates such a text?'.

Lacanian feminism has suggested that both genders can take up the masculine position, precisely because no one has the phallus. For **Lacan**, the phallus is the signifier of lack, not an organ. Even though the male subject possesses the penis, he does not have access to the phallus. Lacan refuted biologism by repudiating a conflation between the phallus and the penis, but what has problematised Lacanian feminism is that on a visual level the penis continues to stand in for the phallus, because it is more visible. The psychoanalytic feminist theorist Parveen Adams has wittily suggested that the phallus could have been equally signified as DNA (the Y chromosome) in order to destabilise the assumption that, on a linguistic as well as a visual level, the penis represents the phallus.

Anti-essentialist gender theorists have taken up the position that gender does not express an inner essence about the subject. Judith Butler, in her book *Gender Trouble* (1990), poses the argument that gender gives the effect of being the norm through the repudiation of its performance. Butler's notion of performative identification is informed by the famous paper 'Womanliness as Masquerade', written in 1939 by the psychoanalyst Joan Riviere. In this paper, Riviere draws on a case study of a successful professional woman, who every time she performed publicly sought reassurance from men by flirting. Riviere suggested that the woman became phallic through her 'masculine' success, but she attempted to conceal this by flirting, and so taking up a 'feminine' **masquerade**. Riviere pioneered the idea that gender is constructed according to social codes, where the subject becomes gendered by a process of mimesis.

Butler says that gender repetition may indeed reinforce conservative culture. But it may also draw attention to it and hence parody that same conservative culture. She refers to Fredric Jameson's notion of post-modern parody, in which he differentiates between a 'postmodern parody of resistance' and a 'postmodern parody of reaction'. He suggests that the repetition of the former serves the interests of a conservative culture by emphasising its foundational narratives, while in the latter, repetition can resist dominant cultural signification by emphasising, and therefore repeating, its fictions.

Butler's notion of performative identification functions in the same way, by either being employed to establish a normative notion of gender and sexuality as compulsory, or as a way of revealing its fictitious nature. For Butler, not all parody is subversive because its various effects rely on context and reception. She uses Jameson's notion of parody in order to suggest that it can be used to either subvert, destabilise, or perpetuate received meaning and values.

In this way, gender is not represented as 'real', but as a boundary which is politically regulated. Sex is seen as an obligatory injunction for the body to become a cultural sign, and it has to repeatedly define itself as such. Therefore, she argues that sex becomes a 'corporeal project', a sustained performative act. The notion of an 'authentic' essential masculinity or femininity is replaced by the notion that all gender/sexual configurations are performed, constructed by a recycling of gendered signs of sexuality and desire. There is no essential masculine subject, just as there is no essential feminine subject. For Butler, the subject can either opt for mimetic subject-positioning which sustains the notion of credible gender identification, or 'camp it up', and so perform gender as excess in order to reveal gender identification as masquerade. Therefore, both genders can take up masculine or feminine subject-positioning. At the same time, according to Butler, masculine and feminine sexualities are signified by strategies which are culturally received, and she therefore proposes that gender can only be understood as a fiction. She writes,

> If gender attributes and acts, the various ways in which the body shows or produces its cultural signification, are performative, then there is no pre-existing identity by which an act or attribute might be measured; there would be no true or false, real or distorted acts of gender, and the postulations of a true gender identity would be revealed as a regulatory fiction.

Butler's statement destabilises the certainties inscribed in the construction of the gendered heterosexual subject, suggesting that both gender and heterosexuality are performed. Thus she challenges **compulsory heterosexuality** and gender identification.

Notions of gender and sexuality were reconfigured with the emergence of queer studies in the 1990s. Following from the discourses raised by anti-essentialist feminism, **queer theory** put to question all reigning schemes of gendered/sexual normativity. A regulatory understanding of sexuality not only refers to heterosexual culture, but also includes gay desires for normativity. So queer theory does not stand for the emancipatory struggles for equality which are often the focus of gay discourses; instead, it interrogates all reigning schemes of gendered/sexual normativity. Queer theorist Eve Kosofsky Sedgwick has proposed some radical configurations of gender/sexual mapping which destabilise the foundational narratives of sexual and gendered identities, and has established some exciting new ways in which subject positioning may be reformulated.

In 'Epistemology of the Closet' (1990), Eve Kosofsky Sedgwick draws on Michel **Foucault's** claim that homosexuality began circa 1870. Obviously, this does not mean that same-sex sex did not occur before this date. It also doesn't mean that homosexuality was not acknowledged before the 1870s – as we know, Classical Greece was notorious for its celebration of homoeroticism. But according to Kosofsky Sedgwick, Foucault flamboyantly dates the pathologising, institutionalising and classifying of homosexuals as starting in the 1870s. As in the past, everyone was assigned to a gendered category, and it became necessary to include another regulatory homo/heterosexual categorisation. This category became inscribed in a discourse conditioned by notions of the private/public. Kosofsky Sedgwick has deconstructed sexual and gender categories by referring to 'allo- and auto-identification', where same-sex sex and different-sex sex involve both kinds of identification.

In the seemingly obvious section entitled 'People are Different from Each Other', Kosofsky Sedgwick has argued that, though we have elaborated a range of crude categories to contain identity, such as gender, race, **class**, nationality and sexual orientation, even if a subject were to share all of these categories with another, the differences may still remain significant. In a challenge to received classifications of identity, she provocatively proposes thirteen categories in order to reconfigure the map of sexual/gendered identification. Included below is a sample of some of her ideas on sexual configurations:

- Even identical genital acts mean very different things to different people.
- Some people spend a lot of time thinking about sex, others little.
- Some people like to have a lot of sex, others little or none.
- Many people have their richest mental/emotional involvement with sexual acts that they don't do, or even don't *want* to do.
- For some people, the possibility of bad sex is aversive enough that their lives are strongly marked by its avoidance; for others, it isn't.
- Some people like spontaneous sexual scenes, others like highly scripted ones, others like spontaneous-sounding ones that are nonetheless totally predictable.
- Some people's sexual orientation is intensely marked by auto-erotic pleasures and histories – sometimes more so than by any aspect of alloerotic object choice. For others auto-erotic possibility seems secondary or fragile, if it exists at all.
- Some people, homo-, hetero- and bisexual, experience their sexuality as deeply embedded in a matrix of gender meanings and gender differentials. Others of each sexuality do not.

Kosofsky Sedgwick's list of sexual identification allows for a mapping of sexuality which does not rely on the triad homo/hetero/bisexual. As such, it divests those categories from the received axiom of 'normative' versus 'perverse' that has historically described the sexual subject. Kosofsky Sedgwick goes on to unpack the categories of sex, gender and sexuality. She describes the former as 'chromosomal sex – the raw material', which is immutable and biologically based. On the other hand, she argues that gender is inscribed in a binary structure that shapes and informs a range of dual systems. This has little or nothing to do with 'chromosomal sex'.

According to Kosofsky Sedgwick, gender is shaped by gender and power relations. She therefore refutes the notion of biologism or the 'natural'. Gender is determined by the binary framework of masculinity and femininity. Sexuality, on the other hand, is determined by its slippage from semantic meaning, traversing both sides of the sex/gender dyad, but also exceeding them. However, she argues that, although sexuality and gender are informed by one another, they must also exist as distinct from one another. So while affiliations between different groups cannot be assumed because of common experience such as oppression, Kosofsky Sedgwick also argues that feminist anti-essentialist deconstructive strategies have meant that we should not be restricted to only same sex/gender identification. We have therefore found 'ways to ask the question of gender about texts even where the culturally "marked" gender (female) is not present as either author or thematic'.

Developments in technology have seen the emergence of cybertheory informed by the virtual world of computers and the Internet. Although **cyberspace** is technologically led, and traditionally **technology** is a male-dominated area, cyberspace has also been claimed by **cyberfeminism**. This has offered women an interesting way of inscribing Kosofsky Sedgwick's idea of the female mark on a male-identified thematic. Donna Haraway's 'A Cyborg Manifesto' (in *Simians, Cyborgs and Women: the Reinvention of Nature*, 1991), stands as a cult classic in feminist theory. In this essay, Haraway explores the collision between the postmodern digital information revolution and feminism. She employs Marxist, psychoanalytic and feminist methodologies in order to analyse how notions of race, gender and class have been transformed by technological developments. She rejects Marxist humanism on the grounds that the subject is understood in terms of a western notion of labour theory and value. Marxism does not recognise the subject in terms of cultural difference as articulated in feminist and anti-colonial theories. Haraway is also critical of psychoanalysis, because it regards woman as 'other', and therefore idealised or undermined.

Like Spivak, Haraway argues that there is nothing that encompasses all women, or men, under one unifying banner. Feminism has assumed that being female unites all women without taking into account differences between women, such as racial and class differences. By universalising sexual difference, all other cultural differences are erased.

Haraway destabilises a binary notion of femininity or masculinity by stating that there is no such thing as 'being' female or male. Gender categories are in fact highly complex notions, constructed by scientific discourses and other social practices which are now being challenged.

The **cyborg** has emerged as a postmodern metaphor for the contemporary subject. As postmodern digital technologies are restructuring the world, the cyborg is a reconfiguration of the subject which has been disassembled and reassembled. The cyborg is for Haraway the 'illegitimate child of patriarchy, colonialism and capitalism'. The cyborg disrupts traditional humanist barriers: human versus animal, human versus machine, and physical versus non-physical. Haraway's cyborg colonises and negates the organic subject. Cyborg replication is not conditional on sexual reproduction or the nuclear family: by reconceptualising the dualism between organic and machinic, all objects become interchangeable coded signs. In this way Haraway contests the essentialism which inscribes difference in organic knowledge. In Haraway's cyberculture, masculinity is circulated as sign, where both machinic and organic configurations of the subject are given equal status.

The years spanning 1975-91 produced some of the most interesting theories on sexual identity. **Anglo-American** feminist theory has been the focus of this paper, although this clearly does not encompass feminist thinking over this period. However, the theorists mentioned above trace a trajectory of contemporary thinking which situates masculinity in relation to feminist theory. Mulvey's notion of trans-sex identification, Spivak's postcolonial deconstruction of the gendered subject, Butler's performative identification, Kosofsky Sedgwick's allo- and auto-identification, and Haraway's cyborg are all examples of how feminist theorists have explored ways in which sexual difference constructs identity in relation to both genders.

Mulvey referred to Freud in order to show how the early shaping of the female subject's unconscious allows for trans-sex identification, meaning that the female subject can overcome the oppressive social constraints of passivity her gender has ascribed to her. However, Mulvey's argument was still contained within an essential binarism between the sexes. By the 1990s, however, deconstructive anti-essentialist feminism had destabilised a notion of essential sexual/gendered categories, offering a range of exciting and polymorphous configurations of sexual identities. The category of masculinity, like femininity, has been reconfigured; in a performative sense, according to Butler; as a transient identification amongst a plurality of configurations, according to

Kosofsky Sedgwick; or as a cyborg which no longer claims an organic identity, according to Haraway. By eliminating an ontological understanding of the masculine in order to reveal gender as a fictitious construct, deconstructive feminism has invited the male subject to reject the tropes of essential masculinity, and participate in what Stephen Heath has called a necessary process of 'change' if men are to embrace feminism.

6

FEMINISM AND THE
DEVELOPING WORLD

ALKA KURIAN

While **feminists** would surely not deny that the oppression of women is a matter of international concern, the west has tended to dominate both the theoretical and practical aspects of the movement. The customary division of the history of feminism into 'waves' stands as a good example of this, since these categorisations are conventionally organised around American and European events and personalities. Thus, however unintentionally, the 'grand narrative' of feminism becomes the story of western endeavour, and relegates the experience of non-western women to the margins of feminist discourse.

However, the growing influence of **postcolonial** theorists such as Gayatri Chakravorty **Spivak**, Trinh T. **Minh-ha** and Chandra Talpade Mohanty has led to increased discussion about the role of feminism in different cultural contexts. Chandra Talpade Mohanty's essay 'Under Western Eyes', first published in 1984, has been a particularly important intervention in such debates, because it explicitly addresses the whole notion of the 'third world woman' as she is constructed in western feminist discourses. Mohanty argues that 'Western feminisms appropriate and "colonise" the constitutive complexities which characterize the lives of women in these countries', thus ending up with a crudely reductive 'notion of **gender** or sexual difference ... which can be applied universally and cross-culturally'. Yet Mohanty herself is trapped within such discourses. Reluctant to use the term 'third world' at all – since, as she says, it implicitly reinforces 'existing economic, cultural and **ideological** hierarchies' – she can nevertheless find no other designation, 'because this is the terminology available to us at the moment'. The best form of protest available to her is to persistently place 'third world' in quotation marks in order 'to suggest a continuous questioning of the designation'.

However, an examination of the influence of feminism on any so-called 'third world' culture is to uncover a narrative which, at once vibrant and problematic, contradicts the easy assumptions implied by the designation. This essay is about the growth of feminism in one country customarily classified as 'third world' – India. Male dominance over women is deeply ingrained within the many facets of Indian culture and, contrary to the experience of women in the western world – where women's struggles for equal political and legal rights were conducted against the background of largely successful interventions within political, economic, social and military systems – it was inevitable that the ambivalences, conflicts and changes introduced into economic and social life in India by the durability of the colonial culture had its impact on the character of women's movements in India.

Despite the unstinting efforts of social reformers like Ram Mohan Roy in the nineteenth century, and other unsung but well-meaning administrators, the traditional and unforgiving picture of the Indian male afforded by the colonial situation was an unappetising combination of the powerless princeling, the desperate coolie, and the obsequious *babu* mercilessly caricatured by the Imperialist writer *par excellence*, Rudyard Kipling. It was only natural that the predominantly liberal leadership of the nationalist Congress, radicalised by Gandhi's influence after the First World War, visualised a society where Indians would have the opportunity to manage their own affairs – but which also acknowledged the crucial place of women if the national movement was to seize the moral and strategic high ground.

India is the birthplace of some of the most influential and articulate postcolonial theorists, including Mohanty and Spivak, yet they are not wholly representative of Indian feminism, which for the most part has not (yet) developed the overt interest in theorisation which has become such a defining feature of western feminism. Indeed, it is interesting to note that theorists such as Spivak and Mohanty work to subvert the dominant intellectual paradigm of the 'first world' from within, choosing to speak from western, rather than Indian, institutions. This essay will argue that, for the most part, the history of Indian feminism has been one of social and political agitation directed against specific and concrete areas of injustice such as political under-representation, domestic violence and adherence to misogynistic traditions such as *sati* (the self-immolation of widows), and only now may it be reaching a point at which the widespread formulation of theorisation is being seen as desirable.

POLITICAL MARGINALISATION

In 1931 women's right to vote was accepted during the Karachi session of the Congress. Gandhi's role in feminising politics, by encouraging women to leave the narrow confines of their homes and kitchens, is not negligible. He saw the immense potential that lay untapped in women and by relying on what he viewed as their inherent non-violence and natural tenacity under duress, he brought them to the centre stage of his self-rule movement. Coming from a cross-section of Indian society, most of these women belonged to families that were committed to the cause of the freedom struggle. Consequently there were no taboos attached to their rising to the occasion when the male members of their families went to jail. In her essay 'Women and Politics' (in Singh, Serbjeet Singh and Jyoti Sabbarwal, eds., *The Fiftieth Milestone: A Feminist Critique*, 1998) Neerja Chowdhary sees the role of most women in the nationalist movement more as a duty and less as an exercise of a choice to enter the public arena. However, despite the nature of this struggle, which brought together men and women from different back-grounds, the achievement of independence did not lead to a marked improvement in the political participation and social situation of ordinary women across the country.

Chowdhary holds that though Gandhi was all for women's political participation, he was not comfortable with the idea of them entering the power game. He saw women's role as cleansing politics rather than starting their own movements. This was a natural by-product of Gandhi's curious mixture of political radicalism and apparently benign social conservatism. Owing to a lack of awareness of the possible roles that they could have been fitted into, the primacy of the **family** over the individual meant that women's potential and abilities honed in the political arena during the nationalist movement were not put to effective use in immediate post-independence India. This situation was not helped by the crucial demarcation made between power and social reform. Rather than claiming their rightful place in the political power structure, middle-class women got involved in worthy social and welfare reform programmes such as refugee rehabilitation (a consequence of the country's partition) and the Sarvodaya and Bhoodan movements, all programmes inspired by generous communitarian ideals.

Getting a party ticket is not easy for women owing to differences in religion, caste and **class**, as well as the **gender** discrimination entrenched in Indian society. Social and domestic responsibilities, fear of character-assassination, family disapproval and party bias all make a woman's choice difficult. It is for no other reason that despite remarkable strides made in all sectors of the economy, the number of women in politics has continued to dwindle in the post-independence period. From being ranked third in 1973, India today occupies a dismal sixty-fifth position internationally in terms of women's representation in the parliament. Women like Sarojini Naidu who participated in the national movement with zeal and fervour, and who was appointed as President of the Congress Party in 1924, as well as several other prominent women leaders eminently qualified to take on the political mantle, were all relegated to secondary, tokenistic political positions in independent India. This was a consequence of the erosion of liberal political and social values amongst the dominant national political parties and the unfortunate relegation of the once mighty Congress to being the handmaiden of the Nehru-Gandhi family.

Apart from the separation of political power from social reform, the competitive and representative electoral politics that were introduced in the country after 1947 meant that it inevitably came to rely on people's affiliations such as caste, class, community, religion, geographical identity and their economic and muscle-power, an atmosphere not entirely conducive to encouraging women to join the political fray. Further, the male bias of the parties means that women are weeded out during the selection process. The case of Congress, the party that brought women to the forefront during India's national movement and which has ruled the country for most of the post-independence period, is a striking example. Congress gave only token representation to women in the party and never involved them in real decision-making processes. Under Rajiv Gandhi the scenario improved, because he regarded women as a sizeable vote bank that he could rely on, and thus made more allowances for them. Apart from setting up the National Commission for Women and the National Perspective Plan for Women, he ushered in a motion to give 30% reservation to women in the village governing bodies, or *panchayats*. But he undid his good intentions by passing the notorious Women's Protection of Rights on Divorce Act (1986) to placate the conservative sections of the Muslim community. The record of other political parties is not good either. In the conservative nationalist Bharatiya Janata Party, only 10 out of 147 members of its National Executive are women and the left-wing parties fare no better in this regard. The Communist Party of India (Marxist), for example, has no women representatives in the Politburo.

Under Indira Gandhi's prime ministership, the espousal of communitarian, populist and nationalist ideals went along with the disintegration of liberal political principles and the destruction of the democratic decision-making process of the Congress. The debasement and vulgarisation of the Congress was certainly not conducive to the advancement of women in national politics because Indira Gandhi's charismatic power had its sources in her family's central place in the nationalist movement for independence. In a traditional and modernising society like India that still hangs on to traces of feudalism marked by the concept of inherited rule, the rise of women like Indira Gandhi or Jayalalitha is due to family connections. Interestingly, despite the opportunity conferred upon them, women rulers have rarely aligned themselves with a feminist agenda due to the fear of destabilising the structures that sustain their position.

Indian social life has always been marked by protests and movements that have caught the imagination of the masses. The most notable of these, especially in the late sixties and early seventies, that brought in their wake millions of farmers, landless labourers, dalits, members of the Scheduled Castes and Tribes and students all over India, have been those of the mass land-grab movements led by the Communist Party of India, the Anti-Price Rise agitation in Maharashtra and Gujarat, and the grassroots movement for political, economic and social change in Bihar led by the Sarvodaya leader J. P. Narayan. These mass movements became a common platform for previously voiceless people; most important amongst whom were women, particularly from the working classes, lower-middle classes, the backward castes and the Dalits. Their participation marked a dramatic change in the kind of women identified with activism, since the nationalist movement predominantly attracted women from the upper and middle classes. The Left-wing Anti-Price Rise Movement (APRM), a women-only campaign that was sparked off in Maharashtra in 1972, is a case in point. Around 20,000 women in different parts of the state participated in several *Latni Morchas* ('rolling-pin demonstrations') in which they challenged senior state administrators by wielding basic kitchen implements such as plates, rolling pins and spoons, thereby giving a **feminine** spin to their protest. By virtue of the very nature of their agitation, these *Latni Morchas* attracted a lot of media attention and began to be interpreted as part of a 'new women's movement'. Unfortunately, once the agitation was over, these very women withdrew from the public arena and went back to the humdrum of domestic duties without drawing any political mileage out of their endeavours.

In a study on the political participation of women, 'Masses of Women: But Where is the Movement?' (in Saskia Wieringa, ed., *Subversive Women: Women's Movements in Africa, Asia, Latin America and the Caribbean*, 1995), Nandita Gandhi gives an insight into this commonly observed phenomenon where women 'appear only in flashes through centuries of oral and written material'. She maintains that because of the social and domestic responsibilities imposed on women's lives, they have little opportunity to join formal politics. Their political participation remains unrecorded due to the sporadic and supportive, rather than consistent, nature of their participation. This leads to their political participation not being given due recognition by the social sciences. Moreover, she points to two major weaknesses inherent in the APRM that were essentially responsible for its inability to sustain itself.

First, its leaders remained reliant on the mass **ideologies** of Gandhism and Marxism to comprehend and criticise the nature of women's oppression. For Nandita Gandhi, both these ideologies, with their underlying assumption about the sexual division of labour, have an 'inbuilt structure of reasoning which theoretically marginalises women . . . or keeps them at the periphery of exploitative relationships'.

Second, the APRM underlined its belief in this sexual division of labour and a woman's disadvantageous situation at home, by resorting to the use of kitchen implements during its populist campaigns. The strategy was to focus on the question of price rises and softening the burdens imposed on housewives by societal pressures. By doing so, it missed the crucial opportunity of politicising the question of household work and its relationship with 'the production process and the capital and with men and the family'. Such populist movements prompted by economic and political crises relied on women's mass participation, but their marginal status was emphasised by the fact that their struggles did not result in the reform of the social and cultural position of women, particularly from the most disadvantaged sections of society.

The advent in the 1970s of the **second wave** of Indian feminism can be attributed to several factors. First and foremost, from being appendages of larger movements (such as the nationalist and other populist struggles), the Indian women's movement saw a shift towards a predominantly feminist agenda. The United Nation's declaration of 1975 as International Woman's Year, and later of 1975–85 as the International Woman's Decade, gave an impetus to the growing consciousness amongst women for the need to do something to redress their subordinate position in Indian society. The publication in 1975, at the behest of the United Nations, of *Towards Equality*, a seminal report on the status of women in India, proved to be a watershed in the history of the Indian Women's Movement. This report, which for the first time tackled the issues of the average Indian woman's existence – such as female infant mortality, child marriages, illiteracy, and dowry – came up with certain startling revelations. It showed that, despite the liberal and communitarian ideas of the Indian constitution, and the various developmental programmes initiated by the state, social attitudes and practices at the level of communities had only worsened with respect to women.

The decade that followed the publication of the above report was marked by intense social and political turmoil. It was as if not just women but also other underprivileged sections of the society, such as the poor and middle-ranking peasants, members of the lower and backward castes, were all simultaneously imbued with a sense of collective consciousness to voice their discontentment with the political regime. The increasingly common usage of the term 'women's movement' heralded the onset of a new consciousness. Their activities, which were part of the general struggles carried out by other marginalised groups, concretised around several motifs, most important of which were struggles against violence and the question of gender and communal identity.

THE STRUGGLE AGAINST VIOLENCE

In 1979, an open letter written by four lawyers publicly underlining their disapproval of the manner in which the Supreme Court of India had shown an instance of its 'cold-blooded legalism' in acquitting two policemen accused of raping 14-year-old Mathura, a tribal girl from Maharashtra, gave momentum to the campaign against violence that had been gathering pace for some time: a campaign led by several civil liberties and women's groups who were determined to bring to light countless instances of miscarriages of justice, police atrocities and general anarchy that had marked the Emergency period.

This instance of 'custodial **rape**' was not the first of its kind where uniformed men had abused their position of authority in victimising the weak and silent sections of the society. Nor was it the first time that a court had come to a judgement on the basis of lack of evidence and by making presumptions about the victim's sexual promiscuity. By singling out the Mathura case, the activists for the first time attracted enormous media attention that highlighted the legal system's inherent **sexism**, hypocrisy and blindness to the terrible violence perpetuated on women. The spontaneous public outcry provoked by this case led to a series of protests and demonstrations – some of them led by academic staff of leading universities – across the country. The unprecedented media coverage and support that came from various quarters enabled women to value the strength of their collective consciousness. A string of women's organisations such as Saheli in Delhi, and the Forum Against Rape (later renamed as Forum Against Oppression of Women – FAOW) in Mumbai came into being almost in direct response to the

Mathura rape case. FAOW organised a national conference in the same year which opened a public debate on the need for legal reforms by focusing on the nature of women's oppression, insensitivity of the courts while dealing with cases of sexual violence, and the insurmountable legal difficulties that women face while seeking justice. The outrage generated by the Mathura rape case forced the government to amend the rape law.

Such highly publicised cases overshadow the day-to-day instances of sexual violence perpetrated by ordinary men that go unrecorded, either because the police do not bother to investigate the crime or because of the victim's silence due to fear of social stigma. According to Nandita Gandhi, 'the extreme vulnerability of women, the sexual nature of the crime, societal attitudes regarding chastity, the indifference of the police and judicial procedures interact with each other to curiously reverse the roles of the victim and violator'. This works to disclaim the relationship between rape and sexual gratification, claiming that 'it is not nature but human society, its laws and institutions, which have created hierarchies between men and women, class and caste; that rape is not a random unpremeditated act but a form of violence by the powerful on those who are powerless, poor and disadvantaged'. And women being the weakest amongst the latter, they tend to be victimised more than the men.

The second campaign that hit the headlines around the same time was the one against dowry deaths when a coalition of around thirty women's groups collectively called the Dahej Virodhi Chetna Manch (Anti-Dowry Consciousness-Raising Platform), brought to light a spate of mysterious suicides or accidental deaths of young married girls that unfolded in major metropolitan cities almost like an epidemic. On the basis of investigations and research carried out in 1977, the Mahila Dakshata Samiti (Women's Enlightenment Committee) in Delhi went on to claim that most of the cases that were being passed off as 'stove deaths' or suicides were in fact murders committed by the girl's marital family, who hoped to get a better deal through their son's marriage next time round. From resorting to humiliating and publicly shaming the in-laws and the husband by staging demonstrations in the neighbourhood, the anti-dowry campaign focused on consciousness-raising through organising a series of seminars, plays, poster campaigns and mass pledges against dowry. By pointing out the court's sexism and insensitivity to women's vulnerability, its insistence on evidence, the personal nature of the crime (where the woman even in her dying declaration hesitated to implicate her husband), the campaign demanded that the State revise its law on dowry.

Traditionally, a social custom practised only among the upper caste, landed, Hindu families, dowry has, over the years, been adopted by other castes and religious communities. Moreover, from being understood as *streedhan*, or woman's property given her at the time of her marriage, the very nature of the term has undergone a dramatic change. Most arranged marriages have today become a business transaction that involve crude negotiations on exchange of items such as furniture, clothes and kitchen implements needed to start a new home as well as extravagant wedding feasts, entertainment of guests, consumer goods, gold and hard cash that the bride's family (depending on the groom's profession and family status) feels obliged to give to his family. Eradication of dowry from the Indian society has always been a losing battle for social reformers. Although it has long been recognised as a social evil, the dowry system has nevertheless spread through the entire cross-section of the society. Several attempts have been made to define the system and relevance of dowry. Indian liberals such as Nandita Gandhi see it as the exemplification of modern Indian materialism and greed for consumer goods, and argue that 'the system of dowry degrades and commodifies women and is one of the manifestations of the low status of women in Indian society'. The radical liberal criticism holds 'dowry as a manifestation of a backward, semi-feudal society on which a capitalist economy has been imposed . . . dowry . . . then takes on a commercialised, consumeristic and capitalist character'.

But discounting materialistic assumptions that smack of moralism, Madhu Kishwar, one of India's leading feminists and founding member of India's first feminist journal, *Manushi*, argues that dowry contributes neither to secure a comfortable existence for the bride (as in most cases she has no right over her own dowry) or to improving the economic status of the groom or his family. By pointing out its prevalence even among those sections of the society who find dowry transactions 'morally wrong and socially harmful', she holds that most girls' parents are eager to give dowry and to meet the in-laws' incessant demands for gifts after the marriage. This only goes to prove the extent to which girls are seen as an economic liability for whom parents have to bribe the groom to keep her in his family at any cost. In an essay published in *Manushi* in 1986, 'Dowry: To Ensure her Happiness or to Disinherit Her?', Kishwar argues that dowry is thus 'a transfer of wealth from men of a family to those of another, with women acting as vehicle of transfer (as brides) or as watchdogs (as mother-in-law and sister-in-law), its significance is not primarily economic but political in the sense that it defines a power relation between the man and woman'. The woman's unhappiness due to being constantly harassed by her in-laws highlights her vulnerability and complete dependence on her marital family.

This sense of being helpless and subordinate in a context where the husband provides no support, moral or otherwise – for no other reason but the fact that he too is a cog in the **patriarchal** set-up – leads to many female suicides. Madhu Kishwar proposes several ways of reducing a woman's vulnerability, such as ensuring that a daughter is not excluded from her father's property, and family investing in the **education** and careers of daughters as well as sons, so that women will have the means to walk out of a difficult **marriage** and lead independent lives. An unconditional moral support by her natal family where she can have refuge, would also go a long way in making sure that the woman is neither killed at the hands of her marital family nor that she has to resort to the extreme measure of suicide.

GENDER AND COMMUNAL IDENTITY

In 1987, the incident in Deorala, a small village in Rajasthan, of a 17-year-old Rajput bride being burned alive on her husband's funeral pyre was not very different to those tragic cases of young married women killed in their own homes, women who are treated as burdens, and thus 'dispensable and replaceable'. But the reason why this case was loaded with a whole set of different 'social and cultural' implications was the fact that rather than the heinous acts of violence that are carried out on women behind closed doors, the *sati* of Roop Kanwar was performed in full public gaze. Kanwar was killed with the apparent sanctity of custom, even though *sati* had been banned since the early nineteenth century by the British administration in one of its few instances of social intervention. According to Madhu Kishwar in her essay 'The Burning of Roop Kanwar' (*Manushi* 42–3, 1987), 'if the wide-spread implicit acceptance of wife murder in our society today expresses the low value set on women's lives, the public burning to death of a woman is an open endorsement of that devaluation'.

The anti-*sati* women's campaign came in for criticism from those, such as Ashis Nandy and Patrick Harrigan, who saw 'Indian feminists . . . as agents of modernity who were attempting to impose crass market-dominated views of equality and liberty on a society which once gave the noble, the self-sacrificing and the spiritual the respect they deserve', and who defined 'these views of equality and liberty as being drawn from the west, so Indian feminists stood accused of being westernists, colonialists, cultural imperialists, and – indirectly – supporters of capitalist ideology' (in Radha Kumar, *The History of Doing: An Illustrated Account of Movements for Women's Rights and Feminism in India*, 1998).

This was of course not the first time that a *sati* had been committed in modern India. In the previous instances, the state machinery had successfully intervened to stop such acts. But the Deorala incident, which elicited no intervention from the state (it would appear that the local authorities knew of the imminent immolation), provoked unprecedented outcry from both anti- and pro-*sati* campaigners. Though *sati* is supposed to be a voluntary act, there were rumours of Roop Kanwar's resistance to it and of her parents not being informed of this supposedly public decision on the widow's part to immolate herself on her husband's funeral pyre. Roop Kanwar was drugged, clothed in bridal finery and dragged out of the house. Eyewitnesses remember her being shoved into the fire that was lit by her brother-in-law.

After the incident that glorified and mythified Roop Kanwar, the *sati*-site (later known as *Sati*-Sthal) became a place of pilgrimage where an entire infrastructure came into being that allowed for brisk business activity, organising accommodation for the *sati*-worshipers who thronged the place in their thousands, and the selling of Kanwar's photographs, religious offerings and food. In short, *sati* became a money-spinner, revealing, in Radha Kumar's words, 'the gruesome materialism of a society which permitted the production of "sacrifice" for profit'. The State government turned a blind eye to the demand made by the Joint Action Forum Against *Sati* that the 'ideologues and profiteers of *sati*' be punished according to the law that exists to discourage such activities. It was yet another instance of the state selling out to placate, in this case, the Rajput electoral base within the much larger context of the Hindu vote bank: a 'process of communal formations in India which shows how issues of gender can become central to these'.

The controversial case of Shah Bano is another example of this kind. A 74-year-old Muslim woman appealed in 1985 for maintenance under the secular criminal law in the Indian Penal Code after being divorced by her husband of forty years. The court granted her maintenance under section 125 of the Criminal Procedure Code as it 'cut across the barriers of religion and transcended the personal laws of the religious communities'. But in his judgement Justice Chandrachud, one of the judges involved, made controversial remarks about the treatment of Muslim women by the men in their community, and was critical of the manner in which Muslim women were unfairly treated by men in their community. The court also recommended that the government introduce a Uniform Civil Code. In doing so, the court aroused the anger of conservative

Muslims, who interpreted the court's decision as an attack upon their personal law – in spite of the fact that the Indian Constitution guarantees the right to freedom of religion.

Feminist, liberal and secular groups criticised the judgement for having shown insensitivity towards the Muslim community. As Madhu Kishwar argued in 'Pro-Women or Anti-Muslim?: The Shah Bano Controversy' (*Manushi* 77, 1986), 'By singling out Muslim men and Islam in this way, Justice Chandrachud converts what is essentially a women's rights issue into an occasion for gratuitous attack upon the community'. This couldn't have happened at a worse time. The mid-eighties saw a steep rise of Hindu communalism linked both to the anti-Sikh riots that took place in the aftermath of Indira Gandhi's assassination and the *Ram Janmabhoomi* agitation that sought to declare the site of the Babri mosque as the birthplace of the Hindu god Rama. This period also coincided with the dramatic rise of the Hindu nationalist Bharatiya Janata Party, which was building up its support through calculated campaigns to win over conservative Hindu opinion. Not surprisingly, these tactics only served to legitimise the fears of orthodox Muslims, and effectively marginalised liberal Muslim views and values. Rajiv Gandhi's government, with a view to placating the conservative Muslim leadership, overlooked the chance to rationalise and do away with gender inequality from the inherently discriminatory personal laws, and allowed instead for the Muslim Women Protection on Divorce Act to be passed which excluded divorced Muslim women from the ambit of Section 125 of the Criminal Procedures Code. Feminist groups and civil rights activists all over the country led campaigns in support of the upholding of Section 125 and strengthening of legal rights of Muslim women but to no avail. Moreover, Shah Bano, the hapless pawn in the controversy who had spent 10 years fighting for her right to maintenance, requested the court to reverse its decision for fear of being exploited by the media, communalists and other activist groups.

CONCLUSION

The Indian women's movement is thus a collection of several smaller movements, which have grown out of a series of spontaneous reactions – organised or otherwise – of thousands of women across the length and breadth of the country against injustices of which they have been victims through the centuries. The dominance of patriarchal attitudes and the complexity of caste, class and religious identities in India have been responsible for subjecting women to **stereotypical** roles.

However, the trend which started during the nationalist struggle for the country's independence began to change in the seventies, and marked the onset of the 'second wave' of the movement that involved mass participation of women from the lower sections of society. The debate shifted from women's welfare to development in an atmosphere where more and more women were voicing their discontent with the existing system and were laying emphasis on the need for political participation and social empowerment. Education has contributed the most in this shift, thanks to which lower and middle-class women have been rescued from being trapped within a sense of passivity and fatalism. The big metropolitan cities such as Delhi, Calcutta, Bangalore, Chennai and Mumbai, as well as certain smaller cities like Hyderabad, Chandigarh, Pune and Ahmedabad, have seen over the years the growth of a 'critical core' of articulate, educated women who, endowed with the ability to critically analyse their marginalised situation within the exploitative patriarchal culture, are now making informed choices about the role they want to adopt and the positions of power from which they do not want to see themselves excluded.

The present-day '**third wave**' of the Indian Women's Movement is an indication of the onset of independent issue-based responses by feminist groups, who began to tackle urban and rural women's dilemmas and conflicts as a part of the larger struggle to assert the personal, social and cultural implications of a feminist consciousness. By moving from awareness-raising campaigns, women's groups underlined the need for developing structures to provide help and support to women in need. The increasing number of women working in various branches of the media has enabled them to bring the previously 'secondary and marginal' women-related issues to the forefront of public consciousness. The late seventies and eighties saw the coming into being of several feminist publishing and research organisations such as *Manushi* and Kali for Women (the first Indian feminist journal and publishing house respectively) and several Women's Studies Centres in universities and non-governmental organisations.

As previously suggested, the involvement of women – particularly from educated, middle and working-class backgrounds – in the sphere of social reform after independence marginalised their influence over the political process. While this was a retrograde development, the gradual absorption of educated women into the administrative structures of the government has been a positive development. A striking feature of the post-1947 political settlement has been the acceptance of positive discrimination in favour of backward castes, *dalits* and other disadvantaged communities. Though such a system would eventually tend to help women from marginalised groups to assume positions of responsibility, it is interesting that the predominance of upper caste and middle-class women and the pervasiveness of Gandhian ideology during the nationalist struggle meant that women were not seen as being in need of quota systems to support them in their endeavours to secure employment in government institutions and representation in the political decision-making process. The present-day dismal 7% representation of women in Parliament is a glaring testimony to the exclusion of women from politics. In order to reverse this trend, women's organisations in India are today asking for a 33% reservation in the Parliament and State Assemblies. It will require a tremendous sustained fight to force the dominant political parties to accept this demand.

Thus the women's movement in twentieth-century India has moved from participation in liberal nationalist political struggles and social reform to a wider populist, even if at times reactionary, agenda which has helped in the eighties and nineties to highlight the tensions between the requirements of modern life and traditional conceptions of womanhood. This is increasingly leading to a healthy and often acrimonious debate about the impact of women's economic, cultural and social empowerment and marginalisation within gender relations, the structure of families and communities.

7

WOMEN AND NEW
TECHNOLOGIES

LIZA TSALIKI

INTRODUCTION

The relationship between women and **technology** has always been an
uneasy one, since the traditional perception of technology is heavily
weighted against women. In most cases, the symbolic representation of
technology reproduces the **stereotype** of women as technologically
ignorant and inept. Much technological equipment tends to be **gender-**
typed, with some tools being regarded as more 'suitable' for men (e.g.,
saws, trucks, wrenches, guns); and others more 'suitable' for women
(e.g., vacuum cleaners, typewriters, irons).

More importantly, though, it is men who are in control of technology,
since women are usually excluded from an understanding of technique
and the physical principles by which machines operate. Nevertheless,
the history of technological developments has shown that the dynamics
and slippages between intended designs and unintended users give rise
to new notions of the ideal user. In fact, as Judy Wajcman argues in
Feminism Confronts Technology (1991), 'the designers and promoters of
a technology can never completely predict or control its final uses.
Technology may well lead a "double life"'.

Nowhere is this more evident than within domestic technologies.
Domestic technologies are targeted primarily at women, who are treated
as technological users and consumers, while men play the roles of
technology's creators and designers. The majority of these technologies
were not specifically designed for household (and, more specifically,
female) use, but originated in very different spheres in order to meet
commercial, industrial and even defence purposes. It was only later that
they were adapted for home use as manufacturers sought to expand
their markets. Hence, the automatic washing machine, the vacuum
cleaner and the refrigerator were widely available in naval and commercial ships long before they were introduced into the home, while
microwave ovens were initially developed for food preparation in
submarines by the U.S. Navy.

The telephone, one of the earlier forms of information and communication technologies (ICTs), is another example of a technology with a 'double life'. It was originally designed for making business transactions between men, and the industry long resisted its 'trivialisation' by women, who were using it for 'frivolous gossip'. By the 1920s, however, the telephone had become a powerful means for enhancing social contacts between otherwise isolated housewives. As soon as the industry realised the power of the female market, the telephone was advertised for both business *and* pleasure uses. The technology of the telephone brought with it rising concerns about the blurring of boundaries between the public and the private, and created unprecedented opportunities for unregulated courtship outside existing social norms. Women were considered especially vulnerable to this new form of communication technology, as their worldly inexperience in gauging trustworthiness made them susceptible to males manipulating the intimacy of the telephone.

In this sense, the inability to comprehend the operating principles and ethos of technology has always been associated with women. This is because technical competence is central to dominant perceptions of masculinity which see a 'natural' polarity between male/female, rationality/emotion, hard/soft. This social construction draws from a wider system of sexual stereotypes within western culture which identify men with **culture** and science and women with **nature** and **intuition**. Following a psychoanalytic approach, the relationship between **masculinity** and technology (technological warfare in particular) has been explained in terms of 'womb envy', whereby, in the words of Judy Wacjman, 'men "give birth" to science and weapons to compensate for their lack of the "magical power" of giving birth to babies'.

However, the notion of technology as masculine culture runs deeper than **psychoanalysis** and into the traditional processes of women's socialisation into relationships with technological objects. Different forms of childhood exposure to technology take place initially in the home where 'toys for the boys' lay the foundations for mathematical, scientific and technological knowledge, while 'toys for the girls' foster their caring and social interactions skills. Schools further reinforce the early socialisation into gender roles that the family has introduced, only to be followed by the gender segregation of the labour and advertising markets. In this context, it is not surprising that even the new ICTs remain a male preserve. Male executives, for example, refused for years to use the typewriter since the latter was seen as female technology. With the advent of electronic office systems, however, 'typing' was replaced by 'keyboarding', which is okay for executives to do, since a computer is involved.

The development of microelectronics and the declining significance of the muscular period of the 'heroic age of mechanization' (where you had to be physically strong to work with machines) was coupled with expectations that the gender stereotyping of technology would decrease. Computers, for example, could have been gender-free, with no differentiation between male and female users. Alternatively they could have been appropriated by women, their technology fitting with 'feminine' rote tasks, detail, precision and nimble typing fingers. The harsh reality, though, is that western culture has already contextualised computer culture as masculine culture. Girls are seriously outnumbered by boys when it comes to computer use and expertise, usually because computers are associated with maths and science – traditionally male subjects. Even when girls use computers, their interaction with and experience of computers is different from that of boys. When girls play computer games, for example, they do not engage in 'computer talk' and do not develop the computer culture boys usually do. As L. Haddon argues in 'Explaining ICT Consumption' (Roger Silverstone and Eric Hirsch, eds., *Consuming Technologies*, 1992), computer games are predominantly a male preserve, as they are part of an 'amorphous boy's "culture" of school and leisure', and follow gender differences experienced in video game playing.

As a result of this process of socialisation, women learn as young girls that the domain of computers belongs primarily to boys and men, and the dismal statistics for women in computer science stand to prove that. In the USA, women routinely receive a third of the bachelor's degrees allocated in computer science, 27% of the master's degrees and 13% of Ph.D.s. They comprise only 7.8% of computer science and computer engineering faculties.

It comes as no surprise, therefore, that women quickly develop a built-in resistance to computer technology that is manifested in anxieties, phobias, and a sense of technological ineptitude. In addition, there are other features that restrict further female participation in computer culture, such as the legacy of the computer hacker. Hacking, with its preoccupation with competition and winning, describes a male world that takes the machine as a partner in an intimate relationship and discourages female users.

Things, though, are changing, as women have started to dynamically explore the new technologies. According to Sherri Turkle in *The Second Self: Computers and the Human Spirit* (1988), the issue for the future relationship of women with computer technology may no longer be about 'computerphobia', triggered by feelings of fear and panic, but about 'computer reticence', in itself the result of the need to 'stay away because the computer becomes a personal and cultural symbol of what a woman is not'. Still, as Donna **Haraway** observes in 'A Cyborg Manifesto' (1991), we are now living in a world marked by 'a movement from an organic, industrial society to a polymorphous, information system – from all work to all play, a deadly game', in which computer technology is everywhere. Within this networked reality, polarities such as nature/culture, animal/human/machine are redefined in boundary-shifting terms. Enter the Internet and the world of **cyberspace** wherein technology is opening up the possibility for female emancipation.

CYBERFEMINISM: TECHNOLOGY AS EMPOWERMENT

'On the Internet, nobody knows you're a dog.' (a cartoon discussion between a dog Internet surfer and his dog-friend, *The New Yorker*, July 5, 1993)

Cyberfeminism is information technology as a fluid attack, an onslaught on human agency and the solidity of identity. Its flows breach the boundaries between man and machine. . . . Cyberfeminism is simply the acknowledgement that **patriarchy** is doomed. (Sadie **Plant,** 'Beyond the Screens: Film, Cyberpunk and Cyberfeminism', *Variant* (14), 1993)

In her now classic essay 'A Cyborg Manifesto' (1991), Donna Haraway, partly inspired by the gender-free utopias of feminist **science fiction**, identifies a new feminism and invokes the image of the cyborg – 'a cybernetic organism, a hybrid of machine and organism'. She concludes by saying that she 'would rather be a cyborg than a **goddess**'. Her vision is that the blurring of boundaries between human and machine will eventually make the categories of male and female obsolete, and open up the way towards a world of freedom, beyond gender.

The **cyborg** imagery suggests that electronic technology makes possible the escape from the confines of the body, and from the boundaries that have separated organic form from inorganic matter. In 'Will the Real Body Please Stand Up? Boundary Stories about Virtual Cultures' (in Michael Benedikt, ed., *Cyberspace: First Steps*, 1991), Allucquere Rosanne Stone characterises the desire to cross the human/machine boundary as 'cyborg envy'. The merging with the computer involves a change from the 'physical, biological space of the embodied viewer to the symbolic "consensual hallucination" of cyberspace [where there is a] desire for refigured embodiment'. Therefore, when humans interface with computer technology, the self is transformed into something entirely new, combining technological with human **identity**. The fusion of the human element with technology is represented in popular culture as a pleasurable experience – 'the pleasure of the interface' in Claudia Springer's terms, leading to a 'microelectronic Imagery where our bodies are obliterated and our consciousness integrated into the matrix' ('The Pleasure of the Interface', *Screen* 32 (3), 1991). As the boundaries between technology and nature are in the midst of a deep restructuring, Cartesian principles no longer hold, and the distinctions between biological/technological, natural/artificial, human/mechanical become unreliable. It is at this point that

> cyborg consciousness can be understood as the technological embodiment of a particular and specific form of oppositional consciousness. . . . An oppositional cyborg politics, then, could very well bring the politics of the alienated, white, male subject into alliance with the subaltern politics of US third world feminism. (C. Sandoval, 'New Sciences: Cyborg Feminism and the Methodology of the Oppressed' in Cheris Kramarae, ed., *Technology and Women's Voices*, 1988)

The cyborg metaphor, in this line of thought, provides a way to overcome divisions among feminists, alienated white males, and the third world in a movement where oppression is overthrown and egalitarianism becomes feasible. Therefore, it is no coincidence that many social groups have embraced the computer, and cyberspace by extension, as a cultural icon wherein physical distinctions of **gender**, race or sexual orientation become obsolete.

One feminist response to the emerging computer-mediated-communication, influenced by discussions on gender fluidity by feminist and queer theorists, is 'liberal cyberfeminism'. This approach sees the computer as a liberating **utopia** that goes beyond the polarity of male/female, heterosexual/homosexual, and cyberculture as a new frontier of sexual activism and rebellion. Liberal **cyberfeminism**, having been influenced by **liberal feminism, postmodernism** and **queer theory**, has extended the notion of cyberspace as a democratic forum wherein users are freed from the constraints of the physical world – a notion already identified with the **cyberpunk** movement – to sexuality. In this sense, cyberspace allows 'gender fluidity' rather than 'gender categorisation', thereby liberating participants from the binarism of maleness/femaleness. Despite, then, a long-standing feminist tradition claiming that technology is inscribed in masculine terms, the cyborg metaphor is not just another toy for the boys, and many feminists have turned to cyberspace at large in search of liberation and agency.

In this context, cyberspace has been compared to a new public sphere, comparable to the seventeenth-century coffee houses and salons in Britain and France, and the eighteenth-century press in Britain and the US – the realms wherein, as Jürgen Habermas has noted, participatory democracy was shaped through rational public debate. However, the Habermasian public sphere has been heavily criticised for being restrictive and exclusionary, and of failing to recognise other co-existing, non-bourgeois public spheres of 'subaltern counterpublics', consisting of women, plebeian men and of racialised ethnicities. Cyberspace, though, becomes the forum of a new public sphere through its various IRC groups, Usenet groups, listserves and other subscriber bulletin boards which serve as institutionalised forums for public debate and exchange on a variety of issues. This form of public debate helps shape participatory democracy, especially if we consider that cyberspace has provided access to the various 'subaltern counterpublics' which, as mentioned above, were previously excluded from the dominant sphere of public debate. Women quickly appropriated the Web and created electronic networks that function to set up a 'Virtual **Sisterhood**', linking women's groups, feminist activist groups and social forums together. As N. Wakeford writes in an essay included in Jennifer Terry and Melodie Calvert's collection, *Processed Lives: Gender and Technology in Everyday Life* (1997),

> Networking, activism and support are interwoven as we push ourselves to learn to work with the new electronic tools we are encountering. Together we anticipate a future where growing numbers of women can access and use the global connections to promote women's equality.

A number of cyber-presences created by women have come in direct response to stereotypical understandings of computing culture. Sites such as Cybergrrrl, geekgrrrl and Netchick explore the possibility of a close relationship between women and computer culture wherein a discourse of 'problems' is not reproduced and traditional **stereotypes** are defied. In fact, Wakeford observes that 'grrrls' dissociate themselves from 'an older style feminist rhetoric', and 'don't blame men for anything. [I]nstead [they] focus on ways to improve and strengthen [them]selves. Grrrls enjoy their **femininity** and kick ass at the same time . . . without acting like women are victims'.

Hence there is a multiplicity of public spheres in cyberspace, where dissonance is welcome and tolerance is exhibited. That said, public spheres are not only arenas for the formation of discursive opinion, but they are also arenas for the formation and enactment of social identities. The potential for anonymity and 'gender-bending' offered in cyberspace further illustrate this and attest to its democratising and liberating potential. More specifically, despite its problematic aspect (in the sense that people can be more insulting when using anonymous computer-mediated communication), the anonymity found in cyberspace is valued because it creates opportunities to invent alternative versions of the self and engage in untried forms of interaction which social inhibitions would generally suppress. The absence of the physical in cyberspace invites infinite possibilities which open up new, and sometimes disturbing, meanings for the physical body. On the Net, grounding a persona in a physical body is meaningless, and men routinely use female personae to communicate, and vice versa. This 'computer **cross-dressing**' means that though gendered modes of communication remain operative, who uses which of the two socially recognised modes has become more plastic. As Allucquere Rosanne Stone observes:

> A woman who has appropriated a male conversational style may be assumed to be male at that place and time, so that her/his on-line persona takes on a kind of quasi life of its own, separate from the person's embodied life in the 'real' world.

As a result, there is an 'in-between' gender awareness on cyberspace which can actually work not simply in the form of male-to-female or female-to-male personae, but also in terms of homosexual-to-heterosexual, heterosexual-to-homosexual or **transsexual** ones. In all cases of 'gender-bending', participants also need to practice 'cross-expressing'. The term refers to 'verbal' gender-shifting, since the success of the acquired identity depends on the user's ability to 'pass' textually; therefore, cross-expressers need to become fluent in discursive fields which are normally foreign to them, as this excerpt from an electronic communication reveals:

> Heh heh heh!! Yeah, I've done cross-expressing . . . I've played a couple of different male characters, a bi woman (I'm lesbian), and also an asexual seal named Selkie . . . I was in an LDR [long distance relationship] with a woman in San Diego, and she had a female character that took my male character as a consort. . . . I'm still exploring my boundaries. . . .

(quoted in K. Hall, 'Cyberfeminism', in Susan Herring, ed., *Computer-Mediated Communication: Linguistic, Social and Cross-Cultural Perspectives*, 1996)

So far, I have explored the liberating and democratising potential of technology by looking at the cyborg icon as the medium of dreams and hopes; by discussing cyberspace as a realm for an emergent new public sphere; by looking into the possibilities offered in cyberspace for circumventing social inhibitions through the features of anonymity and cross-expressing. Network technology, though, is Janus-faced and alongside the vision of cyberspace as heaven lies a vision of cyberspace as hell.

VISIONS OF DYSTOPIA: BURSTING THE CYBERBUBBLE?

The metaphor of the information superhighway often invokes romantic connotations of the open road as a new frontier in the same way that the interstate highway system did in the Eisenhower era. However, despite the promise of a prosperous future that they both entail, it is feared that the information superhighway will have the same detrimental effects on social formation that P. Patton in *Open Road* (1991) identifies with the interstate highway:

> [Highways] have had monstrous side effects. They have often rolled . . . through cities, splitting communities off into ghettos, displacing people, and crushing the intimacies of old cities . . . While promising to bring us closer, highways in fact cater to our sense of separateness.

Furthermore, the notion of cyberspace as an electronic frontier draws on a concept of war, conquest and extermination, and reflects an image of the Wild West. Hackers and their pursuers represent cowboys, law and lawlessness, while various large US corporations, which took interest in constructing proprietary networks in cyberspace, become the equivalent of the railroad companies in the West who encouraged people to settle in frontier lands near the railroad (thus being responsible for the pioneers' total dependence on the railroad for communications and supplies). The frontier metaphor is related to a specific moment in American history which was highly gendered. No wonder that women in cyberspace are positioned as lacking in agency: they exist within a classic Western narrative of individualistic masculinity. The image of cyberspace as a frontier invokes a need for its defence, and allows women to be associated with powerlessness and vulnerability.

The dystopic image of cyberspace becomes more pronounced once we take into account that the Internet has in fact inherited a problematic relationship with gender originating from its roots within the military-industrial complex. Given this inheritance, it comes as no surprise that many women experience the Internet as 'male space'. As Allucquere Rosanne Stone says,

> Many of the engineers currently debating the form and nature of cyberspace are the young turks of computer engineering, men in their late teens and twenties, preoccupied with the things with which postpubescent men have always been preoccupied. This rather steamy group will generate the codes and descriptors by which bodies in cyberspace are represented.

The low visibility of women on the Internet, and within the domain of the new ICTs for that matter, and the cultural dominance of masculinity in electronic spaces, particularly when it comes to linguistic styles and conventions, offer a disconcerting proof of that experience.

In effect, one view suggests that we treat with caution the optimism of the likes of Sadie Plant or Nell Tenhaaf, who argue that cyberspace is a feminine territory, and notes that, instead of (mis)reading the inclusion of the culturally marginal as democracy, we should be aware that commercial culture thrives on the construction of new myths and audiences. The argument of cyberspace as female space is further problematised by the tendency in academic writing to sidestep the enormous structural inequalities in access to communications and computing infrastructures that are deeply woven into modern urban social landscapes. Very often, debates on globalisation, electronic democracy and telematics-based social networks seem to imply a (utopian) degree of uniformity in social access to information technology.

The truth is, though, that given the ever-increasing complexity of digital technology, power in cyberspace is based on expertise, and is available to technologically-adept users – in itself leading toward the creation of a cyber-elite which is, nevertheless, primarily male-dominated. The archetypal computer user is male, in paid employment in a well-defined organisational setting. On the other hand, women in the ICT labour market are segregated into low-paid, low-status, clerical jobs, while they are seriously under-represented in managerial and scientific posts. Gender segregation is reinforced by changes in the timing and location of work brought by developments in ICTs which ensure geographical flexibility and the relocation of a number of tasks and information. This, in turn, facilitates an international labour force divided along gender and racial lines. The use of subcontracted female labour in the software industry means that women in many third world countries are employed for the lower-level, standardised tasks of programming at pay rates which are much lower than in the west. This reality strengthens the traditional perception of women's office work as 'deskilled', resulting in limited agency and autonomy for women in professional roles in relation to men.

This is more so in the case of teleworking where, despite the notion of a greater degree of control over working and domestic lives, research – such as that carried out by Leslie Haddon and Roger Silverstone in *Teleworking in the 1990s: A View from the Home* (1993) – has shown that it reproduces the traditional gender division of labour at home. In this context, female teleworkers are in a child-rearing age, doing clerical work combined with domestic chores and childcare, while male teleworkers are professionals who have set up consultancies or become self-employed. This serves to show that both access to and use of ICTs are equally important in terms of agency. The profile of the average Internet surfer, for example, is white, male, middle-class and well-educated, and company directors are proportionately ten times more likely to be on-line than housewives. Despise the fact that the position of women as Internet users is improving, access to network technology can take place at a number of levels. Women need to have access to computer technology, either at home or at work, which implies that they must have considerable control of their time in order to use and become proficient in ICTs in either environment. At the same time, though, simple access to computer infrastructure does not guarantee any advantages for its users. Heavy users, for example, may merely represent routine telework on piece rates, in non-union conditions, with the responsibility for heating and lighting costs thrown in. Therefore, actual 'use' needs to be taken into account.

Furthermore, Susan Herring's research on gender participation in networking, published in C. Ess, ed., *Philosophical Perspectives on Computer-Mediated Communication* (1996), has shown that cyberspace is not gender-free and that, on the contrary, traditional gendered interactions are maintained, and even magnified, in cyberspace. The majority of linguistic studies on gender differentiation in computer-mediated communication have come up with results similar to those of feminist studies on face-to-face communication in mixed-sex groups. This means that male participation in cyberspace very often **silences** female participants by following largely the same techniques men follow to 'neutralise' women in real life (ignoring topics introduced by women, producing hierarchical structures of discussion, dismissing women's responses as irrelevant). Furthermore, Herring's research in female participation in networking within academia has shown that men and women academics do not take part in equal terms in academic CMC. In 'Gender and Democracy in Computer-Mediated Communication' (*Electronic Journal of Communication*, 1993), she argues that men tend to dominate the discourse by ignoring or delegitimising the contributions of their female colleagues. Women, on the other hand, tend to be intimidated by such practices and restrain themselves from participating. This power-based and hierarchical operation of academic CMC suggests that pre-existing patterns of male dominance in academia, and in society as a whole, are in fact replicated within networking environments.

And as if it was not enough that men 'talk' more in cyberspace, there is growing evidence that female sexual harassment is happening in the virtual world. Stories of cyberstalking and cyber**rape** abound (as in the case of lamdaMOO, an interactive game site, in which a character called 'Mr Bungle' 'raped' a female character), and web sites are set up to halt the abuse of women on-line by offering policies and information on harassment prevention (see http://whoa.femail.com).

In an attempt to debunk such tendencies, increasing numbers of women have taken up separatist cyber-initiatives, and set up women-only lists and bulletin board systems as exclusively female spaces, thus initiating a new strand of feminist counterculture sometimes called 'radical cyberfeminism'. Such initiatives, nonetheless, have been viewed as putting women on the defensive, consolidating the stereotype of the 'harassed female' and reifying the victimisation of women. In that respect, cyberculture has done little to change already existing gender stereotypes. It looks, then, as if despite its promise of deliverance from patriarchal **oppression**, feminist cyberculture is not everybody's answer to the problems women face. As K. Hall comments,

> One of the great contradictions of cyber-images is that they . . . promis[e] marvels and wonders of a gender-free world or a multi-gender world; and yet, such images not only reproduce some of the most banal, flat images of gender behaviour imaginable, they intensify the differences between the sexes.

The irony is that, contrary to Haraway's vision of the cyborg as going beyond gender, the cyborg has been appropriated by cyberfeminists as an essential female being. 'If the male human is the only human, the female cyborg is the only cyborg,' argues Sadie Plant in 'Beyond the Screens: Film, Cyberpunk and Cyberfeminism', and Allucquere Rosanne Stone adds that 'to become a cyborg . . . is to put on the female'. The problem, though, is that the cyberfeminist invasion of patriarchy is not seen as a political project, having neither theory, goals nor principles. This apolitical understanding of cyberimagery has caused concern and scepticism amongst feminist theorists, who argue that the redrawing of the boundaries of the self is, in fact, a political process, and how these will be drawn will depend on who has the agenda-setting power. Therefore, instead of being taken in by technophoric cyberdrool, we should take feminism for what it is: in the words of Cary Elwes, 'the death of feminism and a post-political world' ('Is Technology Coded in Gender Specific Terms?', *Variant*, 1993). Since contemporary society is patriarchal, divided by race, class and gender, it follows that a cybernetic future will be cut out of the same mould, and thus some cyborgs will be more equal than others.

Another problem with cyberfeminism is that it heralds an escape from difference, taking us into a genderless world. However, the very experience of masculinity and femininity is founded on difference, since as Elwes points out, 'it is only interesting to try out masculinity if your experience until now has been that of a woman . . . an experience of marginalization'. Hence, if difference is lost, the experience of how it feels to be a woman will also disappear. After all, and contrary to notions of the human body as 'meat' which becomes obsolete once uploaded in cyberspace, to quote Allucquere Rosanne Stone, 'life is lived through bodies'.

CONCLUSION

In this chapter, I have discussed the notion that technology is encoded in gender-specific terms, and looked at cyberspace in particular as a forum which women can claim as their own. This vision of technology as empowerment was followed by a more dystopian account of cyberspace. The question to ask now is: is there a future of agency for women in cyberspace, or will cyberfeminism prove to be an empty promise? The case is that new technologies, in the form of cyberspace, seem to offer women a means of control over their lives, and hence increase their agency. The downside, as we have seen, is that this seems to occur in severely circumscribed terms, as women are yet to participate in equal terms within cyberculture. If we truly want women to explore the democratising and liberating potential of cyberspace, perhaps public policy initiatives could be the first step towards the decrease of the electronic marginalisation of women. In this context, government measures that provide computer and network access for women in terms of technological infrastructure and expertise, as well as in terms of cultural capital, become a necessary condition to span the electronic ghetto.

8

FEMINISM AND FILM

SUE THORNHAM

In 1972 the first issue of a short-lived American journal called *Women and Film* was published. Appearing just two years after the publication of Kate **Millett**'s *Sexual Politics*, Shulamith **Firestone**'s *The Dialectic of Sex*, Germaine **Greer**'s *The Female Eunuch*, and Robin Morgan's anthology, *Sisterhood is Powerful*, it too declares itself to be part of feminism's '**second wave**'. 'The women in this magazine,' states the first editorial, 'as part of the women's movement, are aware of the political, psychological, social and economic **oppression** of women. The struggle begins on all fronts and we are taking up the struggle with women's image in film and women's roles in the film industry – the ways in which we are exploited and the ways to transform the derogatory and immoral attitudes the ruling **class** and their male lackys [*sic*] have towards women and other oppressed peoples.'

Women, the editors go on, are oppressed within the film *industry* (they are 'receptionists, secretaries, odd job girls, prop girls', etc.); they are oppressed by being packaged as images (sex objects, victims or vampires); and they are oppressed within **film** *theory*, by male critics who celebrate directors like Hitchcock or Sirk for their complexity or irony, or for in some other way rising above their material – often the humble 'woman's picture' or 'weepie'. The editors' own project is threefold: a transformation in film-making practice, an end to oppressive **ideology** and **stereotyping**, and the creation of a **feminist** critical aesthetics. The three are, they write, inseparable.

It is in this climate, then, that feminism's engagement with film begins – as an urgent political act. Without analytical tools, we cannot begin to transform existing myths and practices, and feminists from Simone de **Beauvoir** onwards had seen cinema as a key carrier of contemporary cultural **myths**. It is through these myths – found in 'religions, traditions, **language**, tales, songs, movies' – argues de Beauvoir in *The Second Sex* (1949), that we not only interpret but also experience our material existences as men or women. And though '[r]epresentation of the world, like the world itself, is the work of men; they describe it from their own point of view, which they confuse with absolute truth', women, too, must inevitably see themselves through these representations.

If *Women and Film*'s first editorial is polemically satisfying, however, it raises some crucial questions. *Which* analytical tools will best serve the political goals the editors outline, and can non-feminist or pre-feminist theory be appropriated for this purpose? What is the relationship between the different types of oppression which they describe, and between the different forms of transformation they envisage? In particular, what is the precise relationship between oppressive images, representations, or structures of looking, and the material inequalities which women – and 'other oppressed peoples' – experience as social beings? What, finally, has *looking* to do with sexuality, with power and with **masculinity/femininity**? Why is it that the circulation of images of women's bodies can in itself seem an act of oppression?

Over thirty-five years later we can no longer assume, as the *Women and Film* editors did, a straightforward relationship between the film theorist and the political **activist**, between the theorist and the 'ordinary woman', between 'women and other oppressed peoples', and between the feminist theorist/critic and the feminist film-maker. Nor can we envisage a **utopian** moment when 'images of women' will 'reflect' the realities of women's lives: cinematic representations have proved to be far more complex than this. But questions about these relationships form the terms of the debates which can be charted in feminist writing on film from 1972 onwards. Moreover, because a vital part of feminism's project has been to transform women's position from that of *object* of knowledge into that of subject capable of producing and transforming knowledge, and because *seeing* is so crucial to knowledge in western culture, cinema has been, in Laura **Mulvey**'s words, 'the crucial terrain' on which feminist debates about culture, representation and **identity** have been fought out ('British Feminist Film Theory's Female Spectators: Presence and Absence', in *Camera Obscura* 20/2 (1989)).

Early concerns within American feminism, then, centred on film representations as false *images* of women. Sharon Smith's 'The Image of Women in Film: Some Suggestions for Future Research', which appeared in the first issue of *Women and Film*, Marjorie Rosen's *Popcorn Venus* (1973), and Molly Haskell's *From Reverence to Rape* (1974) all employ a survey methodology, and take as the focus of their attack the issue of 'sex-role stereotyping'. Their concern is to expose as both false and oppressive the limited range of images of women offered by film. In these accounts, films both *reflect* social structures and changes, and *misrepresent* them according to the fantasies and fears of their male creators. The resultant stereotypes serve to reinforce and/or create the prejudices of their male audiences, and to damage the self-perceptions and limit the social aspirations of women. The writers' concern is to link the power of cinematic representations to the social context that produces and receives them, and to insist on women's collective power to instigate change. Yet they lack any developed theoretical framework. At times film representations appear to be the product of deliberate propaganda; at times they seem the result of unconscious fantasy. Film stereotypes are seen as the product of unconscious assumptions too deep-rooted to be changed simply by having more women in positions of power within the film industry, yet the 'vicious circle' of its cultural effects can, it seems, be broken by a combination of rational persuasion and stereotype-correction. What is missing in these accounts is a theoretical framework capable of both explaining the persistence and power of these representations in structuring women's sense of identity *and* seeing them as culturally constructed and thus open to change. But the development of such a framework would necessitate a shift of focus: away from a focus on *mis*representation via 'oppressive images', and towards a consideration of *how* cinema structures meaning and pleasure in such a way as to reinforce, or help to construct, our gendered identities. This in turn would have implications for a feminist film *practice*, which will need to do more than simply offer positive images of women, and instead find ways of reorganising film's visual and narrative structures if it is to genuinely challenge mainstream representations.

Claire Johnston's *Notes on Women's Cinema* was published in Britain in 1973. Like her counterparts in the USA, Johnston clearly signals her political engagement. 'From the outset the Women's Movement has assumed without question the importance of film in the women's struggle,' she writes. 'The reason for this interest in the media is not difficult to locate: it has been at the level of the image that the violence of sexism and capitalism has been experienced.' Her approach – and that of other British feminists – is, however, very different. 'If film criticism is to have any use,' she writes, 'it is that it should provide a greater understanding of how film operates which will ultimately feed back into film-making itself.' To further that understanding, she draws on developments within European film and cultural theory: on structuralism and semiotics, on Marxist concepts of ideology, and on **psychoanalytic** theory. Such approaches insist that film representations should not be viewed, as in the American 'sociological' approach, as *reflections* of reality, whether 'true' or 'distorted'. Films are *texts* – complex structures of linguistic and visual codes organised to produce specific meanings. They are not merely collections of images or stereotypes. To evaluate cinematic images of women in terms of their greater or lesser 'truth' or their degrees of 'distortion' is therefore, argues Johnston, to miss the point. Films structure meaning through their organisation of visual and verbal signs. It is these textual structures which we must examine because it is here, rather than in any conscious manipulation, that meaning is produced. Films, in short, are bearers of *ideology*. Ideology can be defined as that representational system, or 'way of seeing' the world which appears to us to be 'universal' or 'natural' but which is in fact the product of the specific power structures which constitute our society. The sign 'woman', then, acquires its meaning within a sexist, or patriarchal, ideology. Its meaning is derived from that structure and the meanings it generates. It is therefore unproductive to compare film stereotypes of women with the reality of women's lives: that 'reality' is lived within the same ideological structure. What should be examined is *how* the sign 'woman' operates within the specific film text – *what* meanings it is made to bear and what desires and fantasies it carries. Only through such critical detachment can we begin the process of change.

Published two years after *Notes on Women's Cinema*, Laura Mulvey's 'Visual Pleasure and Narrative Cinema' has become the most anthologised article in feminist film theory. In it Mulvey adds to Johnston's account of woman as *sign* an analysis of how cinema as an 'apparatus' creates a position for the film spectator, drawing on psychoanalytic theory to explain this positioning. In so doing, she also produced a further shift in analytic focus, away from a purely textual analysis and towards a concern with the structures of identification and visual **pleasure** to be found in cinema: in other words, towards the spectator-screen relationship.

Mulvey's interest in psychoanalytic theory was one shared by a number of French film theorists in the early 1970s. Christian Metz and Jean-Louis Baudry had both compared the operation of the 'cinematic apparatus' upon the spectator to that of the dream. 'Taking into account the darkness of the movie theater, the relative passivity of the situation, the forced immobility of the cine-subject, and the effects which result from the projection of images, moving images', argues Baudry in 'The Apparatus', film viewing offers remarkable parallels to the state of dreaming (*Camera Obscura* No. 1 (1976)). As with dreams and hallucinations, cinema offers us powerful but illusory perceptions (sound, images, movement) which give access to unconscious desires and fantasies, keeping at bay the 'reality principle' which would repress them. The spectator's entry to this realm of **desire** and fantasy, argues Metz in 'The Imaginary Signifier', is via identification with the all-powerful gaze of the camera: 'At the cinema, it is always the other who is on the screen; as for me, I am there to look at him. I take no part in the perceived, on the contrary, I am *all-perceiving*' (*Screen* 16:2 (1975)).

Metz's account of the film spectator's 'all-perceiving' gaze at the *Other* offers particular resonances for the feminist critic. Simone de Beauvoir's account in *The Second Sex* of the process by which 'One is not born, but rather becomes, a woman' centred on the cultural construction of woman as *Other*, and it is this which had underpinned much of the feminist theory developed in the early 1970s (see 'Second Wave Feminism'). For both Baudry and Metz the film spectator envisaged is male – but this 'masculinisation' remains implicit, unanalysed. Mulvey's appropriation of psychoanalytic theory, in contrast, places the issue of sexual **difference** at its centre. Her essay sets out to demonstrate 'the way the unconscious of **patriarchal** society has structured film form'. Like Johnston, she argues that the sign 'woman' in film is one constructed by and for a patriarchal **culture**, enabling man to 'live out his fantasies and obsessions . . . by imposing them on the silent image of woman' (*Visual and Other Pleasures* (1989)). Cinema's pleasures include voyeurism, fetishism, and a return to the **narcissistic** pleasures of infancy's 'mirror phase'. In this phase, as described by psychoanalyst Jacques **Lacan**, the child imagines itself to be a whole and powerful individual by identifying with its own more perfect mirror image – an image provided in film, argues Mulvey, by the figure of the hero. But these are pleasures provided only for the *male* spectator. Women are objects, not subjects, of the **gaze**, their bodies eroticised and often fragmented. This division between active/male and passive/female, argues Mulvey, also structures film narrative. It is the film's hero who advances the story, controlling events, the woman, and the erotic gaze. Woman, in contrast, functions as erotic spectacle, interrupting rather than advancing the narrative. For this to be countered, conventional cinematic pleasures must be destroyed, oppressive forms transcended, and 'a new language of desire' conceived.

Mulvey's 1975 article, then, placed sexual difference at its analytic centre. In arguing that women are objects, not subjects of the gaze, however, it said nothing about the *female* spectator. Mary Ann Doane's work during the 1980s sought to extend Mulvey's use of psychoanalytic theory into an account of this shadowy figure, and in particular to an analysis of the viewing pleasures offered by a genre aimed specifically at her: the 'woman's film' of the 1940s. Films which address the female spectator, argues Doane, cannot rely on the same psychic mechanisms (voyeurism, fetishism and narcissistic identification) as those which address her male counterpart, since these are mechanisms by which the masculine psyche, according to **Freud**, protects itself from the knowledge of woman's difference (her 'castration'). Instead of the all-powerful and eroticised *distance* which characterises the masculine viewing position, then, what these films offer their spectator is a masochistic *overidentification* with the cinematic image – hence the term 'weepies' as a description. The distinction between the spectator and the object of her gaze is collapsed: she is not offered – as with the male spectator – an eroticised image as object of her gaze, but instead an identification with herself *as* image, as object of desire or of suffering. The female protagonist of these films may begin as active agent only to become passive object; the films may begin with her voice-over only to erase it; they offer us identification with her gaze only to invest it not with desire but with anxiety and fear. Hitchcock's *Rebecca* (1940), with its nameless protagonist, interrupted voice-over and anxious investigating gaze, serves as an example. When, in the sequence of the masquerade ball, its central character seeks to assert her **identity**, she can do so only through assuming that of her predecessor, Rebecca, and by offering herself as object of her husband's – and our – gaze. When she descends the staircase dressed in a costume identical to that worn previously by Rebecca, she becomes – as in so many similar film sequences – object of spectacle. As spectators, we are asked to identify with that objectification, and with the humiliation that follows.

Powerful as these explanations may be as theorisations of the ways in which film plays on unconscious mechanisms of identification in order to confirm **gendered** identities, they bring with them their own problems. How, if film draws on *unconscious* structures for its identifications, can we effect any change? In an exasperated summary, American film critic B. Ruby Rich characterises the problem thus:

> According to Mulvey, the woman is not visible in the audience which is perceived as male; according to Johnston, the woman is not visible on the screen. She is merely a surrogate for the phallus, a signifier for something else, etc. As a woman going into the movie theater, you are faced with a context that is coded wholly for your invisibility, and yet, obviously, you are sitting there and bringing along a certain coding from life outside the theater. . . . the cinematic codes have structured our absence to such an extent that the only choice allowed to us is to identify either with Marilyn

Monroe or with the man behind me hitting the back of my seat with his knees. How does one formulate an understanding of a structure that insists on our absence even in the face of our presence? What is there in a film with which a woman viewer identifies? (in Michelle Citron *et al.*, 'Women and Film: A Discussion of Feminist Aesthetics', in *New German Critique* No. 13 (1978))

Women in this account, she argues, have no presence, no specific experience, and no possibility of active intervention at all. On the contrary, argue Rich and others, the female viewer is a social being as well as a cinematically constructed spectator. She does not slip passively into acceptance of the ideological structures of the text but actively engages with them, constructing her own readings, often 'against the grain'. She is, moreover, no single identity, 'woman', though that might be how the text would like to see her. Instead, our identities as *women* are constructed along lines of multiple differences – of 'race', **class**, **language**, location, for example – and not just along the single divide of sexual difference. To say that we are all embodied female is not to say that we share a single relationship to images of that embodiment. What is needed, then, is a theoretical language that can encompass these contradictions, and not become entrapped by either an activist optimism or a theoretical pessimism.

The 1980s saw a number of responses to the *impasse* into which feminist film theory's use of psychoanalytic concepts seemed to have led. Some, whilst remaining within a psychoanalytic framework, sought to rethink its terms. Increasingly, then, Freud's work on dream and fantasy has been reinterpreted, to become the theoretical underpinning not for cinema's power to 'fix' its spectators within the structures of sexual difference, but for the reverse: for the shifting and multiple positions which cinema offers to its fantasising spectator. In Linda Williams' (1991) study of what she calls popular 'body genres' or 'genres of gender fantasy' (**pornography**, horror and melodrama), for example, she argues that although these genres share a quality of excess in which it is the bodies of *women* which have 'functioned traditionally as the primary *embodiments* of pleasure, fear, and pain', the viewing positions which they offer are not as gender-linked and as gender-fixed as has been supposed. Instead, they are marked by an *oscillation* of identificatory positions, an oscillation between the poles of sadism and masochism, powerlessness and power. Female spectators are not fixed in an identification with the suffering female body; nor are male spectators tied to the sadistic position suggested by the 'male gaze'. For both, she argues, there is a strong mixture of passivity and activity, and a bisexual oscillation between the poles of each.

Other responses have involved a move away from 'cine-psycho-analysis', and towards an engagement with the perspectives emerging within British Cultural Studies. In a 1973 paper, Stuart Hall, then director of the Centre for Contemporary Cultural Studies (CCCS) at Birmingham University, argued that if we are to understand the process by which film or television texts produce meaning, what we need is a model which will account for the *whole* of the communicative process, not just for the meanings inscribed in texts, or for their ideological or behavioural 'effects'. Hall's model sees this process as operating through three linked but distinctive 'moments'. The first is the 'moment' of production, the second that of the text, and the third the moment of viewing. Each is envisaged as the site of struggle or negotiation over meaning: the meanings 'encoded' by the text's producers; the meanings embodied in the text; and the meanings 'decoded' by the viewer. Although Hall envisaged this 'struggle' as operating along class lines, his model was quickly appropriated for a feminist analysis.

What this model suggests is that neither textual meanings nor the ideological structures to which they refer are uncontested. We need only note the appearance within a year of each other of two popular films as different as, say *Pretty Woman* (1990) and *Thelma and Louise* (1991), to see that the ideological terrain on which their meanings circulate is a complex and contested one. Equally, argues Christine Gledhill, we may trace that same struggle – between competing meanings, frames of reference or ideological positions – within the individual film. Popular texts, she argues, do not offer a *single* position for their spectator to occupy. Their representations may derive their meaning from the textual and ideological structures in which they are embedded, but they refer outwards too, to a social reality in which power – whether socio-political or ideological – is not simply imposed but contested. If we take this view we might still argue, like the 'cine-psychoanalysts', that as film spectators we construct and confirm our sense of identity through cinematic identifications, but we might also wish to argue for greater agency in this process. If the text does not present a single position from which it must be understood and enjoyed, it might be appropriated for new readings, for the production of new, perhaps more contingent, partial and fragmented identities, or for a feminist politics of reading.

This last point has led a number of feminist writers to move away from the analysis of film texts and towards an exploration of women as film spectators who are *historically* situated – that is, of women as cinema audiences rather than – or as well as – textual spectators. It is a move provoked also by a growing recognition of the inability of a psycho-analytically-based feminist film theory to deal with two groups of female spectators whose cinematic pleasures and identifications seem literally unthinkable within its terms: black women and lesbian women. As Jane Gaines has pointed out in 'White Privilege and Looking Relations: Race and Gender in Feminist Film Theory' (1988), the opposition male/female, so central to feminist theory, 'is a powerful, but sometimes blinding construct' (*Screen* 29:4)). It can blind the theorist, for example, to the inability of feminist theories based on a 'male gaze' to concep-tualise a lesbian viewing position. It can blind her, too, to what goes on when white feminists use Freud's description of woman as 'the dark continent' to characterise their positioning as *Other* within patriarchy. As Lola Young has put it in *Fear of the Dark: 'Race', Gender and Sexuality in the Cinema* (1996), this 'overinvestment in the gender component of the "dark continent" . . . has resulted in the virtual elimination of the racial and colonial implications. Thus this most racialized of sexual metaphors has become synonymous with the concerns of white women'.

For black feminists, race, rather than gender, is often seen as the primary structuring principle of oppression, so that white women, rather than sharing a common situation, may be regarded as themselves oppressors, and black men may be seen to share a common history of oppression under slavery. Moreover, femininity within Western culture has been defined as *white* femininity, so that, whilst white feminists have been preoccupied by women's reduction to the status of image and spectacle, it is the *invisibility* of black women within the category 'woman' which has been the issue for black feminists. If white women in film have served as signifiers of male desire, black women, when present at all, have served quite different functions. Most frequently they have served as an embodiment of either female sexuality (black female body as sexualised body) or the maternal (black female body as procreative body). Elsewhere, as *unfeminine* women, they seem to be coded – as in the history of slavery – as not really women at all.

Equally, if we consider the position of the black female spectator, our theorisation of structures of identification and of the cinematic gaze must change. If, argues black feminist bell **hooks**, processes of identification depend on the imaginary closing of the gap between self and image, then the gap between black female spectator and idealised *white* image of femininity is one which can be imaginatively closed only through 'the masochistic look of victimization'. The black female spectator, however, more often resists that process, she argues, placing herself *outside* the structures of cinematic visual pleasure proposed by Laura Mulvey or Mary Ann Doane, and developing instead a critical or oppositional gaze. For black feminists like bell hooks, then, the power of the gaze must be seen as materially as well as psychoanalytically constructed. If the politics of slavery denied the slave the right to look, then a 'critical' or oppositional gaze has long been a strategy of resistance and an assertion of agency in the face of domination. For black men, in the darkened space of the cinema, this might mean the possibility of a fantasised phallocentric power denied them in a **racist** society. Black *female* spectators, however, refusing to identify with 'the phallocentric gaze of desire and possession', can create a critical space where Mulvey's opposition of 'woman as image, man as bearer of the look' can be deconstructed and negative images of black women reclaimed.

For the past thirty years, then, cinema has been, in Laura Mulvey's words, 'the crucial terrain' on which feminist debates about **culture**, representation and identity have been fought through. What, finally, of the intervention in film-making *practice* which the editors of *Women and Film* saw as equally important? As the following chronology drawn from Mary Ann Doane's essay 'The "Woman's Film": Possession and Address' (1984) indicates, early developments in feminist film criticism and in feminist film-making went hand in hand:

1971 Release of *Growing Up Female, Janie's Janie, Three Lives* and *The Woman's Film* – first generation of feminist documentaries.

1972 First New York International Festival of Women's Films and the Women's Event at Edinburgh Film Festival. First issue of *Women and Film*; special issues on women and film in *Take One, Film Library Quarterly* and *The Velvet Light Trap*; filmography of women directors in *Film Comment*.

1973 Toronto Women and Film Festival. Washington Women's Film Festival, season of women's cinema at National Film Theatre in London and Buffalo women's film conference. Marjorie Rosen's *Popcorn Venus* and Claire Johnston's *Notes on Women's Cinema*.

1974 Chicago Films by Women Festival. First issue of *Jump Cut* (quarterly on contemporary film emphasizing feminist perspective); two books on images of women in film: Molly Haskell's *From Reverence to Rape* and Joan Mellen's *Women and their Sexuality in the New Film*. (In Mary Ann Doane, *et al.*, eds., *Re-Vision: Essays in Film Criticism*.)

To this chronology we might add that the 1971 documentary *Three Lives* was produced by Kate Millett, author of *Sexual Politics* (1970), and that

Laura Mulvey's own films, *Penthesilea, Queen of the Amazons* (1974), and *Riddle of the Sphinx* (1977) were concerned to explore the same theoretical issues as her critical writing.

By the 1990s, however, this interrelationship had been lost. Writing in 1989, Laura Mulvey argues that by the late 1980s, feminist film theory had 'lost touch with feminist filmmaking, that which had hitherto acted as its utopian other'. The move of feminist (and non-feminist women) film-makers 'into the mainstream' of narrative film production has added to this divorce. Michelle Citron, whose work in the 1970s formed an important part of independent feminist film-making, describes her own move in this direction and her feelings of ambivalence about it. In the 1970s, she writes, she felt that she 'wanted to make films that articulated women's experiences and saw the need for a new film language with which to do so', but in retrospect she is less convinced of their value. The films made in the 1970s were, she feels, 'theoretically interesting and politically sound, but flat. They offer intellectual pleasure but rarely emotional pleasure'. The move into the mainstream, she writes, has its dangers: the feminist film-maker is trading control for power. But power means 'the opportunity to reach a larger audience, the potential of using mainstream culture to critique or subvert it, the freedom to define and test one's own personal boundaries as film-maker'. Above all, it means the move from an overly didactic approach into an engagement with the 'contradictions, paradoxes, uncertainties' of mainstream narrative film (1988: 62). Yet if we look at the recent films of Sally **Potter**, who with *Orlando* made a similar move, or Jane **Campion** (*The Piano*, 1993), it would be difficult to maintain that these films do *not* manifest a preoccupation with concerns central to feminist theory: the relationship of women to language, and to public and private histories; sexual difference and its relationship to other forms of difference; the limits and possibilities of desire; the relationship between women – in particular between **mothers and daughters**. At the same time, they engage fully – if subversively – with the conventions of popular film. Perhaps, then, this divorce, whilst bringing losses, is also a sign of success. Finally, the effect of feminism may also be charted – however ambiguously – within male-directed mainstream film, in the feminisation of popular genres and return of the 'women's picture' during the 1980s and 1990s. As Pam Cook remarks in 'Border Crossings: Women and Film in Context' (in Pam Cook and P. Dodd, eds., *Women and Film: A Sight and Sound Reader* (1993)), these developments, whilst they are an attempt to capitalise on and control feminism, are also a recognition of its cultural power and of the 'politics of vision' which has been so central to it.

9

FEMINISM AND POPULAR CULTURE

NATALIE FENTON

This chapter traces the development of **feminist** theories in relation
to the study of popular **culture**. Feminists researching popular culture
have come from a broad range of disciplines but over the last decade the
term 'feminist **media** studies' has come to stand for a range of
approaches to popular culture that have the political project of feminism at their core. Feminist media studies have followed and sometimes
led feminist theoretical debates more generally. Feminism has moved
from a focus on the repression of all women in general and a politics
based on the concept of shared female experience, to the recognition
and embracing of **difference** within the category 'woman' which removes
the possibility of there being a singular truth about womanhood. This
move from sameness to difference can be charted through a critique of
the politics of representation – a move that can broadly be categorised
as one from structuralism to **poststructuralism** to **postmodernism**.
This development has not been linear or straightforward but has
resulted in more complex accounts of media practice, representation
and consumption. As Charlotte Brundson *et al.* note in *Feminist
Television Criticism* (1997), feminist media studies reject

> the **ideology** and scientism that so many television historians, audience
> researchers and policy analysts [have] employed when media studies was
> dominated by the male-centred concerns and empiricist/positivist
> methods of the 1930s–1960s. . . . The idea of difference – sexual, racial,
> ethnic and otherwise – so central to feminism, mitigates against universal
> truth and the methods that aspire to it.

The chapter will attempt to survey three main areas of feminist
approaches to popular culture – *production*, namely the gender
differentiation, organisation and working practices within the cultural
industries; *textual representation*, including studies of the misrepresentation and under-representation of women in popular culture as well
as studies of female genres (in particular, **soap opera**); and *reception*.

REPRESENTING WOMEN IN PRODUCTION

Concern with women's employment in the mass media springs from two preoccupations: an interest in the development of job opportunities for women at all levels and in the removal of obstacles to their equal participation in every field of work; and an assumption that there is a link between media output and the producers of that output. Since the presence of women in creative and decision-making roles in the media industries continues to be far less than that of men, it is assumed that the images of women disseminated by the mass media reflect and express male concerns. Similarly, if women were to gain positions of power on a larger scale, the implication is that images will change for the better. Early studies such as Gallagher's *Unequal Opportunities: the Case of Women and the Media* (1981) noted that both in terms of overall numbers and distribution across and within specific occupations, as well as in terms of salary, women media workers are at a distinct disadvantage when compared to their male counterparts. Gallagher's research on 22 broadcasting organisations in nine European countries found that women accounted for only six per cent of the top three grade jobs and most were clustered in the lowest three. There is no evidence that the proportion of women is increasing. In a 1990 study, 'Women and Men in the Media' (*Communication Research Trends* 12:1 (1992)), Gallagher found that although women comprised 36 per cent of personnel in European broadcasting (looking at 71 organisations in 12 EC member states), over 50 per cent of these were in administrative roles, that women were at the bottom of the hierarchy in every professional job, and that the number of women on part time and temporary contracts far exceeded that of men. In 1994 the British National Union of Journalists (NUJ) did a survey of their members to discover that men outnumbered women in every job and women were concentrated in the lowest-paid positions (except in the book trade where women dominated, but notably, this is also the lowest-paid media sector).

However, despite the indisputable inequality in employment in the media industries, there is little evidence to support the proposition of a direct correspondence between women working in the media and the representations produced. The overly simple correlation of **gender** of the producer impacting upon the product has been explained in three main ways.

Firstly, it is imperative to take account of the institutional and professional constraints on women working in a male-dominated media industry. If the economic imperatives of profit are the first criteria of

105

meaning construction, then the importance of the gender of the creator may be subsumed. Furthermore, it is difficult for women to resist ideas and attitudes associated with success in their profession, even if such ideas demean them as women in the audience. Secondly, such a perspective fails to recognise a more complex concern with the language of representation and the need to identify: 'a specific women's perspective or aesthetic which could radically transform – rather than simply adapt to – discriminatory structures and practices in the media industry' (Helen Baehr and A. Gray, *Turning It On: A Reader in Women and Media* (1997)). In other words, it takes the given male world as it is, accepting a certain structure of communication, of hierarchical organisation, of power and control. Thirdly, the extent to which a feminist critique can be used to negotiate alternative representations in the media opens up the question of whether women have a distinctive and different contribution to make to media content. Embracing difference within feminism has taught us that all women do not see the world in the same way nor do all women see the world differently from all men. Women and men share cultural outlooks.

The extent to which any engagement with the mainstream can produce new representations of women continues to be questioned by some critics who argue that this type of intervention only results in 'a modest allotment of institutional legitimation... bought at the price of reducing the contradictory complexity (of feminism) for simpler and more acceptable ideas already existing in the dominant culture' (Teresa de **Lauretis**, *Technologies of Gender: Essays on Theory, Film and Fiction* (1987)).

TEXTUAL REPRESENTATIONS OF WOMEN

The women's movement of the 60s and 70s produced a political framework for feminists to challenge the media for their demeaning and stereotypical images of women. Research revealed images to be both an under-representation and misrepresentation of women. This 'symbolic annihilation' (Tuchman, *Hearth and Home: Images of Women and the Media* (1978)) by the mass media was held to be deeply implicated in the patterns of discrimination operating against women in society.

The aim of these feminist studies of the media was gender equality. Put crudely, traditional research on women and the media viewed mass mediated communications as a major source for the general reproduction of patriarchal social relations. Studies of representation revealed that males dominated media content and that, as Busby notes in 'Sex

Role Research on the Mass Media', 'roles of males in the mass media have been shown to be dominant, active, authoritative, while females have been shown to be submissive, passive and completely contented to subjugate their wills to the wills of the media males' (*Journal of Communication*, Autumn 1975). The early work on media images of women has been severely critiqued on the basis of three main assumptions (not all of which are present in every instance):

1. That mass media imagery consists of unrealistic messages about women whose meanings are unambiguous and straightforward (for example, Betty **Friedan**, *The Feminine Mystique* (1963), and Germaine **Greer**, *The Female Eunuch* (1971)). In 'Research on Sex-Roles in the Mass Media: Toward a Critical Approach' (*Insurgent Socialist* 7:3 (1977)) Janus accuses certain studies of women's representation in the media of being consistent with a **liberal** feminist perspective which sets up male versus female categories. The implication is that media content might be less sexist if women characters were shown to have the same occupational distribution as male characters. In her view, this perspective only leads to cosmetic changes in the representation of women because it defines 'male-ness' as the goal for women in media images. Addressing those feminists who complain about 'sexist images in the media' Tuchman replies that images of women cannot be assessed or judged in terms of how they 'reflect' or 'distort' reality. To argue that the media distort images of women assumes that the media should somehow reflect 'reality' as if it were a mirror on the world. To expect media to provide accurate representations of women is to oversimplify women's complex relationship with the media and the symbolic processes involved in representation.

2. That women (and men) passively and indiscriminately absorb these messages and meanings (for example, Andrea **Dworkin**, *Pornography: Men Possessing Women* (1981)).

3. That we as researchers have some privileged access whereby we can recognise and resist such images (for example, Ferguson, *Forever Feminine: Women's Magazines and the Cult of Femininity* (1983)).

Effects of the mass media were thereby generally conceived as detrimental to the general population and in particular to women. However, as Gallagher points out in 'Women and Men in the Media', 'Evaluated in historical context, its contribution is clear. Its disclosure and condemnation of **sexism** in media content provided a first, essential springboard.' The conception of a text with a unitary meaning gave way to a more sophisticated textual analysis that recognised multiplicity of cultural definitions within a media text.

WOMEN REPRESENTED IN FEMALE GENRES

In the late 1970s women's **genres** were recognised as giving a voice to women's experiences. The focus on women's genres was a political advance for feminist media studies. Genres such as soap opera and **romance**, which focused on women's experiences and were largely consumed by women, had previously been labelled as 'trash', but were now given a new legitimacy. To claim such genres as worthy of study was seen as commensurate with claiming the personal as political in the general feminist struggle. The themes and values associated with so-called women's genres where narratives are located mainly in the private and public spheres were heralded by feminists as legitimate of study in their own right, leading Joke Hermes in *Reading Women's Magazines* (1995) to state that feminism's 'overriding motivation should be to respect women and women's genres, and to demand respect for them from the world at large'.

In *Loving With a Vengeance: Mass Produced Fantasies for Women* (1984), Tania **Modleski** seeks to connect the forms of daytime television in the USA to patterns of female domestic labour. Both, she argues, are based upon interruption and distraction. Furthermore, daytime programming such as soaps and quiz shows deal in 'traditional feminine' currency celebrating and confirming particular skills and competencies, thus serving the demands of **patriarchy**.

In 'Housewives and the Mass Media' (in Stuart Hall *et al.,* eds., *Culture, Media Language* (1980)) Hobson indicates the significance of media output in terms of imposing structure upon domestic work, of providing company and combating the isolation experienced by women at home. She also points towards the notion of gendered television output.

Gray, in her study of the use of videocassette recorders ('Behind Closed Doors: Videorecorders in the Home', in Helen Baehr and G. Dyer, eds., *Boxed In: Women and Television* (1987)) argues that attention should be paid to the many determining factors which shape women's domestic consumption of popular forms. These include domestic commitments, the significance of the VCR as **technology** and the general denigration of women's genres.

Early work on female genres was criticised for adhering to a 'conceptualisation of gender as a dichotomous category with a historic-ally stable and universal meaning' whereby the female experience is still seen as being pretty much the same for all women. In *Screen Tastes: Soap Opera to Satellite Dishes* (1997), Charlotte Brundson argues that work emerging from the feminist insistence on examining specific and especially popular generic characteristics and the pleasures they offered to women, initiated a much broader attention to popular **pleasures** and related questions of **identity**. The move from considering gender as a dichotomous category to a focus on identity formation with multiple possibilities was a move from structuralism to poststructuralism.

For poststructuralist feminists the emphasis shifted from a deter-minist model of social structure (i.e., the patriarchal order of the media industries impacts negatively on images produced and on women in general) to how discourses comprising of words and statements and other representational forms brought together into a field of coherent textual regularity actively produce social realities as we know them. This perspective was influenced largely by **Foucault** who challenged the familiar hierarchy of value of the materialist perspective, counter-poising the 'dumb' existence of reality with the ability of groups of signs (discourses) to act as 'practices that systematically form the objects of which they speak'. The material existence of women is seen to be borne through different, often competing discursive strategies which in naming, classifying or speaking the truth of women, also bring her into being. Power is conceptualised as highly dispersed rather than concen-trated in identifiable places or groups.

Many postmodern theorists take the foregrounding of **discourse** one step further to claim that contemporary communication practices are non-representational and non-referential. In other words they have no purchase outside of the text; they have no separate external domain. Rather, they are self-reflexive and self-referential. Contemporary mediated culture, then, is no more than a constant recycling of images previously constituted by the media. The idea is that popular cultural signs and media images increasingly dominate our sense of reality and the way we define ourselves and the world around us. Postmodern perspectives try to come to terms with and understand a media-saturated society. Society has become subsumed within the mass media. It is no longer a question of the media distorting reality; rather the media has become reality – the only reality we have. So there is little point in studying the content of the mass media to see how it may affect our everyday lives; little point in counting instances of mediated hegemonic femininity and making an argument that this sustains the status quo; little point even in studying how people understand the media since, as van Soonen states, 'one interpretation is not by definition better or more valid than another'. The media is reality, is inescapable, is our femininity.

The idea that the mass media take over reality has been accused of exaggerating their importance. Women's experiences are framed by many institutions, the mass media being but one of them. The notion that reality has imploded inside the media such that it can only be defined by the media is also questioned. Most people, it is claimed, would probably still be able to distinguish between the reality created by the media and that which exists elsewhere. Dominic Strinati is typical of this retort when he states in *An Introduction to Theories of Popular Culture* (1995) that 'if reality has really imploded into the media how would we know it has happened?'.

To claim that the media *is* our reality is further criticised by those who wish to point to the oppression of women as real. In this retort reality is recognised as disorderly and fragmented but as also showing patterns of inequality. If the media is our reality it is argued that we effectively deny the existence of material inequalities unless they occur in representation:

> Feminists struggled for decades to name 'sexism' and 'anti-lesbianism'. We said that particular images of women – bound and gagged in **pornography** magazines, draped over cars in advertisements, caricatured as mothers-in-law or nagging wives in sitcoms – were oppressive and degrading. The deconstructionist insistence that texts have no inherent meanings leaves us unable to make such claims. This denial of oppressive meanings is, in effect, a refusal to engage with the conditions under which texts are produced, and the uses to which they are put in the dominant culture. (Kitzinger and Kitzinger, '"Doing It": Representations of Lesbian Sex' in G. Griffin, ed., *Outwrite: Lesbianism and Popular Culture* (1993))

The world according to postmodernists is lived on the surface with nothing that hides behind appearances. This is where the media audience comes into its own – if experience only comes to us in textual form, if all reality is through representation – then the study of the way meaning is made in everyday life is crucial.

THE AUDIENCE OF WOMEN

The role of the audience in the construction of meaning has been subject to differing analytical perspectives. Each tackles in its own way the tension between the audiences' constructive capabilities and the constraining potential of culture and ideology (expressed through the mass media). For the sake of simplicity, two intertwined strands can be distinguished. The first emphasises the capacity of texts to position readers, thus ensuring that the limitations of response are provided by the texts themselves. Readers are thus 'held in ideology' (A. Tudor, 'Culture, Mass Communication and Social Agency', *Theory, Culture and Society*, Vol. 12 (1995)) by their textual placement. This audience positioning has led to texts being described as having 'inscribed readers'. In feminist thinking the main thrust of this analysis was to see texts as instruments of patriarchy through their capacity to situate the reader. The second strand shifts emphasis from the power of texts to confer meaning to the interpretative power of the audience.

MEDIA EFFECTS – THE AUDIENCE AS POWERLESS

Media effects research suggests that mass media texts are very powerful and that their messages are more or less irresistible; the media are seen to behave like a hypodermic needle, injecting audiences with their messages. For example, a study of a girls' magazine called *Jackie* was undertaken by Angela McRobbie in 1982 wherein *Jackie* was conceived of as a system of signs that work to 'position' the female readers for their later roles as wives and mothers by means of the ideology of teenage **femininity** it cultivates. Through a semiological analysis McRobbie uncovers the 'culture of femininity' which as 'part of the dominant ideology' 'has saturated' the lives of the young girls, 'colouring the way they dress, they way they act and the way they talk to each other'. (*Feminism and Youth Culture: From Jackie to Just Seventeen* (1991)). McRobbie then argues that this ideological representation acts as a powerful force on the lives of its readers involving (among others) the search for (heterosexual) romance, finding the right boy and thus placing yourself in a competitive relationship with your girlfriends, and the code of fashion and beauty which instructs readers on how to dress and look in order to be able to meet the demands of this ideology.

This type of media effects theory has been widely criticised as textual determinism which robs readers of their social context and critical agency, leaving no room for interpretative manoeuvre. In the extreme it leaves the audience as no more than cultural dupes, blank slates waiting to be written on. Media effects research is also criticised for only studying one type of effect – that which is more or less immediate, behavioural and measurable. The effects measured are confined to those intended by the sender, thus lacking a critique of the production of messages from within the power relations of society. Media effects research is said to take messages as neutral and non-problematic givens and to be overly simplistic in dimensions of messages selected for study. Ironically media effects research is criticised most of all for being unable to understand the effects of the mass media because it fails to take account of cumulative, delayed, long-term and unintended effects, including those which stabilise the status quo. For example, images of femininity in the mass media may not change the way we actually dress, but they may influence the way we think about what it means to be a woman. Similarly, the fact that sexist imagery in the media can not be directly correlated to sexist attitudes in society does not mean that it is of no consequence.

The downfall of 'effects' research leads theories of communication away from sender-receiver objectivist models to subjectivist theories which start from the premise that reality is socially constructed. In other words, theorists rejected the idea that 'reality' somehow exists 'out there' and all that the media do is act as a mirror to reflect it, to a more sophisticated understanding of 'reality' as something that is constantly changing, constructed and manipulated by all social players.

Feminist researchers reacted against the simplistic conception of the process of mass communication as one of linear transmission from sender to receiver to claim that female audiences play a productive role in constructing textual meanings and pleasures. Women do not simply take in or reject media messages, but use and interpret them according to their own social, cultural and individual circumstances – the audience is involved in making sense of the images they see – the message does not have the total monopoly on meaning.

Research that attributes power to the audience has become known as 'active audience theory'. This type of research, epitomised in the work of Ien Ang's *Watching Dallas: Soap Opera and the Melodramatic Imagination* (1985) and Janice Radway's *Reading the Romance: Women, Patriarchy and Popular Literature* (1984)), involves a celebration of the audience. Audiences are seen as actively constructing meaning so that texts which appear on the face of it to be reactionary or patriarchal can be subverted. In the case of Ang the subversion comes through the pleasures that are gained from it. The world of fantasy is the 'place of excess where the unimaginable can be imagined'.

Active audience theorists in media studies have been accused of relativism gone mad, as an interpretative free-for-all in which the audience possesses an unlimited potential to read any meaning at will from a given text. In 'Active Audience Theory: Pendulums and Pitfalls' (*Journal of Communication* 43 (1993)), David Morley has criticised the neglect in most active audience research of 'the economic, political and ideological forces acting on the construction of texts'. By drawing attention away from the media and texts generally as instruments of power, they have been accused of a lack of appreciation of wider political factors and hence of political quietism and ideological desertion.

Ang has attempted to overcome these criticisms by using Foucault's notion of discourse to undertake a poststructuralist analysis of the audience. As mentioned above, for Foucault, discourses are particular ways of organising knowledge in the context of serving specific types of power relationships. Foucault acknowledges that the real exists but maintains that since reality is only appropriated through discourse, it is discourse which is important. Ang's analysis concentrates upon institutional discourses about television audiences. These audiences do not exist naturally, nor can they be taken for granted. Rather they are constructed by particular discourses which seek to know them in order to exert power over them. For example, advertisers define audiences as consumers, and gather knowledge about their purchasing habits, because they want to sell to them. However, because audiences are constructed in this manner by the combination of knowledge and power within these discourses, it does not mean that real audiences will behave in the way predicted. Audiences can also be understood by the way they resist the discursive powers which try to construct them in ways which suit those powers. To achieve this it is necessary for research to look at 'the social world of actual audiences' and 'to develop the forms of knowledge about television audiencehood that move away from those informed by the institutional point of view' (Ien Ang, *Desperately Seeking the Audience* (1991)).

However, Ang's use of the concept of power remains vague and abstract. The extent to which the space of fantasy is unconstrained and open to resistant readings is difficult to both accept and judge since the fantasies of romance readers to which Ang refers are more or less based on the romantic idyll promoted by romance novels. If power is vested in the hands of television institutions that seek to control audiences by discursive forms of knowledge, what are the particular reasons that make them do this? Is there a particular drive to exercise power which characterises certain institutions? Similarly, why should the power of institutions be resisted? What are the interests which motivate resistance to discursive power?

The active audience approach sits well with postmodern theory's emphasis on plurality and difference. Power rests with diverse audiences, not media barons or institutions. Active audiences produce local meanings from polysemic communications. The postmodern condition becomes characterised by a decentred **subjectivity** dispersed in time and space. In its most extreme this provides a vulgar reduction of Foucault, in which power is pluralistic and can be used by anybody, any time, any place, any where. It takes no account of the increasing power of multinationals and media conglomerates (mostly owned and controlled by men), increasing intervention by the state (operating firmly within patriarchy) and vastly unequal economic realities (working largely in favour of men). Or as Seiter *et al.* remind us in *Remote Control* (1989), 'soap operas allow women to take pleasure in the character of the villainous, but they do not provide characters that radically challenge the ideology of femininity'.

Much postmodernism insists everyone is always actively resisting mediated reality through our knowledge of images and their construction. In other words we know we can't escape it, we know that it is as real as our material existence, but we also know that it is constructed and that we can play a part in the meanings given to it. Each of us plays with the notion of constructedness, taking whatever we choose from the bits and pieces at our disposal. Achieving the ideal is now a contradictory mix of rigorous bodily control and playful experimentation with dress, make-up and accessories. While this is liberating in freeing image for self-expression, it has also been accused of masking the gap between the image and women's continuing socio-economic struggles. With the move to postmodernism, spectacle works to enlarge our fantasies, not bring us closer to identification with the particular or the material. Reverential attitudes and aspirations have been unsettled by a new awareness of the processes of image construction. In a postmodern age, fashion and cosmetics bring new freedoms in experimentation and play. Consumer culture is an arena of female participation and enjoyment; a route to developing multiple subjectivities for women from work to leisure that ensures women feel freed from the obligations of less liberated periods.

The radical ability of the audience to create and play with meaning is said to release the reader from predictable, confirming signifieds. Or in the words of Ang, 'since a subject is always multiply positioned in relation to a whole range of discourses, many of which do not concern gender, women do not always live in the prison house of gender' (*Living Room Wars: Rethinking Media Audiences for a Post-modern World* (1996)). Furthermore, those moments where we can define ourselves despite our gender are declared as the truly liberatory ones. Based on the assumption that discourse is reality and there are always multiple discourses to choose from, the individual becomes a self-made jigsaw of bits and pieces. This frequently relegates to insignificance the fact that someone made the jigsaw pieces in the first place, shaped them, drew particular configurations on them, and gave them to us in particular packaging designed to appeal and to sell. The decentred self that resists and self-constructs at all times and is unbound by gender still reads the soap operas or the romantic novels and largely conforms to ideologies of femininity. Women are addressed and positioned by media texts in terms of their cultural expertise. To the extent that we respond to this invocation we are positioned as female spectators (listeners, etc.).

Much recent work on audiences has recognised the rampant relativism of previous active audience theory and sought to recoup the role of the media in the meaning-making process. Such work states that the meanings of mediated imagery are tied to a community and its shared experiences and to the actual ability of individuals to actively interpret it. This ability may depend on many things, not least educational and cultural capital, national, local and personal socio-economic realities. The concept of gender as discourse allows for the possibility of multiple subjectivities in women and men that may not always be gender-dominated. But are these discourses ever gender-neutral? An important point to remember from Foucault is that discourses reflect and produce power and certain discourses claim legitimacy over others. Aspects of contemporary mass media practices can be used to reproduce a repressive social system.

CONCLUSION

If there can be one single achievement of feminist media studies over the last two decades, it is that it is now impossible to make any sense of the mass media without paying attention to gender. This chapter has shown that early feminist media research on women and popular culture viewed mass mediated communications as a major source for the general reproduction of patriarchal social relations whether through representation in the text or representation in the labour force. The end result was the same for all women – increased oppression through negative representation. Then, as the idea of a singular, essential form of female experience has been increasingly challenged, reflection theories that suggest a fit between representation and 'real' women have been replaced by a critique that focuses on identity and multiple subjectivities whereby women can think their own thoughts and respond to popular culture in a manner that is not self-evident.

So, the impact feminism has had on media and communication theory is considerable. Unfortunately what all this research also reveals is that the impact of feminism on the media itself is more questionable.

10

FEMINISM AND THE BODY

FIONA CARSON

The body has become the locus of a great deal of theorising in recent years, with writers such as Jacques **Derrida** and Michel **Foucault** challenging the traditional Cartesian dualism which subordinates body to mind. Instead, they postulate the body as the central object through which power relations are both formulated and resisted. Such arguments have been taken up by **feminist** thinkers, who argue that the act of theorising the body is especially pertinent to women, as the **gender** conventionally aligned with the body. While men lay claim to the supposedly 'superior' category of mind, the biological processes – **menstruation**, gestation – are writ large upon the surface of the female body, and thus become the means by which 'woman' is defined. The work of Julia **Kristeva**, for example, is crucially concerned with analysing the materiality of the female body; its drives, pulsations and emanations, which she argues are regarded with revulsion within a culture which wishes to divorce the 'pure' subject of Cartesian rationalism from its fleshy corporeality. On a purely materialistic level, too, feminism is crucially concerned with the ways in which women's bodies are controlled within a **patriarchal** system, which regulates women's access to such services as **contraception** and **abortion**, while at the same time idealised forms of their bodies are **objectified**, by various means, for male consumption and sexual delectation.

It is this latter point which will be the concern of this essay, which concentrates on the issue of representation. It will look at traditional forms of representation of the **feminine**, such as the painted **nude**, as well as at **postmodern** theorising about the ways in which such representations can be subverted. Artists and theorists informed by feminism do not reject the traditional alignment between women and body. Instead, they give it a subversive twist by playing on the concept of idealised femininity in such a way as to embrace the Kristevan notion of the female body as unruly, **grotesque**, and resistant to categorisation.

OBJECTIFICATION AND PROTEST

Challenging the dominant ideological representations of femininity was a cornerstone of **second wave** feminist theory. Today in the nineties it could be argued that, despite thirty years of agitation and analysis, not a lot has changed. One of the major issues of the second wave feminist movement of the 1970s was how women were represented negatively as **stereotypes** and objects of the male **gaze** in the visual conventions of both high art and popular **culture**. The key symbolic gestures which are most remembered attacked visible symbols of the beauty industry or oppressive forms of objectification. At the Miss America **beauty contest** of 1968, feminist protestors trashed the oppressive paraphernalia of femininity (such as bras, girdles, false eyelashes, curlers, wigs and fashion magazines) to criticise a system that measured female value by appearance. Allen Jones's sculpture series 'women as furniture', which portrayed highly fetishised dummies as supports for coffee tables, was denounced by a group of British feminists as deeply misogynistic and offensive. At the ICA in 1978 they claimed 'the right to intervene by presenting a show of women's attitudes towards men' (Laura Mulvey, in Rozsika **Parker** and Griselda **Pollock**, *Framing Feminism*, 1987). The resulting exhibition, *Images of Men*, held there in 1980, was a major feminist grassroots intervention into high culture. The continuing importance of this ideological struggle over representation lies in the powerful relationship between idealised or denigrating images of women in the media and the internalisation of these by female consumers.

THE IDEAL BODY

The ideal body of the 1990s is the winnowy, youthful body of the sylph, personified by the model Kate Moss. The materialism and power dressing of the affluent, glossy, competitive eighties were discarded in the eco-friendly 'purity' of the early nineties. More recently, **girl power**'s brash glamour is paired with laddishness in a period where girls must act like boys to get ahead; evidence of some elements of vitality and variety to the relentless idealisation of the thin body underpinned by the billion-dollar **fashion**, cosmetic and slimming industries. Writing in 1990, Naomi **Wolf** argued in *The Beauty Myth* that 'the more legal and material hindrances women have broken through, the more strictly and heavily and cruelly images of female beauty have come to weigh upon us'. She points to the self-hatred, feelings of imperfection and fear of ageing 'inside the majority of the West's controlled, attractive, successful working women'. She calls this the 'Iron Maiden' – what need of the Victorian corset, when we have an internalised, invisible, psychological and physiological corset? Wolf argues that the virtuous domesticity of the 1950s has been replaced by virtuous beauty, quoting a 1984 *Glamour* survey of 33,000 women that revealed obsession with losing one stone in weight as rating above success in work or in love as the most desired goal. The gap between actual bodyweight and desired/ideal bodyweight was in 50% of cases a stone below natural healthy bodyweight. This desire for an unnatural thinness is supported and encouraged by the beauty industries and glamour fashion photography, which promotes female beauty icons who weigh 25% less than the average American woman. Fashion icons like Twiggy in the sixties and 'heroin chic' in the nineties exemplify what Ann Hollander describes as 'the look of sickness, the look of poverty and the look of nervous exhaustion'. A similar aesthetic ideal based on the adolescent body-type is to be found in the cult of thinness, lightness and aerial grace in classical ballet. The pressure to maintain a low bodyweight amongst fashion models in particular leads to a high incidence of **eating disorders** amongst models and a dangerous co-relation with eating disorders amongst teenage girls, who now find moral virtue in 'good looks' rather than the 'good works' of a century ago.

In *Fat is a Feminist Issue* (1978), Susie Orbach interprets the opposite extreme of fatness as an act of fear or refusal to conform to sexual objectification. Issues of the continuing objectification and exploitation of the female body are starkly embodied in the short and mythic life of **Diana** Spencer, whose therapist was Orbach. The struggle for ownership of Diana's body was dramatised both in public, in media discussion of her workouts and her cellulite, and in private, in the war she waged with herself in the very fabric of her body. Her bulimic refusal of the constraining role of the perfect lie, the virgin princess trapped in the confines of one of history's most objectified bodies, was an act of refusal and, ultimately, liberation, as she learnt to reshape her sense of **identity** in a mould shaped by psychotherapy and feminism, only to be hounded to death by the paparazzi.

In *Ways of Seeing* (1972), John Berger made the connection between the visual language of **advertising** and publicity, with its emphasis on idealised, objectified bodies, and the conventions of Old Master painting. One of the most enduring idealisations of the female body is the high art cultural form of the painted or sculpted nude.

HIGH ART CONVENTIONS OF THE NUDE

Henry Moore's *Memorial Figure* of 1945-6, which stands in the grounds of Dartington Hall, was sculpted as a 'memorial to a friend who loved the quiet mellowness of this Devonshire landscape' (Philip James, ed., *Henry Moore on Sculpture*, 1996). It stands in a long line of reclining nudes which use the female body to express ideas about harmony, order and civilisation. Moore monumentalises the female body – in this case, the maternal body – to express the classic unity of woman and **nature**. He wishes to convey 'a sense of permanent tranquility, from which the stir and fret of human ways had been withdrawn'. This ideal of peace and timelessness was particularly poignant in the aftermath of the Second World War.

A similar desire for continuity and order is conveyed in Kenneth Clark's *The Nude: A Study of Ideal Art*, published in 1956. Clark finds the origin of the reclining nude in the High Renaissance paintings by Giorgione, *The Dresden Venus*, voluptuous nude reclining in a glowing Venetian landscape, and its indoor equivalent, Titian's *Venus of Urbino*. For Clark 'the cylindrical smoothness of every form' and the 'perfect ease of transition from one comprehensible shape to another' are evidence of a classical canon linking Giorgione with Praxiteles, Winckelmann and Ingres. This trajectory of the female nude as embodiment of the humanist spirit culminates, surprisingly, in the buxom nudes of late Renoir. In Clark's account, the female body is ordered and perfected into an idealised form, which stands as a symbol of objectified female beauty. In this discourse of perfection, there is no hint of power politics, irregularity or individuality to disturb the gaze.

Protest against this idealisation and objectification of the female body in its most conspicuous and long-lived form, the Old Master painting tradition of the nude, is not new to feminism. The militant **suffragette**, Mary Richardson, took an axe to Velasquez's *Rokeby Venus* at the National Gallery in 1914. In 1952 she finally gave her reason for this attack as being 'I didn't like the way men visitors to the gallery gaped at it all day.' This clash between 'patriarchal' and 'feminist' perspectives on the objectification of the female body continues. In 1989, the authority of this Old Master tradition of the nude was called upon by right-wing MPs to justify the *Sun*'s topless Page 3 girls, under attack from Clare Short's anti-**pornography** campaign. Norman Tebbit defended Page 3 girls as the working-**class** version of naked women in art galleries.

OBJECTIFICATION AND POSSESSION

It was John Berger in *Ways of Seeing* who initiated a different political discussion of the nude by contrasting the power relations implicit in the representation of men and women. A man's presence was promise of power, whereas a woman's presence implied self-conscious display, her sense of self split between the surveyor and the surveyed. 'Men act and women appear. Women watch themselves being looked at.' Berger linked the reappearance of the nude in the Renaissance with the growth of capitalism and the portrayal of possessions, including women, in the new medium of oil paint. He also made connections between the visual and symbolic language of figurative oil painting and the imagery of advertising publicity. The spectator/owner was replaced by the spectator/buyer. In both forms, the idealised and objectified bodies of women had an important role to play. In 1865, Berger argues, 'the ideal was broken' by the 'realism' of Manet's contemporary nude, *Olympia*, who in her assertive pose and returning gaze, appears to be questioning her passive role as object of the gaze.

THE GAZE

Theories about the objectification of the female body have become highly developed in the wake of Laura **Mulvey**'s seminal essay 'Visual **Pleasure** and Narrative Cinema' (1975), which analysed the representation of female stars such as Marlene Dietrich in terms of their objectification by the male gaze within Hollywood narrative cinema. Drawing on **psychoanalytic** and structuralist theory, Mulvey argued that the cinematic pleasures of seeing were primarily a male fantasy. The voyeuristic pleasures of cinematic fantasy constructed women characters and female stars as fetishised objects of a 'masculine' gaze irrespective of the spectator's gender. Mulvey's ideas opened up the field for much more subject-specific research into audience-identification, revealing far more complex processes than she initially proposed. The main questions for feminists were how to intervene actively in this regime of looking, how to subvert dominant discourses of objectification, and what happened when women looked.

RECLAIMING THE FEMALE BODY

For feminist artists of the 1970s who were active in the making of images, one of the key issues was recuperating the representation of the female body from objectification and **stereotyping**. This proved to be a much more complex issue than at first appeared. In an article published in *Art History* in 1978, 'The Body Politic', Lisa **Tickner** proposed that the 'occupied territory' of the female body must be 'reclaimed from masculine fantasy and reintegrated in opposition to its more familiar role as raw material for the men'. Strategies adopted by contemporary women artists to achieve these aims were described by Tickner as role reversal; performance and body art that questioned female identities; parody; and virginal iconography. This last strategy was to become deeply contentious when it was developed into a feminine aesthetic by Judy **Chicago** and Lucy Lippard, because of its universalising and **essentialising** tendencies.

As theoretical developments became more sophisticated, particularly in the 1980s, deconstructing the workings of dominant **ideology** in order to address the 'structural and deep-seated causes of women's **oppression** rather than . . . its effects' came to be seen as the most pressing strategy for social change. In 'Textual Strategies: the Politics of Art-Making' (Parker and Pollock, eds., *Framing Feminism*), Barry and Flitterman proposed the creation of 'an aesthetics designed to subvert the production of "woman" as a commodity'. It was necessary to expose the workings of ideology by analysing the production and consumption of representations of women, as well as analysing the social conditions that produced them. This theoretical position of 'deconstruction' was bitterly opposed to the 'essentialising' body-based aesthetic associated with Judy Chicago's *Dinner Party*. Deconstructive strategies tended to use photographic media and to employ strategies of distantiation, parody and elliptical reference to the body.

Jo **Spence**'s collaborative project, *The History Lesson* (1982), which exemplifies this approach, embarks upon a critique of photographic representations and practices while questioning the role of women in the family. Her working-class heroine is the owner of the gaze, dissecting a paperback of **Freud** with goggles on and turning the binoculars of scrutiny onto the spectator. Her idealised mother, the Madonna, suckles a fully-grown male. As a standing nude, Spence positions herself backview against an industrial landscape, appropriating the pose of Michelangelo's classic male nude, David. As a backview reclining nude, she parodies the post of the *Rokeby Venus*, a forty-seven-year-old naked woman alone in a vast man-made landscape, questioning the history and ideology of the classical nude. In *Cultural Sniping* (1995), Spence uses feminist, Marxist and **psychoanalytic** theory to deconstruct dominant myths about **class**, race and sexuality.

ORDERING THE FEMALE BODY

Lynda Nead's analysis of *The Female Nude* of 1992 reflects the sophistication and theoretical complexity of the debates about representation
and the gaze that dominated the eighties, and reflected the psychoanalytic writings of **Lacan** and his followers, and the deconstruction
theories of **Derrida**. However, what underpins Nead's analysis of the
nude are the much older structuralist ideas of Mary **Douglas**'s *Purity and
Danger* (1966), inflected by Julia Kristeva's writings on the **abject** and
the maternal body in *Powers of Horror* (1982). Douglas perceived a
fundamental dichotomy between 'order=purity' and 'disorder=
pollution' in the social structuring of different societies. Male elites
used this dichotomy to reinforce their power over women, by transcrib-
ing this value system symbolically onto the female body, expressing
anxiety around signs of difference such as menstruation and childbirth.
Of particular threat and therefore of symbolic loading are bodily fluids
and points of entry and exit from the body. Interpreted from a Kristevan
psychoanalytic perspective, there is a correspondence between the
integrity of the body and the integrity of the self. The idea of the self is
formulated in the course of differentiation and separation from the
mother, a process which involves in Kristeva's account a 'mapping of the
clean and proper body' of the child. Thus, as Nead expresses it, 'subjectivity and sociality are based on the expulsion of what is considered
unclean and impure from the clean and proper self'. The provisionality
of this structuring produces the powerful threat of the abject – that
which is dispelled by the social order – particularly liquids and waste
substances produced by the body, like tears, urine, sexual fluids, faeces,
etc., which are viewed as abject waste products and a source of revulsion.
Lynda Nead uses the theories of Douglas and Kristeva to throw light on
the representation of the female body in the high art nude. The nude is
conceived of as a sealed container, a perfected, rationally-organised
formulation of the female body, not subject to individuality or change.
The abject aspects of the female body are hidden and denied. Thus when
Lisa Tickner reminds us that Titian's *Venus of Urbino* menstruated, we
experience the shock of abjection.

In attempting to speak of the lived body of experience, women artists
inevitably begin to transgress the confinement of the idealised body
which exercises a visual tyranny everywhere, from the pages of **women's
magazines**, from commercial breaks on television or from advertising
hoardings on the way to work. While feminist artists from the eighties
used deconstructive strategies to expose the workings of dominant

ideology in representation, other artists still working more directly with the body began to challenge the confines of the Kristevan 'clean and proper body'.

Helen Chadwick reclaims the abjected aspects of the female body in her installation *Of Mutability* 1984–6 (*Enfleshings*, 1989), which she premises with the subtitle 'Before I was bounded, now I've begun to leak . . .' In life-size photocopies of her own body spewing out fruit and embracing dead animals, Chadwick used the age-old theme of Vanitas, the impermanence and perishability of human flesh, to explore a fluid, sensual, unbounded idea of herself, the opposite of the specular narcissus in the mirror, the well-manicured High Art nude. 'What if dangerous fluids were to spill out, displacing logic, refuting a coherent narrative, into a landscape on the brink of "I"?' In this bulimic spewing-out, 'the boundaries have dissolved, between self and other, the living and the corpse'. Chadwick was one of the first women artists to work with abjection and to recognise its power to disrupt categories, and to question the dominant formations of ideology by threatening the integrity of subjecthood with the transgressive power of the abject.

THE GROTESQUE BODY

When the French philosopher Luce **Irigaray** seeks a new symbol for the female body that resists patriarchal definition, she chooses 'volume fluidity', the open container, the volume without contours, as opposed to the controllable closed volume of the female and maternal body of masculine fantasy. Some of the most challenging writing and creative work being done in the nineties explores this territory of abjection and non-idealised representations of femininity in the pursuit of alternative and powerful representations of femininity with which to challenge patriarchal representation. Interesting correspondences can be found between the abject fantasy body of the medieval **witch**, the leaky abjected body of Chadwick's installation *Of Mutability*, and the anarchic fluid body of feminist post-Lacanian theory. In *The Witch in History* (1996), Diane Purkiss describes the unruly body of the witch as the leaky vessel, 'a fantasy image of the huge, controlling, scattered and polluted leaky fantasy of the maternal body of the imaginary'. The shapeshifting, boundless body of the witch threatens the territorial boundaries of the good, clean housewife, especially around areas that need to be kept clean, like the milk churn. There is absolute polarisation between the two models. As Marina **Warner** argues in *Alone of All Her Sex* (1978), this image of the witch as 'bad, lactating mother' is twin to the good, ideal, bodiless virgin mother of Christianity, the second Eve, the Madonna. Echoes of the same polarisation can perhaps be found in the corresponding pairing between Mary Richardson, the 'hysterical suffragette', and the unsullied perfection of the *Rokeby Venus* which Mary tried to destroy.

The visceral, fluid and boundless body of the witch has much in common with the grotesque, carnivalesque body which has always existed in popular culture as a corrective to the contained and idealised body of high culture. In *The Unruly Woman* (1995), Kathleen Rowe argues that the ribald excess of the 'unruly' woman of **comedy** personified in characters such as Roseanne and Dawn French can be used 'affirmatively, to destabilise the idealization of female beauty', and to return the male gaze by 'exposing and making a spectacle of the gazer'. She applies Mary Douglas's categories of purity and danger to melodrama (which, in its valorisation of passivity and suffering, is 'pure'), and comedy (which uses radical negation, imposture and masquerade, and is therefore 'dangerous'). For Rowe, the visual power and spectacle of the unruly woman is an alternative to 'feminist film theory's obsession with Lacanian-based psychoanalysis which takes as given women's identification with loss'. Also writing in 1995, Mary Russo, in *The Female Grotesque*, contrasts the classical body and the grotesque body as two sides of the same coin:

> The classical body is transcendent, monumental, closed, static, self-contained, symmetrical and sleek; it is identified with the 'high' or official culture of the Renaissance, and later, with rationalism, individualism, and normalizing aspirations of the bourgeoisie. The grotesque body is open, protruding, irregular, secreting, multiple, and changing; it is identified with non-official 'low' culture, or the carnivalesque, and with social transformation.

Russo characterises the grotesque body as associated with 'the lower body stratum', connected with animals, degradation, filth, death, and rebirth, and it is in this sense that the category 'grotesque' has been applied to the vast fleshy nudes of the contemporary painter Jenny Saville. The fact that they were painted for the contemporary 'high art' collection of Charles Saatchi poses an interesting question about the possibilities for renegotiation of definitions of the nude. On the one hand, Saville's images revel in fleshly excess, and in the power of physicality and the return of the gaze; on the other, they conform to the internalised self-hatred imposed by society. The monumental model in *Plan* towers over the viewers and gazes down upon them like a female cyclops. Her body might seem a celebration of dominant flesh, but she is marked up for lyposuction. Alison Rowley describes the painting as 'the memory of a mismatch, as it is lived day by day, between a female body of a particular appearance and the culture's sign for the desirable, feminine body' ('On Viewing Three Paintings by Jenny Saville', in Griselda Pollock, ed., *Generations and Geographies*, 1996).

Rosemary Betterton, in *An Intimate Distance* (1996), draws together a number of examples of the use of abjection in the work by women artists about the female body in the nineties. She acknowledges its importance as a continuing strategy of challenging and critiquing 'what is excluded or defined as inferior within male culture', but she also recognises its ultimate limitation, concluding that 'its use in art remains a deeply ambivalent process'.

THE POSTMODERN BODY

In her sociological study of **dance**, Gabriele Klein identifies a pattern in European history, whereby periods of *Korper-entfesselung* (liberation of the body) alternate with *korperdisziplin* (restriction of the body). For Elizabeth **Wilson** in *Adorned in Dreams* (1995), fashion oscillates between the two poles of the 'natural' and the 'artificial'. The 'naturalism' of the hippie fashion of the seventies is shaped by an ideology of 'authenticity'. A similar motivation shaped second wave feminism's resistance to objectification and consequent rejection of fashion, only to create a fashion statement of their own in the form of cropped hair, boilersuits and pierced ears. Janet Radcliffe Richards, writing in *The Sceptical Feminist* (1980), commented on seventies feminists' distrust of artifice: 'trying to make the most of oneself is to create a false impression, somehow to deceive the world, i.e., setting up the natural as superior to the artificial'. From Wilson's perspective, artifice is a more appropriate response than the puritanism and refusal of seventies feminism which she sees as a continuation of the nineteenth-century dress reform's desire to 'get out of fashion'. She sees the polysemy of pluralism and the playfulness of artifice in the dresscodes of **postmodern** culture as a more appropriate strategy for advertising the individual's consensual or dissident body politics. Just as you can rearrange identity in the shifting signifiers of postmodern fashion codes, so increasingly you can rearrange the body as well. Susan Bordo describes the 'plasticity' of the body as *the* postmodern paradigm. In 'Material Girl: the Effacements of Postmodern Culture' (in Schwichtenberg, ed., *The Madonna Collection*, 1993), she quotes *Fit* magazine: 'the challenge presents itself to rearrange things, it's up to you to do the chiselling, become the master sculptress'. This 'sculpting' process might involve working out at a health club or plastic surgery, an increasing phenomenon amongst the under-35s. Thus the ideal body is reinvented in the nineties as 'lean, strong, **androgynous** and physically fit; conveying core western cultural values of autonomy, toughness, competitiveness, youth, self-control'; a masculinisation of the female body in keeping with her new competitiveness in the workplace.

Some feminist critics express reservations about postmodern theory, particularly its view of the dissolution of the unified subject, and with it in some cases the binarism of gender, appearing to leave feminism without a project. For others, the deconstruction of grand narratives, the fragmentation of identities and dissolution of the binary oppositions of gender in postmodern theory are a welcome confirmation of an identity politics based in differences of ethnicity and sexuality, which enables people to reclaim agency and power. For this new feminism of difference to work, Razia Aziz argues in 'Feminism and the Challenge of **Racism**' (in H. S. Mirza, ed., *Black British Feminism*, 1997), it needs to incorporate both the deconstruction of subjectivity, and the political necessity of asserting identity.

A postmodern eclecticism informs the fragmented subjectivities of Chila Kumari Burman's British Asian identity. In her autoprints she uses her body in a multiplicity of symbolic forms, ranging from exoticised bodyprints to the imagery of powerful Indian warriors and Japanese martial arts, to create visual images of resistance to incorporation and marginalisation by the dominant culture. Sonia Boyce and other Afro-Caribbean artists use Afro hair as a symbol of black culture and a starting-point for questioning the **racist** history of assumptions about the black body. Seeking to deconstruct gender binarism and 'heteroreality', Judith **Butler** views all gender positions as forms of performance. Della Grace's *The Three Disgraces* parodies the Old Master tradition of idealised femininity in the paintings of Botticelli and Raphael. Challenging the conventional boundaries of gender difference, she represents Venus's aerial followers as fashionable lesbians, robust nudes with bald heads wearing Doc Martens.

The performance artist **Orlan**'s interventions in **cosmetic surgery** might be viewed as the ultimate form of postmodern gender performance, in which she alters her identity via the fabric of her body. Orlan views identity as 'nomadic and multiple'. She sets about deconstructing two art-forms which idealise and perfect the objectified female body: the Old Master tradition of female beauty and plastic surgery. She sets out to give herself the 'perfect' face, computer-generated by selecting the features of Old Master paintings of Mona Lisa, Diana, Venus, Europa and Psyche, and proceeds to implement them in a series of well-publicised operations. By dramatising the gory process of plastic surgery, she implicates the audience as voyeuristic spectators in this painful process and deconstructs cosmetic surgery's 'myth of magic transformation'. As she says, 'In plastic surgery, nobody sees what you go through and what you look like.' In the process, she stretches our notions of the integrity of body and self to its limits and beyond.

As we have seen, the field of representation of the female body as 'contemplated object' is a complex and deeply political issue. The feminist critique has evolved over the last thirty years as a counterweight to the constant process of objectification and idealisation generated by industry and the media, which through processes of internalisation has become the cultural censor within. As time has passed, the critical voices have diversified to reflect the differences of perspective within feminism. The struggle continues.

11

FEMINISM AND LITERATURE

JILL LeBIHAN

It is difficult to express concisely the enormous impact that feminism has
had on academic literary studies. It is even more difficult to explain why
it should be within English departments in particular that **feminist**
textual criticism, in a variety of forms, has found and retains some
footholds, even in the **backlash** of the nineties. In *Feminism and Its
Fictions* (1998), Lisa Maria Hogeland explains the phenomenon by
seeing feminism 'as a kind of literacy, a way of reading both texts and
everyday life from a particular stance', whilst Cora Kaplan, in *Sea
Changes: Culture and Feminism* (1986), sees writing as part of a political
process of resistance, arguing that 'defiance is a component of the act of
writing for women'.

The field of English literature as taught within British universities
was, until the 1980s, excessively dominated by male-authored works.
Canonical authors, taught reliably on core courses (rather than options)
included George Eliot and Jane Austen as essentials, but many departments got by without teaching both Emily and Charlotte Brontë and
many avoided Virginia **Woolf**. Even when works by these few writers
appeared on reading lists, they were often taught with an indifference to
the feminist issues raised both by their token inclusion and their
thematic content.

Women students and teachers working within the **patriarchal** institution of the university English department began integrating explicitly
feminist-oriented approaches to texts as part of the **second wave**, at the
end of the 1960s in a few pioneering cases and, more widely, into the
1970s and 80s. Because there were so few women-authored texts on the
curriculum, the critical attention of these feminists focused on representations of women in male-authored works. This kind of criticism is
now quite commonplace, and often takes the form of hunting out
stereotypes of women and using them as a means of identifying the ways
in which these restricted cultural representations underpin women's
oppression. By representing women as sexual objects, for instance,

rather than politically powerful subjects, women receive a version of **femininity** and womanhood that is perpetually limited and therefore limiting.

Many feminist critics argued that, in canonical texts, women were usually represented as part of a crude sexual binary: they were virgins or whores. By and large, the whores came to miserable ends, and the virgins got married. Kate **Millett**'s analysis of such negatively sexualised representations of women in texts by men in *Sexual Politics* (1969) remains infamous for her attack on the **phallocentric** D.H. Lawrence, but has since been heavily criticised for its lack of sophistication. However, Germaine **Greer**'s *The Female Eunuch*, despite being first published in 1970, remains very pertinent to a nineties audience in its witty identification of stereotypes of women in a variety of cultural media. Greer argues that

> there are stringent limits to the variations on the stereotype, for nothing must interfere with her function as sex object. She may wear leather, as long as she cannot actually handle a motorbike; she may wear rubber, but it ought not to indicate that she is an expert diver or water-skier. If she wears athletic clothes the purpose is to underline her unathleticism. She may sit astride a horse, looking soft and curvy, but she must not crouch over its neck with her rump in the air.

Greer makes an important point about the emphasis on women's passivity and their **objectification**, and feminist critics have continued this 'images of women' approach to male-authored, canonical texts. They have studied anything from Chaucer and Shakespeare right up to contemporary works, looking principally for victimised or stereotypically passive representations to criticise, or else searching for radical breaks from the mould to celebrate.

This revisioning of classic works of literature through the newly-raised consciousness developed by feminism was an important step in developing a new critical tradition, but in order to achieve a true reformation of canonical curricula, feminist criticism had to do something more than reread the same, old, tired texts. So the work of feminist critics began to focus on texts by women, in a process both of rediscovering long-forgotten and undervalued women's writing from history, and of developing aesthetic criteria applicable to women's texts being produced in the present.

Significant in the process of recovering undervalued work from the past was the establishment of the Virago Press in London by Carmen Callil. This press, originally independent although now owned by a conglomerate, published only work by women, and the Virago Modern Classics series reissued British and American texts from the nineteenth and twentieth centuries that had long been unavailable in modern editions. Often produced reasonably cheaply – in facsimile format and without critical introductions – these texts changed the kind of works available for teaching in higher education and thus began to have an influence on the curriculum. The excuses for not including women's writing on courses, outlined very clearly by Joanna **Russ** in *How To Suppress Women's Writing* (1984), included the idea that women did not write very much, and that what they did write was of dubious quality. The republication of 'lost' texts not only made available an enormous quantity of work, of considerable variety, but also demonstrated the need for literary critics to revisit their critical frameworks.

Feminist critics argue that aesthetic standards for cultural production have been set by white, middle-**class**, heterosexual men in reference to work by white, middle-class, heterosexual writers. In order to transform the content of literary studies, feminists have argued that we need to transform our critical approaches. The American critic Elaine **Showalter** has been one of the most prominent and successful figures in bringing about this transformation. Her landmark work is *A Literature of Their Own: British Women Novelists from Brontë to Lessing* (1978), in which she argues that women's different lives and duties necessarily produce different content in their literary work, and that there are enough features in common to formulate a specific tradition. She points out that 'when we look at women writers collectively, we can see an imaginative continuum, the recurrence of certain patterns, themes, problems, and images from generation to generation' (1996:14). Showalter rejects the idea that the shared content of women's writing is anything to do with a stereotypical 'female sensibility', but links their writing instead to the material conditions of production: 'the female literary tradition comes from the still-evolving relationships between women writers and their society'. Showalter argues that women's writing is like that of any other subculture, and that it goes through three phases of development: '*imitation* of the prevailing modes of the dominant tradition', '*protest* against these standards and values', and finally, '*self-discovery*', 'a search for identity'. Showalter labels these stages 'Feminine', 'Feminist' and 'Female'. Clearly, it is the last of these, texts that fall into the category of the 'female', that Showalter privileges. These texts represent not merely mimicry or retaliation but offer women 'a literature of their own'. In a later, equally influential work, *The New Feminist Criticism* (1986), Showalter argues this point further, in her call for the establishment of '**gynocritics**', 'a female framework for the analysis of women's literature, to develop new models based on the study of female experience, rather than to adapt male models and theories'. If Showalter's work can be used as a gauge for the development of mainstream, **Anglo-American**, literary feminism, though, it is significant that, in a newspaper article on contemporary women's fiction at the end of the twentieth century, she takes up what could easily be interpreted as the '**postfeminist**' stance characteristic of the *fin de siècle*:

> But it may also be that as we reach the millennium, British women's writing may be coming to the end of its history as a separate and distinct 'literature of its own'. The self-consciousness that is the legacy of two decades of feminist literary criticism has made British women's writing self-reflexive in a new way. Now, every book is written in the shadow of feminist theory as well as Jane Austen, and in the consciousness of such female themes, metaphors, and iconographies as the mother tongue, embroidery, cookery, **eating disorders**, sisterhood, madwomen in the attic, lesbian eroticism and mother-daughter attachment.
>
> (*The Guardian*, Tuesday 11 May, 1999)

Showalter here declares the end of the age of separatism, and suggests a decline of the need for separate courses on women's writing, although the kind of issues she lists as concerns of women's writing (**sisterhood**, lesbian eroticism, madwomen and so on) remain, even at the turn of the new Millennium, within a very restricted domain of literary discussion.

The critical view that women's writing can be considered as a subgenre of literature on its own terms has not found universal support amongst all feminists working in the field, and work in the 'gynocritics' tradition has perhaps faced more protest from within the feminist ranks than from without. One of the early and most successful counter-critiques can be found in Toril **Moi**'s *Sexual/Textual Politics* (1985), which was, and to some extent remains, an enormously influential text in what has become the established canon of feminist literary theory. Moi's now classic work provides an early narrative of feminist criticism, and was one of the first to articulate a clear binary divide between 'Anglo-American Feminist Criticism' and '**French Feminist** Theory'. This split is a structuring force in Moi's text, as she reviews what she labels *criticism* by Millett, Showalter, Sandra M. **Gilbert** and Susan **Gubar** amongst others, and *theory*, by Simone de **Beauvoir**, Luce **Irigaray**, Hélène **Cixous** and Julia **Kristeva**. The continental schism, as well as the division between theory and criticism, has had a lasting effect on the view of feminist work in literary studies, playing off the supposedly pragmatic and coherent Anglo-American critics against the esoteric and inaccessible European theorists. Moi claims that 'Anglo-American feminist critics have been mostly indifferent or even hostile towards literary theory, which they have often regarded as a hopelessly abstract "male" activity', although she recognises that, in the early 1980s, this was an attitude that was beginning to change. With the mainstreaming of critical theory in general, feminist academics increasingly adopted assorted textual approaches in their writing, with feminism developing very strong affinities with particular theories, notably **psychoanalysis** and deconstruction. Moi's work might even be credited with facilitating this shift towards the theoretical. *Sexual/Textual Politics*, published originally by Methuen in its New Accents series, provides one of the most compact introductions to the two main strands of feminist literary criticism and theory even now, and effectively made feminism teachable by providing something that could easily become a set text on a specialist English course.

One of Moi's main criticisms of the kind of Anglo-American feminism represented by Showalter is that ultimately it does not radically challenge bourgeois, humanist critical practices: it merely replaces a male-dominated canon of classics with a female-dominated one. Moi argues that the humanist critical position reads 'great literature' in order to learn about

> an authentic vision of life; and the role of the reader or critic is to listen respectfully to the voice of the author as it is expressed in the text. The literary canon of 'great literature' ensures that it is this 'representative experience' (one selected by male bourgeois critics) that is transmitted to future generations, rather than those deviant, unrepresentative experiences discoverable in much female, ethnic and working-class writing. Anglo-American feminist criticism has waged war on this self-sufficient canonization of middle-class male values. But they have rarely challenged the very notion of such a canon.

'Gynocritics' and other practices encourage similar ways of reading to those enforced by patriarchal humanism: the reader's life is to be enriched by learning from the writing of great authors. The fact that these authors are women, under Anglo-American feminism, does not, for Moi, make a great deal of difference. But the kind of theoretically-informed analytical practices Moi advocates, that treat both reading and writing as textual processes, produce a dilemma for the 'gynocritic', catching her 'between the "new" feminists with their "male" theories and the male humanist empiricists with their patriarchal politics' (Moi 1985:79).

There is consensus evident between the 'theorists' and the 'critics' in their rejection of traditional humanism, but the most effective formulation of resistance is the point of disagreement. Whereas Showalter sees women's writing as taking its place under traditionally formulated aesthetic categories, Cora Kaplan argues in *Sea Changes: Culture and Feminism* that women's marginalised status under patriarchal humanism necessarily makes them less subject to its ideological sway, and therefore places their writing outside the canonical embrace:

> Within contemporary western culture the act of writing and the romantic ideologies of individual agency and power are tightly bound together, although that which is written frequently resists and exposes this unit of the self as **ideology**. At both the psychic and the social level, always intertwined, women's subordinate place within culture makes them less able to embrace or be held by romantic individualism with all its pleasures and dangers.

The work of articulating this marginalised position, and, in some cases, of celebrating it, has largely fallen to those that Moi labels the 'French Feminists'. The names most clearly associated with this term remain Hélène Cixous and Luce Irigaray, although in *Language and Sexual Difference: Feminist Writing in France* (1991), Susan Sellars gives details of the work of many more theorists who could be included.

Écriture féminine – 'feminine writing', or 'writing the body' as it has been variously termed – is the practice associated with French feminism and a discourse concerned with **subjectivity**, sexuality and **language**. Its arguments are influenced most strongly by deconstruction and post-**Freudian** psychoanalysis, and following these philosophies, it suggests that all systems of representation, the most prominent of these being language, relentlessly position femininity outside symbolisation, as somehow exceeding or defying representation under patriarchal structures. It is significant that it is 'femininity' that is the excluded term, rather than 'women', in that femininity, for these theorists, is not necessarily bound to sexed **identity**. By and large, femininity is associated with women and deemed to be an ideological structure that governs femaleness rather than maleness, but this is a matter of cultural convention rather than biological necessity.

Hélène Cixous argues that there is a patriarchal hierarchy that orders language into positively- and negatively-charged binary terms, ones which always favour the **masculine** dimension. Her list of binary oppositions includes activity/passivity, father/mother, head/heart, and culture/**nature** (Cixous and Clément 1986: 115). Cixous argues, firstly, that the association of one part of the binary with femininity and one part with masculinity is conventional rather than fixed; secondly, she argues that the negative status attached to terms such as 'passivity', as opposed to positively-charged 'activity', is a result of phallogocentrism (the patriarchal, fixed, monologic structure of symbolic systems). The arbitrary link between women and femininity established by *écriture féminine* has the effect of shifting feminist debate from the focus on women as a coherent, biological mass with common concerns that inform their writing, and refocuses attention on the effects of femininity in writing itself (regardless of the **gender** of the author). Thus, for Cixous, *écriture féminine* can be created by both men and women. However, Cixous maintains that the current symbolic structures we have cannot contain or adequately encode *écriture féminine*, and so finding a working definition of the practice continues to be a problem:

> It is impossible to define a feminine practice of writing, and this is an impossibility that will remain, for this practice can never be theorized, enclosed, coded – which doesn't mean that it doesn't exist. But it will always surpass the discourse that regulates the phallocentric system. ('The Laugh of the Medusa', 1981)

Luce Irigaray shares Cixous's belief that femininity is not adequately articulated within the patriarchal symbolic, but Irigaray refuses the position of the outsider offered to her by Cixous's formulation. She argues that the only strategy for women to adopt is resistance from within, a dismantling of the symbolic structure in its own terms. She does this through parody and mimicry, writing from within the white space between men's lines. Thus, her work has included parodic rewritings of essays by Plato, Sophocles, Freud, Hegel and **Lacan** amongst others. Perhaps her most well-known text is an essay entitled 'This Sex Which Is Not One' (1985), a title which playfully contests the Freudian psychoanalytic position that women have no positive sex of their own (they are always not-men), and which also asserts that women's sexuality and identity do not conform to the monologic structure offered by **phallogocentrism** (this sex which is not *one*, but many):

> Whence the mystery that woman represents in a culture claiming to count everything as individualities. *She is neither one nor two.* Rigorously speaking, she cannot be identified as either one person, or as two. She resists all adequate definition. Further, she has no 'proper' name. And her sexual organ, which is not *one* organ, is counted as *none*.

Irigaray exploits the negative position cast for women to her own advantage. The exclusion of women is interpreted as politicised resistance. The lack of a proper name, a reference primarily to patronyms, means that women can evade the structures that would be forced upon them. The lack of a single sexual organ is replaced, in Irigarary's understanding, by a multiple and fluid sexuality which takes in labia, vagina, breasts and mouth.

Such work, relying as it does on a broad knowledge of a male-dominated tradition of knowledge, has been seen as abstract and difficult to interpret into grassroots political strategies. However, the value of this work is that it contests, on its own terms, the masculine philosophical and psychoanalytic structures that have consistently denied women a place in their discourse and in their academies. It is important that feminism intervenes at all levels of **oppression**, from the practical to the esoteric. And in terms of literary studies, *écriture féminine* has had the effect of moving discussion away from the issues of authorship and canon formation, and creating an emphasis on interpretative strategies, and reformulation of the means of representation.

At the heart of both 'Anglo-American' criticism and 'French feminist' theory is the issue of adequate representation for women and femininity, whether that be within a patriarchal structure or within a new kind of structure formed entirely outside the existing ones. But what has not been addressed until this point is the differences between women. The blanket assumption that all women share in their oppression was one that was made too easily by middle-class, white academics, who followed the models of exclusion provided for them by traditional, male-dominated practices. Throughout the years of feminist development, the voices of working-**class** women, disabled women, women of colour, lesbians and bisexual women have been less prominent than those of their white, middle-class, heterosexual, able-bodied counterparts. These differences within feminism, especially when systematically ignored, threatened to pull the movement apart, particularly as the women's movement began to gain recognition. The argument that women needed to reinforce their commonality rather than their differences, to form a politics based on a strong identity, was a persuasive one for many, but it also resulted in cosily reproducing too many of the oppressive practices associated with patriarchy.

In *Finger-Licking Good: The Ins and Outs of Lesbian Sex* (1996), Tamsin Wilton argues that feminism has often had a detrimental effect on lesbian sexual and political identities. In the 1970s, it was possible for many straight feminists to embrace 'political lesbianism', an attitude which rejected masculinity and male-oriented heterosexuality, but had nothing to do with women's sexual relationships with other women. Indeed, certain kinds of feminists have scrutinised lesbian relationships, notably those involving butch/femme roles, and sadomasochistic sexual practices, and judged them anti-feminist, as unthinking replications of violent heterosexual relations. Lesbians who have been open about their sexual desires have often found themselves ostracised by feminist groups. Coupled with the homophobic attitudes that have prevailed in the last two centuries, the feminist rejection of certain lesbian practices has had a significant effect on the kind of representations available to queer women, of themselves, and to the kind of criticism that has developed in response to lesbian artistic production.

Identifying lesbian writing in itself presents some problems. Historic-ally, the lesbian has been excluded from legal statutes, and cultural representations of women's love for one another have been ignored, or interpreted as friendship rather than anything potentially more trans-gressive. Given society's hostility towards queer relationships, writers have often had to be deliberately evasive in their representation of them, resorting to codes and symbolism not easily recognised by straight culture. Whilst critics generally agree that lesbian writing may not necessarily have to include an explicit sexual relationship between women, they have also been conscious of the need to develop some criteria that constitute the subgenre, for fear that any woman-centred text could be labelled lesbian, and subsumed under the 'women's writing' category in an undifferentiated way.

Texts that include explicit lesbian storylines can be identified most clearly. These might include the growing areas of formula fiction, such as lesbian **romance**, erotica, or detective narratives. These kinds of novels adhere to many of the conventions that readers would expect from popular fiction, but the protagonists are replaced with lesbian characters, and the settings often explore common dimensions of queer life. **Autobiographies**, life-writing and coming-out stories form a valuable part of the lesbian canon, although it is significant that all these subgenres are ones that are less valued by academic institutions. Challenging dominant literary discourses remains an extremely difficult task, and for many lesbian critics, the idea of creating counter-canons, merely reproducing the same set of critical values, has a dubious value. For the critic, questions must be asked about political effects of any texts identified as lesbian: how far is lesbian writing always going to be a form of resistance literature? Is lesbian writing, even formula fiction, neces-sarily radical? Is a lesbian aesthetic applicable to all texts, including texts by men, for instance? Of course, exactly the same questions might be asked about women's writing in general, and the conclusions one comes to may well be the same.

Just as feminist criticism began with an examination of women in fiction by men, and lesbian criticism concerned itself with representations of queer characters in texts from history, so black feminist literary criticism has been concerned with representations of black women characters in canonical works. In similar ways too, black critics have also been concerned with establishing counter-canons, and black women's writing has grown in representation on literature courses, both in the form of specialist options and as part of core literature modules. African-American writers such as Toni **Morrison** and Alice **Walker** have had a particular impact on literary studies, although less powerful groups, such as First Nations writers from Australia and Canada, are not considered within core curricula, and might only gain recognition on less visible courses.

The work of feminist critics on issues of cultural identity has been both in terms of reading work by white writers and of developing appropriate aesthetic judgements for black writing. It has also included producing a critique of black male commentators who have systematically ignored the different position that black women occupy under white, patriarchal dominance. Jane Miller, for instance, argues in *Seductions: Studies in Reading and Culture* (1990) that black feminists have been criticised for detracting from anti-racist arguments, when they insist that women must be taken into account as well as, and as distinct from, men in critiques of imperialism, colonisation and **racism**. This taking-into-account of the voices of black women may be easier said than done, since critics such as bell **hooks** and Gayatri Chakravorty **Spivak** agree that often they are allowed to speak only when it suits a white audience, and only when what they say is what a white audience is prepared to hear. Spivak says that who speaks 'is less crucial than "Who will listen?"' (Sarah Harasym, ed., *The Post-Colonial Critic*, 1990), and hooks argues that 'much that is potentially radical is undermined, turned into commodity, fashionable speech as in "black women writers are in right now"' (*Talking Back: Thinking Feminist – Thinking Black*, 1989).

At the end of the twentieth century, it might be possible to join with Showalter in her confident assumption that the time for separate women's literature and criticism courses is over. She insists that feminist reading practices have transformed approaches to *all* literature, and that the integration of their voices is complete. But in her list of issues for mainstream critics to consider, referred to earlier in this section, though she lists 'lesbian eroticism' as a 'female theme', she nowhere makes a reference to cultural identity, 'race' or ethnicity as having a key role in feminist literary concerns. It seems that feminist literary criticism might not have transformed as much as it needs to do just yet.

12

FEMINISM AND LANGUAGE

MARY M. TALBOT

In its rewriting of academic research, feminism can been viewed *as* language, as Terry Threadgold does in *Feminist Poetics* (1997), when she traces the rewriting of **patriarchal** knowledges in Teresa de **Lauretis**'s feminist work on semiosis. The academy as a discursive community depends on such rewriting, on constant reworkings in the form of critiques, on argument and counter-argument: commentary, in Michel **Foucault**'s sense. Coming from the mouths and pens of **feminists**, all this arguing – being women's complaints about the patriarchal academy – has tended to construct them as scolds. It places them, as Meaghan **Morris** says in *The Pirate's Fiancée* (1988), in 'a speech genre all too familiar in daily life . . . the woman's complaint or *nagging*. One of the defining generic rules of "nagging" is unsuccessful repetition of the same statements'.

One strand of such commentary has contributed to the developing interdisciplinary field of **language** and **gender**: feminism *on* language. As feminists began to search for existing scholarship on women, men and language, what little they found was highly **androcentric**. Linguistics has a long tradition of interest in language change, so that is what they encountered. However, the accounts of women's contribution to language shifts were little more than articulations of the writers' prejudices and reiterations of the **stereotypes** from the period in which they were writing. A classic example is a chapter on 'The Woman' in Otto Jespersen's book *Language: Its Nature and Development* (1922), in which he states as a fact beyond doubt that women's contribution to language is to maintain its 'purity' through 'their instinctive shrinking from coarse and vulgar expressions' whereas men's contributions are vigour, imagination and creativity. He continues with more specific claims about differences in the language used by men and women, establishing the intelligence and importance of men and the empty-headed foolishness of women. On the basis of such scholarly conjectures about language in the patriarchal academy, Jennifer Coates in *Women,*

Men and Language (1986) posited an androcentric rule: 'Men will be seen to behave linguistically in a way that fits the writer's view of what is desirable or admirable; women on the other hand will be blamed for any linguistic state or development which is regarded by the writer as negative or reprehensible.'

Feminist sociolinguists, such as Deborah Cameron, Jennifer Coates and Margaret Deuchar, have critiqued social variationist studies, particularly social stratification studies based on social dialect data taking sex as a sociolinguistic variable. These large-scale studies focused on aspects of pronunciation and grammar and identified an intriguing gender-differentiated pattern, namely that women consistently tend toward the prestige 'Standard' variety of a language more than men do. Feminist critics have pointed out flaws in both method and explanation. The phenomenon presented as in need of explanation is women's greater use of Standard forms, rather than men's lesser use of them. In *Women in their Speech Communities* (1988), Deborah Cameron and Jennifer Coates have remarked on the implication here that male speech is the norm from which women deviate, since it is not clear why the behaviour of those using the Standard forms more often should be what needs accounting for. The explanation given is, in brief, that women are more status-conscious than men, a claim which has been widely criticised. The way the surveys were conducted influenced the nature of the findings. Traditional family structure was assumed in assigning **class** categories, so that whole families took their social position from the fathers. As a consequence, it is likely that some women were wrongly classified. The sociolinguistic interview was the same for all informants, regardless of sex or class. For many it would have been an 'unequal encounter' with an educated middle-class interviewer; for many more, it would have been a cross-sex encounter. Such contextual variables influence the formality of the speech situation and hence the extent to which speakers would use prestige forms. Other feminist sociolinguists, such as Lesley Milroy in *Language and Social Networks* (1980), and Jenny Cheshire in *Variation in an English Dialect* (1982), conducted research which approached the research question differently. These studies accounted for speech patterns in terms of solidarity and tightness of social network membership, thereby avoiding the 'social climbing' view built into the social stratification studies. However, the definition of social network on which it depends runs into similar problems of male bias. Feminists in search of scholarship on the language of women and men, then, repeatedly encountered the male-as-norm and the androcentric rule in operation.

Another feminist critique was pitched not so much at the academy as at the semantic system of English and its usage. Challengers of **sexist** language observed similar tendencies: the pseudo-generic usage of *man*, for instance, enshrines the male-as-norm. In her essay 'The Semantic Derogation of Women' (in Barrie Thorne and Nancy Henley, eds., *Language and Sex: Difference and Dominance*, 1975), Muriel Schulz argues that terms marked as female in English are systematically downgraded, so that apparent pairs like *master/mistress* and *bachelor/ spinster* are not used symmetrically and do not carry the same connotations. Other issues are occupational stereotyping and andro-centric assumptions surrounding work and family ties. Classification is part of the naming and ordering of experience and both reflects and sustains existing social relations and **identities**. In critiquing sexist language, feminists have politicised classifications that were previously considered to be neutral ones. Feminism, then, has gone some way towards undermining a powerful normative force. This has met with fierce resistance both in the academic world and in the mass media. Its critiquing of current usage and suggesting alternatives have inevitably positioned feminist **discourse** on sexist language as scolding. A powerful counter-discourse has developed, recently identified by Deborah Cameron in *Verbal Hygiene* (1995) as 'anti-PC discourse'.

Robin Lakoff's *Language and Women's Place* (1975) was an influential early work on gender and language from a feminist perspective; it explores two avenues: **sexism** in the English language and women's language use. Ironically, early **Anglo-American** feminist scholarship on women's language and on gender differences worked with the same androcentric male-as-norm encountered in pre-feminist scholarship. Lakoff implicitly establishes men's language as a norm to which women's does not match up. She argues that the way women use particular language forms (e.g., hedges such as *you know, sort of,* euphemisms) projects uncertainty, lack of confidence and weakness. The claim has since been refuted with attention to the range of possible functions of such forms (see, for example, Jennifer Coates and Deborah Cameron, eds., *Women in their Speech Communities*, 1988). However, the deficit framework – the assumption that women's language is deficient – can still be found in contemporary assertiveness training, and is used in self-help manuals.

Subsequent research on gendered patterns of language use moved away from the early tendency to focus on language forms to a new focus on language functions (influenced by the developing fields of **discourse** analysis and pragmatics). Language and gender researchers have drawn upon the methods and approaches of many disciplines, including linguistics, anthropology, social psychology and sociology. They all assert the importance of investigating patterns of communication, some explicitly exploring the maintenance of male dominance. A range of studies in the late seventies and early eighties began to address issues relating to the dynamics of power. One microsociological analysis of power in interaction which is still frequently referred to is Pamela Fishman's study of three couples talking at home, 'Interaction: the Work Women Do' (in Barrie Thorne, Cheris Kramarae and Nancy Henley, eds., *Language, Gender and Society*, 1983). This early attempt to make links between macro and micro levels of investigation is strongly influenced by writing on power as reality-defining and, more specifically, on the importance of intimate relationships as reality-maintaining settings. Fishman attends to the division of labour in the conversations and observes the women doing a great deal of support work for their partners. She does so by attending to topic initiation and uptake and to the distribution of questions, attention-getters and minimal responses (e.g., *mm, yeah*). The conversations tended to centre around the men's interests: the women were working on them, asking frequent questions, using minimal responses supportively to develop the men's topics. Fishman presents this detail on interaction among intimates as evidence of reality-maintenance in operation: 'the definition of what is appropriate or inappropriate conversation becomes the man's choice. What part of the world the interactants orient to, construct, and maintain the reality of, is his choice, not hers'.

Other explorations of male dominance through language have addressed issues surrounding women's silence and the silencing of women, sometimes confusing the two (notably Dale **Spender** in *Man Made Language*, 1980). The silencing of women in positions of authority, by talking over them, is the subject of a range of studies; e.g., male patients interrupting women doctors, male employees interrupting women managers. The earliest research on interruptions, as ways of 'doing power' in interaction, is now generally considered to be flawed, however, since it is based on a rather simplistic notion of what constitutes an interruption (see the work of Candace West and Don Zimmerman in Barrie Thorne, Cheris Kramarae and Nancy Henley, eds., *Language, Gender and Society*). They cannot be identified solely by mechanical means, such as by looking for where people are speaking at the same time. Simultaneous speech can be far from disruptive, as shown by studies of high-involvement style (Deborah Tannen, *Conversational Style*, 1984) and of conversations among women (Jennifer Coates, *Women Talk*, 1996).

Research within psychology has tended to use experimental settings with controlled variables. For example, Helena Leet Pelligrini's experimental study of conversational dominance examines the verbal behaviour of male and female 'experts', using 'expertise' as a variable. The results show, as one might expect, that all the 'experts' talked more. However, the female and male 'experts' acted differently; the men talked more and interrupted more than the women did; the women used more supportive minimal responses. Studies such as this one have been used to advance the view that men and women tend to use interactional styles based on power and solidarity respectively. There is evidence of males talking more than females in a wide range of public contexts, including university seminars, school classrooms, managerial meetings, and television and Internet discussions. There is other evidence of women being more supportive than men.

The idea that women and men have distinct interactional styles has proved popular. It is, however, problematic. While there is extensive research to support such a view, including research on politeness and on physical alignment and eye contact in conversations, it needs contextual grounding, as ethnographic studies of women in specific speech communities emphasise. 'Women' and 'men' are not homogeneous groups. Overall, there is support for the view that women in many speech communities and settings tend to be less competitive conversationalists than men, but there is a tendency to overgeneralise and disregard contextual differences. This is basically a problem of allowing gender to override other considerations.

The notion of distinct male and female interactional styles, most fully articulated by Deborah Tannen, is accompanied with an assumption of distinct subcultures into which men and women have been socialised. This two-cultures theory was first put forward by Daniel Maltz and Ruth Borker in their 1982 essay, 'A Cultural Approach to Male-Female Miscommunication', to account for miscommunication among adults. Their claim is that gender segregation in childhood leads to differing patterns of interaction and hence differing discoursal expectations. They then reinterpret Fishman's findings on the conversational division of labour (briefly presented above) in terms of cross-cultural misunderstanding rather than male dominance.

Tannen has brought these alleged male and female interactional styles to a wide audience beyond the academy, in a series of books marketed as self-help: *That's Not What I Meant!* (1986); *You Just Don't Understand: Women and Men in Conversation* (1991); and *Talking From Nine to Five* (1995). Feminist criticism of these popularising books focuses attention on the problems of the two alleged styles and the cross-cultural miscommunication account. The two main problems are the suppression of power, which presents an illusion of men and women being 'equal but different', and the reification of gender *as* difference. In neglecting power the approach loses contact with feminism; behaviour perceived as oppressive is reinterpreted in terms of neutral difference and 'innocent' misunderstanding. This depoliticisation seriously undermines feminist discourse on language. Power issues are also lost in the two-cultures notion itself; a feminist perspective requires reasons for such sexual segregation. Gender is reified as **difference** when the agenda is set solely in terms of identifying male and female differences. This preoccupation inevitably confirms rather than challenges differences and tends to reinforce stereotypes. It shores up essentialism in the perception of gender and this too is a problem for feminism, since it effectively undermines its emancipatory aim. Suppression of power issues and the confirmation of gender as difference permit the appropriation of feminist research on language for non-feminist purposes. Gender-differences work can be used to support accounts of men and women using very traditional sexual dichotomies (e.g., John Gray's *Men are from Mars, Women Are from Venus*).

For contemporary language and gender researchers the challenge is how to conceptualise gender without such polarisation. As Cameron has remarked, *'gender is a problem, not a solution.* "Men do this, women do that" is not only overgeneralised and stereotypical, it fails utterly to address the question of where "men" and "women" come from' ('Rethinking Language and Gender Studies: Some Issues for the 90s', in Sara Mills, ed., *Language and Gender*, 1995). Feminist research on language and gender in the Anglo-American tradition over the past 25 years or so has been of value in stimulating political and social changes. It has been of great value in inspiring equal opportunities and anti-sexist initiatives. In feminism, as Cameron has noted, the focus on 'dominance' and on 'difference' can be seen to embody particular 'moments': feminist outrage and the naming of the oppressor on the one hand, the celebratory reclamation and positive reassessment of women's cultural traditions on the other. However, it is now time to move on. I have already noted some key problems with the 'difference' framework. The 'dominance' framework also has limitations. Its users have sometimes tended to work with a monolithic conception of male dominance and man as oppressor which is all too easily refuted. Detailed attention to the specificities of context is essential. In order to explore patterns of male dominance effectively, we need to do so by examining the institutions, situations and genres which establish men in positions where they can dominate women. Some recent research by Elinor Ochs and Carolyn Taylor on the patriarchal **family** structure, for example, examines the dynamics of dinner-table talk in white American families. It does not reveal monolithic patriarchal power wielded by fathers over families, but practices establishing fathers in positions of dominance much more subtly, including the collusion of mothers in manoeuvring fathers into positions of panopticon-like control and invulnerability.

The main problem with the Anglo-American tradition of language and gender research, however, lies with the polarisation of gender categories. None of the research in the 'difference and dominance' tradition begins to address how language, personal identity and social context interact or how that interaction sustains unequal gender relations. Some recent researchers have turned to **poststructuralism** in order to address this issue. For feminist criticism with a poststructuralist perspective, language is the site of the cultural production of gender identity. Rather than dealing with a notion of static, fixed gender identities, it presents identities as an effect of discourse, constantly in production and therefore changeable. Gender is a process and verbal interaction (both speech and writing) is where it takes place. Individuals take up positions as gendered subjects in their enactments of discourse practices. This marks an important shift away from commonsensical categorisations and points towards the study of how people *gender* themselves and others.

Research on language and gender influenced by poststructuralism examines, not gender difference, but the construction of gender identities. Research carried out by Joan Pujolar i Cos on young men in working-class neighbourhoods in Barcelona, for example, examines how they actively construct their masculine identities in interaction. This examination of masculinity in a multilingual context illustrates the extent to which gender identities are embedded in local practices and the importance of examining gender in conjunction with other considerations, particularly class and ethnicity. In her essay 'Performing Gender Identity: Young Men's Talk and the Construction of Heterosexual Masculinity' (in Sally Johnson and Ulrike Hanna Meinhof, eds. *Language and Masculinity*, 1997), Deborah Cameron refers to **performance** theory in her examination of young Americans' enactment of heterosexual masculine identities. Cameron uses this performative gender work in a critique of the notion of distinct male and female interactional styles. She does so by exploring the young men's co-operative, supportive talk about 'fags'. An advantage of a fluid conception of gender identities and their construction is that it can accommodate contradictory tendencies and permits exploration of how subversiveness can be undermined/contained.

As academic feminists are beginning to theorise the fluidity of gender identities, it is perhaps ironic that it is the earliest feminist scholarship on language and gender which has found its way into gender-bending subversions outside the academy. Lakoff herself has long moved on from her early speculations about a distinct 'women's language'. However, they are now being used (selectively) in an instructional genre for conscious reconstruction of gender identity: in an advisory text for male-to-female **cross-dressers** (Laing 1989).

13

FEMINISM AND PHILOSOPHY

PAMELA SUE ANDERSON

Feminism and the ever-expanding activities of **feminist** philosophy are still often thought to be 'the other' of philosophy by both Anglo-American and European philosophers. One implication of this assumed lack of relevance of feminist debate for philosophers in the west is that '**postfeminism**', albeit a highly contested concept, is an inappropriate label for the state of affairs in philosophy today. 'Pre-feminist' might be a more appropriate adjective to describe much of the dominant philosophy in Europe and the English-speaking world. And yet the philosophers themselves might claim to be 'non-feminist' insofar as western philosophy has been premised on a supposed neutrality or impartiality. The political nature of feminism presumably renders it partial and so 'other' to much of Anglo-American analytic philosophy in particular, which has insisted upon its ability to achieve detached thought about the world.

Consider the situation. Feminist philosophy emerged gradually in the United States during the 1970s, generated by the distinctive questions and perspectives of **first wave** feminists on equality and, to some degree, **second wave** feminists on **identity** and **gender** hierarchy. The initial impact of feminist questions was felt on ethics and political philosophy – two of the so-called 'soft' branches of traditional Anglo-American philosophy (see *The Monist* (1973)). One could trace a parallel, but different, emergence of feminist philosophy in France during the 1960-70s focusing first on ethical and political issues. Yet, in contrast with the detached thought of Anglo-American analytic philosophers, European philosophers typically celebrate engaged thought as evident in the development of existentialism, Marxism, structuralism and **post-structuralism** in France – with which feminists from Simone de **Beauvoir** to Luce **Irigaray** and Michèle **Le Doeuff** famously engage. In the United Kingdom, feminism's impact upon analytic philosophy may be more accurately traced to the 1980s–90s. Yet whatever the geographical context, feminist philosophy would seem to follow three stages, resulting in its three enduring aspects.

The first stage and crucial aspect of feminist philosophy consist in developing critiques of the existing philosophical canon. Feminist critiques in philosophy include questioning the dominant interpretations of the philosophical texts privileged by the western canon of philosophers, interrogating the way in which that canon has been defined by way of the exclusion of women, and exposing the masculinist biases in specific philosophical conceptions and arguments. Conceptions of public and private life, **equal rights**, the role of the **family** and maternal thought in political philosophy are among those criticised for biases. The feminist critiques of philosophical arguments which exclude women generally offer, at the same time, implicit suggestions for the reconstruction of western philosophy, its canon, conceptions and claims.

For example, in 1984 the Australian philosopher Genevieve Lloyd published a groundbreaking feminist critique of reason, *The Man of Reason: "Male" and "Female" in Western Philosophy*. Lloyd's book analyses the nature of reason in the philosophical canon from Plato to Simone de Beauvoir, revealing the ways in which rationality has come to be associated with 'maleness'. Historically, maleness as represented in western philosophy does not carry the same symbolic associations with body, **nature** and passion as it does with mind and reason; but embodiment has been conceived as closely associated with women. Philosophers might agree that the capacity to reason is sex-neutral, in the sense that the mind has no sex; but because human minds are embodied minds, differences in rationality are explained by bodily differences. For instance, take Aristotle and Descartes on reason. Lloyd points out that Descartes rejects Aristotle's account of souls containing both rational and irrational elements; he replaces the Aristotelian soul with a dualism of rational mind and irrational body. Although Descartes' alternative is different from Aristotle's, it does not have much better implications for the philosopher's understanding of women's symbolic gender. On the one hand, Aristotle thought of rationality on a continuum on which women, as defective males, were less rational than men; and yet women's souls would always contain a rational element. On the other hand, despite Descartes' own concern to create an equalitarian philosophy whereby reason is *a priori* possessed equally by all human minds, given that women were symbolically associated with the body, his dualistic conception of the rational mind and irrational body aligns women symbolically with irrationality and men with rationality. So the Cartesian legacy, although perhaps not Descartes' intentions, serves to justify a sexual division of labour in the realm of knowledge. Basically, Lloyd's critique reveals that reason in western philosophy has been symbolically male and that the symbolic connections of reason and gender are complex; these conclusions are meant to encourage the rereading and reconstruction of the philosophical canon with sensitivity to the contingency of the maleness of reason. Nevertheless, some feminist philosophers read Lloyd as advocating the rejection of reason as male. Ultimately Lloyd's feminist critique of reason has had dramatic as well as controversial consequences. The intimate connection between the ideals of reason and the self-definition of philosophy itself render the outcomes of ongoing feminist critiques of reason decisive for the future of philosophy, whether there are reconstructions or not of philosophy's canon and claims.

The second stage and still prevalent aspect of feminist philosophy involves the creation of new philosophical interpretations, arguments and approaches. Notable here are the considerable advances not only in ethics and political philosophy, but in epistemology, metaphysics and philosophy of science; both the former, soft branches of philosophy and the latter, 'hard core' of philosophy are challenged by feminist perspectives. In particular, Canadian philosopher Lorraine Code singles out the introduction to Sandra **Harding** and Merrill Hintikka's *Discovering Reality: Feminist Perspectives on Epistemology, Metaphysics, Methodology, and Philosophy of Science* (1983) as having sounded a 'rallying call' to feminist philosophers that was 'nothing short of revolutionary' (in Janet A. Kourany, ed., *Philosophy in a Feminist Voice: Critiques and Reconstructions* (1998)). The call was '[to] root out sexist distortions and perversions in . . . the "hard core" of abstract reasoning thought most immune to infiltration by social values' and '[to] identify how masculine perspectives . . . have shaped . . . the aspects of thought supposedly most gender-neutral'. This second stage or aspect of feminist philosophy remains contained within various, discrete subdivisions of the main branches of philosophy; hence there exist feminist ethics, feminist epistemology, feminist philosophy of science; and each of these subdivisions is shaped by a specific problematic, key texts, and specialist insight.

For example, feminist epistemology is a vital, new subdivision. In the 1980s Lorraine Code asked the then highly outrageous question, 'Is the sex of the knower epistemologically significant?' (in *Metaphilosophy*, 12 (July/October 1981)). The answer at that date would have been assumed by any serious epistemologist to be emphatically 'No!'. However, the question gradually received affirmative answers. At the outset 'feminist epistemology' sounded like a crass oxymoron to English-speaking philosophers, since epistemology properly conceived must avoid any political or subjective alignment – then suddenly a new subdivision of epistemology emerged. The epistemologist by definition was thought to preserve a detachment – i.e., an objectivity or impartiality – that could justify its apolitical self-presentation. In a direct challenge to this conception, feminist epistemology would give up neither its concern with an attachment to women's agency and embodiment – i.e., with subjectivity – nor its commitment to a meticulously worked out theory of knowledge. Since the mid-1980s the proliferation of feminist epistemological projects have contested the most fundamental presuppositions of traditional epistemology, with highly detailed and varied alternatives. In Code's own words, 'Feminist epistemological projects are located both within and in oppositions to the received epistemologies of Anglo-American philosophy: they often move in and out of these theories, drawing on those of their resources that can withstand critical scrutiny, even as they work to eradicate their exclusionary, oppressive effects' (in Alison M. Jaggar and Iris Marion **Young**, eds., *A Companion to Feminist Philosophy* (1998)). These projects draw upon already existing frameworks including empiricist epistemologies, philosophy of science, Marxist theory and naturalised epistemology. Hence feminist epistemology includes feminist empiricism, feminist philosophy of science, feminist standpoint epistemology and feminist social epistemology – each of which together constitute this distinctive subdivision, in challenging epistemology as traditionally conceived.

The third stage of feminist philosophy, or its gradually emerging aspect, is its incorporation within the more general domain of philosophy. The challenge is no longer to maintain feminist subdivisions within the separate domains of philosophy. Instead the need is for the general assimilation into philosophy of feminist critiques, reconstructions and novel insights; and yet the impact of feminism has still to be felt on a regular and vigorous level in philosophy generally. The goal of feminist incorporation and assimilation has not been realised in most branches of philosophy. Women philosophers, whether feminist or non-feminist, have probably had the most significant, general impact upon ethics. But ethics has been traditionally considered one of the softer branches of philosophy and so more amenable to women. In contrast, feminist interventions in logic, part of the hard core of philosophy, have not been so evident. Yet ironically aesthetics is also considered to be a soft branch of philosophy, while the contributions of women and feminism on the philosophy of art is seriously lacking in all three aspects of critique, creation and incorporation.

151

As a positive example Genevieve Lloyd could figure again at this third stage. In 1994, Lloyd returned to refine and expand her earlier feminist critique of rationality, elaborating the significance of the distinctions between literal and symbolic or metaphorical. She moved her previous work from the first stage of critical intervention to assimilation of feminist insights into philosophical discussions of metaphor and truth. Lloyd both criticises feminist philosophers for taking too literally the 'maleness of reason' and joins company with the likes of Descartes and **Derrida** in debating the play of metaphor in philosophical texts. Moreover, Lloyd has entered the general domain of philosophy with her most recent work on Spinoza. Notably she beckons philosophers generally to discover in Spinoza new conceptions of old philosophical problems, especially concerning human embodiment.

Notwithstanding the clear evidence of the first and second aspects of feminist philosophy, it is important to realise the students, lecturers and professors in departments of philosophy in the United Kingdom and United States today do not often have a good knowledge of the fundamental challenges to, and revisions of, philosophy being made by feminist philosophers. The basic ignorance of feminist philosophy's basic impact upon philosophy generally tends to create a resistance to feminism as something – wrongly – feared. Again the exception is ethics. Students tend to have at least a distinctive awareness of the feminist influence on both ethical theory and practice. But more than the fear of feminism borne out of ignorance, the lack of accurate knowledge also results in a failure to recognise that feminist philosophy is not about peripheral issues. Instead feminist philosophers are doing some of the most vital work in philosophy today, transforming conceptions at its very heart, including objectivity, reason, intuition and imagination. In short, feminists are working on the essentially contested concepts at the core of philosophy, giving new life to a discipline that thrives on intellectual debate and critique.

Yet the exigency persists to ensure that feminist philosophy is not relegated to the other of philosophy, but is an integral element in the ever-developing history of philosophy as it moves into the twenty-first century. Evidence exists demonstrating that when properly presented, feminist philosophy can entice and engage both non-philosophers and philosophers in contemporary cultural debates on feminism and postfeminism. Philosophical analysis of and attention to notions such as knowledge, power, reason and experience, which remain central to how students and teachers think, will be immediately attractive to any discipline which tries to take on board the appropriate impact of

152

feminist and other contemporary cultural critiques of its subject-matter and its methodology. Good, accessible accounts of feminist critiques and reconstructions should be welcomed, not necessarily by tutors in analytic philosophy generally, but by at least a few culturally aware lecturers in philosophy, whether at large or small, new or traditional universities.

When it comes to interdisciplinarity, feminist philosophy – which by definition should be clear and accessible – is potentially invaluable to other disciplines, to **women's studies**, literature, sociology, cultural studies, religious studies, politics, even history; basically, to any discipline which endeavours to bring in central feminist concepts or issues. But equally the plurality of debates in feminism as shaped by various disciplines and subjects, practical and theoretical, should – and have – informed philosophy. In particular three areas could be singled out here as potentially formative for feminist philosophy: psycholinguistics (as shaped by feminists after Jacques **Lacan** and Jacques Derrida), discourse analysis (as informed by Michel **Foucault**) and **film theory** (especially its tools for exploring **subjectivity**).

First, 'psycholinguistic' describes the account of reality that takes language as the condition for all meaning and value. The feminist psycholinguists who have done the most to broaden the concerns of feminist philosophers include Luce Irigaray and Julia **Kristeva**. However different their own writings, Irigaray and Kristeva have forced women to rethink the role of language, the place of gender symbolism and the 'neutrality' of the rational subject. They are often known in popular circles as postmodern representatives of '**French feminism**', especially of *écriture féminine*, which would seem to herald the end of philosophy. Yet both Irigaray and Kristeva write on matters with profound insight for philosophical accounts of reason, knowledge and science. Feminist and non-feminist philosophers ignore their constructive insights at their own loss.

Second, my reference to discourse analysis is directed to Foucault's analyses of the ways in which discourse constructs identity and subjectivity. The impact of Foucault on feminism has been both good and bad for philosophy. Many feminists have been definitively shaped by Foucault's analyses of power and of the body; but their relationship to modern philosophy is, then, either non-existent or dubious. These feminist 'philosophers', who include, most famously, Judith **Butler**, might be more accurately named 'gender theorists'. While those women who have become Foucauldian postfeminists aim to retain the name 'philosopher' as well, the relationship of feminist philosophy to

Foucault has to be highly ambivalent and tenuous. The potentially decisive question is, if Foucault is correct and there exist no 'natural' foundations for either gender or sex, what happens to 'woman' or 'women'? Can there be a feminist philosopher if 'thinking women' are fundamentally put into question? Obviously, one response is 'post-feminism' – to which I will return.

Third, feminist film theory has much to contribute to the explorations of subjectivity by feminism and philosophy. Laura **Mulvey**'s accounts of visual **pleasure** and 'the **gaze**', for instance, could inform a feminist philosopher's account of the body, as well as feminist critiques of epistemological biases in both canonical texts such as Descartes' *Meditations*, in which the intellect is an attentive gaze, and contemporary philosophers' texts such as Stanley Cavell's *Pursuits of Happiness: The Hollywood Comedy of Remarriage*. In fact feminist philosopher Naomi Scheman has engaged with Cavell's philosophy of film, arguing that he focuses upon the genres of remarriage comedies and melodramas of the unknown woman, which reflect a feminine but not a feminist gaze. Basically, film theory could be put in a fruitful dialogue with philosophy, enabling explorations of visual and theorisation of gendered experience. This would allow philosophers to probe aspects of subjectivity that they have only touched upon in the past. So in the case of feminist film theory, it is not first philosophy that can clarify culture but, however shocking a suggestion for traditional philosophers, a cultural media that can develop and criticise philosophical conceptions. A similar argument could be made about feminism and **technology** – this area of feminist work could fruitfully form coalitions with feminist philosophers. How does technology influence gender roles? From personal computers and **cyberspace** to artificial wombs and sex reassignment surgery, technology has opened up the possibility that sex roles, as well as the gendered notions which philosophers have of human identity, are subject to radical challenge from the non-philosopher.

Perhaps ironically, it is ultimately more difficult to break through the barriers of tough-minded Anglo-American analytic philosophers with the value of feminist philosophy, than to influence academics in disciplines other than philosophy. In turn, this makes feminists less likely to see analytic philosophy as anything other than a bastion of male power and patriarchal domination. Interestingly, it is far easier to encourage and enable students to consider the compatibility or incompatibility of feminism and philosophy than to persuade the analytic philosopher of such critical debate. Generally, given the opportunity, philosophy students become easily involved with the excitement of debating feminist critiques and transformations of traditional philosophy. Nevertheless, there are positive signs of engagement with feminist philosophy by serious analytic philosophers such as the American Thomas Nagel, as well as by **third wave** feminists such as the African-American theorist bell **hooks**. Here I think of the American feminist philosopher Drucilla **Cornell**'s discussions with, on the one hand, Nagel on equality and the view-from-nowhere and, on the other hand, hooks on the imagination of a place where imposed personas of race, **class**, ethnicity and sexual orientation could be contested. Both of these inform Cornell's **radical feminist** project for achieving freedom in *At the Heart of Freedom: Feminism, Sex and Equality* (1998). This powerful and passionate work has far-reaching implications for feminism and philosophy, practically and theoretically.

It could be argued that in the United Kingdom, the lack of awareness of feminist challenges to philosophy has been significantly ameliorated in the past seven years. This improvement can be measured against the date in 1992 when Margaret Whitford asks whether 'the feminist philosopher' is a contradiction in terms, and when Christine Battersby describes philosophy as 'the recalcitrant discipline' in resisting the contemporary debates of feminism. Clearly British philosophers have begun to assimilate some of the feminist critiques of central concepts and images in philosophical texts which have often unwittingly excluded women from western philosophy.

For example, in the United Kingdom the Faculty of Philosophy at Cambridge University now has papers in feminist philosophy covering the main branches of philosophy, i.e., philosophy of mind, politics, ethics, epistemology, language. Other traditional universities in the United Kingdom may not always have feminist philosophers in their departments, but as evident from a study of the background of current members of the Society of Women in Philosophy (SWIP) in the United Kingdom, women philosophers have jobs in a variety of departments, including politics, literature, modern languages, cultural studies, media studies, religious studies, sociology or gender studies; and this includes women who not only research in feminist philosophy but are actively teaching it. Possibly in the United Kingdom feminist philosophers may find themselves working outside of traditional departments of philosophy. Yet consider Cambridge, where philosophers are known to be trained to the highest level of the hard core of British analytic philosophy. If Cambridge is anything to go by, then gradually feminism is having an impact upon even the best philosophers in the United Kingdom.

Moreover, the UK SWIP has worked to give women philosophers not only a distinctive platform for voicing feminist concerns, but a network for expressing common experiences of isolation and struggle in philosophy. Still the evidence is unambiguous: philosophy as a discipline has a definite gender bias. In 1996 the results of a questionnaire on Jobs for Women in Philosophy compiled by *Women's Philosophy Review* (published by UK SWIP) concluded that 'If you want a job in philosophy, your bet is to be a man. Failing that, resemble a man as much as possible.' Nevertheless, the *Women's Philosophy Review* is having a positive impact on women's teaching, research and publishing in philosophy, even though it is not as well supported materially either by university departments indirectly, or directly by a publisher, as is its USA equivalent, *Hypatia: A Journal of Feminist Philosophy*. This is evident in both the number of feminist philosophy books reviewed and the variety of philosophical backgrounds of the reviewers.

However gradual, the impact of encouraging more women, whether feminist or not, to 'do philosophy' has become evident in a more fundamental way. Philosophy generally appears more amenable to certain cultural changes. Whether admitted or not, changes in philosophy itself have tended to come from the consistently growing and constantly improving work of women in philosophy. New trends in ethics, notably bioethics including debates on new **reproductive technology**, are clearly indebted to the work and insight of women philosophers. Increasingly obvious recognition of the gendered nature of images and ideas of rationality are due to feminist philosophers. Greater emphasis upon the social positioning of knowers and the decentring of any privileged point of view in philosophy should be traced back to feminists.

Returning to my initial claim concerning the inappropriateness of postfeminism to philosophy, consider a closer look at the label itself. As generally understood, 'postfeminism' describes the contemporary manoeuvres to discredit feminism as *passé* and bad. Specifically, the uncritical and absolutist employment of postfeminism as a term is essentially unphilosophical – and more seriously, regressive for women. Admittedly, this may not be the assumption of women who follow Foucault and embrace 'postfeminism'. However, if women accept as a minimal definition that given by the French philosopher Michèle Le Doeuff, 'a feminist [philosopher] is a woman who does not allow anyone to think in her place', then the very idea of postfeminism would seem to be unacceptable for women who insist upon the possibility of thinking for themselves. To support this incompatibility, the postfeminist would seem to accept unthinkingly the contention that the dangers and damage of feminism 'prove' women are wrong to seek equality with men in a man's world. This so-called proof is not only ungrounded, but it involves a deep contradiction. In particular, postfeminism is propagated as a commodity of the mass media by both pronouncing the official equality of women and cataloguing the ills that this equality brings. Postfeminist doctrine has been popularised by encouraging women to blame feminism for their exhaustion and disillusionment with equality. But here the postfeminist is duped by emotional or psychological forms of persuasion into giving up the possibility of autonomous thinking, and so the very possibility of philosophy. For instance, **women's magazines** make unfounded, postfeminist assertions such as the following: feminism spoiled women's right to be sexually attractive, to flirt, to enjoy domestic bliss; it damaged the family, leaving young children to grow up without correct moral standards; it resulted in violence against women and women killing. However, acceptance of such media messages reveals women's failure to recognise a political structure that profits, literally, from the inequalities and lack of ethics it promotes.

Postfeminism may claim to promote 'the new' in sexual ethics and politics, e.g., 'the new femininity' or 'the new monogamy'. But the moral and political feminist philosopher must assert that the opposite is the reality. In promoting dangerous half-truths and loaded terms, postfeminism would have to be rejected by any woman who thinks for herself. The half-truths include the claims that feminism as anti-family has destroyed what most people see as the essential foundation of a healthy and just society; that feminism is the disease of 'the terminally single woman'; and that women's liberation is the source of an endless catalogue of contemporary personal, social and economic evils. Clearly, as I've understood the term, 'postfeminism' is part of the **backlash** against feminism. But more than this, for women in philosophy, postfeminism threatens the very progress in philosophy made by feminist philosophers who have fought to demonstrate that women can think, that they are not hopelessly condemned to irrationality and the manipulation of patriarchal capitalism. Postfeminism defends men who refuse to acknowledge the **oppression** of women, encouraging reversals of freedom and justice: without accurate evidence and valid arguments, the movement for **women's liberation** is made to appear – to the unthinking – as tyrannical and unrepresentative of the demands of women. If there is any philosophical lesson to be learned from postfeminism, it is that the play and celebration of **postmodern** relativism in defiance of coherent and careful thinking can be co-opted into its opposite: an uncritical and highly restrictive absolutism.

14

FEMINISM AND RELIGION

ALISON JASPER

INTRODUCTION

Although difficult to define, the term 'religion' refers, in general, to beliefs and practices through which people express their understanding of divine powers or of the spiritual dimension of human existence and structure an appropriate response. In discussions of religion in the western world, the emphasis still tends to be placed on belief in a single transcendent and **masculine** divine being as creator and sustainer of human life within and beyond terrestrial existence and on the corresponding institutional structure; that is, the Christian Church. In the broader sense, of course, important differences exist between the various world religions or in less formalised religious positions. Having a belief in a single divinity which is justified on basically empirical grounds, for example, may be regarded by some people as the benchmark for a religious position. But, of course, amongst individuals and groups which regard themselves as religious, some will certainly not accept this as definitive and may cite quite different factors such as growth of self-knowledge or participation in ordained rituals. Nevertheless, it could be said that **feminists** in the field use a common methodology that cuts across these divisions.

First of all, feminists offer a critique of existing religious belief and practice based on exposing the effects of privileging a particular perspective, typically a male perspective. Escaping from the privileged perspective is a key methodological concern because in terms of both the actual beliefs and practices of different world religions and also in terms of the way in which these beliefs and practices are recorded and interpreted, those at the margins of this perspective have difficulty in being seen or heard at all, yet alone being invited to participate in the larger conversation.

Feminists in the field of religion recognise, increasingly, that privileging the views of groups on the basis of race, colour or social **class** is ultimately another symptom of the same syndrome that seeks definition and **identity** by excluding what is viewed as '**Other**'. In the early years of the modern feminist movement, most of those involved were educated and affluent white women. Consequently, feminists have had to come to terms with the **silencing** and marginalising effects of a number of other factors besides **gender**, such as race, poverty, lack of basic **education**, handicap or sexual orientation. Nevertheless, this represents not so much any '**postfeminist**' dilution of the earlier form of feminist analysis as an application and expansion of it.

Another central aspect of this feminist critique cutting across religions identifies the gendered character of symbols that give significance within human **culture**. These symbols might be viewed in terms of discrete events or objects such as the form or occasion of enlightenment or the names and characteristics of the divine, or they might include every aspect of a religious culture from its language, practices of worship, liturgy and organisational structures to its theological or cosmological presuppositions. The aim is to make explicit when gender-related symbols take on a hierarchical character, devaluing or even demonising what is associated with woman and the **feminine**.

Feminist methodology in religion is not simply a matter of critique. It also has a pragmatic and constructive aspect. This pragmatic and constructive aspect is founded in a confidence that what has been represented and devalued in gendered terms or lost to sight because of a privileged male perspective, is of intrinsic value for women or for humankind as a whole, providing resources for an alternative human **imaginary**. That is to say, brought to light and given attention, such qualities, skills and desires can stimulate the development of an alternative set or framework of related symbols for giving value and significance.

For example, feminists will tend to stress the spiritual and ethical dimensions of human existence in relation to the divine or spiritual, over and above the discussion of the nature of God's existence in itself or as, perhaps, a justification for human obedience. By using the word 'spiritual' in this context, they go beyond a disembodied or non-material realm. This different view of spirituality characteristically incorporates human desire for emancipation and transcendence through the material and erotic realms of human existence rather than through their exclusion by ascetic practices or body-denying scales of value. And correspondingly by using the term 'ethical' in this context, feminists emphasise the justification of moral language in terms of fundamental values of equality, love and justice, understanding that these can equally be embodied in material and erotic forms that recognise our communal interdependence as human beings.

In other words, what lies behind the change of definition is an attempt to reverse the existing privilege given, especially in the west, to the non-embodied, disconnected, individualistic masculine-identified spiritualities of the past. Feminists are anxious to make this attempt on the grounds that whole human communities need liberating into aspects of themselves and their relationship with the divine or spiritual that have been repressed or unexplored for generations due to a persistent symbolic identification of woman and the feminine with the excess or Otherness that defines human experience from a male-centred perspective.

A number of strategies illustrating these various methodological procedures have already been developed to address religious issues both critically and constructively:

1 A CRITIQUE OF RELIGIOUS HERMENEUTICS

Feminist critiques of religious scripture are growing in number. Elisabeth Schüssler Fiorenza is one of the best-known feminist biblical scholars writing within the Christian tradition. She has attempted, by exercising what she calls the hermeneutics of suspicion, to reveal how processes of censorship and redaction have often served to preserve the masculine tradition within Christianity. She is suspicious of all forms of interpretation that marginalise women or their concerns. In her earlier work, in particular, she showed how, when the privileged view is abandoned, the writings of the earliest Christian Church in the New Testament reveal traces of a much stronger female presence and the formulation of a radical emancipatory praxis.

Riffat Hassan has done similar work on the Qu'ran (the book of Revelation believed by Muslims to be the word of God) and the Hadith (the sayings attributed to the Prophet Mohammed). She reads the Qur'anic creation story against the accumulation of fundamentally non-Qur'anic material in the Hadith literature which has, she argues, been affected by misogynistic – particularly Christian – readings of Genesis 2–3. She reveals a commitment to justice and equality in the Qur'an, overlaid by interpretation which has a vested interest in the **patriarchal** *status quo*.

2 A CRITIQUE OF RELIGIOUS MYTHS, METAPHORS, THEOLOGIES AND DOGMAS

Amongst those feminists who are hoping to find resources for a new way of conceptualising the divine or the spiritual within existing religious scriptures, Phyllis Trible problematises powerful, yet uncritical, notions of divine masculinity that still influence the lives of women and men and highlights lesser known metaphors for God within the Old Testament. For example, in an essay published in *The Christian Century* in February 1982, she draws attention to descriptions of God in terms of a mother who labours to give birth (Deut 32:18) or as a midwife (Psalms 22: 9–10) helping in the process of childbirth. Janet Morley incorporates similar insights into a maternal God taken from the Old Testament into her liturgical writings.

Other feminists within Christianity and Judaism have found the female personification of Wisdom from the Wisdom literature of the Hebrew Bible/Old Testament and the Apocrypha (Proverbs, Ecclesiastes, Job, Sirach (Ecclesiasticus), and Wisdom of Solomon) a source of empowerment. As the figure of Wisdom represents God's divine power in creation, it gives legitimacy, to some extent, to the feminine within the monotheistic divine and identifies that feminine as positively creative.

Some feminists exercise a critical methodology by looking at specific themes or theologies developed within religious communities which are based on traditions of theology or dogma as well as foundational texts. Sallie McFague, for example, is another scholar working within the Christian tradition who has developed metaphors for a human relationship with God that do not reinforce an uncritical view of divine masculinity, and thus, as she would see it, draw worshippers into idolatry. In her book, *Models of God* (1987), for example, she puts forward a number of different ideas for configuring this relationship. For example, she takes the traditional view of God as creator, but gives the idea an innovative slant by regarding the world as a metaphor for God's body. From this basic metaphor, she develops both a view of a creator-mother and the fraternal/**sisterly** responsibility of humankind towards all creation. Other models she proposes for the relationship between God and humankind remain personal but are not restricted to either male or female. Thus McFague develops the idea of God as healer, insisting on the health of the body as the condition for other kinds of well-being and undercutting traditional body/spirit dualisms within Christianity by recalling the non-judgemental healing ministry of Jesus of Nazareth.

Within other religious traditions women similarly work to recover mythic constructions of the feminine that are not simply a product of privileged male imagination and desire. Lina Gupta, for example, writing in Paula M. Cooey *et al.*, eds., *After Patriarchy: Feminist Transformations of the World Religions* (1991), reviews the nature of the Hindu Divine revealed as the **goddess** Kali. She shows that this female figure repeatedly adopts patterns of behaviour that do not fit with the proper role of women within Hindu tradition. She is a wife but she is rarely found with her partner, Siva. She has no children, lives mostly outdoors and has no fixed household. Her iconography portrays her as wearing necklaces of skulls and severed heads, and she is associated with graveyards and battlefields. Moreover, she appears very often as the personified wrath of other goddesses whose conduct is, normally, very much more conventional. Lina Gupta suggests that this anger represents a deep and repressed rage against the felt injustice of women in particular. She argues that Kali's bad reputation and questionable behaviour cannot be simply dismissed as due to malevolence, and she believes that Kali's 'unfeminine' behaviour is largely problematic from the privileged perspective of the male. In particular she suggests that it is the presumption of certain gender roles associated with women that makes Kali appear violent and bloodthirsty. A male god behaving in such a way would more probably be regarded as bold and strong. Rather Kali is 'out of patriarchal control' and therefore a powerful model for women of strength and self-liberation.

Within the Buddhist tradition, of course, there is no deity and life is sustained not by any external saviour or saviour God but by a combination of inspiration provided by the Buddha, a purposeful structure for living expressed in the *Dharma*, and a formative community, the *Sangha*. In 'Buddhism After Patriarchy' (Cooey *et al.*, eds., 1991), Rita Gross reworks the Buddhist concept of community or *Sangha* which she argues has remained substantially unexplored within more traditional forms of Buddhism, although it has always been regarded as one of the three foundational categories within that religion. She challenges interpretations of the *Sangha* which regard it solely as a context for developing self-reliance. This sort of interpretation she sees as symptomatic of the alienation and hyper-masculinity of our present condition. Taking very seriously the value which Buddhism has placed on this category of *Sangha*, she interprets it in terms of what she believes to be the feminine values of nurturance, communication, relationship and friendship, which, she suggests, have always been important within the Buddhist community. The fact that this importance has not been explicitly acknowledged, she explains by suggesting that it simply has not figured within the privileged view of the male adherents, since, on the whole, they have not been responsible for maintaining domestic order and nurturance but simply taken these as given. She learns through her understanding of feminism that communication, relationship and friendship are attachments worth having in pursuit of a spirituality defined as freedom within the world.

3 BETWEEN CRITIQUE AND CONSTRUCT: TRADITIONS NOT CONFORMING ABSOLUTELY TO THE MALE-CENTRED MODEL

The basic methodological principles already outlined reveal that all cultures have not privileged the masculine or the male point of view in the same way or to the same extent. Women have lived in religious communities as long as men and there are undoubtedly situations in which women, without any form of modern feminist critique, have avoided, circumvented or compensated for the widespread practice of privileging the male. In an essay published in Pat Holden, ed., *Women's Religious Experience* (1983) Susan Whyte writes, for example, about the way in which a group of peasant agriculturists, the Nyole, living in Eastern Uganda in the 1970s maintained separate gender-related perspectives on their relationship with the spirit world within one community. In her study she draws attention to the way in which, whilst the women expressed religious faith and commitment to spiritual values within a society in which the male was viewed as normative and in which the privileged point of view was male, there were areas of their lives in which these structures were simply not relevant. This aspect of the women's lives was not necessarily seen by them as a focus for subversion nor particularly of female solidarity. The social relations of the group were not essentially challenged. Nevertheless, the spirits involved and the rituals performed were symbolic of a different order of concern having to do with **marriage**, fertility and health, particularly of the very young. Admittedly, this fits with a view of the symbolic association between women and the bodily, material realm which is fraught with great dangers for a male-centred spirituality, and beyond the control of the men. Moreover, these spirits were still referred to, by the whole community, in terms that stress their marginality. They were 'little' and 'foreign' spirits and bore no relationship to clan spirits, the satisfaction or neglect of whose needs formed a central element of the community's moral matrix and the explanation of many forms of suffering and misfortune. However, for the women of the group, these 'little' and 'foreign' spirits continued to play a major role in their lives and therefore, in the lives of the whole community. However, their significance for the women of the group lay, at many points, along different lines from that which they had for the privileged male-centred perspective. In other words, whilst the women inhabited the same structures of spirit/human relationships as the men, they were able to reinvest a part of its central symbolism with their own independent meanings within a woman-centred sphere of power and influence. In this example, women's special relationship to a category of spirit on the margins of the dominant morality is accepted by the whole community as a sort of formal and symbolic acceptance of female discontinuity within a highly patrilinear and virilocal social context.

Some women would claim, however, that there are religious traditions which maintain a far more explicit and publicly acknowledged balance between men and women and in the symbolic use of gender within religious practice and teaching. Ines Talamantez, for example, would claim this much for the traditions of the American Apaches. In 'Images of the Feminine in Apache Religious Tradition' (in Cooey *et al.*, eds., 1991), she observes that the Apache deity is the female 'Isanaklesh', who ensures the strength and virtue of Apache culture. Within this **culture**, women, whilst fulfilling predictably domestic roles, have always also maintained a balanced sense of power alongside the men. Talamantez attributes this balance to rituals and ceremonies that take place at various points, all through a woman's life. These rituals, and particularly the rite called *'Isanaklesh Gotal'* which celebrates a woman's coming of age, reinforce the sense in which women are celebrated and cared for by the community. This value relates in some sense to their fertility and thus to the continuation of the culture in a physical sense, but there is also a corresponding expectation that, as adults, these women will take on roles of power and responsibility. In their turn, they will be responsible for caring for and preserving the traditions of the community that will continue to support them, strengthening their link to the divine 'Isanaklesh' through whom they are thought to gain the skills and wisdom to do their own particular job.

4   CONSTRUCTING NEW RELIGIOUS PERSPECTIVES

Nevertheless, many feminists have felt the need for a more radical alternative to traditional religions that will enable them to exercise an authentic choice in the expression of their relationship to the divine and to their own spirituality which might be defined in terms of desiring or yearning in the deepest sense, including the erotic. One consequence of this dissatisfaction with existing forms of religion has been the development of what is called 'thealogy', a term coined by Naomi Goldenberg in

'The Return of the Goddess: Psychoanalytic Reflections on the Shift from Theology to Thealogy' (*Studies in Religion/Sciences religieuses* 16:1, 1987) and associated especially with Carol Christ (see *The Laughter of Aphrodite*, 1987). They have developed a distinctively woman-centred vision of the divine with both a descriptive and a polemic intention, drawing attention, particularly, to the absence of the feminine within the Christian and Jewish theologies of the west and drawing on various, often ancient, forms of **goddess** worship, in order to construct a new form of life-affirming spirituality. In other words, the figure of the Goddess is invoked to challenge male hegemony in religion and, effectively, to legitimise the claims of women for power and justice on an equal footing with men. Worship of the Goddess deliberately re-valorises the connections of ancient goddesses with the earth and with the material, physical, sexual and bodily energies of human living that have been downgraded or devalued in the past. In contrast to typically Christian, Jewish or Islamic ways of describing God, Christ describes the Goddess as personifying change, rather than changeless. She emphasises cycles of birth, death and regeneration within this life and argues for ways of addressing present social problems now, rather than focusing on a life after death as western monotheism has frequently tended to do. Moreover, Christ argues for the historical continuity of the Goddess as a power which has never been entirely obliterated. She suggests new and imaginative rituals in order to shape and encourage the development of a wisdom that has its roots in ancient forms of goddess worship.

Amongst modern feminist theorists, Luce **Irigaray**, in particular, has been prominent in discussing the issue of religion, in contrast to some of her feminist contemporaries who have regarded religion as irredeemably entangled within patriarchal structures and masculinist ways of thinking. Irigaray's work incorporates both elements of critique and reconstruction. She argues that the existing symbolic framework in the west does not simply associate masculinity with the divine but makes the ideal of masculinity the measure of all human aspirations. This in turn lends legitimacy to cultural practices and social policies which privilege these male aspirations at the expense of other human desires associated with women. In her essay, 'Divine Women' (1993), Irigaray discusses the idea that in order for women actually to be able to develop an understanding of their own **subjectivity** or identity as women – rather than simply as factors or features which relate to a masculine subjectivity – they need a divine representation of the ideal to which, as women, they aspire. Putting it rather simply, Irigaray's idea of the

Divine is a form of projection without which women cannot achieve a genuine sense of their legitimacy as women, apart from their relationship with men.

At the same time, Irigaray believes that 'the passage from one era to the next cannot be made simply by negating what already exists'. Whatever comes next will, inevitably, be constructed out of what existed before. To ignore this, she says, will simply reproduce the same situation from which feminists have tried to escape, in which a privileged point of view marginalises or excludes all other cultural dimensions. Therefore it is important to, in some sense, reconstruct the existing traditions rather than abandon them.

One way in which Irigaray approaches the reconstructive aspect of her work is through a process of mimesis or miming female roles within patriarchal myths related to the divine. Her purpose is to subvert them but not, as Christ might advise, to do away with them altogether. For example, she treats the story of Antigone from Sophocles' 5th century Greek tragedy in this way in *Thinking the Difference: Towards a Peaceful Revolution* (1994). What is mimed or imitated, of course, is the role of Antigone. Her reading of Antigone's behaviour in the story is subversive in two respects. In the first place she presents multiple and conflicting interpretations, refusing to consign certain interpretations to the margins or exclude them altogether. But secondly, included within the multiple readings, is the suggestion that by burying the body of her brother and defying her uncle Creon's edict, Antigone displays loyalty to profound and ancient burial customs belonging to her maternal ancestry in its divine aspect. The dominant reading of the **myth** has tended to interpret Antigone's actions in the light of a fundamentally patriarchal familial piety. But, for Irigaray, one layer or level of this mythic tale represents a deadly struggle between Creon's power located in the male-centred structures of the city-state and a different source of female-centred power located at or beyond the margins of the privileged viewpoint. The myth remains tragic but yet, read in this way, the symbolic monopoly of the masculine is challenged and thus transformed into a potential resource for women searching for the traces of the divine or of the divine possibilities within themselves.

Conclusion

Religion continues to be understood, generally, in rather narrow terms related closely to the existence of a divine being conceived in terms of western monotheism and the corresponding structures which have, until recently, been largely or completely male-dominated. This concept clearly does not reflect the diversity of actual religious praxis and belief where that is related to the complete spectrum of spiritual, symbolic and ethical aspirations worldwide. Women have always had a part to play in this variety of religious experience, but a modern feminist methodology has developed a way of showing how privileging the male, male-identified structures and the male point of view has marginalised or excluded women from power or the means of making their lives independently or even equally meaningful. A second strand within this feminist methodology in the field of religion and spirituality works more constructively to find ways of transforming the symbolic frameworks through which human beings acquire significance and value, so that they truly reflect the aspirations and desires of women as well as men. This aspect of feminism within the field of religion is consequently concerned with ethical issues of love, equality and justice and with the ways in which these concepts have often been defined in line with a masculinist rejection of the material, bodily and physical terms. Changes are taking place within the structures of various world religions as some women are beginning to gain power and influence on a more equal level with men. Some feminists, however, remain sceptical about the idea that the existing structures and frameworks can bear the weight of the necessary transformation and are seeking new ways of responding to the divine or the spiritual in their lives.

15

FEMINISM AND PSYCHOANALYSIS

DANIELLE RAMSEY

> The greater part of the feminist movement has identified Freud as the enemy. Psychoanalysis is seen as the justification for the status quo, bourgeois and patriarchal, [but] a rejection of psychoanalysis and of Freud's work is fatal for feminism. . . . Psychoanalysis is not a recommendation for a patriarchal society but an analysis of one.
>
> Juliet Mitchell, *Psychoanalysis and Feminism* (1974)

OVERVIEW

In *The Second Sex* (1949) Simone de **Beauvoir** famously claimed that 'One is not born a woman; one becomes one.' Her main contention was that 'woman' was a concept that existed merely in relation to man. The idea that our conscious selves – our **subjectivity** – is not the innate, irreducible essence of humanist philosophy, but is formed through our relationships with others is of central importance in psychoanalytic theory; yet de Beauvoir, clearly aware of this, was hostile to Freudian theory. Like many feminists before and after her, she saw Freud's theories of **femininity** as deeply suspect, both a product of and an **ideological** bolster to the patriarchal society into which **Freud** had been born. There were a number of important female psychoanalysts contributing to the theory of female sexuality in the wake of Freud's work, but it was with the radicalisation of social theory at the end of the 1960s that a tremendous growth occurred in the study of the politics of sexuality. At first seen as a shatterer of taboos and of sexual repressions, a critique of Freudian theory was developed, in particular challenging his contentious view of female **identity** as marked by passivity and in particular **penis envy**, a life-long feeling of psychic inferiority and physical **lack**.

By and large, this is the image of **psychoanalysis** many feminists inherited from de Beauvoir and others, and it was only with the work of Juliet **Mitchell** in the early 1970s that the **feminist** rehabilitation of Freud began. Mitchell argued that many feminist critics had conflated popularisations and the deviations of post-Freudians for the work of Freud himself. Re-examined, it had much to say to feminists who wished to understand women's oppression. Mitchell (along with Jacqueline Rose, another socialist feminist) translated an important collection of essays on feminine sexuality by the French psychoanalyst Jacques **Lacan** and members of his école Freudienne. In many ways, Lacan is as controversial a figure in feminist circles as Freud himself; his work is seen by some as deeply misogynistic and by others as an insight into the psychic routes of **patriarchy**. Nevertheless, a large and influential body of feminist writing has emerged under the umbrella term '**French feminism**' which extends and critiques Lacanian **psychoanalysis** and would be hard to imagine without it. However, the starting point for any account of psychoanalysis and feminism must begin with the father of psychoanalysis himself.

FREUD AND FEMININITY

Our identity is intimately bound up with our notions of sexuality and **gender** and it is Freud's understanding of the construction of our psychic life, primarily through his notion of the unconscious shaping of familial relations, that makes him one of the most influential thinkers of the twentieth century. What attracts feminists and others to the theory is that Freud sees '**masculinity**' and 'femininity' as largely cultural categories or social constructs. Unlike that of many of his followers, Freud's whole theory is a rejection of **biological determinism**, hence its interest for feminists who want to argue against certain ideas of feminine as natural. In a well-known letter to Carl Muller-Braunschweig he wrote,

> I object to all of you . . . that you do not distinguish between what is psychic and what is biological . . . I would only like to emphasise that we must keep psychoanalysis separate from biology just as we have kept it separate from anatomy and physiology.

It was the publication of *The Interpretation of Dreams* (1900) which was to radically challenge the humanist perception of the 'unified' self. If seventeenth-century French philosopher Descartes doubted all he could, what he was left with was the doubter's very act of thinking, something that could not be doubted: 'I think therefore I am.' Freud suggested that the thinking 'I', the self, was not an irreducible essence but the conscious part of a tripartite structure – the *ego* (everyday consciousness, the 'self'), the *super-ego* (our conscience, internalised social rules) and the *id* (the realm of untrammelled desire). Freud's unconscious is the place of repressed, painful knowledge and forbidden **desire**. Freud's ideas about the unconscious would become more structured and were published in *The Ego and the Id* (1923). Freud linked the unconscious with sexuality. Infantile sexuality was inseparable from a subject's identity and their development into sexual adulthood. Subversively for feminists, this meant that adult sexuality was not the result of biology, but was constructed through the repression of infantile polymorphous drives. Thus the sexes may be born biologically different (as males or females), but their identities (masculine or feminine) are moulded as they emerge from different developmental stages particular to their cultural environment.

Freud discerned four phases of infantile sexuality: the *oral phase*, where pleasure is gained through sucking the mother's breast; the *anal stage*, where the child gains pleasure from control over its faeces; and the third, the *phallic phase*. This is a contentious stage for many feminists and psychoanalysts. Freud believed that up to this point both children are active in their sexuality, in gaining bodily pleasure from their clitoris or penis. Interestingly, Freud does concern himself with the difficulty of such terms as 'masculinity' and 'femininity', since at this stage girl and boy are responsive both actively and passively towards their object (the mother). It is during this stage that the children discover sexual **difference** and believe the mother to be in possession of a penis – it is not until the following Oedipal stage that the girl-child realises she is without a penis. The girl-child perceives the father to be a rival in its relationship with the mother. The Oedipal crisis is brought on by the boy's fear of castration by the father for his incestuous desire for his mother and the 'discovery' of the mother as castrated. The little boy surrenders his desire for the mother and identifies with the father, entering into the symbolic role of manhood. The realisation of the threat of castration and the repression of desire for the mother is the moment at which the unconscious is born.

Freud's theory of the little girl's passage through the Oedipus complex was developed later in Freud's career in three papers, 'Some Psychical Consequences of the Anatomical Distinction Between the Sexes' (1925), 'Female Sexuality' (1931) and 'Femininity' (1933). The girl-child understands that the mother lacks and wants a penis. She rejects the mother for not favouring her with a penis. The girl will proceed to replace the mother as the love object with the father. She does so by fantasising that she will be able to get a penis from him in order to satisfy the mother. This wish for a penis can be gratified through the father giving the girl a baby (a symbolic penis). This is Freud's controversial theory of penis envy, which might be defined as the expression of the castration complex in the girl. Yet this fantasy is shattered when she has to acknowledge that the father will not give her a penis because it is the mother who is the father's love object. To achieve the culturally accepted status of 'femininity' she must accept that one day she will get her penis/baby from a man like her father. Unlike the boy, who identifies solely with the father, the girl must now turn from the father back to re-identify with the mother so she will succeed in becoming a 'feminine' woman.

Freud's fourth and concluding phase, then, is genital sexuality, when the pubescent girl realises that not only does she have a clitoris but she has a vagina. For Freud, despite the bisexual tendencies of the girl in childhood, genital sexuality is now defined through heterosexuality. In essence, it is what is seen as the rather demeaning concept of penis envy that has most exercised women analysts such as Joan Riviere, Karen Horney and Melanie **Klein**. From the 1920s on, they sought to modify Freud's original position.

POST-FREUDIAN WOMEN: RIVIERE, KLEIN, HORNEY

Freud's female colleagues criticised his theory of femininity, in particular the female Oedipal crisis – the unconscious rites of passage that illicit penis envy in a girl. Analysts such as Karen Horney and Ernest Jones (Freud's biographer) engaged in a debate over Freud's representation of femininity. Horney, Riviere and Klein were by no means feminists, yet they were all aware of women's position within patriarchy. Joan Riviere, a distinguished psychoanalyst and translator of Freud, published an article in 1929 in which the term '**masquerade**' was coined in reference to femininity. Riviere's article, 'Womanliness as a Masquerade', claimed that women wore the mask(s) of femininity to gain approval and acceptance. She argued that

> womanliness therefore could be assumed and worn as a mask, both to hide the possession of masculinity and to avert the reprisals expected if she was found to possess it . . . how do I define womanliness or where I draw the line between genuine womanliness and the 'masquerade' . . . they are the same thing.

Riviere suggests (in a similar vein to the later Jacques Lacan) that gender-masquerading is a means of protecting/desiring, not the penis, but what the penis represents – patriarchal power, which for Lacan is represented by the phallus.

Melanie Klein located femininity in the innate drives; in other words, in biology rather than in culture. However, Klein's shifting of the emphasis away from penis envy (which represents woman as lack – an incomplete man, so to speak) to focus on the mother-daughter relationship has enriched contemporary feminist theory, which seeks to analyse the construction of femininity. In the early forties, Klein was to set up a training programme separate from the Freudian school led by Freud's daughter Anna **Freud**, whose work basically elaborated upon his theories of penis envy and the Oedipus Complex.

Klein became famous for her work with children in the first year of life and the theoretical product of this work, **'object relations theory'**, which examines the development of the self through its relationships with others. Rather than following Freud's dictum that until the castration complex 'the little girl is a little man', Klein saw a primary feminine phase where children of both sexes identify with the mother. In 'A Study of Envy and Gratitude' (1957), Klein was to repudiate Freud's theory of penis envy and claimed that girls and boys suffered from breast and womb envy.

Karen Horney was to present the first critique of Freud's theory of female psychology. Again like Klein, Horney was not a feminist, but felt that Freud's account of the unconscious socialisation of the child was partial and male-biased. Horney suggested that the theory of penis envy was a symptom of male envy and fear of the womb. The womb envy felt by all men results in the devaluation of motherhood. It was male narcissism that inclined females to devalue their genitalia. The girl's envy at the boy's ability to touch and display his genitalia is a stage through which the majority of girls pass without psychic damage.

Along with Dorothy **Dinnerstein**, who in *The Mermaid and the Minotaur* (1975) uses Klein to discuss misogyny, female sexuality and women's acceptance of patriarchy, the most important contemporary figure whose work grows out of these early women psychoanalysts' critique of feminine sexuality is the American psychoanalytic sociologist Nancy **Chodorow**, best known for her book *The Reproduction of Mothering: Psychoanalysis and the Sociology of Gender* (1978). Chodorow introduced the British school of object relations theorists to a US audience and was instrumental in making psychoanalysis an acceptable tool for feminism. For Chodorow, it is the pre-Oedipal stage that is paramount and the mother who is pivotal in the child's construction of identity. As we have seen before, this prioritising of the mother-child relationship in the context of identity formation runs contrary to Freud's focus on the Oedipal transition and subsequently the phallus, the desired symbol of power. After a period when the early women analysts seemed to have been overlooked in the excitement of the discovery of French versions of psychoanalysis, their work is being reprinted and widely discussed. They are 'post-Freudian' in the sense that although some were contemporaries of Freud, they used his work as a starting point for their own. The story of the feminist response to Freud must turn to the time when it was at its most controversial – in the late 1960s.

FREUD AND THE WOMEN'S MOVEMENT: MILLETT AND MITCHELL

It would not be until the late 1960s when the **radical feminists** of the burgeoning women's movement began to look at Freud's work closely. Initially, Freud's work was seen as broadly supporting the lifting of sexual repression, but it was not long before there was a whole series of books (Eva **Figes**'s *Patriarchal Attitudes* (1970), Shulamith **Firestone**'s *The Dialectic of Sex* (1970) and Germaine **Greer**'s *The Female Eunuch* (1971), for example) who produced forthright criticisms of Freud's theories on femininity, the castration complex and of course penis envy, criticising Freud's work as a patriarchal theory that saw women as unconsciously incomplete and envious men. It was however Kate **Millett**'s *Sexual Politics* (1970) which was to have the most impact. Her book discusses canonical male authors, highlighting their profoundly misogynistic representations of women and feminine sexuality. It was a devastating and salutary critique. More importantly for psychoanalysts, Millett went on to attack Freud, who it turns out is the real villain of the piece. Millett argues that Freud's work attempts 'to rationalise the invidious relationship between the sexes, to ratify traditional roles, and to validate temperamental difference'. Furthermore, Millett claimed that Freud's theories were highly improbable and we can catch an echo here of the early women analysts' critique of Freud:

> It would seem that Freud has managed in this highly unlikely hypothesis to assume that young females negate the validity, and even, to some extent the existence, of female sexual characteristics altogether. Surely the first thing all children notice is that the mother has breasts, while father has none. What is possibly the rather impressive effect of childbirth on young minds is overlooked, together with the girl's knowledge not only of her

clitoris, but her vagina as well . . . Nearly the entirety of feminine development, adjusted or maladjusted, is now seen in terms of the cataclysmic
moment of discovered castration.

Millett saw the 'passive' nature of Freud's post-Oepidal woman as
supporting the patriarchal status quo. It was at the height of Millett's
fame, however, that the most systematic and thoroughgoing defence of
Freud from a feminist perspective was published. British **Marxist-
feminist** Juliet Mitchell's landmark work *Psychoanalysis and Feminism*
(1974) re-evaluated Freud in terms of feminism and catalogued the
misreadings of psychoanalysis in the earlier feminist works mentioned
above. Her book began the process of unpicking the web of misrepre-
sentations that surrounded Freud's work and its popularisations and in
the use of Freudian concepts outside of their important contexts.
Mitchell argued that Freud did not claim that women were biologically
inferior to men, but offered a 'scientific' means as to understanding why
women were constructed as such in a patriarchal society. At base,
Mitchell claims that Freudian theory is an expose, not a defence of
patriarchy. It is something of a tribute to the effectiveness of Mitchell's
polemic (along with Jacqueline Rose's defence of Freud in the pages of
New Left Review in the mid-1980s), that there are now few feminist
studies that do not use psychoanalytic concepts of some kind. The value
of this 'double articulation', as it is sometimes called, is well-caught by
Jane Gallop in *Feminism and Psychoanalysis: The Daughter's Seduction*
(1982): 'Psychoanalysis . . . can unsettle feminism's tendency to accept a
unified, rational, puritanical self . . . feminism can shake up psychoanalysis's tendency to think itself apolitical but in fact be conservative by
encouraging people to adopt to an unjust social structure.' Gallop
herself draws on a radical notion of subjectivity to be found in the work
of Jacques Lacan, whose influence on French and **Anglo-American
feminism** is far-reaching and to whose work we now turn.

JACQUES LACAN AND FRENCH FEMINISM: KRISTEVA, IRIGARAY, CIXOUS

It might appear odd that a theorist as contemptuous of feminism as
Jacques Lacan (1901–1981) could be considered a major influence on
contemporary feminism, but it is nevertheless true. It was the
publication of *Écrits* in 1966 that solidified Lacan's reputation, and it
was Freud's writings on the construction of sexual difference that was
the basis for Lacan's work. Lacan pursued the anti-humanist element in

174

Freud that led to an examination of the construction of the self, which for previous thinkers in the humanist tradition was the irreducible core of the human. Lacan's work might be summarised as a study of the effect of unconscious desires as they are articulated through language. Lacan rewrites Descartes's 'I think therefore I am,' as 'I am not where I think, and I think where I am not'. His concepts of the **Imaginary**, the **Symbolic** and the Phallus have been used by many of the most important French feminists, so a brief account of them here seems appropriate.

Lacan rereads Freud's concept of the Oedipal crisis in terms of the acquisition of **language**. Lacan calls the pre-Oedipal stage, where the child sees itself as part of the mother and sees no separation between itself and the world, as the Imaginary. The Oedipal crisis, when the father breaks the blissful dyadic relationship between mother and child, is for Lacan the moment of the child's entry into the Symbolic Order, which entails the child entering into the differential system of language and taking up a subject-position there. In other words, the child learns to speak, to say 'I am, you are, they are' and to have repressed its desire for the maternal body and the unity felt in the Imaginary order. This unconscious surrender is the moment of primary repression, the birth of the unconscious itself and the birth of a desire that can never be fulfilled, for the desire for the mother is forbidden by what Lacan calls 'the Law of the Father'. This is the Freudian threat of castration and is represented by the Phallus. In some versions of psychoanalysis, penis envy refers to both the anatomical part and an imaginary organ of fantasy. For the child in Lacan's account, the Phallus is an imaginary object in possession of the father; while it seems to represent masculine power, it in fact represents absence or lack. The Phallus should be understood as a cultural construction that attributes symbolic power to the biological penis. Men (by definition) have a penis, but this does not mean that they possess the Phallus. Only through another's desire does the man feel he has the Phallus.

In Lacanian theory, no one has the Phallus, and this kind of thinking has appealed to a number of feminists. In a sense, the 'castrated' woman is the less deluded, one who sees that the phallus (in Lacanian theory) represents an illusion of power. Lacan strips bare masculinity for the cultural construction it is, and shows how it can only exist narcissistically in relation to femininity. All this has a great deal of mileage in it for feminists who wish to examine the psychic roots of patriarchy. As Juliet Mitchell suggests in her introduction to *Feminine Sexuality*, a collection of articles on femininity from Lacan's école Freudienne, it was Lacan's belief that 'psychoanalysis should not subscribe to ideas about how men

175

and women do or should live as sexually differentiated beings, but instead should analyse how they come to be such beings in the first place'.

This is the approach much French feminism took towards psychoanalysis and Lacan in particular. Although none of the three writers discussed below were born in France, that is where they made their intellectual careers. In the mid-1970s in France, feminists both attacked psychoanalysis for its **phallocentrism** (seeing masculinity as the norm and femininity as deviation) and appropriating it as a means of understanding gender formation. Bulgarian Linguist and analyst Julia **Kristeva**, who has lived in France since the mid-1960s, took up Lacan's concepts of the Symbolic and the Imaginary to develop a theory of **subjectivity**. She called the realm of the pre-symbolic (roughly equivalent to Lacan's Imaginary) the **semiotic**, a space in which impulses and drives circulate through the child's body. The Symbolic, the realm in which we function as rational creatures, is where 'repressive political structures' (such as patriarchy) operate. Kristeva rejects the label 'feminist' because she rejects the dichotomy between masculine and feminine as 'metaphysical'. Rather than say that women should have equality, or that they needed to organise themselves separately from men, she wanted to examine how sexual difference comes into being in our psychic lives. Her influential essay 'Women's Time' (1981) deconstructs the binary opposition of masculine and feminine and opens up current notions of identity. Kristeva asks 'What can "identity", even "sexual identity", mean in a new theoretical and scientific space where the very notion of identity is challenged?' For Kristeva, 'masculinity' and 'femininity' are particular socially constructed subject-positions and have little to do with biological difference.

Luce **Irigaray** (born in Belgium, but a long-time resident of Paris) began as a Lacanian analyst but decided psychoanalytic theory – contra Juliet Mitchell – was not an analysis of patriarchy, but an example of it. While her work is a critique of psychoanalysis, she ambitiously wants to reorientate the very ways we think. As an analyst, she values Freudian theory because 'it gives us something that can shake the whole philosophical order of discourse' but 'it remains submissive to that order when it comes to the definition of sexual difference'. For example, in *Speculum of the Other Woman* (1985), responding to Freud's statement that 'we are now obliged to recognise that the little girl is a little man', she argues that 'The "differentiation" into two sexes derives from a priori assumption of the same, since the little man that the little girl is, must become a man minus certain attributes.' Involving as it does a critique of Freud's concept of penis envy, Irigaray's criticism of Freud is similar to the early women analysts, though in a vastly different context.

In her essay 'Sorties', under the title 'Where Is She?' Algerian-born Hélène **Cixous** highlights women's inferior status under patriarchy. Cixous lists a whole series of terms that operate around a simple binary opposition: woman/passive, man/active. Cixous's work (like Irigaray's) is indebted to psychoanalysis but inflected through the work of Jacques **Derrida**, in particular his deconstruction or unravelling of this kind of binary thinking, which for Derrida is never neutral, but always organised into what he calls a 'violent hierarchy'. Cixous seems to believe that there could be some essential form of the feminine 'behind' language within the girl's pre-Oedipal fantasised relationship with the mother. Cixous, especially her work 'Laugh of the Medusa' (1981), is associated with the term *écriture féminine* (feminine writing), a style of discourse that takes us back to the pre-Symbolic Imaginary. It is the mother-tongue, the female voice. As Cixous writes in *The Newly-Born Woman* (1975), it is a pre-Oedipal idyll, it is 'the voice, a song before the Law, before the breath was split by the symbolic, reappropriated into language under the authority that separates the deepest, most ancient and adorable of visitations'. For Lacanian analysis, however, there is only psychosis in the pre-Symbolic and of the three writers discussed above, this places Cixous furthest away from the roots of psychoanalysis.

CONCLUSION

Though there was much contemporary criticism of Freud's conception of femininity by women from within psychoanalysis itself, they were not feminists in the sense that they believed that women were second-class citizens in society. The turning point comes in the early 1970s with the work of Mitchell and others. After that, with the general explosion of interest in social, political and aesthetic theory later in the decade, feminist engagement with psychoanalysis has grown. This takes us back to Freud's early work and the birth of psychoanalysis itself – his study of **hysteria**, which he sees as bound up with issues of sexuality and identity.

While many feminists would see hysteria as symptomatic of women's confinement within patriarchal definitions of femininity, Freud's and feminism's positions are by no means mutually exclusive: the appeal of psychoanalysis to feminists is summarised by Jacqueline Rose who writes in *Sexuality in the Field of Vision* (1986) that 'psychoanalysis becomes one of the few places in our culture where it is recognised as more than a fact of individual pathology that most women do not painlessly slip into their roles as women, if indeed they do at all'. This pain is a major concern of both psychoanalysis and of feminism and both may be used in a politics that would fight to see the end of the patriarchal phallocentrism that produces **sexism** and misogyny.

SELECT BIBLIOGRAPHY

Ang, Ien, *Living Room Wars: Rethinking Media Audiences for a Postmodern World* (London & NY: Routledge, 1996).

Beauvoir, Simone de, *The Second Sex* (London: Pan, 1988).

Betterton, Rosemary, *An Intimate Distance: Women, Artists and the Body* (London & NY: Routledge, 1996).

Braidotti, Rosi, *Nomadic Subjects* (New York: Columbia, 1994).

Brooks, Ann, *Postfeminisms: Feminism, Cultural Theory and Cultural Forms* (London & NY: Routledge, 1997).

Butler, Judith, *Gender Trouble: Feminism and the Subversion of Identity* (London & NY: Routledge, 1990).

Cameron, Deborah, *Verbal Hygiene* (London & NY: Routledge, 1995).

Chedgzoy, Kate; Hansen, Melanie and Trill, Suzanne, eds., *Voicing Women: Gender and Sexuality in Early Modern Writing* (Keele: Keele University Press, 1996, rpt. Edinburgh: Edinburgh University Press, 1998).

Christ, Carol, *The Laughter of Aphrodite: Reflections on a Journey to the Goddess* (San Francisco: Harper & Row, 1987).

Cixous, Hélène and Clément, Catherine, *The Newly Born Woman*, trans. Betsy Wing (Manchester: Manchester University Press, 1986).

Cooey, Paula M., Easkin, William R. and McDaniel, Jay B., eds., *After Patriarchy: Feminist Transformations of the World Religions* (NY: Maryknoll, 1991).

Coppock, Vicki, *et al.*, *The Illusions of 'Postfeminism': New Women, Old Myths* (London: Taylor & Francis, 1995).

Cornell, Drucilla, *At the Heart of Freedom: Feminism, Sex, and Equality* (Princeton, NJ: Princeton University Press, 1998).

Crawford, Mary, *Talking Difference: On Gender and Language* (London: Sage, 1995).

Davies, Miranda, ed., *Third World – Second Sex* (London: Sen Books Ltd., 1983).

Denfeld, Rene, *The New Victorians: A Young Woman's Challenge to the Old Feminist Order* (NY: Warner Books, 1995).

Dworkin, Andrea, *Pornography: Men Possessing Women* (New York: Perigee, 1981).

Eagleton, Mary, *Working With Feminist Criticism* (Oxford: Blackwell, 1996).

Faludi, Susan, *Backlash: The Undeclared War Against Women* (London: Vintage, 1992).

Ferguson, Moira, ed., *First Feminists: British Women Writers 1578–1799* (Bloomington: Indiana University Press, 1985).

Figes, Eva, *Patriarchal Attitudes* (London: Granada, 1972).

Fiorenza, Elisabeth Schüssler, *In Memory of Her: A Feminist Theological Reconstruction of Christian Origins* (London: SPCK, 1983).

Firestone, Shulamith, *The Dialectic of Sex* (London: The Women's Press, 1979).

Friedan, Betty, *The Feminine Mystique* (Harmondsworth: Penguin, 1965).

Gallop, Jane, *Around 1981: Academic Feminist Literary Theory* (London and New York: Routledge, 1992).

Greene, Gayle, and Kahn, Coppélia, *Changing Subjects: The Making of Feminist Literary Criticism* (London and New York: Routledge, 1993).

Greer, Germaine, *The Female Eunuch* (St. Albans: Paladin, 1971).

The Whole Woman (London: Doubleday, 1999).

Griffiths, Morwenn and Whitford, Margaret, eds., *Feminist Perspectives in Philosophy* (Bloomington: Indiana University Press, 1988).

Haraway, Donna, *Simians, Cyborgs and Women: The Reinvention of Nature* (London: Free Association Books, 1991).

Harding, Sandra and Hintikka, Merrill B., eds., *Discovering Reality: Feminist Perspectives on Epistemology, Metaphysics, Methodology and Philosophy of Science* (Dordrecht, Holland: D. Reidel Publishing Company, 1983).

Haskell, Molly, *From Reverence to Rape: The Treatment of Women in the Movies* (Chicago and London: University of Chicago Press, 1974).

Herring, Susan, ed., *Computer-Mediated Communication: Linguistic, Social and Cross-Cultural Perspectives* (Amsterdam: John Benjamins, 1996).

Irigaray, Luce, *This Sex Which Is Not One*, trans. Catherine Porter (Ithaca: Cornell University Press, 1985).

Jaggar, Alison M. and Young, Iris Marion, eds., *A Companion to Feminist Philosophy* (Oxford: Blackwell, 1998).

Kaplan, Cora, *Sea Changes: Culture and Feminism* (London: Verso, 1986).

Koedt, Anne *et al.*, eds., *Radical Feminism* (New York: Quadrangle, 1973).

Kourany, Janet A., ed., *Philosophy in a Feminist Voice: Critiques and Reconstructions* (Princeton, NY: Princeton University Press, 1998).

Kramarae, Cheris, ed., *Technology and Women's Voices* (London: Routledge, 1988).

Lakoff, Robin, *Language and Woman's Place* (New York: Harper & Row, 1975).

Lauretis, Teresa de, *Alice Doesn't: Feminism, Semiotics, Cinema* (Bloomington: Indiana University Press, 1984).

Technologies of Gender: Essays on Theory, Film and Fiction (Bloomington: Indiana University Press, 1987).

Le Doeuff, Michèle, *The Philosophical Imaginary*, trans. Colin Gordon (Stanford, CA: Stanford University Press, 1990).

Lloyd, Genevieve, *The Man of Reason: "Male" and "Female" in Western Philosophy* (London: Methuen, 1984).

Marks, Elaine and Courtivron, Isabelle de, eds., *New French Feminisms* (Brighton: Harvester Wheatsheaf, 1981).

Millett, Kate, *Sexual Politics* (London: Virago, 1977).

Mitchell, Juliet, *Psychoanalysis and Feminism* (Harmondsworth: Penguin, 1975).

Women: The Longest Revolution (London: Virago, 1984).

Modleski, Tania, *Loving with a Vengeance: Mass Produced Fantasies for Women* (London: Methuen, 1984).

Feminism Without Women: Culture and Criticism in a 'Postfeminist' Age (London and New York: Routledge, 1991).

Moi, Toril, *Sexual/Textual Politics: Feminist Literary Theory* (London: Methuen, 1985).

Morris, Meaghan, *The Pirate's Fiancée: Feminism Reading Postmodernism* (London: Verso, 1988).

Mulvey, Laura, *Visual and Other Pleasures* (Basingstoke: Macmillan, 1989).

Nead, Linda, *The Female Nude: Art, Obscenity and Sexuality* (London and New York: Routledge, 1992).

Radway, Janet, *Reading the Romance: Women, Patriarchy and Popular Literature* (Chapel Hill: University of North Carolina Press, 1984).

Roiphe, Katie, *The Morning After: Sex, Fear and Feminism* (London: Hamish Hamilton, 1994).

Russ, Joanna, *How To Suppress Women's Writing* (London: The Women's Press, 1984).

Russo, Mary, *The Female Grotesque: Risk, Excess and Modernity* (London: Routledge, 1995).

Showalter, Elaine, *A Literature of Their Own: British Women Novelists from Brontë to Lessing* (London: Virago, 1978).

ed., *The New Feminist Criticism: Essays on Women, Literature and Theory* (London: Virago, 1986).

Spender, Dale, *Man Made Language* (London and New York: Routledge & Kegan Paul, 1980).

Spivak, Gayatri Chakravorty, *In Other Worlds: Essays in Cultural Politics* (London: Methuen, 1987).

Thorne, Barrie; Kramarae, Cheris and Henley, Nancy, eds., *Language, Gender and Society* (Rowley, MA: Newbury House, 1983).

Wajcman, Judy, *Feminism Confronts Technology* (Cambridge: Polity Press, 1991).

Wieringa, Saskia, ed., *Subversive Women – Women's Movements in Africa, Asia, Latin America and the Caribbean* (Delhi: Kali for Women, 1995).

Wolf, Naomi, *The Beauty Myth* (London: Vintage, 1990).

Fire With Fire: The New Female Power and How it Will Change the 21st Century (London: Chatto & Windus, 1993).

Wright, Elizabeth, ed., *Feminism and Psychoanalysis: A Critical Dictionary* (Oxford: Blackwells, 1992).

II
A–Z OF
KEY THEMES AND
MAJOR FIGURES

A

ABJECTION In *Powers of Horror: An Essay on Abjection* (1982), the **French feminist** theorist Julia **Kristeva** argues that to take up a position within the **symbolic order**, the individual subject must define itself as independent, and reject anything which threatens that sense of autonomous, unique selfhood. Abjection, however, testifies to the fact that such control is only ever partial. Because it draws attention to the precariousness of **identity**, the abject is associated with all that the subject perceives as being unclean and potentially polluting: food, bodily wastes, and vomit, for example, all of which serve to remind the subject that it cannot escape basic biological drives over which it has no influence. Kristeva aligns the abject with the **semiotic order**, and thus with the female, an implicitly **essentialist** assumption. However, modern feminist artists such as Jo **Spence** have produced work that appropriates the monstrosity of the abject in order to challenge conventional representations of the **feminine**.

ABORTION One of the cornerstones of the **feminist** movement has always been a woman's right to control her own reproductive processes through recourse to such **reproductive technologies** as **contraception**, sterilisation and abortion. Abortion is clearly the most emotive item on this list,

since it involves the termination of a foetus. Campaigns around abortion formed a focal point for **second wave feminism**, and it continues to be a contentious issue.

Ranged against the feminist position are followers of the pro-life movement and various religious organisations which argue for foetal rights. To the fore in such campaigns are iconographic representations of the gestating foetus which render the containing body of the woman invisible, and which thus depict in graphic form the pro-life belief that the embryo is a person whose existence must be preserved, regardless of the wishes of the potential mother.

Although not all feminists would condone a simple 'abortion on demand' policy, a feminist point of view would put the mother first, arguing for woman's right 'to undertake her maternities in freedom' (Simone de **Beauvoir**, *The Second Sex*). For **radical feminists** such as Adrienne **Rich**, abortion is an instrument of male domination, allowing men to control the produce of women's labour.

ACKER, KATHY: PROSE WRITER AND ESSAYIST (1945–1997) Kathy Acker was an innovative and controversial novelist, whose efforts to render female experience in prose brings her close to a radical kind of *écriture* *féminine*. Often accused of pretension, illiteracy and immorality, she saw her writing style as rooted in 'conceptualist' technique, stating that form is determined not by rules but by intention. She read Williams Burroughs' *The Third Mind*, and taught herself to write in a similarly experimental manner, and under Burroughs' influence she became an expert at manipulating text in place of conventional narrative. In works such as *Kathy Goes to Haiti* (1978) and *Blood and Guts in High School* (1984) Acker repeats several pages of text throughout the same novel, fuses countless literary forms within the same page, breaks up the text with illustrations and uses a blend of **autobiography** and historical and literary allusion in place of 'story' (characters in her novels include Rimbaud, Toulouse-Lautrec and Georges Bataille). Her favourite themes include **identity**, **gender**, sexuality, **myth** and corruption.

Acker's deconstructionist impulses extended out of the body of the text to encompass the physical body itself, which she regarded as another text, a story to be written. She was a fanatical **bodybuilder**, and had many piercings and elaborate tattoos. At the first appearance of breast cancer in 1996, she voluntarily underwent a double mastectomy. She turned completely to alternative medicines, but died on 27 November 1997 in New Mexico.

ACTIVISM **Feminist** activists believe that change will not come about through simple negotiation: it must be forced. This is achieved through the staging of activities or protests that will draw attention to issues in a dramatic way, such as the exhibition of bra-burning at the 1968 Miss America **beauty contest**. A more recent example of activism at work would be the **Greenham Common** protest in the 1980s. Although the campaigners themselves were widely derided in the popular press, they were nevertheless successful in creating a dramatic anti-war statement.

ADVERTISING Simply stated, advertising is the process by which people are persuaded to buy things, and are thus transformed into consumers. In order to be effective, however, advertising must surround the product with meanings which extend beyond its simple function. Advertising thus becomes both an expression of dominant **ideological** assumptions within culture, and a means by which such assumptions continue to be perpetuated. Feminists argue that advertising is innately **sexist**, presenting its audience with conservative female **stereotypes** which limit the ways in which women are depicted elsewhere in culture. Moreover, the fact that its aim is to create a perception of lack means that women themselves are duped into trying to live up to unattainable ideals to do with appearance and lifestyle: as Naomi **Wolf** says in *The Beauty Myth*, 'Advertising aimed at women works by lowering our self-esteem.' Although in her later work Wolf has gone on to claim that there has been a shift in advertisers' depictions of women that feature images of female dominance, the issue remains disputed.

AFRICAN-AMERICAN FEMINISM The earliest articulator of black feminism was the ex-slave Sojourner **Truth**, whose legendary speech at the 1851 Women's Rights Convention, Akron, Ohio, questions the exclusion of black women within the **feminist** movement: 'Dat man ober dar say dat womin needs to be helped into carriages, and lifted ober ditches, and to hab de best place everywhar. Nobody eber helps me into carriage, or ober mud-puddles, or gibs me any best place! And a'n't I a woman?' Among other nineteenth-century black feminists were Mary Church Terrell, Amanda Berry Smith and Anna Cooper, who in 1893 gave a remarkably frank and powerful speech about the 'unwritten history' of slave women who suffered a 'double slavery'. They were women in a **patriarchal** society (like their white counterparts) but as black slave women they neither owned their own bodies (and were therefore at the mercy of their master's desires), nor had rights over their own children, who could be sold away from them. With the rise in political consciousness that took place at the end of the 1960s, many black **activists** came to national prominence, including lesbian poet and essayist Audre **Lorde** and most visibly Angela **Davis**, who brought a Marxist interpretation to bear on women's **oppression**. The founding text of contemporary black feminism, however, is bell **hooks**'s *Ain't I a Woman* (1981), whose title quotes Truth's famous Akron speech on the marginalisation of black women within the feminist movement, which is hooks's subject. Many scholarly works have been written about American slave women which was until the 1980s (in Anna Cooper's prescient phrase) 'unwritten history' and which

have in turn enriched black feminist **discourse**. As a critical voice in the heart of the world's richest nation, African-American feminism has contributed significantly to the analysis of women's oppression, and oppression generally.

ALTERITY The term 'alterity' is closely related to the concept of 'othering' and Michel **Foucault**'s notion of the 'exteriority' or marginality of the subject. Often thought of as synonymous with '**Other**', the condition of alterity exemplifies the marginal or peripheral who do not have access to the centres of power. The centre (or centres) represent a point of origin in which meaning is fixed and validated as the determining norm. Those excluded from the centre by virtue of race, caste, **gender** or religion are categorised as irrelevant to normative conventions and designated 'other'. **Feminist** theorists argue that patriarchy has conferred alterity on the experience of women by utilising biologistic and **essentialist** models of women's identity. Thus female experience is homogenised, related to the margins and subjugated to the norm, i.e., male experience, in order to legitimise and naturalise the privileging of **patriarchal** power.

ALTHUSSER, LOUIS: CULTURAL AND LITERARY THEORIST (1918–1990) One of the most influential French Marxist philosophers of the 1960s, whose work began to appear in English translation from 1965 onwards, beginning with *For Marx*. This was followed by *Reading Capital* (1970), *Lenin and Philosophy* (1971), *Politics and History* (1972), *Essays in Self-*

Criticism (1976) and *Essays in Ideology* (1983). Althusser's ideas concerning social institutions, and the place of the human subject within their structures, have influenced feminist deconstructions of **patriarchy** and capitalism. His essay 'Ideology and Ideological State Apparatuses' in *Lenin and Philosophy* lays the foundation for a reconsideration of the female subject's relationship to patriarchal **ideology**, and is famous for introducing the term '**interpellation**', which describes the way in which an individual is identified and positioned within ideological structures.

Althusser's use of the term '**imaginary**' is also useful for **feminist** theory. In his work, the subject misrecognises his or her place in the social order through an ideology which posits as 'natural' a fixed relationship between social **classes**. What is at issue for Althusser is the way in which individual human subjects are constituted by an order which extends beyond the images through which that order is represented to them. In **Lacan**'s psychoanalytical theory the realm of the imaginary is contained within that of the **symbolic order**, and it is the function of **psychoanalysis** to uncover the 'real' relations which exist beneath this series of representations. In Althusser, however, the 'mirror phase' can be equated with 'ideology' in that this is the means through which individual human subjects misrecognise themselves and their positions in the social order.

ANARCHIST FEMINISM Anarchist **feminists** identify church and state with the practice of **patriarchal** oppression. Therefore, for women to assume 'equal' status within existing structures will achieve nothing. Instead, anarchist feminists advocate a society which is non-hierarchical and anti-authoritarian, relying instead on mutual cooperation amongst equal individuals. The founding mother of anarchist feminism is the Russian-American agitator Emma **Goldman**, who argued that the **family** plays a key role in the **oppression** of women, since it is an institution that restricts them sexually, economically and socially. In its place she proposed a society founded on the principles of free love and self-determination. Indeed, it is self-determination that lies at the heart of the feminist anarchist project, since within an anarchist framework each individual must bear responsibility for their society's functioning. As the science fiction writer Ursula K. Le Guin puts it in her short story 'The Day Before the Revolution' (1974), 'What is an anarchist? One, who, choosing, accepts the responsibility of choice.' Some critics, however, see this stress on individual will as itself problematic, since it implies, as Alix Kates Schulman puts it in her essay on Goldman, that 'a failure to change can be seen as a failure of individual will' (in Dale **Spender**, ed., *Feminist Theorists*, 1983).

ANDROCENTRISM Term coined by the American writer Charlotte Perkins **Gilman** in her publication of 1911, *The Man-Made World or Our Androcentric Culture*, which denotes a system of thought centred around male identity and values. Within androcentrism, the female constitutes a deviation from a norm defined by reference to the male: a good example of this in **language** is the way in which 'mankind' is a term used to refer to all people regardless of their **gender**. In her introduction to *Man-Made Language*, Dale **Spender** discusses how the belief that man is the superior sex affects the organisation of social institutions, so that an androcentric system, which automatically rewards the 'superior' gender with more resources, becomes self-perpetuating. The **French feminist** Hélène **Cixous** makes a similar point when she argues that Western thought revolves around the dualism 'man/woman', but that it is not an equal relationship. The superiority of the male half of the equation is predicated upon the subordination of the female half, which is thus exiled from the value paradigm.

ANDROGYNY Greek word from 'andro' (male) and 'gyn' (female), signifying fluidity in the assignation of gender-linked characteristics. **Feminists** have consistently laid claim to androgyny as a potentially liberating concept. In *A Room of One's Own* (1929), Virginia **Woolf** famously claimed that an androgynous consciousness is a precondition for effective artistic expression, for 'it is fatal to be a man or woman pure and simple; one must be woman-manly or man-womanly': a view treated with scepticism by Elaine **Showalter** in *A Literature of Their Own* (1977), who argues that the concept of androgyny enabled Woolf to 'evade confrontation with her own painful femaleness'. Nevertheless, many modern feminists such as Andrea **Dworkin**, Monique **Wittig** and Carolyn **Heilbrun** (whose 1964 publication *Towards Androgyny* is an important early feminist study of the topic) echo Woolf in arguing for the deconstruction of a dualistic conception of **gender**. However, feminists who adhere to separatist ideals advocate quite the opposite – that women should celebrate the possession of a female identity which is quite distinct from its male counterpart. To quote Mary **Daly** in *Gyn/Ecology*: 'attempts to combine **masculinity** and **femininity**, which are **patriarchal** constructs, will result only in pseudointegrity'.

ANGEL IN THE HOUSE The phrase 'angel in the house' entered the language in 1885, as the title of a narrative poem by Coventry Patmore. It tells the story of Honoria, who fulfils all the ideals of Victorian womanhood. Her identity centred wholly on the **domestic** realm, she functions as man's oppositional '**other**': private where he is public, innocent where he is worldly, passive where he is active. Indeed, such is her removal from the outside world that the angel, as her title suggests, takes on a quasi-supernatural aura as the apotheosis of a **feminine** role which is divinely ordained.

The feminist attitude towards this figure is famously expressed by Virginia **Woolf** in her 1931 essay 'Professions for Women', in which the angel features as the internalised pressure to conform experienced by every woman who aspires to a public voice. From this perspective the angel thus becomes a demon, representative of an outdated feminine ideal which, if adhered to, will deny women any chance to gain an **identity** independent of men, home and family.

ANGLO-AMERICAN FEMINIST CRITI-CISM Central to the women's movement is an emphasis on the value of female experience – of **oppression**, of alienation – which, translated into academic terms, has meant the development of a feminism wary of the modern literary theory in which the experience 'behind' the text becomes elided as the experience 'of' the text is foregrounded. Elaine **Showalter**, a critic representative of classic Anglo-American academic feminism, is suspicious of what she terms 'male critical theory', and the **feminist** obsession with correcting, modifying, supplementing and revising it. For her, the male champions of the **poststructuralist** movement are the 'white fathers', the masters from whom feminism must escape and forge its own system, theory and voice. Anglo-American critics like Showalter call for new ways of reading women's texts in order to both recover the experience encoded within it and the greater tradition of women's writing of which it is a part. In her essay 'A Map for Rereading' (1980), Annette Kolodny calls this process 're-visionary rereading', while Showalter has coined the term '**gynocriticism**'.

The Anglo-American school of criticism can be credited with establishing feminist criticism as a distinct academic discipline. However, although its immediate accessibility ensures that it remains influential, it also now seems somewhat dated against the growing influence of a feminist criticism which is informed by poststructuralist and deconstructivist theory, and which seeks to interrogate the grounds upon which a female **identity** itself is constructed.

For critics such as Hélène **Cixous**, Luce **Irigaray** and Julia **Kristeva** (to name the most famous) the female subject is formed in and through the text, which no longer functions as a transparent medium of transmission through which female experience and history can be unproblematically conveyed. A text which was particularly important in outlining the differences between Anglo-American feminism and **French feminist** theory is Toril **Moi**'s *Sexual/Textual Politics* (1985).

ANTHONY, SUSAN B.: AMERICAN SUFFRAGE CAMPAIGNER (1820–1906) A devout Quaker, Susan B. Anthony began her reformist career within the temperance movement She was also involved in the American Anti-Slavery Society, and in 1863 founded her own anti-slavery organisation, the Women's Royal League. Even after the slaves were freed at the conclusion of the American Civil War, she remained concerned with racial issues, arguing, for example, that black women should be allowed to participate in the campaign for the vote.

However, along with Elizabeth Cady **Stanton**, she is remembered primarily for her association with American **first wave feminism**, a movement which was launched at the **Seneca Falls** women's rights convention of 1848. Initially, Anthony and Stanton worked together to reform New York state laws on such issues as **education**, jobs and marital and property rights. In 1869 they founded the National Woman Suffrage Association, and Anthony was its president until the age of 80, although she died before the fight for the vote was finally won in 1920.

ARC, JOAN OF: PATRON SAINT OF FRANCE (1412–1431) It has become difficult to think of Joan of Arc as a real historical figure, as her story has taken on the status of hagiography. At the direction of divinely inspired voices, Joan helped the Dauphin of France (later Charles VII) in his battle against England. Dressed in armour and carrying a white banner, she became the French army's figurehead, credited with inspiring the troops to victory.

In 1430, however, Joan was captured by the English and tried by an ecclesiastical court on charges of heresy and sorcery. That her refusal to conform to acceptable standards of **femininity** lay at the heart of the accusations against her is backed up by the fact that, although she escaped the death penalty by confessing to the crimes of which she was accused, she was retried again when she persisted in dressing in male attire. In 1431, she was burned at the stake in Rouen.

Although there is no evidence that Joan acted from anything other than religious motives, her potential to function as a symbol for the struggle for female independence was spotted by her contemporary, Christine de Pizan, who praised Joan as 'an honour for the female sex'.

ARZNER, DOROTHY: FILM DIRECTOR AND EDITOR (1897–1979) Dorothy Arzner was the first female film director in Hollywood. She began her career as a script typist for William C. DeMille, eventually becoming chief film editor at a subsidiary of Paramount, Realart. A move to Paramount itself followed, for which she edited such films as *Blood and Sand*, starring Rudolph Valentino (1922). By the late 1920s, however, she had moved into directing, with notable success. Although contracted to Paramount, she also lent her talents to the other major Hollywood studios such as RKO, United Artists and MGM and directed, among others, Clara Bow in her first talking picture, *The Wild Party* (1929), Katherine Hepburn in *Christopher Strong* (1933) and Joan Crawford in *The Bride Wore Red* (1937). Her last feature film was *First Come Courage* (1943), although she continued to work in the film business, directing Pepsi-Cola commercials in the 1950s and teaching filmmaking at UCLA in the 1960s.

ATKINSON, TI-GRACE: ACTIVIST FEMINIST (1939–) Ti-Grace Atkinson was one of the more radical members of the **National Organisation for Women** (NOW) in the 1960s. In 1968 she left the organisation, claiming that not only was it was too hierarchical, but was also biased in favour of heterosexual models of emancipation. In publications such as 'The Institution of Sexual Intercourse' (1970) and *Amazon Odyssey* (1974), she argued that men were fundamentally insecure beings who vent their frustrations on women, a process she strikingly termed 'metaphysical cannibalism'. For Atkinson, sexuality is as much political as personal, since it is heterosexual practice which is at the root of women's subordination to men. The adoption of a lesbian perspective is thus the only means by which women can escape **oppression**. Indeed, Atkinson's arguments frequently make lesbianism a precondition of feminism, as in her famous statement, 'Feminism is the theory, lesbianism is the practice.'

AUTOBIOGRAPHY The first use of this term is usually attributed to Robert Southey in the early nineteenth century, although the modern notion of the autobiographical **genre** had begun to emerge with the accounts of spiritual awakening that became popular during the seventeenth century. However, it has subsequently been argued that the earliest forms of self-writing actually date back to the second century AD. Until the 1980s, autobiography tended to be defined as 'the story of a person's life written by *himself*', and the genre was perceived as exclusively **androcentric**; hence its alias, the 'Great Man' tradition.

The strongest influence on the autobiographical genre has been exerted by Western culture's understanding of **subjectivity** which, for centuries, was dominated by the Cartesian notion of the 'universal' subject; that is, a stable, coherent, *essentially male* subject. It has now been suggested that a separate female autobiographical tradition developed along radically different lines because women were unable to identify with universal subjectivity. As a consequence, even the earliest women autobiographers sought to establish alternative subject positions and create new modes of literary self-representation.

The last two decades have seen both the reclamation of the forgotten female autobiographical tradition and the suggestion that the first full-length autobiography to be written in English was actually by a woman: *The Book of Margery Kempe* (1413). Several **feminist** studies charting the development of a distinct female autobiographical tradition have now been published, such as Shari Benstock's *The Private Self: Women's Autobiographical Writing* (1988) and Leigh Gilmore's *Autobiographics: A Feminist Theory of Women's Self-Representation* (1994). Such studies focus on the conflict between women's private and public selves and the tension between their domestic and professional roles in order to illustrate that autobiographical writing has long been considered a feminist act. However, the fact that theories of female subjectivity and sexuality have proliferated since the start of the twentieth century would seem to suggest that women's autobiographical writing will continue to be stylistically innovative and politically motivated.

B

BACKLASH A movement that is a reaction to, or a counter-assault on, something. Some recent **feminist** writers, including Naomi **Wolf** and Susan **Faludi**, have argued that since the late 1970s there has been an anti-feminist backlash in the media that works so as to revoke the gains that the feminist movement has won for women. For example, Faludi writes that within all spheres of society, from health advice guides to Hollywood film, it is the career woman who is shown to be coping with stress-induced illnesses such as hair loss and anxiety attacks, induced, we are told, by loneliness and a deep sense of unfulfilled needs and desires.

Not all feminists agree with this idea because it negates women's responses as active readers or consumers of popular culture. Myra Macdonald, for example, in *Representing Women* (1985), states that 'we need to recognise the part we all play in keeping mythologies and **ideologies** alive. This gets obliterated in conspiracy-theory accounts that see the media as bastions of male privilege, spurred on by the mission of keeping feminism at bay'.

BARRETT, MICHELE: ACADEMIC AND AUTHOR (1949–) Professor Michele Barrett is the Director of Research at City University, London. Barrett teaches and writes in the general fields of social and cultural theory, maintaining a particular interest in **gender studies**. She has worked in the areas of **Marxism**, feminism, the **family**, and contemporary gender studies. Barrett is best known for the books *Women's Oppression Today* (1989) and *The Anti-Social Family* (1991), the latter written with Mary McIntosh. In addition, she is the editor of *The Politics of Truth* (1992) and co-editor (with Anne Phillips) of *Destabilizing Theory* (1992), the latter on contemporary **feminist** debates. Her most recent work is on the implications of **poststructuralist** ideas for sociology. Barrett is also known for her strong interest in the study of modern art and literature, which is reflected in her most recent book, *Imagination in Theory* (1999), a study of writing and **culture**. Barrett has also written on art and aesthetics and anthologised some of Virginia **Woolf**'s most influential essays in *Virginia Woolf on Women and Writing* (1979). She has many international research links and is active in the professional development of sociology, a role that has included being the President of the British Sociological Association.

BARTHES, ROLAND: CULTURAL CRITIC (1915–1980) Barthes is probably the best-known and most influential of all the structuralist and **poststructural-ist** theorists, whose ideas have influenced **feminist** cultural critics such as

Angela McRobbie and Meaghan **Morris**. In books such as *Writing Degree Zero* (1953), *Mythologies* (1957) and *S/Z* (1970), Barthes undertook to expose how **language** functioned, and its relationship with **ideology**. Moreover, he was also concerned to uncover the distinctions between literary texts which operated on the basis of a stable relationship between signified and signifier, and those for whom the act of signification (establishing meaning) itself was of primary importance. The terms he uses to distinguish between the two types of text are 'readerly' (*lisible*), and 'writerly' (*scriptable*). In later works such as *The Pleasure of the Text* (1979) he went on to investigate the sources of **pleasure** which the text affords to the reader, and distinguished between the 'text of pleasure' which does not challenge the reader's cultural assumptions and is therefore comforting, and the 'text of bliss' where the reader experiences a '*jouissance*' from the unsettling effect elicited from the text's representation of the crisis of language. In addition to offering penetrating analyses of literary texts, Barthes concerned himself with the structural analysis of all cultural representations, including **advertising**, film, photography, music and wrestling.

BEAUTY CONTESTS As beauty contests involve the judging of women according to conventional standards of **femininity**, it is not difficult to see why **feminists** have traditionally condemned such events as contributing to the **objectification** of women. Indeed, it was the 1969 Miss America beauty contest that became the focus of one of the first, and most effective, protests of the **second wave** feminist movement. The idea to perform guerrilla theatre outside the contest hall originated from a 'rap group' in New York. To put across their view that women were being judged like cattle by men, they crowned a sheep 'Miss America' and set up a Freedom Trash Can, in which they disposed of objects symbolic of **oppression**, such as girdles, false eyelashes and brassieres. Although this particular bin was not set on fire, the incident spawned the myth of 'bra-burning' in the press. Although feminism has dented the widespread appeal of beauty contests, they are enjoying something of a renaissance in the current **postfeminist** climate, adopting an aura of ironic mock-seriousness in an attempt to deflect criticism.

BEAUTY MYTH Feminist criticism of externally imposed standards of beauty is nothing new: in *A Vindication of the Rights of Woman*, Mary **Wollstonecraft** attacks the 'feathered birds' that were her female contemporaries. The term 'beauty myth' itself, however, has been developed by the American feminist Naomi **Wolf**, who argues in *The Beauty Myth* (1990) that pressures to conform to impossible aesthetic ideals, pressures perpetuated by **advertising** and the media, are inhibiting modern women in their search for social and political advancement. According to Wolf, obsession with the attainment of 'beauty' and the self-hatred engendered by the inevitable failure to do so cause women to turn on their own bodies through invasive **cosmetic surgery** or **eating disorders**; moreover, the myth creates a climate of competitiveness among women that divides them from each other.

BEAUVOIR, SIMONE DE: PHILOSOPHER (1908–1986)

Simone de Beauvoir was born in Paris, went to a Catholic girl's school and eventually enrolled at the Sorbonne. While preparing for her exams she attended philosophy lectures at the prestigious *École Normale Supérieure*, at that time strictly an all-male institution for the education of the academic elite. In 1929, as the youngest ever candidate of either gender for *l'agrégation* in philosophy, Beauvoir received the second-best result of all candidates. However, despite achieving recognition with men at the highest level of national standing in philosophy, Beauvoir never stressed her distinctiveness as a woman or her achievements as a philosopher. In 1949 she published a classic of **feminist** philosophy, *Le deuxième sexe*. Beauvoir offered a new understanding of social relations between men and women, and introduced the philosophical distinction that **femininity** has been a state of being other to oneself, whereas men have been other than the **Other**. Yet Beauvoir herself repeatedly claimed to be only the philosophical disciple of Jean-Paul Sartre.

Beauvoir's most famous statement is her assertion in *The Second Sex* that 'One is not born, but rather becomes, a woman.' Encapsulating the mid-twentieth-century idea that femininity is a social construction, this assertion became central to subsequent feminist politics and fundamental to much social and political inquiry into the sexual division of labour, women's health, familial relations and popular **culture**. In the same book, Beauvoir also asserts that women assume the status of the Other. The problem is that women have been complicit in accepting their subordinate status. To be the Other is to accept the immanence which culturally women become, but do not have to be. But, ultimately, there remains a fundamental tension in Beauvoir's assertions of women being socially constructed and individually free to change their situation.

BIOLOGICAL DETERMINISM

The view that biological or instinctive drives form the basis of men's and women's relationships and other wider social and cultural processes. The notion that it is natural for men to be breadwinners or that traditional **masculine** behaviour is instinctual, and therefore inevitable, is fiercely contested by **feminists**, who argue that men and women are socialised from birth into accepting these roles and codes of behaviour as natural. Feminists emphasise the ways in which **gendered identities** are constructed through **patriarchal** ideology that privileges men and oppresses women. The view that a female's anatomy is her destiny is at the heart of biological determinism. Thus it is opposed to cultural determinism, and these two form the basis of the **nature**/nurture debate.

BISEXUALITY

In relation to sexual behaviour, bisexuality describes a condition whereby an individual can gain pleasure from both heterosexual and homosexual relationships. It is also, however, an important concept in **French feminist** theory. In *The Newly Born Woman* (1975) Hélène

195

Cixous argues that a **phallocentric** epistemology depends on positioning the feminine as **'Other'**. Bisexuality, which she defines as 'the location within oneself of the presence of both sexes, evident and insistent in different ways according to the individual, the non-exclusion of difference or of a sex', is a way in which dualistic systems of thought can be challenged. Bisexuality is not, however, a simple merging of the genders. It does not deny difference – rather, it is plural, playful and polysemous. Cixous goes on to claim that women are closer to a bisexual subject position than men, who have been trained from birth 'to aim for glorious phallic monosexuality'.

Björk Gudmundsdottir: Musician (1965–) With the advent of punk, Björk began to rebel against her homely image as a childhood star. She has since become a **feminist** icon for her unconventionality of appearance and action, which spurns any identification with a passive, male-pleasing **femininity**. She joined a series of punk bands, including Kukl, with whom she caused outrage by performing on television while seven months pregnant. In 1986, she joined a new band, The Sugarcubes, and gained her first taste of international success. When the band split in 1992 she went solo, and soon became the household name that she is today.

A folk historian on the BBC's *South Bank Show* has identified Björk's singing voice as typical of a traditional Icelandic style that is neither sung nor spoken. The sound she has created is unique, and the success of her two solo albums, *Debut* and *Post*, and her numerous, exuberant hit singles –

'Human Behaviour', 'Violently Happy', 'Big Time Sensuality' and 'It's Oh So Quiet' – has turned this singular, diminutive Icelander into an international star, dubbed the **'Madonna** of the Nineties'.

Bly, Robert: Writer and Poet (1926–) A prolific and successful poet from the mid-fifties onwards, Robert Bly came to widespread prominence in 1990 with the publication of *Iron John*. Bly's portrayal of men as a **gender** in crisis has caused this book to become a founding text of the **'men's movement'**. Although he does not attack feminism directly, Bly's argument implies that men have become emasculated by the increasing dominance of women in society, and thus need to regain a relationship with the 'primal, dark energy' of their 'wild' inner selves. *Iron John* influenced the development of 'Wild Men' workshops, which, in their use of masks, drumming and dancing, encourage men to embrace a warrior-tribe identity. Although Bly is anxious to stress that he is not antagonistic towards the women's movement, his work is treated with suspicion by many **feminists**, who remain unconvinced that the 'wild man' represents anything other than another version of unreconstructed **masculinity**. It is a feeling summed up by Bly's own ex-wife in 1989: 'Separatism breeds feelings of superiority and imbalance – male bonding usually offers permission to regress.'

Bodichon, Barbara Leigh-Smith: Educationalist and Social Campaigner (1827–1891) In 1848 Barbara Leigh-Smith Bodichon received the deeds of Westminster school, the start of a lifetime commitment to education. **Education** was generally seen as the best way to further the women's cause and she campaigned for women to be admitted to university examinations and contributed £1,000 towards the establishment of Girton College. She was part of the executive committee until 1885 and left the college £10,000 in her will. In addition, she was concerned with issues such as marriage contracts, discussed in *A brief summary of the most important laws of England concerning women*. This was the basis of a petition in support of the Married Women's Property Bill (1855). She also wrote on the vote in *Reasons for the enfranchisement of women* (1867) and in *Women and Work* (1857) argued for the economic independence of women. She also funded *The English Woman's Journal* which never fulfilled her radical ambitions for it, but was a successful public platform.

BODYBUILDING From a feminist perspective, female bodybuilding can be regarded as an activity which threatens socially constructed definitions of **masculinity** and **femininity**. The 'built' male body is supra-masculine, and in venturing into his province the muscular woman is profoundly disruptive to conventional **gender** paradigms. Hence the ongoing debate in the **sport** of bodybuilding about how far female bodybuilders should be permitted to go in their quest for muscular size and definition: attempts to regulate this include the introduction of women's 'fitness' competitions, in which participants are expected to conform much more

closely to an acceptable 'feminine' ideal. Bodybuilding magazines have also been criticised for curbing the disruptive potential of the built female body, choosing to represent them as **objectified** objects of male desire rather than as serious athletes.

BOURGEOIS, LOUISE: SCULPTOR AND ARTIST (1911–) Born in Paris, Louise Bourgeois took a degree in mathematics at the Sorbonne before studying art. Although she is now known primarily as a sculptor, producing important installation pieces – such as her *Cell* series (1989–93) – she has also produced a great many drawings in a variety of media. Themes central to her work include the **family**, the body and sexuality, as well as her notion of *toi et moi* ('you and me'), which describes the impulse to form connections with other human beings. Indeed, her work, which explicitly draws on her own experience, often portrays relationships between women, or between women and children. The artist Lucy Lippard has identified Bourgeois as a key figure in the development of an *avant-garde* **feminist** aesthetic, and her work is capable of being read as a form of *écriture féminine* translated into three dimensions.

BRAIDOTTI, ROSI: FEMINIST PHILOSOPHER AND CULTURAL THEORIST (1954–) Braidotti describes herself as a 'subject in transit'; an apt description of someone who was born in Italy, raised in Australia, educated in Paris, and currently living and working in the Netherlands. She has developed a distinctively **postmodern** feminism, which postulates a fluid and complex concept of female **subjectivity**. It is a theory she has developed in *Nomadic Subjects* (1995), which seeks to reconcile a postmodern sense of fragmentation and partiality with concrete political and ethical concerns. An example of such concerns in action is a jointly-authored text, *Women, the Environment and Sustainable Development* (1994), in which Braidotti appeals for cooperation between **feminists** and environmental activists, for while she abhors the **essentialist** notion of a primal bond between women and **nature**, she nevertheless maintains that women are linked with the environment insofar as both constitute groups that are persistently excluded from scientific, male-centred discourse. In essays such as 'Cyberfeminism with a Difference' (1996), Braidotti has also intervened in the **cyberfeminism** debate, arguing that **cyberspace** offers women the opportunity to play with multiple images of the self, and thus develop new roles for themselves in a postmodern order. However, it is more than just a high-tech playground – women's presence in the virtual reality scenario is vital in order to challenge the masculine assumption of technological supremacy. In this way, the move into cyberspace adds another dimension to the nomadicy of the female subject.

BRITTAIN, VERA: WRITER AND POLITICAL CAMPAIGNER (1893–1970) Brittain was born in Newcastle-under-Lyme. She attended The Grange, Buxton, and St Monica's School, Surrey, before winning an Exhibition to Somerville College, Oxford. During the First World War she served as a Voluntary Aid Detachment nurse in Buxton, London, Malta and France. The deaths of her brother, her fiancé, and two of their friends inspired *Testament of Youth* (1933), an **autobiographical** account for which she is best remembered. On her return to Oxford, Brittain befriended the writer Winifred Holtby. They frequently lived and worked together until Holtby's death in 1935. Besides working as a freelance journalist (1921–68), Brittain published twenty-nine books, including her biography of Holtby, *Testament of Friendship* (1940).

Brittain married the historian George Caitlan in 1925 but chose to keep her maiden name. The couple pioneered the 'semi-detached marriage', an arrangement whereby they could live apart when their careers demanded it. They had two children: John Edward in 1927 and Shirley (now the Baroness Williams of Crosby) in 1930. A committed **feminist**, socialist and **pacifist**, Brittain worked for the Six Point Group, the Labour Party, and the League of Nations Union, and was a founder member of the Women's International League for Peace and Freedom.

BROWNMILLER, SUSAN: FEMINIST WRITER Susan Brownmiller remains primarily associated with her 1975 publication, *Against Our Will: Men, Women and Rape*, in which she argues that **rape** is more than just an individual crime, but a tactic in a widespread war against women. The threat of rape thus becomes the means by which men can keep the female **gender** in what **patriarchy**

perceives to be their 'proper' place; in Brownmiller's own words, 'the male **ideology** of rape is a conscious process of intimidation by which *all* men keep *all* women in a state of fear'. **Masculinity** is thus primarily defined by reference to a subjugated group, namely women. Her argument has been quoted approvingly by other **feminist** writers such as Andrea **Dworkin** and Marilyn **French**, who similarly regard patriarchy as waging a concentrated campaign against women in which the use or threat of force is a primary tactic.

BURCHILL, JULIE: JOURNALIST AND NOVELIST (1960–) Julie Burchill was born in Bristol, the only child of two factory workers: her father a keen Stalinist trades-union agitator, her mother (in Burchill's own words) a 'diva'. Burchill ran away to London when she was sixteen in response to a *New Musical Express* advertisement for a 'hip, young gunslinger', and almost immediately became a star of the rock press, writing about punk. She moved from rock journalism via *The Face* into mainstream journalism, writing columns for the *Sunday Times*, the *Mail on Sunday* and the *Sunday Express*. She has also published two blockbuster novels, *Ambition* and *No Exit*, and the television screenplay *Prince*, as well as co-founding the *Modern Review* with the journalist Toby Young.

Burchill's private life has been the cause of much publicity (much of it self-generated), which includes the abandonment of two husbands and two sons, on the second occasion for a girlfriend, Charlotte Raven, assistant on the *Modern Review*. Burchill likes to put herself across as a callous heartbreaker, and in her **auto-biography** *I Knew I Was Right* is at pains to stress just how wicked she is. She was, she declares, 'born bad', and she continues to create **mythic** personas for herself. Burchill enjoys a somewhat antagonistic relationship with feminism, in spite of the fact that she parades her independence and addiction to undermining traditional **feminine** conventions at every turn.

BUTLER, JOSEPHINE: SOCIAL CAMPAIGNER (1828–1906) Josephine Butler was born into a prosperous Northumbrian family and married the Reverend George Butler, who was appointed Principal of Liverpool College in 1866. Josephine herself was a passionate advocate of the higher **education** of women, women's suffrage, Irish home rule and slavery; in addition she helped to found a **feminist** magazine, *The Kettledrum*. However, she is principally remembered for her role as leader of the campaign for the repeal of the Contagious Diseases Act, which allowed women suspected of working as prostitutes in garrison towns to be medically examined with or without their consent. The act was repealed in 1886, but for Butler represented only part of her concern that prostitution was an institution which permitted the male abuse of women. As a devout Christian, and an exemplary Victorian wife and mother, she turned the **language** of morality to devastating effect, arguing 'that a large section of female society has to be told off – set aside, so to speak, to minister to the irregularities of the excusable man' (*Social Purity: An Address*, 1879).

**BUTLER, JUDITH: FEMINIST SOCI-
OLOGIST AND PHILOSOPHER** (1956–)
One of the foremost theorists working within the area of deconstructive
feminism, Butler's work interrogates
unproblematic notions of 'femaleness', arguing that **gender** distinctions
only have meaning within a
phallocentric order built on a system
of binary difference. In texts such as
*Gender Trouble: Feminism and the
Subversion of Identity* (1990), she
uses the term '**compulsory heterosexuality**' to describe the institution
which maintains the coherence of
gender **identity** through reference to
the fixed opposition male/female, in
which each category is defined
through its difference to the other.
Butler goes on to suggest that gender
is more fluid than we tend to assume;
far from being innate, gender constitutes a set of gestures which are
performed upon the surface of the
body. She is thus fascinated by
sexualities which differ from the
heterosexual norm, such as homosexual, lesbian or **bisexual** practices,
since in postulating possibilities other
than the male/female dualism, they
expose its reductive nature. In *Bodies
that Matter: On the Discursive Limits
of 'Sex'* (1993), Butler maintains that
the drag queen performs a similar
function, presenting **femininity** as a
set of codes which can be transcribed
upon any body, male or female. This
line of argument has obvious implications for feminism, for if gender is
as unstable as Butler suggests, can
any appeal to 'woman' as a group
remain a tenable proposition?

C

CAMPBELL, BEATRIX: JOURNALIST (1947–) Campbell's work explores a wide variety of contemporary issues from a **socialist–feminist** perspective. Her publications include *Sweet Freedom: The Struggle for Women's Liberation* (1982), which was written with Anna Coote and revised in 1986; *Wigan Pier Revisited: Poverty and Politics in the 80s* (1984), which was inspired by George Orwell's discussion of the Great Depression; *The Iron Ladies: Why Do Women Vote Tory?* (1987), which is a study of women in party politics; *Unofficial Secrets: Child Sexual Abuse – The Cleveland Case* (1988); *Goliath: Britain's Dangerous Places* (1993), which is a **feminist** analysis of the causes of lawlessness and rioting in *fin de siècle* Britain; and, most recently, *Diana, Princess of Wales: How Sexual Politics Shook the Monarchy* (1998).

CAMPION, JANE: FILM DIRECTOR (1954–) After graduating from the Australian School of Film and Television, this New Zealand director first attracted international attention with her 1989 film *Sweetie*, an acerbic study of two sisters in a wildly dysfunctional family. She followed this in 1990 with the television miniseries *An Angel at My Table*, based on the autobiography of New Zealand author Janet Frame. In 1993 in yet another story about an extraordinary woman, Campion made the award-winning film *The Piano*, starring Holly Hunter as the Victorian mail-order bride who refuses to speak. Campion next adapted Henry James's *The Portrait of a Lady* (1997) which was accompanied by a documentary about the making of the film. She received the Academy Award for Best Original Screenplay in 1993 and was the first woman director to win the Palme d'Or at Cannes. Virginia Wright Wexman has produced a series of interviews with the director, published as *Jane Campion Interviews* (1999).

CAPITALIST PATRIARCHY Radical **feminists** and **Marxist feminists** have long debated on whether **patriarchy** or capitalism is the primary reason for women's oppression. Whereas radical feminists would argue that patriarchal **ideology** exists independently of capitalist structures, and that the undermining of the latter would have little effect on the former, Marxist feminists assert that women's **oppression** is rooted in the **class** system, and that true equality cannot be achieved under capitalism. It is a view summarised by Michele **Barrett**, who in *Women's Oppression Today: Problems in Marxist Feminist Analysis* (1980) states that 'women's oppression is entrenched in the structure of capitalism'. A key figure in the analysis of the relationship between patriarchy and capitalism is the American Marxist **feminist** Heidi Hartmann, who published an influential essay, 'The Unhappy Marriage of Marxism and Feminism: Towards a More Progressive Union' in 1979, in which she argues that patriarchy has its basis in male control of female labour power. This control is asserted through a variety of institutions, including heterosexual, monogamous marriage, childbearing and rearing and **domestic** work. Hartmann calls for a strategy of resistance which is both socialist and feminist, and which will thus 'organize a practice which addresses both the struggle against patriarchy and the struggle against capitalism'.

[See also DUAL SYSTEMS THEORY.]

CARTER, ANGELA: AUTHOR, REVIEWER AND JOURNALIST (1947–1992) The list of Angela Carter's achievements is a long one – she wrote novels, short stories, radio plays, screenplays, and a large amount of criticism and cultural commentary. A staunch **feminist** and socialist throughout her life, all of Carter's writing aimed, one way or another, to challenge convention. Her refusal to conform to any kind of party line, even a feminist one, is demonstrated in her 1979 study of the work of the Marquis de Sade, *The Sadeian Woman*, which many feminists, including Andrea **Dworkin**, have condemned for its apparent support of **pornography**. Carter's fiction, too, can be challenging in its eclectic range of reference, mixing fabulation, sex, and humour with an ongoing concern with social oppression and individual mortality. In the short stories collected in *The Bloody*

Chamber (1979), as well as in many of her novels, Carter turned to the fairy tale as a narrative form open to subversive appropriation. Her final novels, *Nights at the Circus* (1984) and *Wise Children* (1991), are both set in the world of showbusiness, and foreground her fascination with the ways in which women, in particular, can manipulate illusion to their own ends.

CHESLER, PHYLLIS: PSYCHOLOGIST AND WRITER (1940–) In her study of women in American mental institutions, *Women and Madness* (1972), Phyllis Chesler argued that women's madness arises out of the female experience of **oppression**, claiming that 'what we consider "madness" . . . is either the acting out of the devalued female role model or the total or partial rejection of one's sex role **stereotype**'. In other words, **patriarchal** society regards the archetypally **feminine** woman as mad, because it draws an implicit parallel between femaleness and madness; however, those women who reject traditional feminine roles also risk being regarded as deviant. Although she remains most widely known for *Women and Madness*, she has also looked at relationships between men in *About Men* (1978); at the personal experience of pregnancy and birth in *With Child: A Diary of Motherhood* (1979); and on the increasingly problematic legal and social issues surrounding motherhood in *Mothers on Trial: the Battle for Children and Custody* (1986) and *Sacred Bond: the Legacy of Baby M.* (1988). In *Letters to a Young Feminist* (1998), Chesler directly addresses a new generation of young women in order to remind them that 'the legacy my generation of **feminists** has bequeathed to you is one of resistance, not compliance'.

CHICAGO, JUDY: ARTIST AND WRITER

(1939–) Judy Chicago is best-known for her work *The Dinner Party* (1974), an installation piece comprising a triangular table laid with place-settings commemorating important female figures. Chicago's description of it as 'a reinterpretation of the Last Supper from the point of view of those who'd done the cooking through-out history', draws attention to the way in which the piece works to both evoke and ironically undermine the **domestic** role traditionally assigned to women. This exploration of those aspects of women's experience and skills which are not usually con-sidered worthy of public record has continued to motivate Chicago's art. From 1980–85 she worked on 'The Birth Project', which, as its title suggests, consists of a series of images centred on the subject of childbirth. As with 'The Dinner Party', the medium in which the images are created constitutes an ironic gesture towards traditional female forms of expression, in this case needlework. The **collective** nature of the piece was also important, since it was sewn by a group of female seamstresses under Chicago's supervision. Chicago has returned to needlework in her latest project, 'Resolutions: A Stitch in Time', which reinterprets traditional proverbs and aphorisms through the medium of sewing and painting, and which constitutes a similarly collabor-ative project. Chicago is also the author of a number of books, including two **autobiographical** volumes, *Through the Flower: My Struggle as a Woman Artist* (1975) and *Beyond the Flower: The Autobiography of a Feminist Artist* (1996).

CHODOROW, NANCY: SOCIOLOGIST

(1944–) In *The Reproduction of Mothering: Psychoanalysis and the Sociology of Gender* (1978) Chodorow argues that boys and girls do not go through parallel Oedipal processes, but that the female continues to derive a sense of **identity** from the mother. Chodorow rejects the determinism of **Freud**; rather, her emphasis is on men and women's early socialisation in relation to the mother. For Chodorow, psychological processes are developed through our experiences of a **culture** in which women shoulder the major responsibility for childcare. Mothers are the first significant '**other**' for both sexes, but whereas boys are en-couraged to construct a **subjectivity** thorough a process of differentiation from the mother, girls experience a continuing identification with the mother through reference to their shared femaleness. Because girls are perceived by the mother in terms of sameness and extensions of the self, mothers encourage traditional female traits such as nurturance and inter-personal relationships in their daugh-ters and independence in their sons. The effects of this socialisation means a woman's sense of self is less differ-entiated than a man's, who defines himself as more separate and distinct from the world.

Chodorow's theory has been drawn upon to account for the popularity of adult **romance** novels, melodrama and women's **autobiographies**, since they perpetuate this process of identifi-

203

cation with the female. However, she has also been criticised for blaming mothers for **gender** inequalities.

CHORA In Plato's *Timaeus*, *chora* is the unnameable, unstable receptacle existing prior to the nameable form of the One. **Feminist** philosophers have appropriated this Greek term for their discussions of the maternal body. Generally for feminists, chora has come to designate a site of undifferentiated being, connoting the experience of continuity with the maternal body as an infinite space. In particular, Julia **Kristeva** defines chora in psycholinguistic terms: chora specifies the pre-signifying traces that underlie and at times break through the order of signification. Within Kristeva's **semiotic** terms, the shared bodily space of mother and child resists representation, yet is experienced as **desire**, the uncanny or the mystical. The chora as maternal desire threatens to destabilise the finite unity and autonomous **identity** of the modern 'man'.

CHRISTIAN FEMINISM In terms of a modern **feminist** approach, Mary **Daly** was perhaps the most revolutionary feminist critic of Christianity in the 1970s. Daly, a white American, brought up and educated within the Roman Catholic tradition, published *Beyond God the Father: Toward a Philosophy of Women's Liberation* in 1973, denouncing Christianity's 'universe of **sexist** suppositions'. For Daly, the worship of God the Father looked like the projection of a male-centred human **ideology** into the realm of the Eternal. Essentially, Daly accused western **patriarchal**

societies of making God in their own image. At the time, Daly hoped for change and transformation, but subsequently, she abandoned religion as implacably hostile to women. Christian feminism is therefore, in some ways, a slightly contentious term. Daly believes that Christianity and feminism are incompatible but among white western feminists, Rosemary Radford Ruether and Elisabeth Schüssler Fiorenza, for example, both remain convinced that, although Christian scriptures, theology and institutions have been read or constructed from a male perspective in the past, it is not necessary to do this any more. Learning to see these things as resources for social justice or for healing the whole planet, they regard the Christian tradition in a far more positive light, although both advocate radical reconstruction.

In more recent years, feminists from Christian Churches in non-white and **third world** contexts, have made a strong case for reading the tradition from their own distinctive perspectives. Feminists from the **African-American** context (Womanist Theologians such as Jacquelyn Grant), from the Latin-American context (*Mujerista* Theologians such as the Hispanic-American, Ada María Isasi-Díaz) as well as from countries as far apart as Africa (such as the Nigerian, Mercy Amba Oduyoye) and the Far East (such as the Chinese, Kwok Pui-lan and the Korean, Chung Hyun Kyung) are increasingly demanding to speak for themselves and their own communities. Characteristically, they have seen the Christian tradition as essentially emancipatory and life-affirming. For many of these feminists, issues such as Jesus's maleness are less problematic in the light of his perceived solidarity with the poor and marginalised.

CIVIL RIGHTS FEMINISM The rebirth or **second wave** of feminism began in earnest in the 1960s. The name 'civil rights' feminism reflects the historical context within which this movement grew. Beginning with educational campaigns, the **Women's Liberation** movement evolved alongside the anti-**racism** crusade. A major reference for this phase of feminism was Simone de **Beauvoir's** *Second Sex* (1949), which argued that the persistent division of the sexes into biological categories had worked to deny women a history of their own. Women's Liberationists sought to highlight and overcome the **oppression** of women by discovering and creating a history for women. They viewed cultural values and beliefs to be the root of women's oppression. This standpoint later developed into a call for **equal rights,** whereby no **gender** is systematically disadvantaged. Differing responses to de Beauvoir's work split this phase of **feminist** thought into two factions, 'women's liberation' and **radical feminism**. The latter argued that male power, rather than cultural beliefs, was more prominently at the root of women's oppression. Key texts of this period are Betty **Friedan's** *The Feminine Mystique* (1965) and Germaine **Greer's** *The Female Eunuch* (1970). The Women's Liberation Movement later became known as the Women's Movement and is largely associated with the birth of **liberal feminism**.

CIXOUS, HÉLÈNE: WRITER AND PHILOSOPHER (1937–) Hélène Cixous is Professor of Literature at the University of Paris III, Vincennes and director of the Centre d'Études Féminines, a research centre she founded in 1976. The author of many novels, plays, short stories and essays, Cixous believes that woman's **difference** from man is both sexual and linguistic, and her aim is to speak and write about a positive representation of **femininity** in a discourse which she terms *écriture féminine*. The social script, she argues, depends upon gendered binary oppositions which relegates the feminine to the role of **Other**, or the negative, in any hierarchies which society constructs. Cixous argues that if women's writing becomes *écriture féminine*, it can subvert **masculine**, symbolic **language**.

Cixous's exhortation to women to write in such a mode is to the fore in essays such as 'The Laugh of the Medusa' (1975), which employs, like all her work, an erotic, fluid syntax and new images, puns and absences in order to release women's bodies from existing representations. In it she claims that this rhetoric of difference which stems from the female body will create new **identities** for women and, eventually, new social institutions.

In her linking of a female writing practice to the mechanisms of the female body – she draws, for example, an analogy between writing and maternity – Cixous's views can seem **essentialist**. Surprisingly, however, she falls short of identifying herself as a **feminist**. As Cixous portrays it, men as well as women can access a female mode of writing; indeed, she cites the work of Jean Genet as an exemplary instance of *écriture féminine* in action.

CLASS In conventional usage, the term 'class' denotes a homogenous group of people of similar economic and educational level. The system is also hierarchical, in that class groupings are not equal in status or power. A Marxist analysis focuses on the oppressive relations between classes and the **ideologies** through which this inequitable situation is maintained. A **feminist** viewpoint, however, adds another dimension to this debate. **Marxist feminist** discussion centres on whether women can be identified as an oppressed class in themselves, in that they are **subordinated** to men within the institution of the **family**. As Michele **Barrett** maintains, 'an aspect of women's relationship to the class structure is that it is mediated, to some extent at least, by the configuration of the family, dependence on men, and **domestic** labour'. However, to go on to argue that it is possible to cut across conventional class divisions in order to find common areas of experience shared by all women may be rather simplistic, since women's experience must inevitably be shaped by the class position they inhabit. In addition, there is an abundance of other factors, such as **race** and sexual orientation, which also complicates a feminist analysis of class.

CLITORIDECTOMY 'Clitoridectomy' denotes the practice of removing the tip of the clitoris, but has become synonymous with the terms 'female circumcision' and 'female genital mutilation' in describing a range of practices that involve the excision of the female genitalia, thus removing woman's ability to experience sexual **pleasure**. The most radical of these procedures is infibulation, in which the inner and outer lips of the vagina and the clitoris are removed and the wound sealed, leaving only a small exit hole for urine and menstrual blood.

It has been estimated that at least two million women and girls are circumcised every year in at least 26 African countries. From the 1970s onwards clitoridectomy has been attacked by feminists and health and development organisations, who argue that it not only violates women's basic human rights, but also carries serious health risks.

However, although the argument against clitoridectomy seems incontrovertible, **third world feminists** have frequently criticised Western attitudes, arguing that their condemnation carries with it a hidden assumption of superiority. That such an assumption is unwarranted is proved by the fact that clitoridectomy was seriously proposed by American and British doctors in the nineteenth century as a means of treating nervous conditions in women.

COLLECTIVE Term used to describe a group of people working together for mutual support or advantage (and a key feature of socialist societies), the contemporary **feminist** use of the term 'collective' first appeared in the 1970s. Women rejected the hierarchical, authoritarian and undemocratic manner in which male-dominated organisations were usually run. Early collectives included Britain's first **Rape** Crisis Centre (1976), historical research and publishing groups like the Women's History Workshop and the editorial boards of magazines and journals like *Spare Rib* and *Feminist Review*. But many working-**class** women also found their voices and the confidence to engage in a wide range of issues, from health, tenants' and black women's rights to factory sit-ins and inner-city employment projects. Women's groups still exist in the west (aided by the Internet for those with access) but in the **third world** they are particularly active in helping women pursue economic and sexual independence.

COMEDY **Feminist** cultural theorists, often appropriating the work of Mikhail Bakhtin and his notion of carnival, have become more interested in the **gender**-subversive potential of comedy in recent years. The carnivalesque can be imagined as a linguistic, textual and performative sensibility, characterised by **laughter** and excess, which is temporary but persistent and potentially subversive. It has been the women writers and performers of comedy who have perhaps most consistently represented women and **femininity** in ways which exceed conventional boundaries.

Carnival foregrounds the body and its excretive and sexual aspects. Since the eighties, female comics like Sandra Bernhard and stand-up Jenny Eclair (who styles herself the 'rotting old whore of comedy'), have wrenched representations of female sexualities away from images of impossible, untouchable beauty and passivity. Carnival's emphasis on the **grotesque** body is also apparent in the female comic body, exemplified by the defiant fatness of Roseanne or Jo Brand who, with other stand-up comediennes, also loudly exceed the boundaries of 'ladylike' speech.

For Bakhtin, the essential subversive component of carnival is the collective laughter of its participants, and an emphasis on **sisterhood** is also a strong component of female-centred comedy, which predominantly features pairs and collectives of sisters, best friends and workmates, such as the relationship between Edina and Patsy in *Absolutely Fabulous*, or Roseanne and Jacky in *Roseanne*.

For women, becoming the teller of the joke is risky in its invocation of laughter. However, female laughter – especially when collective – is empowering for women as self-affirmation, whilst always potentially threatening to the **patriarchal** order.

COMPULSORY HETEROSEXUALITY The term 'compulsory heterosexuality' describes a system whereby women's sexual orientation towards men is considered to be innate, rather than a preference selected from among a range of different options. In her widely-read essay 'Compulsory Heterosexuality and Lesbian Existence' (1980), Adrienne **Rich** argues that heterosexuality has been forced on women by a **patriarchal** system that seeks to convince them 'that marriage and sexual orientation towards men is inevitable'; a view perpetuated by 'the **ideology** of heterosexual **romance**'. This ensures not only that lesbian sexuality is rendered deviant, but also precludes the development of relationships between women on every level.

CONSCIOUSNESS-RAISING Consciousness-raising (or CR) was a primary tactic of **second wave** feminism, which regarded it as a way of developing a shared consciousness of **oppression** among women. Consciousness-raising groups were founded on the credo that 'the personal is political', encouraging participants to share their personal life experiences, such as childhood, motherhood and marriage. The belief was that, far from each story being individual, common patterns would emerge, thus demonstrating that female experience, rather than being exclusive to the individual, was in fact rooted in a wider system of sex inequality. Consciousness-raising groups did not aim for total introspection, but advocated moving on from personal narratives to evolving strategies to deal with oppression. That this did not always happen is demonstrated in an essay by Carol Williams Payne, 'Consciousness Raising: A Dead End?' (1971), in which she describes feeling a sense of 'stagnation' within 'a small group which just talks and does not relate to the rest of the movement'.

CONTRACEPTION Now the most familiar aspect of **reproductive technology**, contraception signifies the prevention of unwanted pregnancy by a range of methods, including *coitus interruptus*, oral contraception ('the Pill'), the IUD (coil), the condom, sterilisation, the 'morning-after' pill and vasectomy. **Abortion** has also been described as a working-**class** woman's means of contraception. The diaphragm (1882) was the first reliable form of birth control used by women themselves and the first means of separating sex from procreation. In the twentieth century emphasis has been placed on contraception as a form of controlling population growth (**family** planning), rather than as a means of liberating women. However, responsibility for contraception has continuously been placed on women, with an accompanying increase in medical intervention, often by unsympathetic male doctors. Birth control clinics started in the 1920s; free contraception in 1974. **Feminists** welcome the degree of control over fertility now possible, especially since the invention of the Pill, but also criticise the responsibility and medical risks involved. With its total ban on any form of contraception apart from the rhythm method, the influence of the Catholic Church, particularly in the developing world, is deplored by feminists. Many other religions, reactionary political systems, poverty and lack of **education** also deny effective birth control to a majority of the world's women.

CORNELL, DRUCILLA: PHILOSOPHER Drucilla Cornell is Professor of Law, Political Science and Women's Studies at Rutgers University. **Radical feminism** and 'Leftist' politics inspired Cornell's books in feminist philosophy, including *Beyond Accommodation: Ethical Feminism, Deconstruction and the Law* (1991), *The Imaginary Domain: Abortion, Pornography and Sexual Harassment* (1995), and *At the Heart of Freedom: Feminism, Sex and Equality* (1998). Intending to be a poet and translator of revolutionary Polish women's poetry, Cornell did not train as a philosopher. Yet poetic and philosophical acumen inform her work on 'the imaginary domain' as a new way of thinking about freedom of sexuality. The imaginary domain is a philosophical concept for the conditions, or the starting place, necessary to articulate the equivalent evaluation of each of us as a sexuate being. 'Sexuate' avoids the loaded meanings of 'sex' and **'gender'**, and 'represent[s] the sexed body of our human being when engaged with a framework by which we orientate ourselves . . . sexually'. Ultimately Cornell returns feminism to some of the earliest aspirations of its **'second wave'**.

COSMETIC SURGERY Cosmetic surgery is becoming an ever more hotly-debated subject within feminism. The issue is many-faceted: firstly, it can be regarded as a practice which persuades women to reconfigure their face and body to fit a male-created perception of beauty; secondly, it persuades them to submit to invasive surgical procedures which are medically unnecessary and which often carry unacknowledged risks; and thirdly, they do so to the often considerable monetary profit of others. In *The Beauty Myth* (1990) Naomi Wolf argues that the business of cosmetic surgery depends on engendering a sense of ugliness in women who do not conform to an aesthetic norm, and then configuring such 'ugliness' as a disease which can be 'cured'. However, other feminists do not immediately equate the quest for beauty with **oppression**. In *Unbearable Weight: Feminism, Western Culture and the Body* (1993), for example,

Susan Bordo reads the surgically-constructed body as one example of a range of practices which constitute an attempt to gain control within a system which denies the female a sense of self-mastery.

CROSS-DRESSING The term 'cross-dressing' is descriptive of a range of behaviour which involves adopting the uniform of the opposite sex: although their motivations may differ widely, drag queens, female impersonators, **transsexuals**, transvestites and butch lesbians are all cross-dressers. Judith **Butler** argues that the practice of cross-dressing serves to draw attention to the essential performativity of all **gender** identity: arguing of drag, for example, that it 'implicitly reveals the imitative structure of gender itself – as well as its contingency' (*Gender Trouble*, 1990)). In *Vested Interests: Cross-Dressing and Cultural Anxiety* (1993), Marjorie Garber similarly reads it as an act which foregrounds the way in which all individuals are constructed within cultural paradigms. However, **feminists** such as bell **hooks** – and even Butler herself in later publications – maintain that male appropriation of female dress is innately misogynistic, in that what they choose to reproduce is an utterly conventional **feminine** appearance.

Nevertheless, from the disguised heroines in Shakespearean comedies to the elegant **androgyny** of the singer k.d. **lang**, cross-dressing retains a persistent presence within **culture**. It is probably the folkloric forms of cross-dressing, such as the pantomime dame of British tradition, which serve to remind us of cross-dressing's association with the carnivalesque, a state in which traditional hierarchies, including those constructed on gender, are rendered topsy-turvy in a violation of established order. Whether such play helps to liberate women in general from the confines of a rigidly feminine aesthetic, however, remains open to question.

CULTURAL STUDIES In direct relation to the increased importance of cultural practices and institutions in every area of society, 'cultural studies' has emerged in recent years as higher **education**'s most upwardly mobile discipline. The growth of the mass media, new global information systems and flows, and new visual forms of communication continue to have a profound impact on the ways our lives are organised and on the ways in which we comprehend and relate to one another and to ourselves.

Within the explanatory hierarchy of the social sciences in general and sociology in particular, **culture** has traditionally been allotted a rather inferior role. In contrast to economic and political processes, for example, which were routinely assumed to alter material conditions in the 'real' world, cultural processes were deemed ephemeral and superficial. Because cultural processes dealt with seemingly less tangible things – signs, images, **language**, beliefs – they were often assumed, particularly by Marxist theorists, to be unlikely to provide social sciences with valid 'real' knowledge.

However, theorists have begun to argue that, because social practices are meaningful practices, they are all fundamentally cultural, since in order to conduct a social practice we need to be able to think meaningfully about it. The production of social meanings is therefore a necessary precondition for the functioning of all social practices, and an account of the cultural conditions of social practices must form part of the sociological explanation of how they work. **Feminist** cultural theory is motivated by the desire to identify, and thus deconstruct, patriarchal practices and customs encoded in a range of cultural productions.

CULTURE One of the major arguments in **feminist** cultural criticism is that woman is traditionally positioned as the '**Other**', or object of man's attention, in mainstream culture. This has the effect of positioning her outside culture, which is gendered male. One feminist response to this may be to go along with Shulamith **Firestone**'s assertion in *The Dialectic of Sex* (1970) that women should be 'proud of the female culture of emotion, intuition, love, personal relationships, etc.', redressing the inequality in the male=culture/female=nature dualism by focusing on the recovery or development of a uniquely female culture in which all women can participate. This involves redefining traditional aesthetic categories by creating a new aesthetics which recovers women's 'invisible' arts, such as quilting or cooking. A crucial contribution to feminist criticism, for example, is the evocation of maternal cultures by **African-American** women, such as Alice **Walker**'s loving description of her mother's gardening skills in *In Search of Our Mother's Gardens* (1983).

210

In opposition to this project it could be argued that it merely reinforces women's extra-cultural status in creating a cosy **utopian** space which avoids them having to confront their experience of subordination within mainstream culture. Moreover, it preserves a notion of 'woman' as a homogenous category, paying little attention to the variety of their experiences. Feminist anthropologists and black feminists are two groups which have argued strongly in support of theories which stress the relativity of female positioning/s within cultural constructs.

CYBERFEMINISM Cyberfeminism has been defined by the British feminist technotheorist Sadie **Plant** as 'an insurrection on the part of the goods and materials of the **patriarchal** emergence composed of links between women, women and computers, computers and communications links, connections and connectionist machines'. It is a comment which indicates the **utopianism** which lies at the heart of cyberfeminism, which argues that **technology** is not inimical to women, and that women should seize control of new information systems. Indeed, Plant argues that information technology has always formed alliances with women. In *Zeros and Ones* (1997), she traces a hidden history of female involvement with the development of computers and their software, from Ada **Lovelace** to Captain Grace Murray Hopper, who was the chief programmer of the computer Mark 1, developed by the United States during the Second World War. Other feminists, such as Rosi **Braidotti**, adopt a slightly differ-

ent position. While she does not argue for quite the same traditional involvement with information technology as Plant, in 'Cyberfeminism with a Difference' Braidotti nevertheless claims that female intervention in the development of **cyberspace** technology is now a necessity, 'if only to make sure that the joy-stick of cyberspace cowboys will not reproduce univocal phallicity under the mask of multiplicity'. The cyberfeminist project, however, is not a unified one, ranging from the trendy and individualistic 'webgrrls' or 'cybergrrrls' to the high **postmodernist** theory of academics like Donna **Haraway**. Currently, cyberfeminism has many issues to contend with, not least the necessity to balance a coherent political agenda with its visions of a **feminist** cyberspace utopia. The multiplicity of feminist resources and communication networks on the web already testify that there is a female presence in cyberspace, although it is yet to be seen whether this will lead to fruitful coalitions and workable strategies in the world outside the computer screen.

CYBERPUNK 'Cyberpunk' is a term pieced together from 'cyber' (relating to electronic communication networks and virtual reality) and 'punk' (an antisocial rebel or hoodlum), and was originally applied to a school of 'hard' **science fiction** in which interactions between the organic and the technological are foregrounded. In any discussion of feminism and cyberpunk, however, there is a crucial difference to be drawn, between women as *characters*, and women as *producers*. Female characters are an integral, but contradictory, part of cyberpunk fiction, beginning with the cyber-mercenary Molly Millions in the first cyberpunk novel, William Gibson's *Neuromancer* (1984). Strong and ruthless, violent and independent, Molly can be seen as a positive female role model, but she is also a fantasy-figure designed to appeal to an implicitly male audience. However, female cyberpunk writers have colonised the genre in recent years, with authors like Gwyneth Jones, Pat Cadigan and Melissa Scott using cyberpunk conventions as way of interrogating the roles assigned to women within a **technological** society.

CYBERSPACE The term 'cyberspace' was first used by William Gibson in his 1994 novel *Neuromancer*. In Gibson's fiction, cyberspace is 'a consensual hallucination' created within the dense matrix of computer networks. Gibson imagines a world in which people can directly 'jack' their nervous systems into this network, vastly increasing the intimacy of connection between mind and electronic matrix.

It has been argued that, in the work of Gibson and others, cyberspace is explicitly configured as *feminine* space; the fantasy world that lies beyond the hardware of the **technology** out of which it is born – a notion which has very different implications depending on the sex of the person (or 'hacker') who enters it. If male, his incursion into cyberspace can be seen as an act of *colonisation*:

but if female, it becomes an act of *appropriation*. This is borne out in the work of many **feminist** cyberpunk writers, such as Marge Piercy (*Body of Glass* (1992)) and Melissa Scott (*Trouble and Her Friends* (1994)), both of whom describe cyberspace as democratic and communal. It is also a place in which the troubling markers of **gender** difference can be transcended, since cyberspace renders the organic body superfluous.

CYBORG As Donna **Haraway** has written in her 'Cyborg Manifesto' (1985), we live in a cyborg world of electronic communications, in which the difference between artificial and natural remains ambiguous: 'our machines . . . disturbingly lively and we ourselves frighteningly inert'. The term is thus indicative of transgressed boundaries, and an interrogation of the assumption of a unified subjectivity.

The term 'cyborg' is a conflation of 'cybernetic organism', and was coined in 1960 by the research space scientist Manfred Clynes. However, cyborgs appeared in **science fiction** stories decades earlier. A 'cyborg' can be anything from a human with a prosthesis to a robot with a thin veneer of skin (as in the *Terminator* films), and according to Donna Haraway, we are all cyborgs to some degree. Thus she postulates a cyborg ontology which takes as its premise the dissolution of traditional boundaries associated with the body.

D

DALY, MARY: RADICAL FEMINIST PHILOSOPHER AND THEOLOGIAN (1928–) Mary Daly's first important work was *Beyond God the Father* (1973), in which she argues that the principal function of God in all religions is to act as a legitimating paradigm for the institution of **patriarchy**. Formed in God's image, only man can lay claim to personhood, in contrast to which woman is conceptualised as *im*personal object, or 'It': a process which Daly terms 'power-over'. In her role as man's inferior **'Other'**, woman can therefore be aligned with negative acts and emotions. **Feminists** must replace the patriarchal concept of a transcendent God with the notion of God as immanence, an act which will detach personhood from **gender**.

Daly develops these arguments further in her most influential book, *Gyn/Ecology* (1978), in which she rejects the term 'God' altogether. She also moves towards a far more **essentialist** position, in that she now urges women to throw off socially constructed notions of **femininity** in order to discover the 'wild woman' within. Arguing that reality is constructed through **language**, she advocates its radical deconstruction, echoed in the idiosyncratic neologisms and linguistic puns she employs throughout the book. Daly's ongoing concern with language has resulted in a feminist dictionary, *Webster's First New Intergalactic Wickedary of the English Language* (1987), and she has also written an **autobiographical** text, *Outercourse* (1993).

DANCE The contradictory urges of the passing-on of specific repertoires, the continued refinements of athleticism, body-image and technique, and the moves against the limited mechanistic virtuosity of privileged techniques such as ballet have produced many forms of dance over the last century. Expressionistic and analytical approaches to choreographic and dance innovation have spawned a variety of hybrid forms of modern and postmodern dance, including the affirmation and appropriation of a range of international and popular conventions. The use of functional and cross-art performance concerns has also influenced the formal and representational considerations of dance. In *Terpsichore in Sneakers* (1987) Sally Banes has indicated some of the many forms and shifts in American and European dance over the last seventy years, including a movement away from conventional **gender** roles, a concern for the dynamics of the body in motion, and the development of a choreography of 'naturalised' and gestural activities. The expressionistic works of Mary Wigman in Germany and Martha

213

Graham in America have influenced generations of dancers as diverse as Pina Bausch and Meredith Monk. The American dancers of the Judson Church, such as Yvonne Rainer, Trisha Brown and Steve Paxton, have also influenced New Dance in Britain and Europe in interrogating the possibilities of pedestrian activity, improvised walking and falling, contact improvisation and the assimilation of non-western movement repertoires – such as Shobana Jeyasingh's combination of Indian gestural choreography and minimal orchestration. Anne Teresa De Keersmaker, Wim Vandekeybus, DV8 and The Cholmondeleys have produced choreographies that have assimilated the anti-mechanistic approach of contact improvisation with the athleticism of other modern dance techniques, coupled with the interrogation of sexed and gendered roles. This combination, also reminiscent of the expressionistic ensembles of Bausch's dance theatre, produces a propensity for 'thrash' dance, which returns to the rigours and idealism related to ballet and the body-image. Whereas dancers associated with the Judson Church questioned the very premises on which dance and dancers ascribe value, the return to theatricality and narrative dance has more forcefully addressed the question of the body as sign.

DAVIS, ANGELA Y.: ACTIVIST AND ACADEMIC (1944–) Brought up in segregated Alabama, Davis went to graduate school in California and became the foremost black woman **activist** of the 1960s. She was wrongly implicated in an escape from a California courthouse and was on the FBI's 'most wanted' list for murder, kidnapping and conspiracy. After two months on the run, vividly described in her **autobiography** published in 1974 when she was only 29, she was arrested and spent sixteen months in jail before successfully co-defending herself in one of the most famous trials in American history. She was acquitted of all charges in 1972. Among her books, *If They Come in the Morning* (1971) analyses racial oppression, while *Women, Race and Class* (1981) is a classic of black **Marxist feminism** that argues that **sexism** and **racism** can only be eradicated through the destruction of the economic system that produced them: capitalism.

DELPHY, CHRISTINE: MARXIST– FEMINIST SOCIOLOGIST (1941–) Christine Delphy is a materialist **feminist** who has criticised the abstract intellectualism of fellow French feminists such as Julia **Kristeva** and Hélène **Cixous**. She is not so much concerned with biological **difference** as with the ways in which the concept of **femininity** arises from actual social conditions, and argues that women as a **gender** constitute a separate **class**, since they are exploited by men within the **domestic** sphere. Delphy's thesis in books such as *The Main Enemy: A Materialist Analysis of Women's Oppression* (1977) and *Close to Home: A Materialist Analysis of Women's Oppression* (1984) is that women's work within the home services the male head of the household, who straightforwardly appropriates it rather than entering into a process of exchange. Women's exclusion from this process comes about because housework, lacking both a fixed salary and negotiated hours, is not a regulated form of labour.

DENFELD, RENE: WRITER (1967–) Along with Naomi **Wolf** and Katie **Roiphe**, Rene Denfeld is associated with a popular brand of **post-feminism**, which is concerned that **second wave feminism** has ceased to appeal to a younger generation of women. Denfeld's name became known following the publication of *The New Victorians: A Young Woman's Challenge to the Old Feminist Order* (1995), a provocative text which combines interviews with a range of young women with Denfeld's own polemic in order to argue that second wave feminism has retreated into the academy, loony new-age practices and sexual puritanism, and has thus ceased to be relevant in the modern world. It is important to note that Denfeld does not reject feminism altogether; rather, she argues that its crime is that it has failed to appreciate all it has gained, and that, in order to advance its cause further, it must modify both its practices and the ideology that underpins them. Denfeld's latest book, *Kill the Body, The Head Will Fall: A Closer Look at Women, Violence and Aggression* (1997), has grown out of her own interest in amateur boxing. It is as consciously contentious as her previous publication in its argument that women can be just as physically violent as men, and that the destructive power of female anger must not be taken lightly.

DERRIDA, JACQUES: PHILOSOPHER (1930–) Operating from a position within structuralism, Derrida is the originator of a mode of reading known as 'deconstruction', a form of analysis applicable to all forms of writing. Traditionally, meaning in **language** is assumed to be anchored to an organising principle, a centre, but Derrida questions this concept and rejects the idea of a 'presence' in which ultimate authority resides and through which meaning is fixed. In works such as *Of Grammatology* (1976) and *Writing and Difference* (1978), Derrida follows Ferdinand de Saussure in focusing on the arbitrariness of meaning in texts: he uses the term *différance* – a pun on two French words *différence* (difference) and *différance* (deferral) – to describe the process whereby meaning is rendered permanently indeterminate, leaving language to refer only to itself.

Derrida's ideas are of value to **feminists** because his denial of ultimate meaning opens up discursive spaces from which conventional patterns of thought can be dismantled. In particular, he challenges a system of binary opposition which situates the male as legitimating principle and the standard against which truth and value are measured: a process he labels '**phallogocentric**'. Derridian concepts have influenced the work of many feminist theorists, including Luce **Irigaray** and Gayatri **Spivak**.

DESIRE The concept of 'desire' derives originally from **Freud**'s notions of the castration complex and **penis envy**, in which females are described as experiencing 'guilt' originating from their recognition that they lack a penis, and the repression of their desire to possess one. This conception of female **subjectivity** represents women as incomplete men, and has been vigorously criticised. It does, however, highlight the notion of *lack*, in which women, upon entry into the **symbolic order**, are forced to identify with that which is absent (the penis), rather than that which is present (the vagina). While males can eventually become representatives of the Name of the Father, females can only fantasise over the missing phallus. Woman is therefore constructed as 'other', and it is this lack which occasions female desire. Alternatively, she must identify herself as an object of male desire, an act which involves **objectification** of, and thus alienation from, her self. This psychoanalytic concept of desire is central to **French feminism**, in which it is reworked in order to yield positive connotations for women.

DIANA, PRINCESS OF WALES: ARISTO-CRAT (1961–1997) Princess Diana's death in a car crash in August 1997 only confirmed her already-existing status as an icon of modern **culture**. Like all icons, her image can be read any number of different ways – fairy-tale princess, tragic heroine, mother, spurned wife, sex symbol and humanitarian saint. But can she also be appropriated for feminism? Biographies such as Andrew Morton's *Diana: A True Story* certainly encouraged women to identify with many aspects of Diana's life: her problematic marriage, her love for her children, her battle with **eating disorders** and her struggle to find an independent image following her divorce. In her essay 'Diana the Huntress', published in the *New Republic* in 1992, Camille **Paglia** argues that she reclaimed a glamorous image for feminism, and in *Diana* (1998), Julie **Burchill** also sees Diana's story as one of empowerment. Yet as a **feminist** icon she remains problematic, for the narrative of her life also associates her with emotional instability and the quest for romantic love, attributes of the traditionally '**feminine**' woman which are the targets of feminist critique.

DIFFÉRANCE Capable of being translated as both 'difference' and 'deferral', *différance* is a term proposed by Jacques **Derrida**, who argues that all systems of thought are built upon a binary pattern which places concepts in opposition, then privileges one over the other, thus producing meaning. *Différance*, however, resists the either/or logic of this system, refusing unity and closure and asserting the ultimate provisionality of meaning. As that which cannot be fully assimilated in order to make an unproblematic whole, *différance* is thus marked by excess. The term is a significant one in feminist theory, particularly **French feminist** theory. Hélène **Cixous**, for example, relates it to her notion of *écriture féminine*, or feminine writing, which similarly attempts to undermine the binary logic upon which the discourse of the **symbolic order** depends.

DIFFERENCE Central to the feminist critique of binary thought is the issue of 'difference'. Most theoretical discussions of difference are indebted to the work on **language** and its signifying processes by Ferdinand de Saussure, Jacques **Derrida**, Jacques **Lacan** and others, who postulate that meaning can be created only by differences and sustained only through reference to other meaning/s. **Postmodernism** tends to assert the plurality of the 'different', thus rejecting the binary opposition of the '**other**'.

Postmodernism's move to rethink margins and borders works to disrupt the notion of centralisation, with its associated concerns of origin and homogenous identity. From a decentred perspective, the 'ex-centric' – whether in terms of class, race, **gender**, sexual orientation or ethnicity – takes on new significance as a result of the implied recognition that our **culture** is not really the homogenous monolith of popular conception. In striving to challenge their position as marginal to the dominant **androcentric** culture, many feminists clearly share with postmodernism an assertion of **difference** rather than binary opposition and exclusion. **Feminist** theory offers perhaps the clearest example of the importance of an awareness of the diversity of history and culture of women, of their overlapping differences in terms of race, ethnic grouping, **class** and sexual preference. However, difference must always remain a contested site if it is not to become fixed into another inflexible discursive construct.

DINNERSTEIN, DOROTHY: PSYCHO-ANALYST (1923–1992) Like Jacques **Lacan** and Julia **Kristeva**, Dorothy Dinnerstein argues that our concepts of **gender** difference are constructed during the pre-Oedipal stage of psychosexual development, the period in which the infant retains a symbiotic attachment to the mother. Her work has therefore been particularly important in the development of **feminist** critiques of motherhood. In *The Mermaid and the Minotaur: Sexual Arrangements and Human Malaise* (1976), she identifies women with 'mermaids' and men with 'minotaurs', each possessing a particular set of gender-linked characteristics which determine their relationship to each other. 'The treacherous mermaid, seductive and impenetrable female representative of the dark and magic underwater world from which our life comes and in which we cannot live, lures voyagers to their doom. The fearsome minotaur, gigantic and eternally mindless, greedy power, insatiably devours live human flesh.' The origins of this disturbing situation, says Dinnerstein, lie in the infant's original view of the mother as someone who has the power to either grant or withhold the satisfaction of the child's need. Men compensate for this period when they were totally under their mother's control by seeking to dominate women, while women desire to be dominated because they have no more desire to re-empower the female figure of the mother than men do. Dinnerstein postulates dual parenting as the only solution to this situation, a conclusion she reiterates in *The Rocking of the Cradle and the Ruling of the World* (1987).

DISCOURSE A term used in critical theory, especially in the writings of Michel **Foucault**, 'discourse' is the name given to the systems of linguistic representations through which power sustains itself. Foucault argues that within individual discourses a series of mechanisms are used as means of controlling **desire** and power, which facilitate classification, ordering and distribution. In this way, a mastery is exerted over what appears to be the randomness of everyday reality. It is thus possible to investigate those discourses which have been used to master reality in the past: e.g., discourses concerned with questions of sexuality, systems of punishment or madness. Foucault perceives the cultural system to be constituted through various discourses to which not all people have equal access, some being able to control this accessibility to others through the exercise of power: a phenomenon of which most disadvantaged groups, at least, are painfully aware. From a **feminist** point of view, the dominant discourse is **patriarchal**, and feminism is crucially concerned with understanding the mechanisms by which discourses are produced, challenging women's subordinate position within it, and formulating alternative discourses within which new meanings can be constructed.

DISCRIMINATION Attitude, behaviour or treatment based on prejudice. Recognition of and opposition to discrimination based on **gender** are key elements of **feminist** theory, although there is disagreement over origins and causes. Campaigners eventually succeeded in arguing that legislation was the only effective strategy and sex discrimination was made illegal in the US in 1964 (Civil Rights Act). The UK Sex Discrimination Act was passed in 1975; the Equal Opportunities Commission was established at the same time. However, significant differentials in pay and workplace conditions still obtain in both societies, as recent statistics quoted by Natasha **Walter** in *The New Feminism* (1998) have shown, and discrimination is still found in every area of life, much of it now covert rather than overt. Some Scandinavian countries have gone further than most in attempting to ensure equality in work and family life, but in many other parts of Europe and beyond discrimination is still inscribed in the **culture**.

DOMESTICITY Pertaining to home life: applied particularly to women's relationship with home and **family**. In England, women's increasing restriction to the domestic sphere stemmed in part from rapid political, economic, demographic and social change accompanying early capitalist development in the 1600s; it was challenged by writers like Aphra Behn and Mary Astell. For the latter, **marriage** represented 'domestic slavery' and later **feminists** took up the theme. From the 1800s, formidable legal, moral and social structures, reinforced by countless images and texts, reified the private, not the public, sphere as the 'natural' milieu for all **classes** of women. Ethnology, anthropology and **patriarchy** conspired to maintain this situation through the 20th century; the role of 'housewife' involved dependency, unpaid work and low status, but the alternative was usually seen as worse. Two World Wars gave many European and American women their first opportunity to experience life outside the home, but attempts to place them back there were largely successful. From de **Beauvoir** on-wards the politics of 'domestic' work, both inside and outside the home, was vigorously debated (see **Oakley** *et al.*). Notwithstanding some changes for the better and the appearance of the 'New Housewife', millions of women worldwide are still trapped by the 'female equals domestic' equation.

DOUBLE STANDARDS Hypocrisy in action: rules which are applied more strictly to some persons than to others or a set of ethical principles by which something seen as unacceptable in one person is condoned or approved in another. Frequently used with reference to sexual behaviour or morality – the **Seneca Falls** Declaration condemned the existence of 'a different code for men and women, by which moral delinquencies which exclude women from society are not only tolerated, but deemed of little account in man'. **Women's magazines** like *Cosmopolitan* have also been accused of double standards, in promoting the idea of the independent woman while simultaneously stressing the importance of sexual attraction and availability. It is also present in the rewarding of equal work with unequal pay and conditions and in society's expectations of women's unpaid work within the **family** and community. Margrit Eichler has made a critical study of the topic entitled *The Double Standard* (1980).

DOUGLAS, MARY: SOCIAL ANTHRO-POLOGIST (1921–) Mary Tew, later Douglas, was born in Italy, but educated at Oxford University. Her early fieldwork focused on the Lele of the Belgian Congo in Zaire (1949–50,

and 1953). She has held the posts of Professor of Social Anthropology at University College, London, and Avalon Professor of the Humanities at Northwestern University.

Her publications include *Purity and Danger* (1966), a study of the beliefs surrounding cultural purity and pollution; *Natural Symbols* (1973), a study of cultural classification systems; *The World of Goods* (1980), a study of economic anthropology; and *Cultural Bias* (1978) and *Risk and Culture* (1982), two studies of moral account-ability. Douglas's *Purity and Danger* influenced the theory of **abjection** advanced by Julia **Kristeva** in *Powers of Horror* (1980).

DUAL SYSTEMS THEORY Dual systems theorists regard **patriarchy** and capitalism as distinct entities, each with their own agenda and sphere of social relations. An analysis of women's **oppression** must take account of this, analysing capitalism and patriarchy separately *before* examining the points at which they intersect. However, dual systems theorists differ in their view of patriarchy. While theorists like Heidi Hartmann regard it as materialist, rooted exploitative reproductive or domestic practices, others, such as Juliet **Mitchell**, approach it as an **ideology** which transcends the material sphere. Dual systems theorists are opposed by unified systems theorists, who attempt to analyse patriarchy and capitalism together: for example, Alison Jaggar in *Feminist Politics and Human Nature* (1983) argues that the concept of alienation is a category broad enough to encompass both phenomena.

DWORKIN, ANDREA: ANTI-PORNOGRAPHY ACTIVIST AND WRITER
(1946–) Andrea Dworkin is one of the most widely recognised personalities of **radical feminism**. Those who are suspicious of feminism see in her all their fears confirmed, as her public image is strident, confrontational and distinctly 'unfeminine'. Dworkin is primarily known for her ongoing struggle against **pornography**: in the mid-1980s she joined forces with the lawyer Catherine **MacKinnon** in drafting the MacKinnon-Dworkin Anti-Pornography Ordinance, which attempted to categorise pornography as a violation against women's civil rights.

Dworkin sets out her views in *Pornography: Men Possessing Women* (1981), in which she emphatically refuses to draw any kind of line between erotica and pornography, since both engage in 'the graphic depiction of women as whores'. It is such depictions, Dworkin argues, which maintain male power over women in all situations, sexual or otherwise.

Dworkin has become a particular target for **postfeminists**, who argue that her fight against pornography helps to perpetuate a negative image of women as the passive victims of men: they also voice unease about the way in which her campaign feeds into the interests of right-wing religious conservatism. Dworkin's fiction, such as *Mercy* (1990), has also been condemned for its inclusion of graphic and often violent sex scenes, which detractors argue reveal her unhealthy fascination with the very material she is attempting to ban.

E

EATING DISORDERS A term that refers to a range of dysfunctional attitudes towards food, from anorexia nervosa (self-starvation) to bulimia (binge eating followed by purging). Anorexia was first identified as a clinical disorder in 1873, when it was observed to be an illness which affected mainly middle-**class** girls between the ages of fifteen and twenty. Doctors at the time interpreted it as a manifestation of **hysteria**, but feminists have attacked this concept of the disease. In *Fasting Girls: The Emergence of Anorexia Nervosa as a Modern Disease* (1988), Joan Jacobs Brumberg estimates that up to one female student in five in American universities is anorexic, and that this is 'an inevitable consequence of a misogynistic society that demeans women . . . by **objectifying** their bodies'. Naomi **Wolf** reiterates Brumberg's figures in *The Beauty Myth* (1990), in which she points out that eating disorders are merely an extreme and life-threatening version of a practice which nearly all western women engage in – dieting. Wolf observes that the vast majority of women in western countries, anorexic or not, are pathologically obsessed with keeping their weight low in an attempt to conform to the cultural demand for **feminine** slenderness.

Other **feminists** are, however, sceptical of this conclusion. In *Who Stole Feminism? How Women Have Betrayed Women* (1994), Christina Hoff Sommers attacks Brumberg's statistics and all arguments based upon them. She not only argues that Brumberg's estimates are incorrect, but also that they have been used in support of a feminist **myth** which paints an exaggerated picture of women as the hapless victims of a **patriarchal** society.

ECOFEMINISM Just as there is not one feminism, there is not one ecofeminism – a term coined by Françoise d'Eubonne in *Le Féminisme ou la mort* (1974). Ecological feminism is the name given to a variety of positions that have roots in various feminist practices and philosophies which reflect different understandings of the nature and solution to pressing environmental problems. What one takes to be a *bona fide* ecofeminist position, then, will depend largely on how one conceptualises feminism.

Nevertheless, all ecofeminists agree that important connections exist between the domination of women and the domination of **nature**, an understanding of which is crucial to feminism, environmentalism and environmental philosophy. The *raison d'être* of ecofeminism is to make visible the existence and methods of the twin dominations of women and nature and, where necessary, to pro-vide corrective analyses and practices. Many ecofeminists claim that this process must include a discussion of **technology**, arguing that consider-ations of science, development and technology are so central to the ecofeminist debate that one might visualise ecofeminism as emerging from the intersection of feminism, science/technology and environmen-tal concerns.

ÉCRITURE FÉMININE A term usually reserved for a particular kind of critical writing by women, emanating from the feminism of contemporary French critics, such as Luce **Irigaray**, Hélène **Cixous** and Julia **Kristeva**. What unites this form of **feminist** criticism is the belief that there is an area of textual production that can be called 'feminine', that it exists beneath the surface of masculine **dis-course**, and only occasionally comes to the fore in the form of disruptions of 'masculine' **language**. A further assumption is that woman is given a specific identity within the masculine structures of language and power, and that she must strive to challenge it.

This particular brand of **radical feminism** has conventionally been read as assuming that there is an 'essential' **femininity** that can be recovered, and that it is also possible to distinguish between a genuine feminine 'writing' and other forms of language. However, critics such as Elizabeth Grosz, in *Jacques Lacan: A Feminist Introduction* (1990), and Margaret Whitford, in *Luce Irigaray: Philosophy in the Feminine* (1991), have argued that it would be a mis-take to take the link made between

the female body and writing in the work of theorists such as Luce Iri-garay too literally. Instead, they stress that Irigaray is being metaphorical in her use of the male/female **gender** binary, thus constructing, as Irigaray herself says in *Speculum of the Other Woman* (1974), 'a symbolic interpre-tation of anatomy'. It is a point made clear by Elizabeth Grosz: 'Irigaray and other "**feminists** of **difference**" do not refer to the female body in biological terms, but only in so far as it is enveloped, produced and made meaningful by language.'

EDUCATION Education is a key issue for all **feminists**, as it raises the question of what exactly women are being educated *for*, and consequently the nature of their overall role in society. It was especially important for the **first wave** group, as it became a vital part of their access to economic independence, power and self-respect. Mary **Wollstonecraft**'s *Vindi-cation*, in a chapter on 'National Education', stresses 'the necessity of establishing proper day-schools' to improve the relations of the sexes, while Victorian novels such as *Jane Eyre* and *The Mill on the Floss* see education as a necessary precondi-tion of dignity and autonomy. Popu-lar medical authorities, however, insisted that prolonged academic work would threaten the repro-ductive capacity of young women and throw their mental balance into disarray: hence the concentration on ornamental 'accomplishments' rather than serious intellectual training. The debate about education, which intensified after 1850, thus entailed a full reconsideration of women's role in society as wives and mothers. Nevertheless, by the end of the nineteenth century women were making steady inroads into educational institutions at all levels.

Thus the twentieth century began with the establishment of women's equal right to education more or less settled; but paradoxically, feminist scepticism grew at the benefits for women of entering an institution still heavily dominated by men and male values. It is famously voiced by Virginia **Woolf**'s questions in *Three Guineas* (1938): 'do we wish to join that [academic] procession, or don't we? On what terms shall we join that procession? Above all, where is it leading us, the procession of educated men?'. In 1975, Adrienne **Rich** published an essay entitled 'Toward a Woman-Centred University', in which she argued that the traditional university system must be 'dehierarchized', flexible and free arrangements for childcare must be provided and the traditional curriculum altered in order to address issues that directly concern the community outside the academy. Only this way, she says, will women 'assume any real equality within the academic world'.

EMANCIPATION Advocates of female emancipation seek equitable treatment within existing social structures, rather than seeking to change the way society itself is organised. Emancipation was the particular goal of **first wave** feminists, who campaigned for legislation that would give women material benefits such as the vote, economic independence, and equal access to **education**. In the words of Winifred **Holtby**, feminism could be summed up in the demand that men 'recognize our full humanity'. Once this state of equality is achieved, Holtby finishes, 'we will trouble you no more'.

Emancipatory theory depends upon a **liberal** conception of the subject as potentially autonomous and self-determining, capable of fulfilling its potential under the right social conditions. It does not go so far as to question the grounds of **subjectivity** itself, as do schools of **feminist** thought influenced by **poststructuralist** theories. **Second wave** feminism went much further than the first wave in theorising the existence of **patriarchal** systems of power which must be overthrown in order to achieve liberation, and it is this ongoing struggle with discursive systems and **ideological** constructions, as well as social campaigning, which continues to preoccupy modern feminists. Today, feminism does not tend to be thought of as a self-limiting project which will disappear once a particular set of goals have been attained.

ENLIGHTENMENT The 'Age of Enlightenment' is a term used to describe a period of heightened philosophical and intellectual activity which can be dated from the English Civil War of 1688 to the outbreak of the French Revolution in 1789. Thinkers of the period believed that they were emerging from a 'dark age' of superstition and ignorance into a new era of scientific rationality, reason and social justice. Philosophers such as John Locke asserted that knowledge could only be gained from observation of natural phenomena, and thus rejected unthinking adherence to traditional sources of authority, such as the Bible. Publications such as Jean Jacques Rousseau's *Social Contract* (1762), developed the concept of civil liberty which was to pave the way for both the American and French revolutions.

Feminism was not part of the Enlightenment project, and its assertions regarding the rights of the individual were largely addressed to men, although the French Revolution spawned some radical **feminist** activists, such as Marie Olympe de Gouges, who overtly drew on Enlightenment discourses in her pamphlet *Declaration of the Rights of Women and Citizens* (1791). She was guillotined by Robespierre for her dangerous extremism, but feminism is nevertheless indebted to the ideas born out of the Enlightenment period. It created a model of humanitarian reform that was to inspire **first wave** feminism, directly influencing some of the movement's key thinkers, such as John Stuart **Mill** and Mary **Wollstonecraft**.

EPISTEMOLOGY Epistemology is the theory of knowledge, something with which feminism has always been crucially concerned, since it is based on a challenge to accepted truths and ways of knowing. So-called 'Enlightenment' epistemology is based on the concept of rationality, reason and objectivity, all concepts which many **feminists** regard as a **masculine** way of viewing the world. Exactly what form a feminist epistemology should take is, however, a matter for debate. In *Theorizing Patriarchy* (1990), Sylvia Walby argues for a 'feminist standpoint epistemology' which is founded in women's own experience, since because 'the way that men have typically constructed what counts as authoritative knowledge is itself **patriarchal** . . . the only basis of unbiased knowledge of the world is women's own direct experience'. A complicating factor here is that all women may not share the same experiences (or will perceive the same experiences very differently) which means that an epistemology constructed on this basis would be variable and subjective, rather than universal. However, philosophers like Jacques **Derrida** and Michel **Foucault** have produced theories which can aid in the formulation of a female knowing subject, since in poststructuralist debate 'truth' is only ever temporarily fixed within a discursive field, formed in and through material power relations. Although this line of thought disperses the notion of a single way of perceiving the world, be it masculine or **feminine**, it does open up the way towards a pluralistic epistemology within which 'truth' is always open to challenge.

EQUAL RIGHTS Early **feminist** theorists saw equal rights as a fundamental goal for female emancipation. This focused on an individual's right to pursue self-fulfilment unconstrained by **gender**; a view which paralleled the racial equality being pursued by **civil rights** activists of the same period. Later feminist **ideologies** argued that this approach deflected attention away from the particular issues that dominated a woman's experience. Thus, many actions have taken the route of specific campaigns against specific inequalities or discriminations. Whilst some strategies have brought rewards, some have not. An Equal Pay act was introduced in Britain and America in the early 1970s and the Right to Equal Pay was recognised by the United Nations and by the International Labour Organisation. However, in the same decade both British and American judges determined that discrimination on the basis of pregnancy did not constitute unlawful sex discrimination. Feminist movements have battled between themselves over what constitutes equal rights, or what the main areas of concern to women are – poverty, violence, childcare, reproductive freedom, professional advancement or domestic pursuits. This has often resulted in disputes between feminists over issues, rather than encouraging a united challenge against social and economic structures. Whilst some ground has been made, true parity between the sexes remains a distant goal.

ESSENTIALISM In relation to **gender**, the term refers to the belief in natural or innate differences between men and women. Essentialism rejects the view that gender differences are socially constructed concepts that have become attached to men and women, and insists that difference is fixed and natural. There is no unified **feminist** position on **essentialism**. Many argue that gender is an effect of **culture**, a view well represented by Judith **Butler**. However, others support the notion that there is such a thing as a unique female **identity**. Mary **Daly**, for example, represents the radical feminist position in her concept of the 'Lusty Woman', who transcends **patriarchal** institutions.

French feminist thought also draws on essentialist concepts in its postulation of the existence of a uniquely female mode of **discourse**, or *écriture féminine*, although the usage made by such theorists as Hélène **Cixous** and Luce **Irigaray** of references to the female body and identity are often highly metaphorical and ironic, and do not necessarily denote belief in the existence of a fundamental female identity.

ETHNOCENTRICITY A way of thinking which derives universal theories of knowledge from a single limited perspective. For **feminists** of colour, it describes the process whereby the bulk of feminist theories have been constructed from a white, western viewpoint. American writers such as bell **hooks** and Audre **Lorde** have been particularly articulate in their condemnation of this bias within feminist debates. In a criticism of Mary **Daly**'s *Gyn/Ecology* in *Sister Outsider* (1984), Audre Lorde attacks the way in which Daly refers to black women only in negative terms, arguing that although 'the oppression of women knows no ethnic nor racial boundaries . . . that does not mean it is identical within these differences'. It is a point echoed by bell hooks in the same year, when she wrote in *Feminist Theory: From Margin to Center* that 'white women may be victimized by **sexism**, but **racism** enables them to act as exploiters and oppressors of black people'.

ETHNOGRAPHY Derived from social anthropology, ethnography is an approach or method of studying

225

groups in order to understand a **culture** as a whole; that is, based on long-term and in-depth fieldwork. More recently, drawing on audience studies, feminists have used the methods and aims of ethnography to examine the meanings and pleasures of women's popular culture such as **romantic** fiction, **soap opera** and **women's magazines**. For example, Ann Gray's (1987) ethnographic study of the use of video-recorders in the domestic context highlights the importance of social relations in understanding gendered audiences. Gray found, for example, that soap opera plays a significant part in women's social lives in relation to other women, in that its role in the construction of a separate, but **collective**, women's culture is crucial. Thus the significance of the study is its revelations concerning the complexity of the ways in which women relate to television and video in their day-to-day lives.

F

FALUDI, SUSAN: JOURNALIST (1960–)
Faludi's best-seller *Backlash: the Undeclared War Against Women* won the
Pulitzer prize in 1992. In her book,
Faludi investigates a variety of **discourses**, ranging from politics to the
law, that have had the effect of
undermining women's progress in
society. Faludi refers to the 1980s as
'the **backlash** decade' during which
an 'undeclared war' was waged against
women's rights. From academic
journals to the political arena, women
were told not only that their struggle
for equal rights had been won, but
also that they were paying the price
in broken relationships, unfulfilled
maternal urges, and debilitating stress.
Faludi claims that the media led the
way in this attempt to deconstruct the
credibility of feminism, for example,
coining the terms 'man shortage',
'biological clock' and '**postfeminism**'
in an attempt 'to push women back
into their "acceptable" roles'. Hollywood joined the 'backlash' a few years
later, in the late eighties, with the
development of a new horror genre
that reiterated the popular image of
feminists as sick and unhappy: for
example, *Fatal Attraction*.

Faludi has been criticised by
postfeminists such as Christina Hoff
Sommers for developing an elaborate
conspiracy theory, and for not recognising alternative discourses that
demonstrate more ambivalent, or
even sympathetic, reactions towards
feminism than the discursive formation she identifies. Indeed, many
feminist writers have pointed out that
culture is never as discursively monolithic as Faludi implies, and attack her
argument as reductive.

FAMILY The focus of research and
fierce debate for successive **feminist**
movements, the family has been
described both as the very locus of
women's **oppression** and of all
meaningful personal life, as well as
the source of male power and means
of socialising children. In post-
industrial societies it is seen as the
basic unit of the community, but
attempts to defend the nuclear family
(two married heterosexual parents
living together with their children) as
a "natural" and inevitable structure,
existing since the origins of humankind, have been challenged and
shown to be false. For nineteenth-
century **utopian** socialists Owen,
Fourier and Saint-Simon (all male),
the family was a bastion of selfish
individualism incompatible with a
cooperative way of life, but theory
was not generally matched by practice
in the socialist communities set up in
USA, France and England. Further
attempts to promote alternative, collective structures of childcare, housework, etc., were made by Charlotte
Perkins **Gilman** and Alexandra

Kollontai; some aspects were later introduced in the former GDR. However, the Victorian notion of family and domesticity as the keystone of society with the woman as wife, mother, nurturer and '**Angel in the House**' predominated. Not until the women's movement of the 1960s and 70s were the politics of the family examined again in detail. Growing state intervention in family planning and child welfare, coupled with a concomitant 'privatisation' of the family, produced pressures and effects that were little documented, let alone understood. The family remains a key feminist issue.

FANTASY In a modern literary context, the term 'fantasy' signifies a particular genre which, to quote Joanna **Russ**, 'contravenes the real and violates it . . . fantasy is what could *not have happened*; i.e., what *cannot* happen, what *cannot* exist'. It is a genre in which women writers have always played a prominent role, from Gothic novelists such as Clara Reeve and Ann Radcliffe in the eighteenth century, to perhaps one of the most influential of all fantastic texts, Mary Wollstonecraft **Shelley**'s *Franken-stein* (1818). In the twentieth century, **feminist** writers have often exploited fantasy's speculative potential to both critique a reality which they perceive as male-dominated, and to offer alternatives. Marge Piercy's *Woman on the Edge of Time* (1976), for example, imagines a future in which perfect equality between the genders has been achieved; Joanna Russ, on the other hand, creates a satirical female-only **utopia** in *The Female Man* (1975).

Fantasy's link to the subconscious, to dream and to **desire**, make it an inherently subversive literary form, showing that which is hidden within the dominant order. An assumption which is fundamental to feminist interventions within the fantastic genre is that in revealing realism's flip side, **patriarchal** definitions of reality can be both challenged and changed.

FASHION Fashion is both an industry and an art: whether it exists for the pleasure or the subordination of women is a matter for debate. The **stereotype** of the bra-burning, dungaree-wearing feminist who has renounced all the trappings of **femininity** retains its currency in the popular imagination, which thus almost automatically assumes feminism and fashion to be mutually exclusive categories. It is certainly true that feminists from the **first wave** onwards have been extremely critical of fashion as a visible sign of female **oppression**, a view summed up in a placard displayed at a feminist conference held in London in 1981: 'Fashion= control=violence against women.' Consequently, the first wave women's movement sought to introduce comfortable, practical clothing for women and rejected the confines of corsetry, in the same way that that many feminists of the **second wave** refused to wear short skirts and high heels. More recently, Susan **Faludi** has argued that fashion is a tool of the **backlash**, and that the industry is constantly shifting tactics in order to retain women as docile consumers.

However, as the punk movement of the seventies proved, fashion has always had the potential to be subverted rather than rejected out-right. One of the leading figures in this subversive reappropriation of fashion must surely be the post-modern icon **Madonna**, whose conically-breasted Gautier corset has become something of a **postfeminist** symbol in itself. In Madonna's performance the most problematic aspects of fashion iconography – the corset, stiletto heels, fishnet tights – was given an added twist by being displayed on the body of a woman who claimed to be fully in control of her own self-fashioning. Likewise, postfeminists point to the **Spice Girl** phenomenon and the rise of the supermodel as evidence that fashion can be a symbol of empowerment as well as a source of pleasure.

FAWCETT, MILLICENT GARRETT: WOMEN'S SUFFRAGE CAMPAIGNER (1847–1929) In contrast to her sister, Elizabeth Garrett Anderson, one of the first women to qualify as a medical doctor, Millicent Garrett Fawcett did not proceed with her education beyond the age of fifteen and was married by the time she was twenty. However, this did not hinder her in her development as a formid-able and influential campaigner for feminist causes. Indeed, her marriage to the Liberal MP and economist Henry Fawcett enabled her to gain an insider's knowledge of the British political system.

Although her **feminist** concerns were wide, Millicent Garrett Fawcett is best remembered for her contri-bution to the struggle for the vote, setting up the National Union of Women's Suffrage Societies (NUWSS) in 1897. Sometimes criticised by more radical sections of the movement, who viewed her as possessing conser-vative views, she was a reluctant supporter of the militant tactics employed by the Women's Social and Political Union (WSPU), led by the **Pankhursts**. Millicent Garrett Faw-cett oversaw the passing of the Representation of the People Act (1918) into law, and continued as an active campaigner until her death at the age of eighty-two.

FEMALE In a literal context, a word which refers to an individual who possesses a particular set of biological characteristics, including the ability to give birth. It is thus to be differ-entiated from '**femininity**', which describes a socially-constructed image of femaleness.

However, **feminists** are concerned with defining a notion of the female that extends beyond her reproductive system, although no universally-agreed-upon alternative exists. A philosophical version of the debate conceptualises women within a **patri-archal** system as existing in a state of estrangement from their 'real' female natures. Instead of a positive and active concept, 'female' has become locked into a dualistic system of thought in which it is constructed as inferior to 'male'. For example, in *Gyn/Ecology* (1978), Mary **Daly** argues that the female principle is rendered silent and powerless within patriarchal **discourse**, which achieves the woman's alienation from her own female nature, and that in order to achieve liberation 'we must struggle to discover this Self as Friend to all that is truly female'.

Hélène **Cixous** propounds the

notion of female writing practice in the theory of *écriture féminine*, arguing in 'The Laugh of the Medusa' that 'by writing her self, woman will return to the body which has been more than confiscated from her'. In 'This Sex Which is Not One', Luce **Irigaray** attempts to define a feminist epistemology which is intimately linked to the auto-erotic rhythms of the female body. For both theorists, the biological female body functions as a highly stylised metaphor which represents the point from which female knowledge can be produced.

FEMININE MYSTIQUE In 1963, the American feminist Betty **Friedan** published a book entitled *The Feminine Mystique*, in which she argued that women were trapped in a system which defined 'proper' **femininity** as little more than domestic fulfilment. Friedan argued that the mystique derived from **psychoanalysis** a simplistic notion of femininity as essentially passive, and was perpetuated through sociological arguments that women be set completely different **educational** and social goals from men. Coerced by seductive media images and limited by their lack of useful training, millions of white middle-**class** women absorbed themselves in home, husband and children, becoming trapped in what Friedan somewhat drastically termed a 'comfortable concentration camp'.

FEMININITY One of Simone de **Beauvoir**'s most famous aphorisms is 'One is not born, but rather becomes, a woman' (*The Second Sex*). It is an apt summary of the **feminist** claim that, while femaleness is a consequence of

biology, femininity originates from within societal structures. Femininity is thus a set of rules governing female behaviour and appearance, the ultimate aim of which is to make women conform to a male ideal of sexual attractiveness. **Masquerading** as 'natural' womanhood, it is actually something imposed upon the female subject, in spite of the fact that the pressure to conform to the culturally dominant feminine ideal is internalised to the extent that women effectively tailor themselves to fit it – hence the existence of an immensely profitable **fashion** and beauty industry. A **postfeminist** twist to this debate, however, (and the essence of '**girl-power**') stresses the pleasure of creating self-aware, even parodic, feminine identities which exploit the potential femininity offers to construct different versions of the self.

Furthermore, the distinction between 'female' and 'feminine' drawn above cannot be made in French, in which the single word *féminine* is capable of conveying both meanings. Playing on this ambiguity, **French feminists** such as Hélène **Cixous** and Julia **Kristeva** have postulated femininity as a theoretical area which represents all that is marginalised within the dominant **patriarchal** order, and is thus a term which describes a position which can be occupied by any peripheral subject, be they male or female.

FEMINIST One who holds the view that women are less valued than men in societies that categorise men and women into differing cultural or economic spheres. A feminist also insists that these inequalities are not fixed or determined, but that women themselves can change the social, economic and political order through collective action. Thus the feminist purpose is an active desire to change women's position in society. The notion that men can be feminists is a contentious one. Tania **Modleski**, for example, distinguishes between male contributions that involve the analysis of male **power**, and male contributions that profess to speak on behalf of women or as women.

In the study of literature, culture and film, feminist criticism takes the form of the analysis of the mechanisms of production and consumption of a particular text or practice from a feminist perspective. But it is important to understand that there are different ways of seeing which are all feminist, allowing for diversity within disciplines and within the feminist movement itself. As Maggie Humm explains in her introduction to *Feminisms: A Reader* (1992), feminism is a diverse movement both culturally and historically and its objectives have been endorsed worldwide. The extent to which feminism has been effective can be evaluated by the extent to which its discourse has become part of everyday thinking.

FEMINIST CRITIQUE Term coined by the American literary critic Elaine **Showalter** in 'Toward a Feminist Poetics' (1979), which describes a form of **feminist** criticism which examines the ways in which women have been represented, or omitted, from male-authored texts. A feminist critique would also examine how a female audience is affected by being represented in reductive or dismissive ways. However, Showalter argues that, valuable though it might be, a feminist critique is necessarily limited, since 'if we study **stereotypes** of women, the **sexism** of male critics and the limited roles women play in literary history, we are not learning what women have felt and experienced, but only what men have thought women should be'. She thus proceeds to propose **gynocriticism** as the solution to this problem, a critical practice that will focus on texts written by women. 'Gynocritics begins at the point when we free ourselves from the linear absolutes of male literary history, stop trying to fit women within the lines of the literary tradition, and focus instead on the newly visible world of female **culture**.'

FIGES, EVA: NOVELIST AND CRITIC (1932–) Figes was one of the first British **feminists** to be influenced by Betty **Friedan**'s *The Feminine Mystique*, published in 1963; her own book *Patriarchal Attitudes* (1970) was to become one of the seminal texts of the period. Becoming a single parent after her marriage ended in divorce was the impetus for her development of a feminist theoretical perspective. In a polemical work profoundly informed by knowledge of history, psychology and literature, she challenged the myth that motherhood was totally fulfilling, and criticised both **Freud**ian **psychoanalysis** and the institution of **marriage**. She examined the roles played by religion, capitalism and philosophy in the creation of a culture in which a woman is taught to desire 'not what her mother desired for herself but what her father and all men find desirable in a woman'. The process by which female **identity** is constructed was, she believed, less to do with inherent biological factors than with the external norms, conditions and power relations which promote and support male domination. She argued that the discovery of the male role in reproduction was the catalyst for the subsequent desire throughout history for control over women. Later work includes *Sex and Subterfuge*, a study of women novelists up to 1850.

FILM NOIR Literally, 'dark film', the term was produced by French film critics in the 1950s to describe a number of films emerging from Hollywood during and after WWII which offered a dark and unrelenting worldview both in narrative form and visual style. Film theorists continue to debate when the classic period of *noir* occurred and whether it may be termed a movement, a genre or a visual style. Much feminist **film theory** has addressed the *femme fatale*, a characteristically ambiguous female character within classic and neo-*noir* film. In classic *noir* the *femme fatale* is a dangerously active sexual figure who brings about the downfall of the male protagonist, often being killed in the process. In neo-*noir* she is also overtly sexual but frequently survives the film; notable examples may be found in *The Last Seduction* (John Dahl, 1993) and *Basic Instinct* (Paul Verhoeven, 1992).

FILM THEORY Although film theory emerged in the 1920s and 1930s, it didn't become established until the 1950s. André Bazin, the editor of the famous French journal *Cahiers du Cinéma* is seen as a key contributor to film theory. Auteur theory emerged during this time, informed by the French New Wave.

In the 1960s and 1970s, film theory developed in response to structuralist and **psychoanalytic** theory. Structuralist approaches were applied to **genre** theory, **ideology** in the cinema, the analysis of narrative structures and avant-garde film. Structuralist film theorists such as Christian Metz drew on **Freud**ian and **Lacan**ian psychoanalysis to explain how films operate at an unconscious level. Structuralist psychoanalysis established a model of cinematic representation which constructs the spectator through the re-enactment of unconscious processes involved in the acquisition of **language** and sexual difference.

The key modes of psychoanalytic film theory are the cinematic apparatus (which refers to all aspects of film reception, including the film, the **spectator** and the context of the screening), the relationship between film texts and spectators, and the structural decoding of film texts.

FIRESTONE, SHULAMITH: RADICAL FEMINIST (1944–) In her most famous publication, *The Dialectic of Sex* (1970) Shulamith Firestone put forward her view that **gender** inequality originates from 'the division of society into two distinct biological classes for procreative reproduction'. The liberation of women from **patriarchy** thus requires a biological revolution, a seizing of the means of reproduction, in a process analogous to the economic revolution called for by Marx. Indeed, Firestone presents her argument as a refinement of

Marxist thought, which she argues ignores the fact that women constitute an oppressed group in themselves: what she terms a 'sex-**class**'. If, however, they assume control over their own reproductive functions, the biological **family** unit will dissolve, heterosexuality will no longer be compulsory, and women will be freed from the demands of domestic labour.

Firestone's argument is of particular interest in the context of contemporary **feminist** concerns regarding **reproductive technology**, since *The Dialectic of Sex* sees 'artificial reproduction' as the gateway to a liberated future in which women will no longer have to experience pregnancy – a process she describes, with brutal succinctness, as 'barbaric . . . the temporary deformation of the body of the individual for the sake of the species'. Firestone's approach to this issue is, however, more thoughtful than some critics have given her credit for, since she does proceed to question the potential of science to act in the liberatory capacity she is proposing, given the male domination of the field. Her work is thus an early call for awareness of the potential and risks involved in reproductive science, and for the necessity of feminist engagement with such issues.

FIRST WAVE FEMINISM This term refers to the first concerted movement working for the reform of women's social and legal inequalities in the nineteenth century. Although individual **feminists** such as Mary **Wollstonecraft** had already argued against the injustices suffered by women, it was not until the 1850s that

something like an organised feminist movement evolved in Britain. Its headquarters was at Langham Place in London, where a group of middle-class women, led by Barbara **Bodichon** (1827–91) and Bessie Rayner Parkes (1829–1925), met to discuss topical issues and publish the *English Woman's Journal* (1858–64). The key concerns of first wave feminists were **education**, employment, the **marriage** laws, and the plight of intelligent middle-**class** single women. They were not primarily concerned with the problems of working-class women, nor did they necessarily see themselves as feminists in the modern sense (the term was not coined until 1895). First wave feminists largely responded to specific injustices they had themselves experienced. Their major achievements were the opening of higher education to women; reform of the girls' secondary-school system, including participation in formal national examinations; the widening of access to the professions, especially medicine; married women's property rights, recognised in the Married Women's Property Act of 1870; and some improvement in divorced and separated women's child custody rights. Active until the First World War, first wave feminists failed, however, to secure the women's vote.

FOUCAULT, MICHEL: PHILOSOPHER, HISTORIAN AND CULTURAL CRITIC (1926–1984) Elected to the Chair of History of Systems of Thought at the prestigious Collège de France in 1970, Foucault's theories regarding power and knowledge have profoundly influenced the development of **postmodernist** thought. His first important book, *Madness and Civilisation*, published in 1961, sets out the concerns which continued to motivate his subsequent work: his interest in marginalised groups and his desire to destabilise unproblematic notions of the self-knowing autonomous subject. Analysing the emergence of a **discourse** of madness in the seventeenth and eighteenth centuries, which enabled insanity to be institutionalised and controlled by the state, Foucault argued that all **subjectivity**, however apparently 'rational', was actually created and controlled through complex structures of power embodied in state apparatuses. Moreover, the discourses through which the subject is constructed are not universal, but are always historically specific.

In *Discipline and Punish* (1975), Foucault anatomises how systems of social control operate through reference to Jeremy Bentham's 'Panopticon', a mechanism for prison surveillance. In the way it both exhibits and conceals the guards' gaze, the panopticon causes prisoners to regulate their own behaviour.

Foucault's final work was *The History of Sexuality*, published in three volumes from 1976-84, in which he puts forward the view that sexual behaviour, far from being innate, is in fact governed by complex **ideological** systems. He also examined the operation of discursive power-formations on the female body, which he argued was subjected to a process of 'hysterization'. Identified wholly with its reproductive functions, the female subject was thus confined to the private, **domestic** sphere.

Although Foucault's work was never explicitly '**feminist**' in orientation, many theorists argue that he has given feminism new ways of thinking about how women are controlled within a **patriarchal** system. Judith **Butler**, Elizabeth Grosz and Michele **Barrett**, for example, have all appropriated and critiqued his ideas within their own work.

FOX-GENOVESE, ELIZABETH: HISTORIAN (1941–) Elizabeth Fox-Genovese is a scholar of women in world history. In particular she focuses on women in the southern United States, and is best known in this area of her interests for the book *Within the Plantation Household: Black and White Women of the Old South* (1988). Fox-Genovese is also credited with changing history studies through the implementation of a programme across America to integrate materials on women into traditional courses. This was supported by the publication of the four-volume work *Restoring Women to History* (1984-86). She then turned her writing focus towards interpreting feminism, in *Feminism Without Illusions: A Critique of Individualism* (1991) and *Feminism Is NOT The Story of My Life: How Today's Feminist Elite Has Lost Touch With the Real Concerns of Women* (1996). The latter focuses on interviews with women who have never felt part of the **feminist** movement and concludes that feminism must shift to meet their needs, thus aligning her ideas with those of so-called '**postfeminists**' such as Christina Hoff Sommers and Rene **Denfeld**.

FRENCH FEMINISM In a theoretical

context, a term which covers a variety of **feminist** writing produced in France from the student revolt of May 1968 onwards. A text which has been influential in defining a French feminist school of thought is Elaine Marks and Isabelle de Courtivron's anthology, *New French Feminisms*, published in 1981, which collects the work of all those women most closely identified with the development of French feminist theory, of whom Hélène **Cixous**, Julia **Kristeva**, and Luce **Irigaray** remain the best-known outside France.

French feminist theory originates from one of the first and most influential of the groups founded by the **second wave** feminist movement in France, *Psychanalyse et Politique*, which established the influential publishing house *des femmes* (later, the group signalled a shift in its agenda by reversing its name, becoming *politique et psychanalyse*). Members of this group questioned the validity of Simone de **Beauvoir**'s demand for social equality and her rejection of male-dominated theory. Instead, they argued that theories such as Marxism, **psychoanalysis** and **poststructuralist** thought could offer a way of deconstructing the opposites (or binaries) – man/woman, rationality/**hysteria** – which are the dominant versions of sexual **difference**, and that differences between men and women are products of **gender** identities formulated through the operation of **discourse** rather than the consequence of biology. Many French feminists, such as Kristeva and Cixous, consider that art and literature offer important evidence of the ways in which differences of thought are structured.

Often allusive, poetic and full of linguistic puns, French feminist thought is often thought of as over-intellectual and 'difficult': however, the idiosyncrasy of their language is a way in which these writers seek to formulate a '**feminine**' (*féminin*) form of expression outside dominant structures of signification.

FRENCH, MARILYN: AMERICAN NOVELIST AND CRITIC (1929–) French's work is characterised by its overt polemicism – Susan **Faludi** has termed it 'a call to arms'. French's view is that all **cultures** are based upon the routine subordination of women in every area of life, and that there are many aspects of **oppression** which feminism has not successfully redressed. Her first novel, *The Woman's Room* (1977), is a fictional companion to Betty **Friedan**'s *The Feminine Mystique* (1963), in that it deals with the lives of women trapped in middle-**class** American suburbia in the fifties and sixties. Under the influence of feminism, her female characters find their way out of the American dream, but French does not simplify the problems and dangers involved in claiming **liberation**. In subsequent books, such as *Her Mother's Daughter* (1987) and *Our Father* (1994), French continues to examine the impact of feminism upon the private lives of individuals.

As well as writing novels, French is also a literary and cultural critic. She published a **feminist** analysis of Shakespeare, *Shakespeare's Division of Experience*, in 1982. In *Beyond Power: On Women, Men and Morals* (1985), she argues that **patriarchy** is the paradigm for all other modes of oppression. In 1992, she published *The War Against Women*, the central thesis of which is that women worldwide continue to suffer under patriarchal systems, which base their authority on female subordination.

FREUD, ANNA: PSYCHOANALYST (1895–1982) Freud was born in Vienna, the youngest child of Martha and Sigmund **Freud**. She had been a reluctant schoolgirl, and this seems to have prompted her later research into school phobia. She spent six years as a teaching apprentice, qualifying in 1915. She taught at the Cottage Lyceum, Vienna, becoming a head teacher in 1917. She gave up teaching in 1920 due to chronic illness, and went on to become a practising **psychoanalyst** and lecturer at the Vienna Psychoanalytic Institute.

Freud and her family emigrated to London in 1939. During the Second World War she was one of the directors of a residential nursery for homeless children, and in 1947 she founded the Hampstead Child Therapy Clinic. Her published works include *The Ego and the Mechanism of Defence* (1937) and *Beyond the Best Interests of the Child* (1973). *The Writings of Anna Freud* span eight volumes, and were published between 1966 and 1980.

FREUD, SIGMUND: NEUROLOGIST AND PSYCHOANALYST (1856–1939) Freud studied medicine at the University of Vienna, before conducting scientific research. Married, and with six children, financial considerations prompted him to become a specialist in neurology at the Vienna General Hospital in 1882. In 1885 Freud studied under Jean Martin Charcot in Paris, and in 1886 he set up in private practice, using hypnosis to treat **hysterics**. He went on to replace hypnosis with his controversial technique of 'free association'. Although Freud's career was prestigious, leading him to being appointed Professor of Neuropathology at the University of Vienna and founding the international Psychoanalytical Association in 1910, this did not stop him from being extricated from Vienna by the Nazis, emigrating to London in 1938, a year before his death.

The relationship of Freudian theory to feminism is a problematic one. His interest in **gender** acquisition led to his development of theories of female sexuality which characterised it in terms of lack in publications such as *Three Essays on the Theory of Sexuality* (1905). This has led to **feminists** such as Kate **Millett** and Shulamith **Firestone** to reject his ideas as misogynistic. Other feminist theorists, however, have adapted Freudian theory to suit their own purposes: Juliet **Mitchell**, for example, makes an important distinction in the preface to *Psychoanalysis and Feminism* when she says that '**psychoanalysis** is not a recommendation *for* a **patriarchal** society, but an analysis *of* one'.

FRIDAY, NANCY: WRITER Nancy Friday is most closely associated with her books detailing men and women's sexual fantasies: *My Secret Garden* (1973), *Forbidden Flowers* (1975), *Men In Love* (1980) and *Women On Top* (1991). Erotica thinly veiled in psychological commentary, they convey Friday's view that sexuality is a fundamental part of **identity**. She presents her work as being particularly significant for women, in that it both charts and contributes to the open expression of female sexuality. Whereas her contributors of 1973 felt their dreams and desires made them 'bad', those whose narratives make up *Women On Top* are more celebratory in their breaking of sexual taboos.

Friday is somewhat reluctant to attribute this change to the women's movement. Although she speaks nostalgically of the period when the **second wave** revolution was at its height, she argues that the **feminist** revolution and the sexual revolution are not synonymous. Instead, she claims that the movement turned against heterosexuality, thus alienating women who continued to retain a sexual attachment to men.

It is this view that informs her 1996 publication, *The Power of Beauty*, a semi-**autobiographical** work in which she seeks to formulate a **feminine** aesthetic which will allow women to enjoy the pleasure of personal display and seductive practices, an approach she believes to be more liberating than feminist puritanism.

FRIEDAN, BETTY: AMERICAN FEMINIST (1921–) A qualified psychologist, Friedan worked as a journalist following her marriage until she was dismissed for becoming pregnant. It was this event, she later said, that made her aware of the inequitable treatment of women in American society. Her first book, *The Feminine Mystique*, was published in 1963, making an immediate impact on the growing **feminist** movement. Friedan dismantled the female version of the American dream, which taught women to aspire to perfect **domesticity**, in order to reveal the frustration and feelings of entrapment beneath. She postulated that **education** was the way in which women could escape from the limitations and hopeless aspirations of domesticity, since it would enable them to take jobs outside the home and assign routine household tasks to others. This last point perhaps illustrates the limitations of Friedan's argument, which as many critics have observed, is biased towards the white middle-**class** experience.

In subsequent books, such as *The Second Stage* (1983), Friedan voices increasing unease about the activities of **radical feminists**, which she fears will alienate mainstream support. Although a key figure in the development of second stage feminism in the United States, a founder member of the **National Organization for Women** and high-profile **activist**, Friedan has since turned her attention to other issues, such as society's treatment of the elderly.

G

GATENS, MOIRA: PHILOSOPHER
Moira Gatens lectures in philosophy at the University of Sydney, Australia. Gatens went to Sydney as a postgraduate to write on the mind/ body problem. Her Ph.D. thesis expanded to cover the relations between reason and passion, **nature** and **culture**, from the seventeenth century to the present. Spinoza's notion of reason as an active emotion became her vital concern. But Gatens was initially discouraged from her reading of the seventeenth-century Dutch Jewish rationalist. Her book *Feminism and Philosophy: Perspectives on Difference and Equality* (1991) excluded what she later says was the most creative element in her doctorate: Spinoza; so it is unsurprising that in *Imaginary Bodies: Ethics, Power and Corporeality* (1996), Spinoza becomes pivotal in Gatens's study of the body and the body politic. 'Imaginary bodies' refers to those images, symbols and metaphors which help construct various forms of subjectivity; Spinoza's notion of imagination is employed to conceive of embodiment in terms of multiple and historically specific social imaginaries.

GAY LIBERATION MOVEMENT The Gay Liberation movement sprang out of the Stonewall Rebellion in New York in 1969. It modelled itself on other radical groups of the sixties, making the rejection of **compulsory heterosexuality** a political decision, and adopting **activist** strategies, such as 'gay pride' parades. Rather than merely pleading for tolerance, gay liberation demanded equal human rights for gay and lesbian people, thus creating a visible communal identity which fought against mainstream society's wish to pathologise non-heterosexual behaviour as 'sick', 'perverted' or 'criminal'. **Lesbian feminists**, however, began to criticise the movement for representing the rights of homosexual men only, in the same way that they critiqued the implicit heterosexual orientation of the women's movement – indeed, in colloquial parlance 'gay' is no longer synonymous with 'lesbian'. Thus, lesbian activism has not always been carried out under the aegis of gay pride but has sought to develop new political strategies of its own.

GAZE According to John Berger in *Ways of Seeing* (1972), women are accustomed to being the object of male regard; however, they do not return the gaze in order to transform *men* into objects of **desire**. Instead, they internalise the male point of view to become self-surveyors: in Berger's words, 'Men look at women. Women watch themselves being looked at.' Drawing on **psychoanalytic** theory, film critics such as Laura **Mulvey** have analysed the way in which films position male and female **spectators** differently. In 'Visual Pleasure in Narrative Cinema' (1975), she argues that women are controlled in films by having to act for men as sexual spectacles and through the assumed gaze of a male hero and male director. In other words, the gaze reproduced in films is voyeuristic in that it makes female subjects the objects of male desire. Female spectators, **interpellated** as the recipients of the male gaze, are similarly erased.

GENDER Whereas **Anglo-American feminists** would distinguish between 'sex' and 'gender', arguing that sex is biological and that gender (like **femininity**) is socially constructed, **feminists** influenced by **psychoanalysis** argue that sex and gender **identity** are closely intertwined. In *Sex, Gender and Society* (1972), Ann **Oakley** was one of the first to argue that gender is not dependent on biology: sex is anatomical in origin, while gender is acquired through a process of acculturation. More recently, Judith **Butler** has critiqued the sex/gender split postulated by Oakley and others as unnecessarily reductive, 'effect[ing] a false stabilization . . . in the interests of heterosexual construction' (*Gender Trouble*, 1990). Butler points to **cross-dressing** as an activity which foregrounds the fictitiousness of gender, and which suggests the possibility of a wider concept of gender **identity** which does not work to normalise the male/ female dualism. What Butler's work emphasises is that the identification of gender as a product of **culture** does not necessarily lead to liberation:

indeed, gender can become one of the mechanisms whereby socially acceptable male and female behaviour is regulated.

GENDER STUDIES Gender studies avoids the exclusivity implicit in the term **'women's studies'**, for its aim is to examine the dynamics of female *and* male experience and **identity**. Elaine **Showalter** publicly proclaimed her allegiance to **gender**, rather than women's, studies in 1989, when she published a book entitled *Speaking of Gender*. She argued that the time for **gynocriticism** – the study of female texts and experience – had passed, and that **feminists** should now 'read male texts, not as documents of sexism and misogyny, but as inscriptions of gender and "renditions of sexual difference"'. According to Showalter's definition, therefore, gender studies would involve analysing **masculinity**, like **femininity**, as a construct. In *Feminism Without Women: Culture and Criticism in a "Postfeminist" Age* (1991), Tania **Modleski** claims that this approach may be problematic, since it implicitly assumes that inequality between the genders is no longer an issue. Reading the new interest in 'gender studies' as an example of a postfeminist **backlash** against feminism, she warns against the dangers of bringing 'men back to center stage' in the academic debate concerning gender construction. For Modleski, gender studies deprives women of the means to formulate any agenda based on an appeal to exclusively female experience, and that 'the once exhilarating proposition that there is no "essential" female nature has been elaborated to the point where it is now often used to scare "women" away from making *any* generalizations about or political claims on behalf of a group called "women"'.

GENRE French for 'kind' or 'type'. In the context of English studies, media studies or film studies, the term implies that texts can be categorised and that they are related to one another in certain ways. Individual texts can be classified as belonging to a particular genre – **romance, science fiction** or Gothic in literature; **soap opera**, sitcom and game show in television, for example. The reason for categorising texts in this way is that insights can be gleaned in understanding their meaning and structure. Genres have key elements from which they are constructed, such as recurring settings, situations, themes and characters. All these mean that **pleasure** is derived from anticipation, expectation and prediction. However, although it is important to look at convention and similarity in structure, we need to recognise that there is always an interplay between repetition and novelty, hence the differences between, for example, *Coronation Street* and *EastEnders*, even though they are both recognisably soap operas.

Genre is often **gender**ed, and those most identified with women, such as the romance or soap opera, are often deemed to be of a lesser intellectual importance than those genres which are male-identified. However, critics such as Tania **Modleski** and Janice Radway have studied the ways in which women can use generic conventions in subversive ways.

GILBERT, SANDRA M.: POET AND LITERARY CRITIC (1936–) Sandra Gilbert was born in New York and educated at Cornell and Columbia Universities. Her publications include several volumes of poetry: *In the Fourth World* (1979); *The Summer Kitchen* (1983); *Emily's Bread* (1984); and *Blood Pressure* (1988). She is, however, best known for her collaborative work with Susan **Gubar**. Their groundbreaking volumes of **feminist** criticism include *The Madwoman in the Attic: The Woman Writer and the Nineteenth-Century Imagination* (1979), and its sequel, the three-volume *No Man's Land: The Place of the Woman Writer in the Twentieth Century* (1988-94). They also jointly edited *Shakespeare's Sisters: Feminist Essays on Women Poets* (1979); *The Norton Anthology of Literature by Women* (1985), and *The Female Imagination and the Modernist Aesthetic* (1986).

The Madwoman in the Attic in particular has become one of the central texts of **Anglo-American** literary criticism. Gilbert and Gubar concentrate on the work of well-known women writers such as the Brontë sisters and Emily Dickinson, intending to uncover an anxiety of authorship originating from the belief that the rightful owner of the pen was male, and that women who wrote were deviant. They argue that this sublimated anxiety surfaces repeatedly in texts written by nineteenth-century women, in which the figure of the madwoman or **hysteric** becomes emblematic both of the guilt involved in transgressing the prohibitions against female authorship, and the rage such a restriction arouses.

GILMAN, CHARLOTTE PERKINS: WRITER (1860–1935) A leading social critic and **feminist** writer of her period in the United States. In her best-known piece, *The Yellow Wallpaper* (1899), Gilman presents the internal dialogue of a woman diagnosed with **hysteria** for whom total rest cure has been prescribed. The patient is slowly driven mad by her cure, cut off from any intellectual pursuits whatsoever. Though it is a work of fiction, it was based on Gilman's own experience after being diagnosed as an hysteric and prescribed a 'rest cure' by the distinguished American neurologist Silas Weir Mitchell, which prohibited her writing and labelled her feminism and social critiques as symptoms of uterine illness. Gilman recovered from her 'cure', and went on to write influential social theses, including *Women and Economics: A Study of the Economic Relation Between Men and Women as a Factor in Social Evolution* (1898), and a feminist **utopian** novel, *Herland* (1915), which, like *The Yellow Wallpaper*, has become a classic of women's **fantasy** literature.

GIRL POWER In *The Female Eunuch* (1970), Germaine **Greer** argued that women were not sexual *subjects*, but sexual *objects*. In the nineties, girl power (a term which has arisen out of the **Spice Girl** phenomenon) would argue precisely the opposite: that women are not sexual objects, but fully sexual subjects. However, in denoting women who lay claim to male privileges while retaining their **femininity**, girl power conveys an implicit rejection of many of the tenets popularly identified with second wave feminism, such as the notion that the beauty and **fashion** industry contributes to women's **objectification**, and attempts to create alternatives to **patriarchal** power constructs.

The **feminist** reaction to the rise of girl power is mixed. In *The New Feminism* (1998), Natasha **Walter** regards it as a movement which is celebratory of feminism's gains. Germaine Greer, on the other hand, devotes an entire chapter of *The Whole Woman* (1999) to an attack on girl power, which she describes as a phenomenon based on the cynical marketing of the traditional trappings of sexualised femininity to pre-teens.

GODDESS The goddess culture aims to celebrate and make manifest primal female power, in contradistinction to phallic law and order. If, as Marilyn **French** asserts in *The War Against Women* (1992), 'all major world religions are **patriarchal**', then the figure of the goddess can come to represent an order of being in which **matriarchal** principles are dominant. Mary **Daly**, for example, argues that the ancient world worshipped various manifestations of the 'Triple Goddess', but that Christianity triumphed by assimilating the goddess's myths and rituals and reworking them within a patriarchal belief structure. In *The New Victorians* (1995), Rene **Denfeld** attacks contemporary feminists for having retreated into wacky New Age versions of goddess-worship, and claims it as a crucial element in young women's increasing alienation from the women's movement.

GOLDMAN, EMMA: ANARCHIST FEMINIST (1869–1940) Goldman was born in Russia, but emigrated to the United States, where she worked as a nurse and midwife when not lecturing or demonstrating on **anarchist** or **feminist** issues. Although opposed to the issue of women's **suffrage** (which she dismissed as a 'fetish'), Goldman was a pioneering advocate of **contraception**, once arrested and jailed for fifteen days for distributing birth control information. Goldman outlined her anarchist views in *The Traffic in Women* (1911), in which she argued for women's rights over their own bodies, and for liberation from the dogmas of religion.

GREENHAM COMMON WOMEN'S PEACE CAMP In 1981 women marched from Cardiff to Greenham Common in Berkshire protesting against the NATO decision to site Cruise Missiles at the RAF base there. On arrival, women set up the Peace Camp outside the Main Gate. This became known as Yellow Gate when other satellite camps sprang up. The Ground Launch Cruise Missiles arrived in 1983, but the Peace Camp was determined to rid the Common of nuclear weapons and the military through non-violent direct action. The last of the Cruise Missiles were flown back to the United States in March 1991 and in September 1992 the USAF left Greenham Common. Yellow Gate continued to challenge the existence of nuclear weapons, turning attention to the Atomic Weapons Establishments at Aldermaston and Burghfield. Non-violent direct actions resulted in legal challenges in the courts which aimed to oppose the threat and use of nuclear weapons. These activities are chronicled in *Greenham Common Women's Peace Camp: A History Of Non-Violent Resistance 1984-1995* (1996) by Beth Junor. A formal planning application has been submitted to West Berkshire Council to build a commemorative site on the land which has now been occupied continuously for nineteen years. More information can be found at http://www.web13.co.uk/greenham/.

GREER, GERMAINE: ACADEMIC, JOURNALIST AND BROADCASTER (1939–) Born in Melbourne, Australia, Germaine Greer was educated at universities in Melbourne and Sydney, and completed her Ph.D. at Cambridge University, where she began to write for counter-cultural magazines such as *Oz*. Her first book, *The Female Eunuch* (1970), established Greer's polemical, assertive approach to **feminist** argument, attracting enormous publicity for the movement. In it, Greer defines heterosexuality as a powerful instrument of female subordination. Women are conditioned to conform to their society's expectations concerning the creation and maintenance of a feminine **identity**, because they only gain value by being valuable to men. Going into the workplace is no escape, argues Greer, as working women remain just as preoccupied with winning and retaining male approval in the office as they do in their marriages. To this end, Greer championed the cause of sexual emancipation, in an attempt to free sexual activity from its confining institutions. Characteristically, however, she changed tack completely in *Sex and Destiny* (1984) and the publications which followed it, in which she argued that chastity was the best form of contraception, clitoral orgasms were 'one-dimensional', and the menopause a liberatory experience.

Greer, however, has never been afraid of controversy or of contradicting herself. Although not all feminists agree with her views, she remains one of the movement's most recognisable figureheads. In addition, she has researched extensively on early women's writing, and is the author of *Slipshod Sibyls* (1995) and editor of *Kissing the Rod: An Anthology of Seventeenth-Century Women's Verse* (1989). Greer's most recent publication is *The Whole Woman* (1999), which argues that the full impact of **second wave** feminism is yet to be felt.

GRIFFIN, SUSAN: POET AND THEORIST (1943–) A published poet (*Like the Iris of an Eye*) and playwright, Griffin's involvement in philosophy and literature is evident in *Rape: The Power of Consciousness* (1979), a wide-ranging discussion of the sources and impact of male violence towards women. *Pornography and Silence* (1981) argued that a male mind and culture 'terrified of woman and **nature**' had created a metaphysics of **pornography**, by which men are desensitised to violence and women internalise a mistaken view of their own sexuality. She developed the notion that women are innately closer to the natural world in *Woman and Nature* (1984) and made an important contribution to '**ecofeminist**' theory, believing that men's treatment of women, marked by violence, hatred, self-interest and domination, equates with their treatment of nature. 'Womanly' values, to do with nurturing and peaceful cooperation, are inherently linked with ecologically friendly activities and avoidance of ecological disaster; nature and women are thus seen as equally **oppressed**.

GROTESQUE Theorisation of the grotesque has become almost exclusively linked to the work of Mikhail Bakhtin, who in *Rabelais and His World* (1965) studies medieval culture in order to argue for an identification of the grotesque with the 'folk'. At certain points in the calendar ordinary people were allowed to temporarily transgress the social order, replacing the regulating 'bodies' of church and state with rituals that foregrounded the irregular, crude and multiple material body. In Bakhtin's argument, therefore, the grotesque becomes associated with all that is exiled to the margins of propriety and acceptability – hence, as Mary Russo has argued in *The Female Grotesque* (1994), achieving an identification with the position of women in a male-dominated culture. Indeed, the female body which exudes both blood and babies is often identified as the ultimate example of the grotesque, as in Bakhtin's image of the 'senile, pregnant hag'. Artists such as Cindy **Sherman** and writers such as Angela **Carter** have, however, played a part in women's own appropriation and deployment of grotesque imagery in order to expose and critique the processes involved in creating socially-acceptable images of the **feminine**.

GUBAR, SUSAN: LITERARY CRITIC (1944–) Distinguished Professor of English and Women's Studies at Indiana University, Susan Gubar has published various essays, most notably '"The Blank Page" and the Issue of Female Creativity' (1981), which ranges from Greek **myths** to **modernism** to make its point that women have always been excluded from the public creative process. However, the blank page of the essay's title is identified with a female creativity which remains unrecorded in male texts and institutions. It is this view which informs the collaborative work with Sandra M. **Gilbert** for which both are best known, beginning with *The Madwoman in the Attic: The Woman Writer and the Nineteenth-Century Imagination* (1979). Although the author-centred focus of this study has been criticised as naïve and over-simplistic, it is still acknowledged as a classic text of **Anglo-American feminism**. Its three-volume sequel, *No Man's Land – The Place of the Woman Writer in the Twentieth Century* (1988–94), responds to this criticism by engaging with some of the subsequent developments in **feminist** literary theory.

GYN/ECOLOGY Term coined in Mary **Daly**'s 1979 publication *Gyn/Ecology: The Metaethics of Radical Feminism*, which argues that women must formulate a collective strength, a female body of knowledge, which will enable them to resist **patriarchal** control in both its physical and psychic manifestations. The book builds on Daly's account of ex-centric spirituality begun in *Beyond God the Father* (1973), to argue that male

dominance relies on sexual violence throughout history and in all cultures. Patriarchy, Daly claims, governs all institutions, including religion, medicine and science, and it erupts in sado-rituals such as foot binding and clitoridectomy. To contest phallic **culture**, women must work together to reverse male myths and renounce male **language** and beliefs. To this end, Daly reclaims the term 'gyn/ecology' itself from male medical discourse as part of her attempt to create a 'gynomorphic' vocabulary for women.

GYNOCRITICISM Term coined by Elaine **Showalter** in an influential essay, 'Feminist Criticism in the Wilderness' (1978), which describes a feminist critical practice which studies women's writing with the aim of tracing a specifically female literary tradition. Showalter argues that **feminist** criticism began with revisionary readings of the **literary canon**, a process she calls 'feminist reading'. Gynocriticism, however, is more ambitious in its theorising of female literary activity: 'its subjects are the history, styles, themes, **genres** and structures of writing by women; the psychodynamics of female creativity; the trajectory of the individual or collective female career; and the evolution and laws of a female literary tradition'. In this way, argues Showalter, feminist literary criticism will emerge as a specialised critical **discourse** capable of challenging the male domination of the field of literary theory. In 'Toward a Feminist Poetics' (1979), Showalter differentiates gynocriticism from what she terms '**feminist critique**', which is concerned with literature written by men.

Influential works of gynocriticism include Ellen Moers's *Literary Women* (1976), Showalter's own study *A Literature of their Own* (1977), and Sandra M. **Gilbert** and Susan **Gubar's** *Madwoman in the Attic* (1979). On the basis of these texts, feminist literary criticism has flourished in the academy, although it has ventured beyond the original agenda set out by Showalter in 1978, participating in the complex and multifaceted theoretical debates springing from **postmodernism, poststructuralism** and **psychoanalysis.**

H

HALDANE, CHARLOTTE: JOURNALIST AND AUTHOR (1894–1969) A suffragette and socialist, Charlotte Haldane worked as a journalist before deciding to write a novel which explored in fictional form her interest in prenatal sex selection. This led her to approach the renowned biochemist J. B. S. Haldane for scientific advice, an encounter which, as she describes in her autobiography *Truth Will Out* (1949), changed her life on both a professional and personal level. Not only did it result in a **science fiction** novel, *Man's World* (1926), but also in marriage to Haldane himself. J. B. S. moved in socialist circles which included both scientists and writers, such as Julian and Aldous Huxley, Naomi Mitcheson and Rebecca **West**, and Charlotte became integrated into this group, which was extremely influential in interwar debates concerning control of reproduction and the role of mothers. Her 1927 publication *Motherhood and Its Enemies* is problematic for its attack on the 'intersex' woman who apes **masculine** behaviour, whom Charlotte blames for devaluing motherhood through her 'abnormal' attitude to **femininity**. However, the book also reveals the same sceptical attitude towards eugenicist policies as her work of dystopian fiction *Man's World*. In 1939 she became the editor of *Woman Today*, a left-wing journal which included essays which promoted science as an important tool for the advancement of socialism.

HALL, RADCLYFFE: AUTHOR (1883–1943) Hall was born in Bournemouth. After her parents separated she suffered physical and sexual abuse from her mother and stepfather, and her education was further marred by undiagnosed dyslexia. At 18, Hall gained her independence when she gained her father's estate.

The first of Hall's five volumes of sentimental poetry appeared in 1906. Some were set to music, becoming popular songs. She subsequently published a collection of short stories and seven novels: *The Forge* (1924), *A Saturday Life* (1925), *Adam's Breed* (1926), *The Well of Loneliness* (1928), *The Master of the House* (1932) and *The Sixth Beatitude* (1936). Hall is best remembered for *The Well of Loneliness*, a groundbreaking portrayal of lesbian sexuality, which became notorious when it was banned under the Obscene Publications Act in 1928. Reissued in 1948, it has since become a lesbian classic.

Hall defined herself as a 'congenital invert' rather than a lesbian; moreover, her understanding of inversion would seem closer to the modern notion of **transsexualism**, as she adopted a **masculine** mode of dress and called herself John. Although

Hall had other lovers, her relation-ship with Lady Una Troughbridge lasted twenty-eight years. They lived together until Hall's death from cancer.

HARAWAY, DONNA: CULTURAL SCIENTIST AND PHILOSOPHER (1944–) Donna Haraway's first degree was in English, philosophy and biology, and in its spanning of the boundaries between the humanities and sciences set the tone for her subsequent work, an entertaining fusion of intellectual disciplines described by Haraway her-self as 'experimental critical fiction'. The research she did for her Ph.D., a dissertation on philosophy, history of science and biology, resulted in her first book, *Crystals, Fabrics and Fields: Metaphors of Organicism in 20th-Century Developmental Biology*.

The publication which made her name, however, was the essay 'The Cyborg Manifesto' (1985), in which she postulates the half-organic, half-technological figure of the **cyborg** as a paradigm for the **postmodern** situ-ation, where the boundaries between **nature** and **culture** are routinely transgressed. Not only are we all, quite literally, cyborgs, in that we are inescapably dependent on **techno-logical** networks, but we have also reached an epistemological impasse in which no truths stand for the whole. The cyborg, therefore, stands for the playful fusion of oppositional concepts and ironic and partial mean-ing. Although the cyborg does not replace dualism with totality, the ease with which it negotiates boundaries and oppositions is potentially liber-ating for women, who have always been relegated to the position of subordinate '**other**' in patriarchal dual-istic thought. 'The Cyborg Manifesto', which has made Haraway's name synonymous with technotheory, has been sometimes misread as a straight-forward celebration of technology. In fact, she asks us to realise that, although we must remain properly critical of technoscientific claims, because we are already bound up in its networks we cannot lay claim to an innocent subject position from which to speak. Thus our critiques cannot help but be compromised. In her latest publication, *Modest Witness@Second_ Millennium* (1997), the figure of the cyborg has mutated into Onco-mouse™ who is not only a visible sign of technological operation upon the 'natural', but, as trademarked organ-ism, foregrounds technoscience's in-volvement with capitalistic practices.

HARDING, SANDRA: PHILOSOPHER (1935–) Sandra Harding is now an American **feminist** philosopher of considerable repute. Focusing upon the American philosopher W. V. O. Quine's attempt and failure to break out of positivist epistemology, Hard-ing's doctoral dissertation was forma-tive for her writings on science and knowledge. Her publication of ground-breaking books in feminist phil-osophy began in 1983, when Harding edited (with Merrill B. Hintakka) *Discovering Reality*, a collection of essays which made a revolutionary impact on the hard-core reasoning in philosophy. In 1986 she published her landmark *The Science Question in Feminism* – winner of the Jessie Bernard Award of the American Sociological Association – arguing that women's social experience provides a unique starting point for discovering certain biases in science. This argument led her to challenge familiar assumptions about both science and knowledge, while seeking a better, more objective, vision of the world in *Whose Science? Whose Knowledge? Thinking from Women's Lives* (1991). By thinking from the lives of women, Harding claims that feminist standpoint epistemology can move us towards less partial thinking. Having established herself as a prominent representative of feminist epistemology, Harding continued to explore science. In 1998, Harding again challenged feminists, scientists and epistemologists by arguing, in *Is Science MultiCultural? Postcolonialisms, Feminisms and Epistemologies*, that different cultures organise the production of knowledge in different ways, and that other local knowledge systems may be better equipped to discover some aspects of the natural world than modern science. Harding's arguments remain contentious. Some feminists want to move the analysis of science beyond epistemology. Others find Harding's notions of a 'feminist standpoint' and 'strong objectivity' either highly innovative or problematic. Whatever the case, her gentle and accessible style continues to encourage feminist thinking.

HEILBRUN, CAROLYN: AUTHOR AND CRITIC (1926–) Carolyn Heilbrun is Avalon Foundation Professor in the Humanities at Columbia University, New York, and has been an influential voice in **feminist** literary criticism from the 1960s onwards. Her first major publication, *Towards Androgyny: Aspects of Male and Female in Literature* (1973), ranges from Greek **myths** to the **modernist** writing of Virginia **Woolf** in order to argue that dualistic conceptions of gender should be challenged, since adherence to a principle of **androgyny** would 'promise an unlimited range of personal destiny available to either sex'. Heilbrun's subsequent academic texts, such as *Reinventing Womanhood* (1979), *Representation of Women in Fiction* (1982), *Writing a Woman's Life* (1988), and *Hamlet's Mother and Other Women* (1990) continue her interest in expanding the literary roles available to women characters and the forms of representation available to women writers.

Heilbrun herself is also a prolific and popular novelist. Under the pseudonym Amanda Cross, she has written a number of mystery novels featuring Kate Fansler, an English professor and amateur detective. In addition, she has published a biography of Gloria **Steinem** (1996) and a collection of essays celebrating advancing age, *The Last Gift of Time: Life Beyond Sixty* (1998).

HEROINISM Term coined by American literary critic Ellen Moers (1928–1979) in *Literary Women* (1976). According to Moers, 'heroinism' describes an act of 'literary feminism': the attempt to develop new forms and literary conventions for women through the creation of active female characters, which resist the passivity of their conventional narrative roles. Moers summed up this project in a quotation drawn from Mary **Wollstonecraft**'s preface to her first novel, *Mary, a Fiction* (1788): 'In delineating the Heroine of this Fiction, the

Author attempts to develop a character different from those generally portrayed.' However, heroinism and feminism are not necessarily synonymous terms, a point Moers illustrates through reference to the Gothic novelist Ann Radcliffe who, although she was never identified with the kind of polemical feminism with which Wollstonecraft was associated, was nevertheless influential in making the Gothic novel a female space which would accommodate women as both writers and characters.

Although Moers dismissed heroinism as 'a word which sounds more like an addiction to drugs than a seal on literary accomplishment', she maintained that the coining of a new term was necessary 'because I could find nothing else in English to serve for the feminine of the heroic principle'.

HETEROSEXISM The assumption that heterosexuality is the only normal mode of behaviour for men and women. Feminists argue that heterosexism, both as an institution and as an **ideology**, is an essential element in the maintenance of **patriarchy**. Catherine **MacKinnon**, for example, in her essay 'Feminism, Marxism, Method and the State: An Agenda for Theory' (1982) asserts that **essentialist** assumptions which perceive the male as dominant and aggressive and the female as submissive and passive are rooted in the institution of heterosexuality, thus validating women's exploitation by men. Lesbian and gay experience is also marginalised within heterosexist ideology: Adrienne **Rich** terms it **'compulsory heterosexuality'**, which, in making male/female interactions the paradigm for all social and sexual relationships, prevents women from forming fruitful relationships amongst themselves.

HITE, SHERE: CULTURAL HISTORIAN (1942–) In an academic capacity, Shere Hite has lectured at universities in Britain and America. From 1972–78 she was director of a **feminist** sexuality project commissioned by the **National Organization for Women** (NOW), and in 1978 set up Hite Research International, a commercial organisation that combines research and publishing with business and family consulting. Hite is most widely associated with her survey on women's sexual behaviour, *The Hite Report on Female Sexuality* (1974), in which she argued that the definition of sex as penetration should be changed in order to take account of the fact that most women need external stimulation to achieve **orgasm**. *The Hite Report on Men and Male Sexuality* (1976) continued the argument from the other side of the **gender** divide, claiming that men, too, would benefit from a broader definition of sexual behaviour.

Hite has expanded her research into sexuality to include those social constructs that arise out of heterosexual practice. *The Hite Report on the Family: Eroticism and Power between Parents and Children* (1994) and *The Hite Report on the Family: Growing up under Patriarchy* (1995) argues that traditional notions of **'family'** are undergoing a process of redefinition, to include reconstructed family groupings which are not dependent on the 'mother/father' paradigm. She also examines how the family indoctrinates children into **patri-archal** power structures. In 1997, she published *Women with Women*, which calls for closer alliances between women on both a personal and professional level.

HOLTBY, WINIFRED: AUTHOR, JOURNALIST AND POLITICAL CAM-PAIGNER (1898–1935) Holtby was born in Rudston, Yorkshire, and grew up on her family's estate. Her mother, the first woman Alderman to serve the East Riding county council, inspired Holtby's best-known and last novel, *South Riding* (1936), a book which employs an epic scope in order to explore the impact of national social and political change on the lives of individuals. In the course of her relatively short life, she published six novels, two volumes of short stories, a collection of poetry, a play and a study of the work of Virginia **Woolf**, as well as a large amount of non-fiction and journalism.

Holtby is also remembered as the lifelong friend of the **feminist** and **pacifist** campaigner Vera **Brittain**. Both contributed to many feminist projects, including the journal *Time and Tide* (of which Holtby became the director in 1926), and were active members of the Six Point Group, an organisation which campaigned on behalf of equal opportunities for women. Holtby's vision was of 'a society in which there is no respect of persons, neither male nor female, but a supreme regard for the importance of the human being'. It was a view she expanded in *Women and a Changing Civilisation* (1934), a publication which strengthened her position as one of the most important figures in the inter-war feminist debate in Britain.

HOOKS, BELL: CRITIC (1952–) A prolific author, hooks (born Gloria Watkins) is a leading black cultural critic. Her first book, *Ain't I a Woman* (1981), on the marginalisation of black women within feminism, made her reputation and she has produced many volumes since on fiction, film, feminism and cultural theory, among them *Feminist Theory* (1984), *Talking Back* (1989), *Yearning* (1990), *Black Looks* (1992), *Outlaw Culture* (1994) and *Bone Black* (1997), an **auto-biography**. Hooks's feminism is not just about delivering **equal rights** for women, but is part of her general struggle against **oppression**. She is unyielding, therefore, in her criticism of **feminists**, such as Betty **Friedan** and Naomi **Wolf**, who leave to one side issues of race and **class** and take their own affluent, white experience for that of all women. Both embrace the opportunities capitalism offers successful women. The 'exclusionary use' of the term 'feminism' by white middle-class women leads hooks to shift from using the phrase 'I am a feminist' to saying 'I advocate feminism', for it serves 'as a way women who are concerned about feminism as well as other political movements could express their support while avoiding linguistic structures that give primacy to one particular group'.

HUTCHEON, LINDA: POSTMODERN THEORIST (1947–) Professor of English and Comparative Literature at the University of Toronto, Linda Hutcheon has published an influential series of studies on **post-**

modernism: *Narcissistic Narrative: The Metafictional Paradox* (1980), *A Poetics of Postmodernism* (1988), and *The Politics of Postmodernism* (1989). It is in *A Poetics of Postmodernism* that she fully develops her theory of 'historiographic metafiction', which she describes as fiction which promotes a view of the world as 'resolutely fictive and yet undeniably historical'. By 'asserting that both history and fiction are discourses, human constructs, signifying systems, and both derive their major claim to truth from that **identity**', historiographic metafiction repositions history as a contingent, rather than an absolute, discourse, and challenges its representational conventions. Thus it allows alternative subjectivities – those which have been exiled to the margins of the dominant cultural paradigm – to be reproduced through the practice of postmodernist fiction. Hutcheon's understanding of postmodernism, therefore, is not concerned with the deconstruction or alienation of the subject. Intend she argues that, on the contrary, it must work to affirm a female or **postcolonial** identity capable of participating in historiographic discourses and of effecting social change. Her most recent publication to date is *Irony's Edge: The Theory and Politics of Irony* (1994).

HYSTERIA A term coined from the Greek word for 'uterus', hysteria was once traditionally the preserve of over-emotional females, thus reinforcing the dualism which equated men with rationality and women with irrationality. However, as Elaine **Showalter** has noted in *The Female Malady* (1985), the advent of the First World War brought about an epidemic of male hysteria, or neurasthenia, which severely shook **gender**ed theories of mental illness. Showalter has since expanded her study of hysteria, and in her controversial study *Hystories: Hysterical Epidemics and Modern Culture* (1997) argues that tales of alien abduction, recovered memories of sexual abuse, chronic fatigue syndrome, multiple personality disorders and Gulf War syndrome are all manifestations of a *fin de siècle* epidemic of hysteria. All are 'hystories' – hysterical narratives that express our millennial angst. Not only is hysteria as prevalent today as it was in Charcot's Paris or **Freud**'s Vienna, but it is also more contagious. Other theorists, however, such as Hélène **Cixous** in *La Jeune Née* (1975) retain hysteria's customary association with women, representing it as an alternative and ambiguous **discourse** which allows female rage at her repression to be voiced.

IDENTITY The concept of identity, more specifically of a female identity, is particularly important within the work of those **feminists** influenced by **psychoanalysis**. **Freud** argued that the child gains a sense of identity within a social order through identification with the father, a process which leaves girls estranged from their mothers and identifying with a power which is not their own. **French feminists** such as Julia **Kristeva** seek to develop a concept of feminine identity by allying it with the anarchic drives that are suppressed within the regulatory dominant order; what she terms the **semiotic**. Such a concept does not, however, lead to the development of a stable **subjectivity**, but rather one which is fluid, amorphous and provisional.

Feminists across a wide spectrum of positions are also concerned with the way in which identity is formulated within **language**, arguing that it is a system which encodes a male, not a female, identity. Thus, Hélène **Cixous** proposes an *écriture féminine* (feminine writing) and Luce **Irigaray** *parler-femme* (speaking as a woman) to work in opposition to conventional linguistic structures; while Dale **Spender** calls for women to refute their muted role within what she terms 'man-made **language**'. First-person narratives such as **autobiography** are often presented by their authors as a way of formulating a more 'authentic' sense of self by recording the experiences of women which remain unrepresented within a **racist** or **sexist** society.

IDEOLOGY A term which gains much of its modern significance from the work of Louis **Althusser**, who defines ideology as the means whereby, at the level of ideas, every social group produces and reproduces the conditions of its own existence. Althusser argues that ideology 'represents the imaginary relationship of individuals to their real conditions of existence', disguising the real material relations between the different social classes. This knowledge can only be retrieved though a theoretically aware analysis of the interrelationships that prevail within society at any one time. Social change occurs when the ideology of the dominant **class** is no longer able to contain the contradictions existing in real social relations. **Feminists** seek, in a variety of different ways, to challenge an '**ideology** of **gender**' which naturalises inequitable divisions between male and female.

IMAGINARY When used in contemporary literary theory, this term originates in Jacques Lacan's rereading of **Freud**, where it refers to the narcissistic stage within which the child makes no differentiation between itself and the maternal body. As a stage in the evolution of an **identity** separate from the mother, the child begins to gain a sense of itself as an individual. However, this image is a myth: it is an imaginary **subjectivity** that allows the ego to speak of itself as 'I', and to indulge in fantasies of omnipotence. In order to achieve full integration within the social order, the child must finally repress this idealised imaginary self, relegating it, and the imaginary self-sufficiency it represents, to the unconscious. Theorists such as Hélène **Cixous** draw on Lacan's ideas in her quest to represent a feminine imaginary which retains a pre-Oedipal unity with the figure of the Mother.

INTERPELLATION A concept introduced by Louis **Althusser** in his essay 'Ideology and Ideological State Apparatuses' (1970). He describes how every individual is 'appointed as a subject' within **ideology** by being 'hailed' in terms of the role that they are expected to adopt. Althusser uses as an example the scenario of a police officer calling after a suspect: 'Hey, you there!'. Once the object of the address responds to that hail, he or she has taken on the role that the summons implicitly assigns to them: they have been 'interpellated' into the police officer's **discourse**.

In Althusser's theory, no one can escape being addressed and positioned within the dominant discourse. **Feminists**, like other resisting groups, seek to foreground the process of interpellation, and thus open up a space from which it can be critiqued. Feminist literary, film and cultural theory, for example, argue that the consumer of a text is invited to identify with it by adopting a particular viewpoint and attitudes which are often inimical to women. It is therefore necessary for them to become, in the words of Judith Fetterley, 'resisting readers', who work 'against the grain' of the text's superficial meanings in order to formulate interpretations which will challenge the values encoded within it.

INTERTEXTUALITY Term employed by Julia **Kristeva** to propose that meaning is always reliant on a range of contextual information. In *Desire in Language* (1980) Kristeva presents intertextuality as a concept which subverts the **symbolic order** by making meaning irreducible to single or stable units. In practice this means that every text is always understood in relation to a range of other texts. As with Jacques **Derrida**'s notion of *différance*, the consequence of this approach is that interpretation is always in process – never finished or finite. While 'intertextual' implies a literary usage the term 'text' is used here in its widest sense to denote any 'sign' or unit of meaning – so that a film, a piece of music or art, or even the self may be 'read' as a text. The concept of intertextuality has been instrumental in forging connections between disciplines such as English, film studies and cultural studies.

INTUITION There is an uncomfortable ambivalence about the way in which the notion of intuition or intuitive knowledge has been viewed, identified as it conventionally is with '**feminine**' ways of knowing. Revered as the basis of truly creative thought, respected as a key to practical, common sense wisdom, intuition is at the same time dismissed as something mysterious and unanalysable, situated outside accepted intellectual constructs. **Radical feminists** of the **second wave** tended to appropriate the concept of intuition as representing an alternative **epistemology** which was exclusive to women. Opponents of this view, however, argue that fascination with intuition merely reinforces the dualistic paradigm that equates women with emotion, men with reason.

IRIGARAY, LUCE: PHILOSOPHER AND PSYCHOANALYST (1932–) Director of Research at the Centre National de Recherches Scientifiques, Irigaray was originally a member of Jacques **Lacan**'s École Freudienne de Paris, but was expelled for her outspoken critiques of **psychoanalysis**. In her subsequent work, beginning with *Speculum of the Other Woman* (1974), she has continued to attempt to formulate an alternative to **masculine** philosophical thought, which she argues, works to alienate women from themselves. She maintains that throughout the entire western philosophical tradition from Plato to Hegel, women are the 'sex which is not one' – the title of a book she published in 1977.

Irigaray resembles Hélène **Cixous** and Julia **Kristeva** in her linking of **language** and sexuality, but she also praises the radical 'otherness' of women's eroticism, which she argues

reveals feminine identity as plural, offering the potential for the foundation of a feminine **symbolic order** which will allow women's difference from men to be celebrated. Her primary argument is founded upon the idea that women have always been forced to repress their sexuality, and that the reclaiming of it will have an enormously liberating effect. Rejecting **Freud**'s notion that women define themselves in terms of **lack** (that is, they see themselves as inferior to men because they do not possess a penis), she claims that, on the contrary, the female sex is composed of 'two lips' which 'embrace continuously'.

Irigaray's ideas have received a large amount of attention from **feminists**, and are also now being claimed for a theoretical **postfeminism**, which constructs female **identity** as **difference**. In *Sexual/Textual Politics* (1985) Toril **Moi** characterises Irigaray as 'struggl[ing] hard to avoid falling into the **essentialist** trap', in danger of perpetuating a **patriarchal** logic which positions woman as man's '**other**'. Moi's opinion has been challenged by such critics as Margaret Whitford, who argues that the irony inherent in Irigaray's formulation of a female **imaginary** is frequently overlooked: rather than 'an essentialist description of what women are really like . . . [it is] a description of the female as she appears in, and is symbolized by the western cultural imaginary' (*Luce Irigaray: Philosophy in the Feminine*, 1991).

J

JARDINE, ALICE: CRITIC (1951–)
Alice Jardine is Professor of Romance
Languages and Literatures at Harvard University. In 1985 she published *Gynesis: Configurations of
Women and Modernity*, in which she
coined the term 'gynesis' to describe
how women are represented in
modernist texts. Jardine criticises
deconstruction for having paid little
attention to women, arguing that 'for
Derrida and his disciples, questions
of how women might accede to
subjecthood, write texts or acquire
their own signatures, are phallogocentric questions'. Thus the 'feminine'
in a text is what has exceeded the
(male) author's meaning. In an essay
published in 1989, 'A Criticism of
Our Own', Elaine **Showalter** differentiates gynesic criticism from
gynocriticism by arguing that, while
gynocriticism is concerned with placing
women's work within a **cultural** context, gynesic criticism follows **poststructuralism** in divorcing the text
from the circumstances of its production; thus 'its **feminist** subjectivity is a
product of the reading process',
rather than considered as a specific
subject operating from within a
particular socio-historical situation.

Jardine was also an early participant in the debate concerning men's
relationship to feminism. Her book
Men in Feminism (1987), co-edited
with Paul Smith, allowed both male

and female academics to voice their
opinions on this complex issue.

JEFFREYS, SHEILA: SOCIOLOGIST
Senior Lecturer in the Department of
Political Science at the University of
Melbourne, Australia, Sheila Jeffreys
is a revolutionary **lesbian feminist**
who has been an activist since the
early 1970s. She has participated in
campaigns against **pornography** and
male violence, in 1980 becoming a
founder member of London Women
Against Violence.

Jeffreys' research has concentrated
on the history of female sexuality. In
The Spinster and Her Enemies (1985),
she examined how **first wave feminism** centred campaigns on sexually-
related issues, such as female purity,
child sexual abuse, **abortion** and
contraception. She concludes that the
sexual revolution which took place
after the First World War did not, in
fact, liberate women, but pressured
them into heterosexual relationships
by labelling those who were not
sexually active 'frigid' or 'prudish'.
Jeffreys develops this argument in
*Anticlimax: A Feminist Perspective on
the Sexual Revolution* (1990), which
claims that the sexual revolution insti-
gated by the feminist **second wave** has
legitimated the sexual exploitation of
women, and has strengthened the institution of heterosexuality. Jeffreys'
most recent work is *The Idea of*

Prostitution (1998), which portrays prostitutes as the sex industry's primary victims.

JEWISH FEMINISM It could be argued that Judaism and feminism have been intertwined at least from the 1960s onwards, since many of the women who were influential in the inception of the **second wave** feminist movement – Betty **Friedan** and Phyllis **Chesler**, for example – are also Jewish. Although the problems involved in reconciling Jewish and **feminist** identities were not necessarily something that such women addressed explicitly, Jewish women's groups began to spring up from 1971 onwards, with the intention to challenge their traditional exclusion from Jewish religious life. In 1972, this resulted in a delegation attending the annual convention of the conservative Rabbinical assembly in order to present a list of demands for equality under Jewish law. The first national Jewish feminist conference was held in 1973.

The Jewish feminist project is twofold – both to gain access to equality within the Jewish faith and to combat the anti-Semitism, which Jews encounter both inside and outside the feminist movement. The struggle with **identity** which lies at the heart of Jewish feminism has been movingly articulated by Adrienne **Rich** in her essay 'Split at the Root: An Essay on Jewish Identity' (1982): 'What did it mean to feel myself . . . both anti-Semite and Jew? And, as a feminist, how was I charting for myself the oppressions within **oppression**?'

Certainly, Jewish feminists have succeeded in making great incursions into their religious institutions. In the Conservative, Reconstructionist and Reform movements, women can now be ordained as rabbis, and moves have been made to create more inclusivist liturgies. Even Orthodox Judaism has granted women increased access to the Torah, thus enabling them to gain status as scholars. However, Jewish feminist theologians such as Judith Plaskow continue to argue that the subordination of women is inscribed deep within the linguistic and narrative structures upon which the Jewish faith is based.

JOUISSANCE In French theory 'jouissance' signifies '**pleasure**' or 'bliss', but the difficulty involved in developing an exact definition illustrates the ambiguity surrounding the term, which **French feminists** situate on the margins of signification. For Julia **Kristeva**, it indicates a female energy which cannot be fully incorporated into the **symbolic order,** and which is identified with a self-eroticism centred in the body of the mother. Hélène **Cixous** locates *jouissance* in the realm of the female **imaginary**, which is based on the **pleasure** of giving. Writing, for Cixous, becomes a way of experiencing *jouissance* by re-establishing a symbiotic relationship with the imaginary mother and a pre-Oedipal **feminine** sexuality.

K

KAHLO, FRIDA: ARTIST (1907–1954) Most of Kahlo's work, painted on canvas, wooden boards and tin, depicts her personal story; perhaps most important are the artist's many self-portraits. In them, Kahlo often portrays herself in native Mexican dress, her forehead or body imprinted with the people and events central to her life. Kahlo's paintings also have the strong silhouettes, insistent detail and bold colours often associated with folk art. In *Frida Kahlo* (1989), Angela **Carter** draws a parallel between Kahlo's work and that of the American performance artist Cindy **Sherman**, arguing that Kahlo deploys a subversive narcissism in her paintings which both appropriates and challenges the male **gaze**. Her use of **cross-dressing** and extravagant Mexican folk costume in her self-portraits also works to subvert conventional representations of **femininity**.

In 1925, at the age of 18, Kahlo was in a bus accident that injured her spine, pelvis and foot, injuries that led to many hospital stays, operations, and, ultimately, her death. In many ways her art is a chronicle of her personal pain and strength in the face of endless medical problems. Along with her partner, the muralist and social activist Diego Rivera, Kahlo was also a dedicated Communist. They were well known for their dedication to Mexico's populist causes and to the country's native culture.

KLEIN, MELANIE: PSYCHOANALYST (1882–1960) After her mother's death in 1914, Klein suffered from depression and was psychoanalysed. She grew interested in **psychoanalysis** herself and became a member of the British Psychoanalytical Society. Her first major book was *The Psychoanalysis of Children* (1931) and it is for her work with children, and in particular her development of play analysis, that she is famous. Klein's work, though rooted in **Freud**, significantly revises him. It is known today as **'object-relations' theory** and deals mainly with the way the child develops in relation to others, seen at various times as either 'good' or 'bad' objects and through which it develops a sense of self. Initially, the baby experiences love and hate in relation to the mother's breast, from whence all other relations come. Klein rejects the concept of **'penis envy'**, which for Freud is the girl-child's understanding of her own **lack**. Instead, she sees children of both sexes as envious of the mother's reproductive and life-giving powers. It is this aspect of Klein's work, her reinterpretation of the primacy of the mother/child relationship, that has been of most interest to feminists, though she could not be classed as a **feminist** herself.

KRISTEVA, JULIA: PSYCHOANALYST, LINGUIST, THEORIST, NOVELIST AND CRITIC (1941–) Julia Kristeva is a practising psychoanalyst and philosopher who teaches linguistics at the Université de Paris VII. Although Kristeva rejects 'feminism' as a term, her writing is primarily concerned with the issue of sexual **difference** and how this affects the constitution and place of the individual in **culture**. Kristeva does not identify **'feminine'** with a biological woman or **'masculine'** with biological man. In an implicitly **feminist** gesture, Kristeva argues that the place of sexual difference is the **semiotic**, which is the time of mother/child bonding, a moment of bodily eroticism, melodies and maternal rhythms, all of which precede the **symbolic** – the paternal zone. The meeting point of the semiotic and the symbolic in art and literature takes place in moments of *jouissance*, or **pleasure**. In 'Desire in Language' (1977), Kristeva suggests that the symbolic represses the semiotic or maternal drives, but that these erupt into language in the forms of puns and verbal slips.

In 'Women's Time' (1979), Kristeva proceeds to describe historical representations of sexual difference. Here the symbolic becomes the 'masculine' time of history, which is linear time, and the feminine is equated with cyclical and monumental time. All language, according to Kristeva, is sexually differentiated. The masculine symbolic retains, and indeed celebrates, logical connections and linearity. This singularity is, however, challenged by the semiotic which contains the 'feminine' drives or voice tones. This means that changes to dominant histories, to capitalism and to **patriarchy**, will depend not only on new political practices (in 'Women's Time' Kristeva discusses terrorist movements), but on new forms of **language** which revalue the feminine.

Kristeva's work seeks a place for women in the intellectual domain. Poetic language is central to Kristeva's endeavour, as it blurs the boundaries between signifying structures and subjective identity.

L

LACAN, JACQUES: PSYCHOANALYST (1901–1981) Lacan's rereadings of **Freud** have become influential within literary studies and **feminist** thought, forming the basis of the **psychoanalytic** theories concerning **feminine** consciousness and **identity** advanced by **French feminists** of the psychoanalytic school such as Julia **Kristeva** and Luce **Irigaray**, and have also aided the development of **queer theory**. Lacan's *The Four Fundamental Concepts of Psychoanalysis* (trans. 1977) and his *Écrits: A Selection* (trans. 1977) outline the nature of his revision of Freudian psychoanalytic method. A further selection of papers appeared under the title *Feminine Sexuality* (trans. 1982). It is to Lacan that we owe the terms '**imaginary**', '**symbolic order**' and '*jouissance*'. Similarly, it is to his investigation of the operations of the unconscious according to the model of **language** that we owe the notion of a 'split' human subject. For Lacan, the **imaginary** is associated with the pre-Oedipal and pre-linguistic relationship between the mother and child, where there appears to be no discrepancy between identity and its outward reflection (the 'mirror stage'). This is succeeded by the entry of the infant into the symbolic order, with its rules and prohibitions centred on the figure of the father, possessor of the ultimate signifier of authority, the phallus. The child's entry into the symbolic order, or '**Law of the Father**' is achieved by the repression of '**desire** of the mother'. This nostalgia for imaginary unity is repressed to form the unconscious, which the interaction between analyst and patient aims to unlock.

LACK A concept first developed by **Freud** in relation to sexuality. Before the Oedipal crisis, that is before the child understands the relationship between mother and father, we have a blissful relationship of psychic plenitude with the mother in which we experience no loss or **lack**. It is only with the primary repression of **desire** for the mother, which both brings the unconscious into being and marks our entry into full subjecthood, that we experience lack. For **feminists**, however, it is Freud's theory of feminine sexuality as lack which has been most often attacked. Sexual **difference** is understood as having/not having a penis, and therefore the female is defined as lack, an incomplete or castrated man and victim of **penis envy**. This deeply contentious idea has been much criticised both by feminists and from within psychoanalysis by a formidable array of influential analysts such as Melanie **Klein**, John Riviere and Ernest Jones, and, more recently, **French feminist** thinkers.

LANG, K.D.: SINGER-SONGWRITER
(1961–) Infatuated with country
music, and particularly Patsy Cline,
lang hooked up with backing band
The Reclines to release her debut
album, *A Truly Western Experience*
(1984). Her live reputation drew the
attention of Sire, and a major label
album, *Angel With a Lariat* (1987)
followed. By *Absolute Torch and
Twang* (1989) lang's status as one of
country music's most versatile and
original performers was established.
In the 1990s increasing attention was
paid to her personal life: long adopted as a lesbian icon, she now 'came
out' publicly. At around the same
time her album *Ingenue* (1992) inflected country with silky sophistication,
and showed her beautiful voice at its
best. Her most recent albums are the
playful *All You Can Eat* (1995) and
Drag (1995). The latter's title is an
obvious pun, for although the word
'drag' ostensibly alludes to the theme
of smoking, which links all the
album's songs together, it is also a
reference to the **androgynous, cross-
dressing** style for which lang is
famous. Lang has also been involved
with film, appearing in *Salmonberries*
(1991) by Percy Adlon, and scoring
the soundtrack to Gus Van Sant's
Even Cowgirls Get the Blues (1993).

LANGUAGE The term 'women's
language' was first used by Robin
Lakoff in her pioneering essay 'Language and Women's Place' (1975),
which argued that language did have
gendered features. **Second wave**
feminism is deeply concerned with
the material and political effects on
women of the everyday sexism we
encounter in social language and

cultural productions. Current **feminist** accounts of language usage follow
on from Kate **Millett**'s analysis of
literary **stereotypes** in *Sexual Politics*
(1970) and Dale **Spender**'s influential
account of the politics of **naming** in
Man Made Language (1980).

Feminist debates about forms of
sexism in language cover a number of
issues, ranging from assessing how
English usage discriminates against
women when 'man' purportedly stands
for both male and female; proposing
a non-sexist vocabulary; examining
literary representations of women and
men; and investigating how gender
ideology is produced and reproduced
in popular **culture**.

It is in language that **femininity**
and **masculinity** disclose themselves.
Gender rules define the limits of our
experiences and hence our subjectivities and our writing worlds. **French
feminists** assert that there are gender
differences in language and these
writers attempt to develop specifically 'feminine' **discourses**. Although
the reasons for male domination of
the language can be explained in
purely social terms, theorists such as
Jacques **Lacan** advance psychological
theories regarding the origin of language. However, as well as those who
believe that women possess their own
delicately-felt non-linguistic language,
there are others who believe that
women in fact have their own form of
essentialist discourse, which is lost
when we reach the stage of intern-
alising **androcentric** symbolism, and
so remains forever undeveloped,
suppressed in our subconscious. Toril
Moi, in *Sexual/Textual Politics* (1985),
claims that this causes differences to
emerge between male and female

writing. Hélène **Cixous** has suggested that women are closer to the mother's body, and hence 'write the body', while **Kristeva** proffers the notion of the pre-Oedipal **'semiotic'**, which works to subvert and undermine dominant male-centred language from the margins of signification.

LAUGHTER In *Rabelais and His World*, Mikhail Bakhtin portrays laughter as possessing the ability to critique authority, and thus able to liberate us from 'fear of the sacred, of prohibitions, of the past, of power'. Bakhtin's argument is reminiscent of **Freud**'s, who in his essay 'Humour' similarly regarded laughter as potentially rebellious, signifying 'not only the triumph of the ego but also of the **pleasure** principle, which is able here to assert itself against the unkindness of the real circumstances'.

For **feminists**, laughter can be a powerfully disruptive force when directed against **patriarchal** restrictions. The **French feminist** Hélène **Cixous**, for example, has created a paradigmatic figure in the Medusa whose laughter, aiming 'to smash everything, to shatter the framework of institutions, to blow up the law, to break up the "truth"', breaks down the prohibitions which work to silence women ('The Laugh of the Medusa', 1976). And in *La Jeune Née*, Cixous and Catherine Clément tell the story of Baubô, who makes Demeter laugh by showing her bare bottom. Demeter is mourning for the loss of her daughter, Persephone, but she laughs in spite of herself because she recognises in Baubô's action 'the mockery of **culture**' which 'is outmaneuvering the **Symbolic order**, overturning it'.

Outside the theoretical arena, the work of modern comediennes such as Victoria Wood, Jo Brand and French and Saunders can also be seen as participating in a redefinition of female roles. Their refusal to behave with propriety, their use of humour as both an analysis of female experience and as a weapon against men, cuts **patriarchy** down to size.

LAURETIS, TERESA DE: FILM THEORIST Teresa de Lauretis is Professor of the History of Consciousness at the University of California, Santa Cruz. Her publications include *Alice Doesn't: Feminism, Semiotics, Cinema* (1984), *Technologies of Gender* (1987), *The Practice of Love: Lesbian Sexuality and Perverse Desire* (1994), and the edited collection, *Feminist Studies/ Critical Studies* (1986). In her theoretical work on film, Teresa de Lauretis draws on **structuralism**, **semiotics** and **psychoanalysis** to explain the workings of narrative and spectator positioning in film texts. Focusing on questions of identification, **pleasure** and **desire** in film, she is also concerned with how these can be related to social and material reality. Arguing that **feminism** is characterised by a tension between 'the critical negativity of its theory' and the 'affirmative positivity of its politics', she has therefore written not only about mainstream film but also about **feminist** filmmakers who seek to offer alternative narratives which will articulate their desire in terms which interrupt or reverse the usual structures of narrative. Her most recent work has been concerned with issues around lesbian desire, in terms both of a theoretical understanding of 'perverse desire' and of its representation within film.

LAW OF THE FATHER A concept associated with Jacques **Lacan**, but taken up by a number of **feminist** thinkers (Luce **Irigaray**, for example) as part of a theory of the psychic roots of **patriarchy**. For Lacan, the Law of the Father is the breaking of the libidinal unity of mother and child and is represented by the Phallus, which is the symbol of castration, the prohibition of the child's **desire** for the mother and, more generally, the sign of the subject's position in the **symbolic order**, where sexual difference is reinforced at the cost of separation and loss. For many, the Law of the Father is not a natural state of affairs but a **cultural** construct, the product of patriarchal society.

LE DOEUFF, MICHÈLE: PHILOSOPHER (1948–) Michèle Le Doeuff has had a formative impact as a French philosopher on Anglo-American philosophy and feminism, especially on relations between male philosophers and women. Le Doeuff discerns a pattern, with far-reaching consequences for women students of philosophy, in the desire of philosophers to present their thought as complete, self-contained and free of any unthought elements. This desire causes male philosophers to project their own necessary lack of knowledge onto another; often the other is a woman student, lover or both. This other on which the philosopher projects his own lack tends to be someone who only has a relation to philosophy

mediated by a mentor who claims complete knowledge. Le Doeuff names this pattern of women's relation to philosophy via a male mentor or lover the 'Héloïse complex', finding an example in the relations of Simone de **Beauvoir** and Jean-Paul Sartre. The philosopher's desire for complete knowledge results in a philosophical practice that is unethical in projecting the necessary deficiencies in knowledge onto others and so creating the image of the other as lacking. The unthought elements in the practice of philosophy are located in what Le Doeuff calls 'the **philosophical imaginary**' or, roughly, in its symbolism or imagery. **Feminist** critiques of the maleness of reason are best placed in the philosophical imaginary, where the symbolic dimensions of the text meet the carefully worked-out claims to knowledge. The philosophical imaginary not only creates the unity of reason, but allows the exploration of neglected aspects of philosophy that are often associated with women.

LENNOX, ANNIE: SINGER, SONGWRITER AND PERFORMER (1954–) Annie Lennox has produced a wide-ranging body of work in music and video. She emerged in the 1970s as a member of The Tourists, and achieved international success in the 1980s with Dave Stewart as part of The Eurythmics. The Eurythmics produced socially conscious music videos that aimed to subvert the practice of constructing the female as object of the male **gaze**. In *Rocking Around the Clock* (1987), Anne E. Kaplin, for example, analyses camera techniques in the Aretha Franklin/Eurythmics video 'Sisters are Doin' It

For Themselves', which shows a montage of representations of women that draw attention to the ways in which images of women are constructed rather than 'natural'. In the video, Franklyn performs in a simple red dress alongside Lennox, who is dressed **androgynously** in white, **masculine**, clothing, thus 'bringing together powerful, current, alternative female images and the past strength of black female **discourses**'.

Since her split with Stewart in the 1990s, Lennox's solo performances and socially conscious videos continue as an important strand in her work, and it is in these that she is most subversive in her attempt to foreground social constructions of **gender** identity.

LESBIAN CONTINUUM Adrienne **Rich**, in her article 'Compulsory Heterosexuality and Lesbian Existence' (1980), defined the lesbian continuum against the 'clinical and limiting' term *lesbianism*, as 'a range – through each woman's life and throughout history – of woman-identified experience; not simply the fact that a woman has had or consciously desired genital sexual experience with another woman'. Woman-identified experience may include friendship, practical and emotional support, and other relationships between women which are not defined by sexual or familial convention. This definition has been criticised for so expanding the term 'lesbian' as to make it virtually indistinguishable from 'straight' practice – specifically by downplaying the role of the erotic in formulations of lesbian **identity**. While it is regarded with some suspicion in contemporary

debates about sexuality, there are explicit connections between this term and **queer theory**, most notably in Judith **Butler**'s use of Rich's phrase '**compulsory heterosexuality**'.

LESBIAN FEMINISM In the mid-1970s a call to political lesbianism by **radical feminists** was based on the principle that heterosexuality, as a social norm, was a further indication of women's oppression. This evolved from the assumption that the only 'true' **feminists** are lesbians because they choose women as sexual partners. Thus, they are truly woman-centred. In America, Charlotte Bunch's *Lesbianism and the Women's Movement* (1975) argued that 'the lesbian rejects male sexual/political domination; she defies his world, his social organisation, his **ideology**, and his definition of her as inferior'. This is achieved by the fact that lesbianism denies heterosexuality and thus closes off the last route of women's subordination – sexual domination. In Britain the political lesbian position was advanced by such as Leeds Revolutionary Feminists, in their publication *Political Lesbianism: The Case Against Patriarchy* (1979). They posited lesbianism as a political preference over and above **desire** and also maintained that lesbians were more **oppressed** than other women. This led to a hierarchy of beliefs and experiences, which placed political lesbianism as a single 'correct' feminist identity. The radical response to this ranged from continued calls for separatism and the recognition of the need to avoid excluding heterosexual women. Continuing debates around gay rights and splits between political lesbians and lesbian sado-masochists over exactly what constitutes gay experience has not helped to clarify the difference between an individual and a political **identity** in feminism. However, it has helped to open debates about heterosexuality and reaffirmed the importance of understanding **difference**.

LIBERAL FEMINISM The term 'liberal feminism' is an unwieldy one, in that it covers a wide range of opinions, not all of them compatible. Broadly speaking, however, liberal feminists work towards an egalitarian society, which would uphold the right of each individual to fulfil their potential. The liberal **feminist** tradition goes back to feminism's earliest days: John Stuart **Mill** and Mary **Wollstonecraft** both argued for the necessity of social reform in order to give women the same status and opportunities as men. They, in their turn, were influenced in the formulation of these ideas by **Enlightenment** philosophers such as Thomas Hobbes, who maintained in *The Citizen* (1651) that 'the right of all men to all things ought not to be retained'.

In the early years of the twentieth century a split emerged in Britain between 'old' feminism – exemplified in the work of Winifred **Holtby** and Vera **Brittain** – which clung to the liberal views of the nineteenth-century feminists, and 'new' feminism, which argued that equality between the sexes could not be achieved by legislation. Indeed, 'new' feminists such as Virginia **Woolf** held that in many areas men's and women's social needs were divergent, given the biological and psychological differences between them. Although these views anticipate the **essentialist** politics that has become identified with **second wave** feminism, the liberal voice has always been retained. The American Betty **Friedan** is considered to be the leading liberal feminist of the second wave, arguing in *The Feminine Mystique* (1963) that the way out of the confines of the home lay in increased access to **education** and the world of work.

Liberal feminism has been widely criticised by those who believe that it concentrates only on the most superficial forms of **sexism**, doing nothing to deconstruct the deeper **ideological** formations which subordinate women to men. It has also been attacked for bias in favour of white, middle-**class** women, ignoring the specific needs of minorities. Nevertheless, it should not be denied that liberal feminists are responsible for welfare, **education**, and health reforms that have benefited the lives of millions of women.

LIBERTARIANISM A term used by Sheila **Jeffreys** in *Anticlimax: A Feminist Perspective on the Sexual Revolution* (1990) to describe women who are against the censorship of pornographic material and the legislation of sexual behaviour. Jeffreys maintains that libertarianism is the **backlash** against the anti-**pornography** campaigns of **radical feminists** such as Andrea **Dworkin** and Catherine **MacKinnon**, and that it is in no way compatible with feminism, since 'libertarian theory does not originate in feminism but in the ideas of the sexologists, the **ideology** of the 1960s "sexual revolution", and the work of gay male theorists such as Michel **Foucault**'. Similarly, Andrea Dworkin terms women who defend pornography 'pseudofeminists' and 'collaborators'.

The term also functions as an apt description of the views of figures such as Susan **Sontag**, who argues that pornography can achieve the status of art, and Camille **Paglia**, who has proclaimed 'I am radically pro-pornography and pro-prostitution.' In 1979 the British novelist Angela **Carter** published an analysis of the work of the Marquis de Sade, *The Sadeian Woman*, which perfectly fits the libertarian mode. In this book, Carter put forward the notion of a hypothetical 'moral pornographer', who would 'use pornography as a critique of current relationships between the sexes'.

LITERARY CANON The word 'canon' derives from the Greek *kanon*, meaning a 'straight stick'. When Athanasius of Alexandria selected twenty-seven works of the New Testament as authoritative within the Christian tradition in 367 AD, he was invoking the notion of a standard or rule for determining which scriptures should be venerated. His main criteria were doctrinal reliability and historical verifiability.

Literary canons have evolved historically as a means of classifying what Matthew Arnold called 'the best that is thought and known in the world'. They are rarely constructed with rigorous criteria, although often the longevity and sustained appreciation of an author or text is enough to justify inclusion.

Feminists attack the institutional-isation of literary canons on the grounds that they are exclusionist and sexist. With the exception of figures such as the Brontës, Jane Austen and George Eliot, women writers have tended to be poorly represented on lists of the great and the good. Consequently, university syllabi seek to redress the balance by ensuring coverage of marginal or neglected female novelists, poets and dramatists. Also, there has been a resurgence of interest in forms of composition such as letters, journals and diaries, modes dominated by women but habitually ignored in the canon.

LORDE, AUDRE: POET AND ACADEMIC (1934–1992) Lorde was born in New York and educated at the University of Mexico, Hunter College and Columbia University. She took her first degree in literature and philosophy and her Master's degree in library science.

Lorde worked as a librarian before embarking on an academic career. She held various posts, including that of Thomas Hunter Professor at Hunter College. She published several volumes of poetry, as well as the **autobiographical** *Cancer Journals* (1980), the 'biomythographical' *Zami: A New Spelling of My Name* (1982) and the influential collection of essays *Sister Outsider* (1984).

The title of the latter indicates the trajectory of most of Lorde's writing, which, located as she was at the intersection of a number of peripheral subject positions – woman, Black, lesbian and, in the last years of her life, cancer sufferer – is largely concerned with the voicing of the experience of marginalisation. In 'An

Open Letter to Mary **Daly**' (1980), Lorde criticises *Gyn/Ecology* for falsely universalising women's experience, and making eurocentric assumptions stand for the whole. Her conclusion that 'beyond sisterhood is still **racism**' shows that, from an Afro-American perspective, feminism is nowhere near as inclusive an **ideology** as it might like to think.

LOVE, COURTNEY: SINGER, SONG-WRITER AND ACTRESS (1965–) Courtney Love was once considered to be no more than a groupie of her husband Kurt Cobain, but since his death, she has emerged as a talent in her own right, with a talent for personal reinvention second only to **Madonna**. Her early style was 'trailer trash chic', and she also invented the 'KinderWhore' look, chosen to make her look like a raped child, which became a favourite with **Riot Grrrl** feminists. However, Love underwent a dramatic makeover in 1997. She admitted to having undergone **cosmetic surgery**, and appeared on the cover of *Harper's Bazaar* and in the pages of *Vogue* as the Versace muse. Love is guitarist and lead vocalist in her band Hole, and has also appeared in several films, including *Sid and Nancy* (1986), *Feeling Minnesota* (1996) and *The People vs. Larry Flynt* (1996).

LOVELACE, ADA: MATHEMATICIAN (1815–1852) Ada Lovelace was the daughter of the poet Lord Byron. Her parents separated five weeks after her birth and she never knew her father. Ada married the Earl of Lovelace in 1835, and had three children; however, confessing in her

letters that she had 'a total deficiency in all natural love of children', her real passion remained mathematics. In 1834, Ada entered into what was to be a long correspondence with Charles Babbage, inventor of the calculating machine, the Analytical Engine, eventually producing an annotated translation of Louis Menabrea's article on Babbage's work. It was out of her deliberation of Menabrea's writing that Ada devised a way of programming the Analytical Engine. Her system, however, remained purely theoretical until the twentieth century: in 1979 a software language developed by the U.S. Defense Department was named 'Ada' in acknowledgement of her achievement at developing the world's first programming language.

Ada Lovelace's life, marred by illness and early death, and distinguished by intellectual achievements which remained largely unrecognised in her time, has become an inspiring fable for **feminist** technotheorists. Sadie **Plant**, in her book *Zeros and Ones* (1997) makes Ada an emblematic figure in her argument that computer **technology** is linked to female arts.

LUXEMBURG, ROSA: MARXIST REVO-LUTIONARY (1871–1919) Luxemburg's life took place during the most revolutionary period in modern history and her writings on the necessity of collective action and revolution continue to influence disparate groups from **anarchists** and socialists to left-wing liberals. Luxemburg, arguing against 'evolutionary' socialists of the day, did not believe that the capitalist system could be reformed to produce a just society. In *Reform or Revolution* (1899) she argued that capitalism was inherently prone to crisis. While the state could be pressurised into delivering reforms such as the vote, trade union rights and health care, through the use of the police and judiciary it was ultimately a weapon in the **class** war. In *The Mass Strike* (1906) which describes the Russian revolution of 1905, Luxemburg saw the role of the **activist** as that of leadership, directing the release of revolutionary energy towards the setting up of a socialist society. Although she fought doggedly for women's rights, true to her **Marxism**, Luxemburg believed that **women's liberation** could only come about in a classless society. Luxemburg co-founded the German Communist party, was imprisoned for anti-war activities and was murdered by Prussian soldiers after the suppression of the German revolution in 1919.

M

MacKinnon, Catherine: Lawyer
(1946–) Catherine MacKinnon is one of America's most famous lawyers, admired and reviled in about equal measure. She is the holder of a J.D. from Yale Law School (1977) and Ph.D. in political science from Yale University Graduate School (1987). She was admitted to the Bar of the U.S. Supreme Court in 1986, and is now Professor at the University of Michigan Law School. Wide-ranging though her career has been, her name will forever be linked with that of Andrea **Dworkin**, with whom she drafted a series of anti-**pornography** ordinances in the mid-1980s. The intention was to make pornography a civil rights issue rather than a moral one, and thus to give victims of pornography the right to legal redress. Although MacKinnon and Dworkin succeeded in getting anti-pornography ordinances passed in some American states they were later overturned by the U.S. Supreme Court on the grounds that they were in opposition to the constitutional right to free speech. From the beginning of her career, however, MacKinnon has fought to introduce legislation to protect women against sexual and physical violence and sex discrimination. Her most recent concern has been with seeking restitution for survivors of the sexual genocide in Bosnia and Croatia.

Madonna (1958–) Born in Michigan in 1958 to a poor Catholic family, Madonna Louise Ciccone transformed herself into the 'Material Girl' of the 1980s, the greed decade's most avaricious symbol. Her rise to fame was conventional enough: a succession of small bands and influential boyfriends led to a record contract and a Number 1 album, *Like a Virgin*. Once in the media gaze, Madonna adroitly manipulated her image to ensure maximum exposure (literally and figuratively). Ripped jeans, crop tops, pointy bras – each accessory toyed with the stuff of male fantasy, yet did so in a way which was ironically self-conscious and appealed to a young female fan-base eager to vindicate expressions of their own empowered sexuality.

The music barely mattered. Songs such as 'Holiday', 'Into the Groove' and 'Justify My Love' sold millions, but were always adjuncts to the visuals. Madonna's videos helped establish MTV as the final arbiter of pop values, and even when banned due to lewd or sacrilegious content generated more interest than the lightweight disco songs themselves.

Madonna's popularity peaked in the early 1990s, when cultural studies departments around the world debated the significance of this particular global marketing phenomenon and its contribution to issues of **gender.**

MARRIAGE In *The Second Sex*, Simone de Beauvoir asserts that marriage is 'the only means of integration in the community' for women, even though it places her under male authority. Those women who remain single are regarded as 'wastage'. Even in an era in which feminism has won many more social and professional opportunities for women, marriage remains an enduring institution. It is shored up by the **ideology** of **romance**, which enshrines it as the fitting end for all narratives, from fairy tale to film. As Angela Carter satirically notes in her novel *Nights at the Circus* (1984), 'True lovers' reunions always end in marriage.'

Feminist thought has long argued that marriage functions as a cornerstone of **patriarchy**. For Marxist feminists such as Christine **Delphy**, it operates as the means by which men gain control of female reproductive functions and women's **domestic** labour. Linguists claim that the western custom whereby the woman changes her name to that of her husband on marriage erases her identity in **language**, while **radical feminists** maintain that marriage is traditionally regarded as a private sphere which exists outside of the scope of public regulation, leaving abused wives with little opportunity of legal redress. Andrea **Dworkin**, for example, asserts that the institution of marriage 'developed from **rape** as a practice', thus upholding the sexual power of men. It is thus a form of **compulsory heterosexuality**, and the means by which the **oppression** of women is perpetuated sexually, economically, and socially. It also informs the way in which state organisations such as welfare and health are organised.

MARXIST FEMINISM As a theory of liberation, Marxism has much to say about women's **oppression**. However, Marxism sees **class** division rather than **gender** as the root of women's **oppression**. Because a great deal of the time and effort needed to reproduce the workforce comes from the private **family**, Marxism sees this as the key to women's oppression: despite **education** and healthcare in advanced capitalist countries, the system largely depends on women's unpaid labour for the creation of a healthy workforce. Women's generally lower economic and social status grows out of this. In the classic Marxist statement of this position, Engels's *The Origin of the Family, Private Property and the State* (1845) argues that the bourgeois family rests on a material foundation of inequality between husband and wife, where the latter is a kind of unpaid prostitute, producing heirs for the transmission of property in exchange for board and lodging. From this position comes *The Communist Manifesto*'s (1848) call for the abolition of the bourgeois family, an aim that chimes in with the aims of **radical feminism**. For Marxists, much feminism is a bourgeois theory that seeks to reform the system to the advantage of some women, rather than get rid of the system that exploits the vast majority of women and men.; see for example Naomi **Wolf**'s call for women to enter the workforce as bosses and as workers in *Fire With Fire* (1993). For Marxists this would result in one class of women bosses exploiting another group of female wage labourers. Nevertheless, feminism sees Marxist economic theory as often blind to gender issues and argues that Marxism has yet to explain with reference to the needs of capitalism how women's oppression seems to exist in all known societies. There are, of course, women who are Marxist-feminists and who are critical of Engels but who broadly agree with his analysis.

MASCULINITY In common with the term **femininity**, with which it is inherently linked as both parallel and opposite, masculinity is an extremely problematic term, in that both articulate the complexities in thinking about the dynamics of **gender**, sexuality, social roles and identifications. Masculinity, in its definition of what is characteristic of or peculiar to men, has recourse to simple biological determinism, essentialising biological distinctions between the sexes.

Sexual political enquiries into masculinity by men have tended to challenge the social expectations imposed on men by the masculine paradigm, and the more reactive 'masculinist' or **'men's' movements** have sought to reaffirm characteristics understood as masculine in the face of a perceived – and possibly politically actual – 'threat' from feminism.

Both **essentialist** feminism and deconstructive feminism have identified the binary structures of thought and culture within which objects and qualities are understood as corresponding to poles of masculinity and femininity, with those gendered masculine generally culturally privileged over the feminine. Essentialist feminism, then, seeks to reverse this hierarchy by reversing dominant cultural values and affirming the 'feminine'. Deconstructive feminism, however, ultimately seeks to undermine the very oppositional polarity between masculinity and femininity, the paradigm of binary thought.

MASCULINITY STUDIES Feminism has brought into being many things, but one which some feminists have already disowned is the growing body of work categorised under the general title 'masculinity studies'. In Kenneth Clatterbaugh's sociological study of what he describes as six contemporary perspectives on masculinity (conservative, profeminist, men's rights, spiritual, socialist, group-specific), *Contemporary Perspectives on Masculinity: Men, Women and Politics in Modern Society* (1990), he notes how each is in a different way a response to contemporary feminism. Most of this work (but by no means all) starts from the assumption that to talk about **masculinity** is to challenge masculinity's power. As Antony Easthope writes in *What a Man's Gotta Do: The Masculine Myth in Popular Culture* (1986): 'It is time to try to speak about masculinity, about what it is and how it works.' Easthope's focus is on what he calls dominant masculinity (the myth of heterosexual masculinity as something essential and self-evident which is tough, masterful, self-possessed, knowing, always in control, etc.). Easthope begins from the proposition that masculinity is a cultural construct; that is, it is not 'natural', 'normal', or 'universal'. He argues that dominant masculinity operates as a **gender** norm, and that it is against this norm that the many other different types of 'lived masculinities' (including gay masculinities) are invited to measure themselves. As part of this argument, he analyses the way dominant masculinity is represented across a range of popular cultural texts: pop songs, popular fiction, films, television and newspapers. From a similar perspective, Sean Nixon's examination of 'new man' masculinity, *Hard Looks: Masculinities, Spectatorship & Contemporary Consumption* (1996) explores it as 'a regime of representation', focusing on four key sites of cultural circulation: television advertising, press advertising, menswear shops and popular magazines for men. Although it is true that **feminists** have always encouraged men to examine their masculinity, many feminists are less than impressed with masculinity studies.

MASQUERADE Jacques **Lacan** uses the term to describe women's role of reflecting or representing the authority of the Phallus, thus legitimating the existence of the masculine subject. A somewhat different view is provided by the psychoanalyst Joan Riviere, who in 'Womanliness as Masquerade' (1929) presents masquerade as part of her case-study of an intellectual woman who feels compelled to put on a seductive performance of **femininity** in order to conceal her assumption of '**masculine**' rationality. Riviere's ideas have been developed, most notably, by Mary Ann Doane who in her essay 'Film and the Masquerade' (1982)

draws on Laura **Mulvey**'s theories of female **spectatorship** and Luce **Irigaray**'s psychoanalytic criticism, as well as Riviere's work, to argue that masquerade is potentially liberating for women. Whereas cinema always constructs the feminine as the object of the **gaze**, thus denying the female subject an objective view of the self, masquerade reveals that 'womanliness is a mask which can be worn or removed', and thus draws attention to the processes whereby it is constructed. Judith **Butler** also makes use of the term in *Gender Trouble* (1990), in which she debates the opposing arguments of Lacan and Riviere in order to question whether masquerade legitimises or deconstructs the existence of an *a priori*, **essentialist** feminine **subjectivity**.

MATRIARCHY A matriarchal society is one led by women, in which the line of descent is traced through the female, rather than the male, line. A number of feminist anthropologists, such as Helen Diner, Elizabeth Gould Davis and Evelyn Reed, have postulated the existence of matriarchal clans which preceded the institution of **patriarchy**.

For proponents of matriarchal systems, the importance of such a social structure is not just that it vindicates female power, but that it creates a social framework modelled on 'female' virtues, such as nurturing and peaceable cooperation and respect for the environment. In *The War Against Women* (1992), for example, Marilyn **French** argues that the earliest human settlements were '**goddess**-worshipping communities living in egalitarian harmony and material well-being', in which 'women had somewhat higher status and more respect than men'. These were superseded by a patriarchal system ruled over by 'king-priests', who created a caste-system which subjugated women. Adrienne **Rich**, on the other hand, prefers not to speculate as to whether a universal matriarchy once existed, but acknowledges that, **myth** or reality, it represents a powerful longing to retrieve a female past from accounts of history which render women silent and their experiences invisible (*Of Woman Born*, 1976). More recently, '**postfeminists**' like Rene **Denfeld** in *The New Victorians* (1995) have attacked the notion of prepatriarchal societies as nonsense, and have condemned modern feminism for promoting spurious New Age theologies based on goddess-worship.

MEDIA We face a growing network of commercial intertextuality, such as the global news coverage offered by CNN, and Japanese acquisition of American software. International marketing leads to a declining emphasis on dialogue: the visual and violent as commodities reach a transnational audience with little in the way of shared **culture**. In the network of global information systems film and television are powerful media. In them, women are, for the most part, represented negatively or not represented at all. Analysis of women's roles in mainstream media and the creation of feminist alternatives to these representations have therefore become an important project in **feminist** theory. Feminist criticism first centred on simple content analysis of sexual **stereotypes** in media,

drawing on **semiotics** in order to deconstruct such images. It can, however, be argued that it is the medium itself as much as the content which enables or creates **sexist** meanings. For example, reference to **psychoanalytical** critiques enables feminist theorists such as Laura **Mulvey** to think about how media's address to specific spectators (usually male) shapes film form.

MEN'S MOVEMENTS While there are as many subdivisions within the men's movement as within feminism, the phenomena began with the Men's Rights Movement of the 1970s, with Jack Sawyer's article 'On Male Liberation' (1970) and Mark Feigen Fasteau's book *The Male Machine* (1975) emerging as key texts. Organisations such as the National Organization for Men Against Sexism (NOMAS) align themselves with feminism, but many sectors of the men's movement react against the female fight for liberation, claiming **masculinity** to be a set of behaviours and attitudes which are either constructed (by men's social role as protectors and providers), or 'natural' and innate. In either case, it is wrong for feminism to attack men for conforming to the dictates of duty and/or nature. Thus, traditional masculinity becomes a defensive posture in the face of the **feminist** threat, an attempt by which men attempt to cope with their own diminishment in the face of the growing empowerment of women. One of the most well-known sectors of the men's movement is that which seeks to reassert the 'mythical', but intrinsic, nature of manhood. Robert **Bly**'s *Iron John* (1990) and R.

Moore and D. Gillette's *The King Within: Accessing the King in the Male Psyche* (1992) encourages men to take time to isolate themselves from the powerful influence of **femininity** in order to rediscover their inner masculine selves. Weekend retreats offer men the time and space to act out the inner aggressions and 'innate' masculine emotions denied in the company of women. Essentially, such a philosophy encourages the reassertion of traditional western cultural norms of heterosexuality, **marriage** and complimentary **gender** roles, with attributes such as aggression, risk-taking and preoccupations with power, money and status reappearing as 'masculine' qualities.

MENSTRUATION In *The Female Eunuch*, Germaine **Greer** famously proclaimed: 'If you think you are emancipated, you might consider the idea of tasting your menstrual blood – if it makes you sick, you've a long way to go, baby.' She represents a **feminist** point of view that seeks to divest the physical process of menstruation with the shameful and unclean associations it has accrued under **patriarchy**. In *Gyn/Ecology*, Mary **Daly** asserts that 'the menstruating woman is called filthy, sick, unbalanced, ritually impure. In patriarchy her bloodshed is made into a badge of shame, a sign of her radical ontological impurity.' **Essentialist** feminism argues that menstruation should be acknowledged as a proud symbol of entry into womanhood, while social reformers argue for the necessity for educative programmes for girls and an increase in research into the biological processes behind menstruation.

MILL, JOHN STUART: POLITICAL THEORIST AND ECONOMIST (1806–1873) In the history of nineteenth-century feminism John Stuart Mill is best known for his essay *The Subjection of Women* (1869), a central document of Victorian sexual politics, although he also examined Benthamism in his *Utilitarianism* (1863) and freedom of the individual in *On Liberty* (1859). Mill worked for most of his adult life in India House, the headquarters of the East India Company. He was elected MP for Westminster from 1865–8, and in 1867 was founder of the first woman's suffrage society.

In 1851 Mill married Harriet Taylor (1807–1858), with whom he had been in love since they met in 1830. After her death in 1858, her daughter Helen urged him to continue her work for women, which he did in the *Subjection*. Directed largely at middle-class married women, Mill's book attacked the 'legal subordination of one sex to the other' based on men's superior strength. He famously compared oppressed wives with slaves, and insisted that the so-called 'true nature of women' could never be known in the artificial society in which they were currently living. 'What is now called the nature of women is an eminently artificial thing', he argued, and the *Subjection* is largely a plea that all impediments to their employment and progress should be removed. Mill maintained that 'the only school of genuine moral sentiment is society between equals'. Where the *Subjection* has disappointed is in its assumption that married women will rarely want to work outside the home; there is also nothing on divorce. Its greatest strength perhaps is its logical argument combined with a certain outspokenness, as when Mill acknowledges that the 'vilest malefactor has some wretched woman tied to him, against whom he can commit any atrocity except killing her'.

MILLETT, KATE: PAINTER, SCULPTOR AND WRITER (1934–) Kate Millett is the author of one of the founding texts of the **second wave feminist** movement, *Sexual Politics* (1970). The radicalism of this publication lay in its claim that personal relationships between men and women are fundamentally political, becoming the paradigm for all other power relationships within **patriarchy**. According to Millett, the differences between the sexes are not biological in origin, but are manufactured within **culture**, with writers such as D. H. Lawrence, Henry Miller, and Norman Mailer producing literature which naturalises the male domination of the female. Although these representations are fictional, Millett argues that fiction functions as a form of **advertising**, in that it invites readings which give it the status of reality. By the same token, *Sexual Politics* attacks **Freud**ian theory for **essentialising** inequalities between the sexes. Millett's ideal, and one which she argued second wave feminists were steadily working towards, was an **androgynous** society, in which neither **gender** would dominate the other. Millett holds up feminism's 'first phase' (from 1830– 1930) as an example of its previous failure to attack the foundations of patriarchal authority, arguing that **first wave feminism** foundered on its failure to destroy the 'socialization process of temperament and role differentiation' which maintained patriarchy as an institution.

Although *Sexual Politics* established an agenda for **radical feminism** in the 1970s, Millett herself, after being diagnosed as a manic-depressive in 1973, moved on to publish more **autobiographical** work. It was an experience she drew on in *The Loony Bin Trip* (1991), which criticises society's treatment of the mentally ill.

MINH-HA, TRINH T.: FILM-MAKER, COMPOSER, POET AND THEORIST (1953–) Born in Vietnam, Trinh T. Minh-ha originally trained as a composer at the University of Illinois, and is currently Professor of Women's Studies and Rhetoric at the University of California, Berkeley. She has made several avant-garde films including *A Tale of Love* (1995), *Surname Viet Given Name Nam* (1989), *Naked Spaces – Living is Round* (1985) and *Reassemblage* (1982). A book of her poetry, *En minuscules*, was published in 1987. Her non-fiction writing focuses on **postcolonial** theory, **gender** and film, and includes *Woman, Native, Other* (1989), *When the Moon Waxes Red* (1991) and *Framer Framed* (1992).

Working at the nexus of postcolonial theory and theories of representation, as well as from a perspective which is both Vietnamese and American, Trinh T. Minh-ha has evolved the concept of the 'inappropriate/d other'; the subject who operates both from within and outside the boundaries of the dominant **culture**. The inappropriate/d other is neither fully displaced nor amalgamated, but can move between margin and centre, articulating the experience of dislocation without succumbing to alienation and exile. In her essay 'The Promises of Monsters: A Regenerative Politics for Inappropriate/d Others' (1992), Donna **Haraway** describes the inappropriate/d other as existing 'within a critical, deconstructive relationality, in a diffracting rather than a reflecting (ratio)nality – as the means of making potent connection that exceeds domination'. For Trinh T. Minh-ha, identity is plural, complex and many-layered, since 'despite our desperate, eternal attempt to separate, contain and mend, categories always leak' (*Woman, Native, Other*).

MITCHELL, JULIET: WRITER (1940–) Mitchell has written on a wide number of topics from **socialist feminism** to literature, but she is most famous for her defence of **Freud** in her pathbreaking and enormously influential book, *Psychoanalysis and Feminism* (1974). Contrary to many **feminists** in the late sixties (such as Germaine **Greer** and Kate **Millett**) who saw Freud's work as the psychological justification and **ideological** underpinning of **patriarchy**, Mitchell argued that 'the greater part of the feminist movement has identified Freud as the enemy . . . [but] a rejection of **psychoanalysis** and of Freud's work is fatal for feminism . . . Psychoanalysis is not a recommendation *for* a patriarchal society but an analysis *of* one'. While detractors may seriously misread Freud, so do some of his admirers who see Freud's work as a form of cultural or **biological determinism**. For Mitchell, Freud's value

lies in his understanding of how patriarchy becomes embedded in the psychic life of the individual, and most importantly, that these structures of thought are the product of a particular epoch in human history and are therefore susceptible to change. Mitchell has edited important collections of the work of Melanie **Klein** and, with Jacqueline Rose, of Jacques **Lacan**'s writings on **feminine** sexuality.

MLF (*MOUVEMENT DE LIBÉRATION DES FEMMES*) The MLF was born out of the student and worker strikes in Paris of May-June 1968. It was initially used by the press to describe a collection of radical women's groups, but by 1970 it had come to denote the **feminist** movement in France as a whole. However, the MLF was never a unified organisation centred on a single agenda, and the two main groups operating under the MLF umbrella represented very different forms of feminism. The *féministes révolutionnaires*, whose major spokesperson was Monique **Wittig**, were radical and confrontational in their politics, believing that **activist** tactics must be employed in order to bring down the **patriarchal** order. Following the American model of **consciousness-raising**, they staged a number of high-profile demonstrations, such as public protests against Mother's Day and Father's Day, and political disruptions. In contrast, the *Psychanalyse et Politique* group (which later become *politique et psychanalyse*, or *po et psyche*), as their name indicates, rejected the anti-**Freud**ian stance of the *féministes révolutionnaires*, and turned to **psychoanalysis**

as a means of interrogating the means by which gender **difference** was constructed within **culture**. They were represented principally by the psychoanalyst Annette Fouque, who was also responsible for setting up the influential feminist publishing house *des femmes*, which has played an important part in the dissemination of feminist psychoanalytic theory. Amidst much controversy, the logo 'MLF' was legally taken over by *po et psyche* in 1975.

MODERNISM An artistic and literary movement that emerged at the beginning of the twentieth century, influenced by developments in **psychoanalysis** and avant-garde representational experimentation. A response to the crisis of modernity, the development of modernism was given added impetus by the catastrophic effects of the First World War. In literature, the poet T. S. Eliot published a highly influential essay, 'Tradition and the Individual Talent' (1919), in which he declared that the true poet wrote from a position of impersonality, acting as a channel for a historical consciousness which excluded feeling and moral judgement. In *No Man's Land* (1988) Sandra M. **Gilbert** and Susan **Gubar** argue that the doctrine of impersonality allowed male modernist writers such as Ezra Pound and D. H. Lawrence, as well as Eliot himself, to construct an elitist and misogynistic concept of literary excellence which excluded women on the grounds of their tendency towards emotionalism. However, women writers refused to regard themselves as separate from the modernist project, regard-

ing its demand for a break with tradition as signifying the possibility of a new start for the female author. Foremost among women modernists was Virginia **Woolf**, who argued in 'Women in Fiction' (1929) that 'the aloofness that was once within the reach of genius and originality is only now coming within the reach of the ordinary woman'. Along with Dorothy **Richardson**, May Sinclair and Katherine Mansfield, Woolf led the way in the attempt to formulate a distinctively **feminine** aesthetic based on new forms of representation that would better convey the workings of the female consciousness: indeed, Woolf's and Richardson's use of 'stream of consciousness' narration (which presents the thoughts of a character unmediated by any framing narrative) anticipates the idea of *écriture féminine* developed by French theorists such as **Kristeva** and **Cixous**.

Other women writers who emerged as important contributors to modernism include Gertrude **Stein**, Djuna Barnes and Mina Loy. Many useful **feminist** analyses of female modernism are in print, including Sandra M. Gilbert and Susan Gubar's three-volume work *No Man's Land: The Place of the Woman Writer in the Twentieth Century* (1987–94) and Bonnie Kime Scott's *The Gender of Modernism* (1990).

MODLESKI, TANIA: CULTURAL CRITIC AND ACADEMIC (1949–) Modleski's earlier publications examine various popular **media** from a primarily **Marxist-feminist** perspective. Her first book, *Loving With A Vengeance* (1982), is a **feminist** study of the more positive aspects of popular, formulaic texts such as Harlequin novels, Gothic romance novels and television soap operas. *The Women Who Knew Too Much: Hitchcock and Feminist Theory* (1988) is a collection of feminist readings of the Hitchcock films *Blackmail, Murder, Rebecca, Notorious, Rear Window, Vertigo* and *Frenzy*. Modleski's latest book, *Feminism Without Women: Culture and Criticism in a "Postfeminist" Age* (1991) is a collection of essays critiquing contemporary images of women in the media that move away from Marxism and instead, controversially, advocate a form of feminist essentialism. She critiques the 'myth of **postfeminism**', warning that the move from women-centred, feminist approaches to **gender** studies is allowing patriarchy to both appropriate and contain feminism for maculinist ends.

Modleski is also the editor of *Studies in Entertainment: Critical Approaches to Mass Culture* (1986). She is currently Professor of Film and Literature at the University of Wisconsin-Milwaukee.

Moi, Toril: Academic (1953–) The Norwegian-born academic Toril Moi is best known for her influential work on **French feminism**: indeed, she was a pivotal figure in bringing the work of theorists such as Hélène **Cixous**, Julia **Kristeva** and Luce **Irigaray** to a wider audience in the mid-1980s. *Sexual/Textual Politics*, published in 1985, not only outlined the often-complex ideas of these three writers, but also influentially compared them with the work of **Anglo-American feminist** critics such as Elaine **Showalter**, Sandra M.

Gilbert and Susan **Gubar**. Moi subsequently edited two influential translations of French feminist writing: *The Kristeva Reader* (1986) and *French Feminist Thought: A Reader* (1987), and is also the author of *Feminist Literary Theory and Simone de Beauvoir* (1990). Toril Moi is also the co-editor, with Janice Radway, of *Materialist Feminism* (1994).

Monstrous Feminine Barbara Creed, in her eponymous book, defines the monstrous feminine in psychoanalytic terms as the figure of feminine excess. Through her reading of Sigmund **Freud** and Julia **Kristeva**, Creed elucidates visual and cultural representations of the excessive **feminine** body which exorcise fears regarding female sexuality and women's ability to procreate. These include representations of the monstrous mother in films such as *Alien* (Ridley Scott, 1979) and *The Brood* (David Cronenberg, 1979), and the vagina dentata, or 'toothed vagina', in **pornography** and horror films. Such representations focus on women's bodies and their difference from the male 'norm', depicting **menstruation**, pregnancy and childbirth as grotesque and horrific. Creed's work builds on and responds to that of other **feminist** film critics and theorists who deal with **abjection**, the phallic woman and the debate between feminism and **psychoanalysis**.

Morris, Meaghan: Cultural Critic (1950–) Currently Australian Research Council Senior Fellow at the University of Technology, Sydney, Meaghan Morris is Australia's most well-known cultural critic. Morris's early work on **Foucault**'s theories concerning knowledge and power has set the tone for much of her subsequent research, which attempts to find a place within **postmodernism** from which a female **subjectivity** can be articulated, and examines how the female subject is constructed through a network of cultural **discourses**. In *The Pirate's Fiancée: Feminism, Reading, Postmodernism* (1988), Morris locates these discourses in a wide range of cultural phenomena, including shopping centres, **fashion** and film. The title of the book is drawn from Nelly Kaplan's 1969 film *La Fiancée du pirate*, which provides Morris with a female figure, who, 'acting critically upon her everyday conditions of existence – to transform her position within them', represents her own discursive intention, which is to appropriate postmodernist discourse and situate it within a **feminist** frame.

Morris is also intrinsically concerned with history, the subject of her most recent publication, *Too Soon Too Late: History in Popular Culture* (1998), in which she critiques feminist analyses of **culture** which overlook specificities of **class**, economy and nation, and a postmodern conception of history as something which is somehow beyond culture. For Morris, history arises from the complex interactions located *within* culture, and thus is always plural, particular and localised.

MORRISON, TONI: NOVELIST AND ESSAYIST (1931–) Morrison was born in Lorain, Ohio, where she set her first novel, *The Bluest Eye* (1970), a grim meditation on the aesthetics of beauty in a **racist** society, and the Pulitzer prize-winning *Beloved* (1987), a historical novel dealing with the psychological consequences for a mother who saves her young daughter from a life of slavery by killing her. From the mid-sixties until the mid-eighties Morrison was a senior editor at the distinguished publishers Random House. There she was able to encourage a new generation of black women writers including Angela **Davis**, Gayl Jones and June Jordan. Awarded many literary prizes and honorary doctorates for her fiction, Morrison is unquestionably the most important African American novelist now writing. In 1993, she became the first African American to receive the Nobel Prize for Literature. Morrison's novels deal with profoundly painful subjects such as child **rape** and murder, and as the Nobel citation says, 'by writing novels characterized by visionary force and poetic import, [Morrison] gives life to an essential aspect of American reality'. She deals with this reality, however, by constructing complex, hybrid texts that draw on the African American oral tradition, South American magic realism and the supernatural and Gothic elements to be found in other American writers such as Hawthorne and Melville to produce fiction that goes far beyond the conventions of contemporary realism. Her other novels are *Sula* (1973), *Song of Solomon* (1977), *Tar Baby* (1981), *Jazz* (1992) and *Paradise* (1998).

MOTHER/DAUGHTER RELATIONSHIP The relationship between mother and daughter is a much-analysed subject in both **feminist** art and theory. There has been a substantial amount of **autobiographical** or semi-autobiographical material published by feminist writers in recent years which is specifically focused around the figure of the mother, such as Carolyn Steedman's *A Landscape for a Good Woman* (1986), Marilyn **French**'s *Her Mother's Daughter* (1987), and Margaret Forster's *Hidden Lives* (1995). In all of these narratives, the mother appears as a problematic figure, towards whom the author experiences contradictory feelings of closeness and distance. In its reconstruction of the mother's history, the text itself is an attempt to bridge the gap between mother and daughter, yet in its 'authoring' of that story also implicitly repudiates the anonymous life the mother represents.

As psychiatrists like **Freud** and **Lacan** would famously have it, the gaining of an adult, social **identity** is predicated upon separation from the mother: a process which may be somewhat more problematic for girls than boys. It is the **psychoanalytic** concept of the mother-daughter relationship which has been taken up by theoretical feminists such as Luce **Irigaray**, who argues that women, in being forced to distance themselves from the figure of the mother, cannot help but become alienated from themselves: in opposition to this, Irigaray postulates an alternative economy in which 'a woman would be directly in intersubjective relation with her mother' (*Sexes et parentés*, 1987). Hélène **Cixous** argues that women retain a closer association with the mother which gives them greater access to the libidinal act of writing, an impulse which arises from the plenitude of the maternal body. In

Gyn/Ecology (1978), Mary **Daly** claims that the aim of **radical feminism** is reunion with the mother and a transformation of the relationship between mother and daughter; what she terms the re-establishment of 'Mother-Right'.

MULVEY, LAURA: FILM THEORIST (1941–) Laura Mulvey is the author of the famous paper 'Visual Pleasure in Narrative Cinema' (1975), where she employs **psychoanalytic** theory to analyse how pre-existing patterns of fascination determine how a film will be read. Lacanian **psychoanalysis** provides her with a methodology to analyse the unconscious, structured like a language in order to deconstruct and therefore reveal the unconscious of **patriarchal** society. Mulvey's aim is to destroy the **pleasure** in the text in order to conceive a new **language** of **desire**. In her essay, Mulvey refers to three key psychoanalytic concepts:

1. **Freud**'s notion of scopophilia (looking as a source of pleasure);
2. **Lacan**'s mirror phase, in which the child perceives its ego ideal, but recognition is mislaid in misrecognition. She argues that this **narcissistic** process is reproduced in cinematic representation.
3. The castration complex, where desire is shaped through sexual **difference**.

Mulvey argues that sexual difference controls how we view film; the woman on the screen connotes to-be-looked-at-ness, both for the male spectator and the character on the screen with whom the protagonist identifies. This means that the female

279

character in film is either fetishised or voyeuristically scrutinised.

In 'Afterthoughts . . . Inspired by *Duel in the Sun*', published in *Framework* in 1981, Mulvey attempts to theorise female visual pleasure, which she resolved shifts between 'active' **masculinity** and 'passive' **femininity**. She refers to this as 'trans-sex identification'.

MYTH In her controversial study of **pornography**, *The Sadeian Woman* (1977), the British writer Angela **Carter** dismissed myth as 'consolatory nonsense'. She was highly sceptical of **feminist** attempts to recover female-centred mythologies, believing that 'it does so at the price of obscuring the real conditions of life'. Views such as this notwithstanding, feminists have long been interested in myth, arguing for either the recovery or invention of empowering myths for women. In *Gyn/Ecology* (1978), for example, the American **radical feminist** Mary **Daly**

asserts that mythic power has been stolen from women by **patriarchy**, and that a connection must be restored with 'gynocentric' myths if women are to truly know themselves. Adrienne **Rich**'s poem 'Diving into the Wreck' portrays a similar project; an attempt to find what lies behind 'a book of myths/ in which/ our names do not appear'. The work of feminist **science fiction** and **fantasy** writers, such as Joanna **Russ**, can also be said to constitute the effort to create new and inspiring myths for women. Some feminist theorists have also appropriated and transformed mythical figures into highly evocative symbols of female transgression and rebellion. In her famous essay 'The Laugh of the Medusa' (1976), for example, the French writer Hélène **Cixous** asks her readers to consider the monstrous snake-headed Medusa of Greek myth, who turns men to stone, as a positive representative of the power of female expression which has been exiled from male **culture**.

N

NAMING In her 1980 novel *On Strike Against God* the **radical feminist** writer Joanna **Russ** asserts that 'it is very important ... *to find out for whom you were named*': a statement which draws attention to the importance of naming as an issue for **feminists**. Russ's point that the history behind one's name can convey significant facts about women's place in **culture** is reiterated in a non-fictional context by Dale **Spender** in *Man Made Language* (1980), which presents a twofold argument. Spender sees the naming process as an inescapable necessity if we are to make sense of our experience – and, indeed, of ourselves – but she also observes that not everyone has equal access to signifying systems. Hence her call for the critique of a system in which **patriarchal** bias is ineradicably inscribed, since 'those who have the power to name the world are in a position to influence reality'. A contemporary, and much criticised, response to this problem is the introduction of '**politically correct**' language, which, in its coining of inclusive terms, attempts to eliminate linguistic bias.

NARCISSISM Commonly a fixated love of one's own image, ego, body or ideal, and a crucial concept in the **psychoanalytical** theory of **subjectivity**. **Freud** takes up Ovid's myth of Nar-

cissus to develop a thesis on morbid self-love, linking the consequence of fixated **identity** thinking to melancholia and the loss of ego. However, there are two strands to his idea of narcissism. Primary narcissism is a necessary aspect of ego development linked to libidinal attachment and dependent on relations with others. Secondary narcissism is understood as a pathological dissolution of the ego connected to the realisation that the absolute demand for love is an impossible one. In melancholia this disappointment becomes a fixation with a lost love object, ego or ideal linked to Thanatos, whereby the judging super-ego takes the ego as its own object for punishment. This form of narcissism disavows the intersubjectivity on which the ego is dependent. Contemporary writers are divided on whether secondary narcissism acts as a critique of the centrality of the ego or is paradigmatic of the infantile demands of contemporary culture. In the context of feminism, ego and agency are understood to be necessary political propositions and yet identity fixation is understood to be authoritarian. Freud's two strands of narcissism articulate this ongoing problematic.

NATIONAL ORGANIZATION FOR WOMEN (NOW) The National

Organization for Women was set up in Washington, D.C. in 1966 by women attending the Third National Conference of the Commission on the Status of Women. The most famous of the original twenty-eight founding members was Betty **Friedan**, author of *The Feminine Mystique* (1963), who became its president. However, she retired from the presidency in 1970, claiming in subsequent publications and interviews that the reason behind her resignation was a difference of opinion with radical elements within the organisation, most notably, Gloria **Steinem**.

Although NOW is too radical for some, and too liberal for others (the **radical feminist** Robin Morgan, for example, accused NOW of adopting anti-lesbian sentiments in an attempt to appear 'respectable'), it remains an influential organisation in America. It has been instrumental in the passing of a great deal of legislation for the benefit of women, and continues to fight for such issues as the right to **abortion,** gay and lesbian rights and race equality. From its inception, NOW has espoused non-violent **activist** tactics – such as marches, demonstrations, rallies, and the bringing of high-profile lawsuits – in order to draw attention to its cause.

NATURE In *The Newly-Born Woman* (1975), Hélène **Cixous** and Catherine **Clément** claim that patriarchal thought is structured around a system of binary oppositions 'related to "the" couple, man/woman'. Nature is firmly relegated to the female side of the equation, leaving **culture** the province of the male. In *Le féminisme ou la mort* (1974), Françoise d'Eubonne

adopts a similarly **essentialist** view, looking back to a pre-patriarchal era in which women controlled agriculture and cared for the land. Once **patriarchy** rose to dominance, however, men took possession of both women's bodies and of the natural world; thus, feminism and ecological concerns are intrinsically linked in d'Eubonne's debate.

Postmodern theorists, though, are sceptical of such assumptions. Donna **Haraway**, for example, claims in *Simians, Cyborgs and Women: The Reinvention of Nature* (1991) that 'rather than marking a categorically determined pole, "nature" or "woman's body" too easily means the saving core of reality distinguishable from the social institutions of patriarchy'. Arguing from a historical materialist standpoint, Haraway links nature and culture together in equal opposition, each apprehensible only through the labour process – therefore, neither nature nor woman represents any kind of essential, or better, 'reality'. A return to a primal past is thus impossible, since it does not exist. Haraway goes on to argue that instead **feminists** should seek to formulate new scientific theories and practices which would lead to the development of a **'cyborg'** consciousness in which 'nature and culture are reworked; the one can no longer be the resource for appropriation or incorporation by the other'.

NEW MAN Although the precise origins of the term are disputable, the idea of the New Man became popularised in the mass **media** during the 1980s. In short, the term describes men whose lifestyles have been influenced by feminism, and who give at least tacit support to **feminist** ideology. Typically, cooperation with the redistribution of **domestic** roles and parenting duties, a countering of traditional patterns of 'male' or '**masculine**' ascribed behaviour and a resistance to **gender** and sexual **stereotyping** are associated with the New Man.

In many ways, the notion of the New Man gave license to journalists to discuss feminism's impact on many facets of contemporary life without having to actually use the term, thus gaining the New Man a disproportionate amount of media interest. Such attention has waned in the late 1990s, with the New Man superseded by his younger brother, the 'New Lad'.

The iconic image of the New Man as consumer and consumable idol was of a semi-naked, muscular torso holding a baby. This image reflects the perceived possibility of retaining 'masculine' strength and sexual desirability, while also cultivating a 'sensitive', 'caring' and 'emotional' side. To this extent it is apparent that the New Man both facilitated the alteration of traditional images of masculinity and men in society, and reaffirmed them. The model's gaze to the camera implies that this marketable image was primarily addressed to the female viewer and represented a constructed image of men as **(post) feminist** women were understood to desire them.

NEW WOMAN The 'New Woman' was a term first coined in 1894 by the novelist Sarah Grand (1854–1943) in the *North American Review* to mark a sense of modern discontent with the traditional stay-at-home life of **marriage** and motherhood deemed appropriate for middle-**class** women. A descendant of the rebellious 'Girl of the Period' invented by Eliza Lynn Linton in 1868, the 'New Woman' was keen to broaden her experiences without submitting to male domination. She particularly deplored male sexual licence and the consequent risk to women's health; adopted comfortable clothes in protest against tight-lacing, took up bicycling and smoking; demanded a university **education**; and demanded full economic independence. Negatively, 'New Women' were seen as neurotic and highly strung: either recoiling from sexual activity altogether, or else claiming the right to enjoy it outside marriage or in irregular relationships. The 'New Woman' debate did much to revive an interest in feminism at the end of the nineteenth century, especially the role of women in marriage. Though initially a journalistic invention, it reflected a genuine crisis in women's construction of their sexuality, a concern that was eventually superseded by the **suffrage** campaigns of the early twentieth century.

NIGHTINGALE, FLORENCE: FOUNDER OF MODERN NURSING (1820–1910) An expert on hospitals and public health, Nightingale was a national heroine in her own day and an unofficial consultant on numerous matters of public policy. As early as the 1860s she had formulated the essential principles of a public health-care system. After her return from the Crimean War in 1860, where her innovations in health-care resulted in the mortality rate amongst the wounded plummeting, she established The Nightingale School. She also wrote extensively on the subject of nursing: for example, *The Nightingale Pledge* (1893). However, she also wrote in many other areas, including applied statistics, philosophy, sociology of religion, and theology. In addition to this, Nightingale is known for her novel *Cassandra*, in which she critiques Victorian society for its confinement of women within the domestic sphere. It is a work that drew on her own fight for independence and a career. Nightingale integrated her scholarly work with political **activism** on issues as diverse as the reform of Army medical services, the regulation of prostitution, public health in India, and medical services in the American Civil War.

NIN, ANAÏS: NOVELIST, SHORT STORY WRITER AND DIARIST (1903–1977) Nin was born in Paris, of a Spanish-Cuban father and a French-Danish mother. Her upbringing took place in Berlin, Brussels and New York. When she returned to France in the early twenties, it was with the distinction of dual nationality: she was at once native and expatriate, both a Frenchwoman and an American-in-Paris. She moved back to the US on the outbreak of the Second World War.

No book by Anaïs Nin is better known today than her slim, posthumous collection of erotic tales, *Delta of Venus*, published after her death in 1977. The stories in that book were not meant to be seen by the public, although they can be read as a serious attempt to inscribe a female sexual **subjectivity** in writing. The semi-autobiographical nature of this work was echoed in her diaries, written between 1931 and 1977, and published in seven volumes from 1966 onwards. Together, they constitute an important intervention in the field of female **autobiography**, and Nin claimed that their publication helped her towards an understanding of the universality of female experience. As she said in 1973, 'I know that you think that you discovered *me* when I published the *Diary*, but actually I discovered *you*.'

NOVEL-WRITING In 1957, the literary critic Ian Watt published an influential study entitled *The Rise of the Novel* in which he claimed Daniel Defoe, Samuel Richardson and Henry Fielding as the first three novelists working in English. This claim has since been taken severely to task by **feminist** critics, who have traced a tradition of women's use of the novel form which runs chronologically parallel to Watt's triumvirate of authors. Conventionally, Jane Austen has been regarded as the first female novelist, and even Watt credits her with playing an important role in developing the form in the early 1800s. Dale **Spender**, however, begins *Mothers of the Novel* (1986) with the statement that, although she had initially intended beginning her study with Jane Austen, further research revealed that women had been writing novels for one hundred and fifty years previously, establishing a tradition of female novel-writing which has since been completely forgotten. For Spender, as for Joanna

Russ in *How To Suppress Women's Writing* (1984), this suppression of a female literary heritage is the result of the systematic devaluing of the figure of the woman who dares lay claim to the authority of authorship. The work of literary historians such as Dale Spender and Germaine **Greer**, as well as Elaine **Showalter** and Ellen Moers, have done much to re-acquaint women with their writing foremothers.

NUDE Visual representations of the female nude have been the subject of much **feminist** critique by artists as well as by art historians. Some of the most powerful debates were sparked by John Berger in his BBC television series and accompanying book *Ways of Seeing* (1972), in which he provocatively likened the erotic objectification of women in post-Renaissance painting (high art) to the strategies of contemporary soft **porn** and mass **culture** (including **advertising** and televised **beauty contests**). For Berger, paintings of the female nude were usually produced by male artists with a male audience in mind – such images tell us more about male heterosexual fantasies and desires than they do about the female body or female sexuality. Berger was writing at a time when women artists too were re-examining the female nude, and trying to reclaim it for a feminist agenda. The body art of, for instance, Carolee Schneemann and Judy **Chicago** began breaking open the closed perfection of the aestheticised female nude, exploring its taboo sexuality, fertility and interior bodily processes, often utilising non-traditional techniques. Such work, however, has in turn been critiqued: many feminist artists and writers are uncomfortable with its perceived **essentialism** and continuing marginalisation from mainstream notions of art. In addition to this ongoing artistic reassessment of the body as subject-matter, recent feminist art historians have also become more aware of the many ways in which earlier women artists represented the female nude differently from male artists.

O

OAKLEY, ANN: SOCIOLOGIST
Ann Oakley is Professor of Sociology
and Social Policy at the Institute of
Education, University of London.
She is the author of numerous books
and articles on various aspects of **feminist** sociology, including *Woman's
Work: The Housewife, Past and Present*
(1974); *From Here to Maternity*
(1981), a collection of interviews with
pregnant women; and *The Captured
Womb: A History of the Medical Care
of Pregnant Women* (1984). Her name
is also associated with that of the
psychoanalyst Juliet **Mitchell**, with
whom she has co-authored three
books: *The Rights and Wrongs of
Women* (1976); *What is Feminism?*
(1986); and *Who's Afraid of Feminism?* (1997). In addition, she has
also published six novels, the most
well-known of which is probably *The
Men's Room* (1988), which is both a
poignant story about infidelity and a
working-out of Oakley's feminist concerns within a fictional context.

OBJECT-RELATIONS THEORY A
response to **Freud**'s model of child
development, largely derived from
the work of Melanie **Klein**. As its
name implies, object-relations theory
focuses on relationships – primarily
that between a child and its mother in
the year after birth – and posits
femininity rather than **masculinity** as
a primary phase. Klein thus gave the

maternal figure a central role in the
Oedipal drama, and argued that if
young girls are subject to **penis envy**
then young boys are also subject to
womb envy. In the late seventies and
early eighties Klein's work was
employed by **feminist** theorists as a
means of analysing **gender** difference. Nancy **Chodorow** and Dorothy
Dinnerstein, amongst others, reinterpreted Klein's work and provided
fertile ground for literary criticism
that investigates the relationship
between women and **language**. More
recently this approach has been
criticised for its cultural **essentialism**
and dependence on a heterosexual
model.

OBJECTIFICATION The group New
York Women Against **Pornography**
define objectification as 'a process
whereby a powerful group establishes
and maintains dominance over a less
powerful group by teaching that the
subordinate group is less than human
or like an object. This precludes the
powerful group from identifying with
or sympathising with the less powerful group.' For anti-pornography
campaigners, therefore, the problem
with pornography is not moral so
much as its tendency to treat women
as objects to be used for men's
pleasure. However, pornography is
only the most extreme manifestation
of a process of objectification that

saturates the culture of represen-tation at every level. The artistic convention of the **nude**, for example, similarly constructs women as the passive recipients of the male gaze. And as **feminists** such as Sheila **Jeffreys** and Ann **Oakley** observe, the habit of objectifying the female in film, art and literature has reper-cussions for real women in real situations. For example, both point to the medical establishment as guilty of routinely treating women as objects to be worked upon rather than as rational partners in the consultation process.

OBJECTIVITY A basic definition of objectivity is detached thought about the world. In fact, objectivity func-tions as both an ontological and an epistemological notion: i.e., a ques-tion of whether or not something exists independent of our subjective grasp of it. **Feminist** philosophers in epistemology, ethics and politics have turned their attention to develop various critiques of objectivity, at the same time seeking to reconfigure the notion. For example, Sandra **Harding** proposes a 'strong objectivity'. Her proposal is that politically informed inquiry from the standpoint of women's lives generates a stronger, less biased objectivity than a weak objectivity that defines itself by circumventing the conditions of its own possibility. Feminist episte-mologists aware of racial, **class** and other variables of our gendered **identity** understand the effects of social and material positioning on the very possibility of achieving reliable knowledge. Other feminist philoso-phers imagine reconfigurations of

objectivity that allow for detachment from their own standpoint, without commitment to the possibility of a way of knowing that transcends all standpoints. Revisionist feminists find neglected resources in philoso-phical texts for bringing imagination, difference and context to bear on reconfigurations of objectivity.

OLSEN, TILLIE: WRITER AND ACADEMIC (1913–) Tillie Olsen was born in Nebraska to Russian immigrant parents. She left school early and held various jobs before becoming a trade unionist and political activist. Her first publication was a collection of short stories, *Tell Me A Riddle* (1961). She went on to publish more short stories, a novella and the novel *Yonnondio: From the Thirties* (1974). *Yonnondio* tells the story of two women's dreams and ambitions being thwarted by sexual inequality and economic recession. Although Olsen had begun writing this novel before her marriage, it remained unfinished for forty years due to the demands of family life.

In *Silences* (1978), Olsen examined the circumstances surrounding liter-ary creation, concluding that domes-ticity and motherhood had effectively 'silenced' many women by sapping their creative energies. Olsen went on to an academic career, campaigning for an inclusive **literary canon** that will record the writing of men and women from different racial groups and **classes**.

OPPRESSION In *Feminist Theory: From Margin to Centre* (1984), bell **hooks** defines feminism as 'the struggle to end sexist oppression'. Hooks claims that the experience of oppression cuts across all boundaries of race, **class** and **culture**; and therefore feminism, as the struggle to *end* oppression, is a cause open to every woman, not the privileged preserve of the educated and articulate few. In *The Science Question in Feminism* (1986) Sandra **Harding** puts forward a similar argument, arguing that, while feminism is united in the attempt to overthrow mechanisms of oppression, that does not mean that it cannot remain a culturally and critically diverse movement. It is an issue also addressed by **third-world feminists**, such as Chandra Talpade Mohanty. In her essay 'Under Western Eyes' (1984), she argues that western **feminists** mistake their particular experience of oppression as representative of the experience of *all* women, and calls instead for an appreciation of 'the historically specific material reality of groups of women'.

ORGASM Freud defined the adult female orgasm as vaginal in origin, and dismissed the clitoral orgasm as adolescent. Women who did not experience vaginal orgasms were 'frigid', for which complaint Freud advised psychiatric treatment. This would help them to renounce the residual envy of men which was preventing them from accepting their biological female role. Followers of Freud, such as Wilhelm Stekel, classified the typically frigid woman as someone who 'wishes to dominate and is afraid to submit'; a statement which foregrounds the Freudian view that women's 'proper' sexual role involved subordination. In the 1970s,

however, a number of **feminist** critiques of Freud appeared, which drew on research done by sex therapists such as Masters and Johnson in the 1960s proving that women did not reach orgasm by vaginal stimulation alone. The most famous of these is Anne Koedt's 'The Myth of the Vaginal Orgasm' (1970), which argued that the 'myth' was of use to men because it keeps the act of intercourse centred around the penis, and thus around the idea of masculine satisfaction; it also axiomatically defines sexual satisfaction as resulting from heterosexual, rather than lesbian, relationships. Also published in 1970 was Mary Jane Sherfey's 'A Theory on Female Sexuality' which claimed that women's capacity for sexual pleasure is limitless, and that the typical woman 'is simply unaware of her sexual capacity'. However, some feminists, such as Sheila **Jeffreys** in *Anticlimax: A Feminist Perspective on the Sexual Revolution* (1990), are suspicious of such theories as reinforcing **essentialist** notions of women as primarily sexual beings, and of reproducing **heterosexist** paradigms.

ORLAN Orlan is a French performance artist whose work radically attacks notions of female beauty. Unlike Naomi **Wolf**, who challenges **stereotypes** verbally through her writings, Orlan has chosen to use her own body as a medium for interrogation and critique. The work entitled 'The Reincarnation of Saint Orlan', begun in 1990, consists of a series of **cosmetic surgery** operations designed to transform herself into an identi-kit self-portrait of **femininity**. Her features have thus been medically altered to give her the forehead of Leonardo's Mona Lisa, the eyes of Gerome's Psyche, the nose of a School of Fontainebleau Diana, the mouth of Boucher's Europa and the chin of Botticelli's Venus. Even more controversially, she later experimented with images of 'deformity' by inserting cheek implants into her temples, like two little horns, and planning to have a nose grafted on to her forehead.

Much of the debate surrounding these cosmetic interventions has focused on the complicity or otherwise of Orlan's relation to the media. Her regular appearances at academic conferences (usually accompanied by uncensored projections of her operations on large screens) and occasional television interviews have led many to suspect that Orlan is the victim of the very 'glamour' she seeks to oppose.

OTHER A term that revolves around the notion of **difference**. For Jacques **Lacan**, the Other relates firstly to the unconscious, which he calls 'the discourse of the Other', and secondly to the construction of **subjectivity** in relation to another. More generally, it is a way of defining oneself by designating a person as 'other' by placing them outside or in opposition to a norm. For Simone de **Beauvoir**, throughout history women have been reduced to objects by men, constructed as the 'other' of man, the negative or abnormal; hence her famous phrase in *The Second Sex* (1949): 'One is not born a woman; one becomes one.' **French feminists** have taken up this notion and explored its creative possibilities by suggesting that the idea of woman's 'otherness' may provide a way of exploring and subverting **patriarchal** discourse. Other feminists see in this strategy merely the reproduction and reinforcement of patriarchal **stereotypes**.

P

PACIFISM There is a long history of association between feminism and pacifism. **Essentialist** feminists identify non-violence as an inherently female trait, with Mary **Daly** proclaiming in *Gyn/Ecology* that 'the state of **Patriarchy** is the State of War', and that gyn/ecology involves the 're-claiming of life-loving female energy'. **Socialist feminists** from the **first wave** onwards have campaigned for pacifist causes: in *Woman and Labour* (1911), Olive **Schreiner** prophesies that 'that day when the woman takes her place beside the man in the governance and arrangement of external affairs of her race, will also be the day that heralds the death of war as a means of arranging human differences'. The British **feminist** Vera **Brittain**, too, was a dedicated anti-war **activist** following her experience as a nurse in the First World War. It is a tradition that has been carried on by such groups as women of the **Greenham Common Peace Camp**. Feminist pacifism is often built on an appeal to women's biological role as the bearers and raisers of children, thus equating the urge for peace with the maternal imperative to nurture: what Sara Ruddick terms 'maternal thinking'.

However, this can be balanced against the campaign being waged by feminist organisations such as NOW for women's equitable treatment within the military, and their repudiation of a passive role in warfare. Such views reject the notion that women are naturally peace-loving, arguing instead for the necessity of their participation in all areas of society.

PAGANISM Although 'pagan' comes from the Latin *paganus*, meaning 'villager' or 'rustic', 'urban paganism' is now on the increase, part of a general resurgence on the part of pagan religions. An increasing number of people are finding spiritual fulfilment in shamanism, druidry, witchcraft and other Norse and Celtic mythologies. Unlike organised religions, paganism does not have a collected system of beliefs and rituals, but is an umbrella term for the many polytheistic religions that believe in the sacredness of the earth and nature, hence its links to environmentalism.

Paganism holds an obvious appeal for **essentialist** feminism and eco-feminism, in which contexts it can represent reunion with an earth mother or **goddess** principle, and a return to **matriarchal** values, including respect for the natural world and 'female' values such as **pacifism** and nurture. One of the leading figures in this combination of paganism, feminism and ecological concerns is the American writer and activist Starhawk. In publications like *The Spiral Dance: A Rebirth of the Ancient Religion of the Great Goddess* (1979), as well as in pagan encounter groups termed 'witch-camps', Starhawk preaches a goddess-centred religion which centres the sacred in both the self and the natural world.

PAGLIA, CAMILLE: CULTURAL THEORIST AND COMMENTATOR (1947–)

Professor of Humanities at the University of the Arts in Philadelphia, Camille Paglia self-consciously situates herself as part of a **backlash** against hegemonic feminism, which she proclaims to have become over-dependent on theory in the academy and neurotically puritanical outside it. Her attempts to draw attention to the limitations of **feminist** thought has led to her identification with **postfeminism**, although she has never applied the label to herself.

Paglia's first book, *Sexual Personae*, was published in 1990. A huge tome which stretched across a wide and eclectic range of reference, it argued for the abandonment of 'the pretense of sexual sameness', replacing it with an awareness of 'the terrible duality of gender'. But this **essentialist** trend in Paglia's thought can lead her into problematic areas: in articles on date **rape**, for example, she has verged on absolving men of any accountability regarding sexual assault by implying that it is up to women to protect themselves from 'primordial male sexuality'.

Paglia's relentless promotion of herself as an outrageous and controversial personality, sidelined by the academic establishment for her proclamation of uncomfortable truths, certainly succeeds in getting her ideas publicity. However, it also detracts from them, as they can be regarded as originating from a thirst for notoriety rather than as serious critiques. But Paglia's constant quest to unsettle assumptions and interrogate orthodoxies, while it may not lead to many outright converts, are of value precisely because she takes nothing for granted.

PANKHURST FAMILY: SUFFRAGE CAMPAIGNERS: EMMELINE (1858–1928); CHRISTABEL (1880–1958); SYLVIA (1882–1960)

Emmeline Pankhurst and two of her daughters, Christabel and Sylvia, have become the best-known names in **suffragette** history. Based initially in Manchester, Emmeline (nee Goulden) had worked with her husband, Dr Richard Pankhurst (d.1898) to found the Women's Franchise League in 1889, and acquired experience in campaigning through her work for the Independent Labour Party. In 1903, she formed the Women's Social and Political Union (WSPU), moving to London in 1907 to be nearer to the centre of political life. Though her daughters Christabel and Sylvia worked with her on the suffrage campaign, and all spent time in prison for what were considered acts of vandalism, their interests and personalities increasingly diverged. Whereas Christabel, a law graduate, was an active militant, Sylvia, who trained at the Manchester Municipal School of Art and the Royal College of Art, came to reject militancy, becoming more interested in socialism. She published *The Worker's Dreadnought*, a paper for working-**class** women, and broke finally with her mother in 1912, the year Christabel fled to Paris to escape arrest. Nevertheless, in *The Suffrage Movement* (1931), Sylvia

291

chronicled her family's involvement in the campaign that she continued to support. She was a keen worker among the poor in London's East End. A **pacifist** during the 1914–18 War, when she formed the Women's Peace Army, Sylvia Pankhurst afterwards extended her interests still further: she worked for Russian socialism, and from 1936 for the Ethiopian cause. Christabel and her mother, however, supported the war effort; afterwards, Christabel stood unsuccessfully as a Parliamentary candidate, and Emmeline joined the Conservative party. After 1939 Christabel lived in America and worked for the Second Adventists. The Pankhursts were all, in their different ways, charismatic leaders whose personal example inspired many women to join the cause. Together they embodied both the vital spirit of the suffragette movement and also its divisive collective history.

PARKER, ROZSIKA: ART HISTORIAN AND PSYCHOTHERAPIST Best known for her writing on women and social history of art, particularly *Old Mistresses: Women, Art and Ideology* (1981) and *Framing Feminism: Art and the Women's Movement, 1970–1985* (1987), both co-authored with Griselda **Pollock**. In addition, Parker's account of embroidery, *The Subversive Stitch: Embroidery and the Making of the Feminine* (1984), traces the history of embroidery as a sign of the shifting ideology of **femininity** from medieval to contemporary England. Along with Griselda Pollock, Parker also formed part of the founding group of the Women's Art History Collective in 1973–5, and she was also one of the original members of the editorial collective of *Spare Rib*, working with them from 1972–80. She has also trained as a psychotherapist, recently producing a book related to this work, *Torn in Two: The Experience of Maternal Ambivalence* (1995).

PARTHENOGENESIS A term that describes the act of reproduction without male intervention, and thus an attractive concept to **feminists** who advocate separatism. Although modern **reproductive technology** has done much to separate reproduction from the sexual act, parthenogenesis, in which the ovum reproduces without fertilisation from sperm, is not (as yet) realisable. Nevertheless, it remains a persistent theme in feminist **fantasy**, such as Charlotte Perkins **Gilman**'s *Herland* (1915), Naomi Mitcheson's *Memoirs of a Space Woman* (1962) and Joanna **Russ**'s *The Female Man* (1975). In the real world, however, parthenogenesis has been reproductive technology's ultimate aim from the 1920s onwards: in 'The Determination of Sex', published in 1926, Julian Huxley was confident that 'artificial parthenogenesis' was 'theoretically possible . . . it would be only a matter of surmounting technical difficulties . . . to apply it to human beings'. Whereas the fantasy writers mentioned above regard parthenogenesis as conferring primacy upon the body of the mother, which becomes self-sufficient in its ability to both create and bear life, in the context of biotechnological debates it could be argued that the authority of the father is (re)introduced through the intervention of the scientist.

PATRIARCHY A system ruled over by men, whose authority is enforced through social, political, economic and religious institutions. All **feminists** oppose patriarchy, although they differ in their conceptualisation of it. **Radical feminists** tend to regard patriarchy as an all-pervasive and ahistorical system, a stance summed up in Marilyn **French**'s introduction to *The War Against Women* (1992), in which she traces the origins of patriarchy back to prehistoric times. She characterises patriarchy as inherently hierarchical and aggressive, and existing independently of social changes – for example, she maintains that the shift from feudalism to capitalism made little difference to women's subjugation. This view has, however, been critiqued by **Marxist** and **socialist feminists** such as Christine **Delphy** and Heidi Hartmann, who seek to locate patriarchy within materialist relations. Delphy sees patriarchy as co-existing with capitalism, originating from male exploitation of women's domestic work. Hartmann similarly regards it as originating specifically from male control of women's labour. Shulamith **Firestone**, however, sees women's construction as a subordinate **class** arising from their reproductive functions, identifying the biological **family** structure as the primary site of women's **oppression** under patriarchy. **Postmodern** feminist theorists draw on **psychoanalysis**, deconstructivist and **poststructuralist** concepts in order to reveal patriarchy as an **ideology** that permeates every area of **culture**.

PENIS ENVY A fundamental if controversial concept in **Freud**ian **psychoanalytic** theory of **femininity**, but one which has been much criticised both by anti-Freudian **feminists** and by many psychoanalytic feminists. It is the theory that the girl's perceived lack of a penis leads her to want to possess a male member and to her subsequent need for a child as a penis-substitute. For many anti-Freudian feminists, the concept of penis envy was deeply insulting to women, seeing them as incomplete men. Other psychoanalysts also disagreed with the theory and saw the attribution of penis envy to women as a symptom of male fear and envy of their reproductive power. Psychoanalysts Juliet **Mitchell** and Jacques **Lacan** see it as envy not of an anatomical penis but of 'the phallus', a signifier of power, which is similar to Simone de **Beauvoir**'s analysis in *The Second Sex* (1949), which argued that women envied not the penis but male power.

PERFORMANCE The emergence of performance as a discrete activity of twentieth-century art practice shares with other artistic modes both a diversity of motivations and a reaction against artistic academicism and hierarchy of form. The performic impulse was manifested in European **modernism** as a refusal to conform to conventional formal orchestrations of narrative, image, pattern and composition, and affirmed the validity of folk forms such as music hall, circus and cabaret.

An international proliferation of performance collaboration during the sixties and seventies articulated a second wave modernism which made reference to **autobiography**, cultural pluralism, popular entertainment forms, the performance lecture, the body as site, and the employment of pedestrian activities. For **feminism**, these interrogations and breaks with institutionalised form continue to produce contestations between progressive idealism and the dada-esque refusal to accede to the pretext of an essential correspondence between form and meaning. Performance crucially foregrounds temporality, and thus effectively articulates the debates in feminism between performative **identity** strategies and the material presentation of performic flux.

PHALLOCENTRISM A term relating to the advancement of the **masculine** as the source of power and meaning through cultural, **ideological** and social systems. Within this conception, advanced primarily through the work of psychoanalysts such as Sigmund **Freud** and Jacques **Lacan**, **patriarchy** is symbolically represented by the phallus. The phallus is not to be confused with the biological penis: instead, it is a construct which advances the Name of the Father as the natural locus of law and meaning, thereby affording symbolic power to the penis. Female **subjectivity** is thereby categorised as naturally subordinate to male **subjectivity**, since women are characterised by *absence* (of a penis), while men are characterised by *presence*. Jacques **Derrida** defines the phallus as a 'transcendental signifier': that is, an extra-linguistic point of meaning which is fixed and unified – the apex of male power. In relation to the definitive phallus, female subjectivity is constituted as '**Other**', or 'marginal'. Thus women are effectively stripped of

agency and consigned to displacement by the discourse of phallocentrism.

PHALLOGOCENTRISM A portmanteau word combining '**phallocentrism**' and 'logocentrism', which connects **patriarchal** authority and self-legitimating systems of thought which define themselves in relation to an authoritative centre. This centre is the source of a 'metaphysics of presence', the unchallengeable originator or source of linguistic meaning. The phallus, representing the **Law of the Father**, is viewed as a name relating to a fundamental 'truth', and as such is designated with presence. Both logocentrism and phallocentrism are monolithic **discourses**, as they desire to limit and fix meaning in the experience of those subject(ed) to these forms of discourse.

Phallogocentrism represents a form of double-bind to the female **subject,** who is constituted linguistically and socially by a male lexicon which makes **masculinity** the measure of normality. **Patriarchy** is thus indivisibly linked to 'the word', and the phallus to the pen, rendering women the *tabula rasa* upon which phallogocentrism inscribes female subjectivity. As Gayatri **Spivak** suggests in her introduction to **Derrida**'s *Of Grammatology*: 'The hymen is the always folded . . . space in which the pen writes its dissemination.'

PHILOSOPHICAL IMAGINARY The philosophical **imaginary** is a style of 'thinking in images' with which past philosophers deny engagement. Unacknowledged elements in the practice of philosophy are located in the imagery and symbolism of a philosophical text. This constitutes the philosophical imaginary that is not incidental to philosophy as a decorative aspect of a text, but functions to mask aspects of philosophy not readily articulated and to organise the values implicit in the text. Uncovering this dual function, Michèle Le Doeuff enables feminist philosophers to confront the dangers and possibilities in critiques of reason. Ignoring elements of their own thought, they run the danger of constructing the unity of 'woman' by masking difference and seeking distinctively female versions of rationality. Instead, **feminist** philosophers should imagine alternative thought patterns and intellectual spaces in which they can glimpse possibilities excluded through polarisations of reason and imagination. This would be an exercise of the philosophical imaginary.

PLANT, SADIE: FEMINIST TECHNO-THEORIST (1964–) Sadie Plant is an academic whose name has become synonymous with **cyberfeminism**, which she defines as 'an insurrection on the part of the goods and materials of the patriarchal emergence composed of links between women, women and computers, computers and communications links, connections and connectionist nets'.

In *Zeros and Ones: Digital Women and the New Technologies* (1997), Plant argues that every time a useful new **technology** is invented, traditional **patriarchal** strength becomes less significant to the ways in which the world is run. Already, men have lost much of their traditional power to computers and **reproductive tech-**nologies. For Plant, the binary digits which form the basis of all computer code act as a metaphor for the current state of male/female relations. 'One', the upright definite, plus 'Zero', the hole, equals One – or as she puts it, 'Male and female add up to man.' There is no female equivalent. But if man is the product, then woman is the process, and as such, she shares a secret relationship with the machine. Going against **feminist** theories which argue that technology entraps women, Plant maintains that it is men who are losing out in a world where centralised control has been subsumed by the peripheral.

PLEASURE A term used in different contexts in different areas of **feminist** theory. Theorists of popular culture examine the pleasures of reading texts: Laura **Mulvey**, for example, in 'Visual Pleasure and Narrative Cinema' analyses the way in which pleasure is constructed in Hollywood cinema. Her aim is 'to negate the relationship between pleasure and the narrative fiction film in order to conceive a new language of **desire**'. Mulvey therefore regards pleasure as working to reinforce the dominant order's conception of **gender**. L. Star, however, represents an alternative way of perceiving the pleasures of viewing. In a study of New Zealand women's experience of watching televised rugby matches, she formulates the concept of 'resisting pleasures', whereby those excluded from the dominant objects of address can view 'against the grain, that is, in contradiction to the messages you are expected to receive from the text' (see Ann Brooks, *Postfeminisms*, 1997).

Drawing on **psychoanalysis, French feminism** theorises a female **discourse** of pleasure centred on the body. In *Parole de femme* (1974), Annie Leclerc represents the exploration of the site of female pleasure as an imperative which will disrupt male-authored paradigms of desire: 'Well, it's too bad for him, but I must talk about the pleasures of my body ... the pleasures of my woman's belly, my woman's vagina, my woman's breasts, luxuriant pleasures that you can't even imagine.' In the same vein, Luce **Irigaray** formulates a female *jouissance* which is multiple and diffuse, symbolised by her sexual organs, 'composed of two lips which embrace continually' ('This Sex Which is Not One', 1977). In essays such as 'The Laugh of the Medusa' (1976), Hélène **Cixous** links the sensual pleasures of the body with a female writing practice, which she terms *écriture féminine*.

POLITICAL CORRECTNESS (PC) It is now customary to ridicule the concept of political correctness. In the popular imagination the term now indicates nothing more than: a) a mildly ridiculous terminology which substitutes tortuous synonyms for the simplest of terms ('metabolically different' for 'dead'; 'chairperson' for 'chairman', and so on); and b) a puritanical movement which, while claiming to be inclusive, actually tries to ban anything that doesn't conform to its own rigid agenda.

In fact, political correctness grew out of the American **feminist** movement in the mid-1980s onwards, and constituted a serious attempt to challenge habitual assumptions encoded

in speech and tradition. In its name, more ethnic writers were included in the literary, artistic and intellectual canons; an attempt was made to make language more inclusive; and positive discrimination in support of minorities was advocated. However well-meaning its intentions might have been, for many PC has become indicative of an earnest totalitarianism which seeks to prohibit free speech and which elevates minor figures on the grounds of their race, colour or sexual orientation.

Political correctness remains a problematic concept both inside and outside the feminist movement. Self-styled 'new' feminists such as Natasha **Walter** regard political correctness as 'puritanical' and humourless; a 'straitjacket' from which feminism must free itself (*The New Feminism*, 1997). Deborah Cameron, on the other hand, maintains that politically correct **language** is liberating, since it 'does not threaten our freedom to speak as we choose. . . . It threatens only our freedom to imagine that our linguistic choices are inconsequential, or to suppose that any one group of people have an inalienable right to prescribe them' (in Sarah Dunant, ed., *The War of the Words*, 1994).

POLLOCK, GRISELDA: ART HISTORIAN (1949–) Professor of Social and Critical Histories of Art in the Department of Fine Art at the University of Leeds. Pollock is prominent for her writing about women and the social history of art, producing the profoundly influential publications, *Old Mistresses: Women, Art and Ideology* (1981), and *Framing Feminism: Art and the Women's Movement, 1970–*

1985, both co-authored with Rozsika **Parker**. These were followed by *Vision and Difference: Femininity, Feminism and the Histories of Art* (1988), in which she studied the work of women artists in the context of the dominant representations of **femininity**. In addition to her extensive writing on the problematic feminine in the fields of social history of art, Pollock also focuses on such issues as part of **cultural** and **psychoanalytic** theory, and has analysed different artistic practices from the mid-nineteenth century to those found in contemporary art.

PORNOGRAPHY The issue of pornography tends to arouse extreme reactions as far as feminism is concerned. **Feminists** differ on whether all sexually-explicit material is defamatory to women, or whether pornographic forms can be used to formulate a discourse of female **desire**. The anti-pornography position has become virtually synonymous with the efforts of the American **radical feminists**, Andrea **Dworkin** and Catherine **MacKinnon**, who have attempted to make the production of pornographic material a civil-rights violation. In *Pornography: Men Possessing Women* (1981) Dworkin defines pornography as encoding misogyny in its most extreme form, revealing 'the ideology of male domination [which] posits that men are superior to women by virtue of their penises . . . that the use of the female body for sexual or reproductive purposes is a natural right of men'. Anti-pornography campaigners also trace a correlation between the consumption of pornography and the sexual abuse of actual women.

Other feminists, however, adopt a more **libertarian** position. Pornographic material is now being produced specifically for a female audience, such as the Black Lace imprint in Britain, launched in 1993; although it tends to be marketed under the euphemism 'erotica'. The distinction between pornography (which **objectifies** and degrades women) and erotica (which is celebratory of female sexuality) is a distinction often made by supporters of sexually-explicit material. Anaïs **Nin**, for example, said erotic writing 'is as beautiful as can be'. An appreciation of erotica is also equated with the principle of liberation: Nancy **Friday**, who has made a career out of documenting women's sexual fantasies, talks of her books as deconstructing the madonna/whore dichotomy, and giving women 'permission' to be bad. One feminist writer who resolutely refused the comforting distinction between erotica and pornography was the British author Angela **Carter**, who proclaimed erotica to be 'the pornography of the elite', and who, in her controversial publication *The Sadeian Woman* (1979) postulated the hypothetical figure of the moral pornographer, who would use pornography as a means of deconstructing the power relationship between the sexes.

POSTCOLONIALISM There are strong parallels between postcolonialism and feminism as both are fundamentally concerned with the politics of **'othering'**, marginalisation and the construction of a **'subaltern'** or subordinated **subjectivity** by colonialism and/or **patriarchy**. Broadly speaking, postcolonial critics have attempted to dismantle naturalised assumptions about **language** and textuality using two main strategies: a denial of the centrality of imperialist **culture** (abrogation), and a seizure and reconstitution of imperial **discourse** (appropriation). These strategies are equally evident in **feminist** theories in which patriarchal norms are rejected and/or subverted.

Language is a central concern of both postcolonial and feminist theory and the theoretical trajectories of both have examined issues of '**silencing**' and enclosure due to the way in which the female/colonised subject has been forced to articulate selfhood in the terms of the oppressor. Both postcolonial and feminist theories interrogate the notion of a standard code by rejecting the binary structures of patriarchy/colonialism in order to posit alternative, but no less valid, centres. This in turn allows the experience of the marginalised to be rendered authentic and offers the possibility of reconstructing the patriarchal/colonial canon.

Postcolonial theory, like feminism, raises vexing questions about **identity** formation, **essentialism**, biologism and constructivism in order to refute the notion of an ontological marginality and inferiority applicable to minority discourses. Both theories attempt to reinstate the marginal in the face of the dominant and unmask the structures of domination in a process of convergent, subversive but not always intersecting evolution.

POSTFEMINISM Definitions of this term, which is currently in wide usage, vary dramatically. Some **feminists** argue that postfeminism participates in the discourse of **postmodernism,** in that both seek to destabilise fixed definitions of **gender**, and to deconstruct authoritative paradigms and practices. In *Introducing Postfeminism* (1999), Sophia Phoca traces the origins of postfeminism back to the split within the **MLF** in Paris in 1968, when members of the *po et psyche* group publicly rejected the feminist struggle for equality with men. Instead, theorists such as Julia **Kristeva** and Hélène **Cixous** argue in support of **difference**, and draw on **psychoanalytical** theory in order to maintain that the feminine subject differs fundamentally from the masculine subject. They also emphasise the fluctuating and multiple nature of that subjectivity.

For others, this alignment of postfeminism with theory is problematic. Instead, they use the term in connection with a distinct group of mostly young British and American feminists who have attacked feminism in its present form as inadequate to address the concerns and experiences of women today. Indeed, this is the context in which the term itself was coined, and is therefore the one in which it is most correctly used. Although these so-called 'postfeminists', which include Naomi **Wolf**, Katie **Roiphe**, Rene **Denfeld** and Natasha **Walter**, are often labelled 'anti-feminist' they characterise themselves as the precursors of a shift in aims and objectives of feminism: what some term a '**third wave**'. Generally, they support an individualistic, liberal agenda rather than a collective and political one, on which grounds their detractors frequently attack them for being pawns of a conservative 'backlash' against feminism, which seeks to limit its effectiveness.

POSTMODERNISM Just as **feminism** cannot be seen as a monolithic movement, it should also be noted that postmodernism is constituted of diverse and often opposing positions. Rosalind Krauss and Douglas Crimp define it as a break with the aesthetic field of **modernism**, whereas Fredric Jameson and Jean Baudrillard detail the postmodern as a new 'schizophrenic' mode of space and time. Others, like Craig Owens and Kenneth Frampton, frame its rise in the fall of modern myths of progress and mastery. Many writers have noted the absence of **feminist** theorists in the postmodern project: Craig Owens, in his essay 'The Discourse of Others: Feminists and Postmodernism' (1983), writes that the absence of discussion of sexual difference together with the fact that few women have engaged in the postmodern debate suggests that 'postmodernism may be another masculine invention to exclude women'.

However, Jean-François Lyotard's definition of postmodernism as the rejection of all universal theories and ideas is a notion that would seem to hold out the opportunity to feminism to rewrite the **patriarchal** script. Postmodernism's project to disrupt traditional boundaries between elite and **popular culture**, theory and practice, art and life, and the dominant and the marginal, is one shared by feminism, which similarly moves to interrogate hierarchical patterns of thought and customary categories of value. Feminist theorists such as Linda **Hutcheon** and Patricia Waugh have sought to define the relationship between feminism and postmodernism. In her analysis of the literary postmodern, *Feminine Fictions* (1989), Patricia Waugh maintains that postmodernist writings by women maintain an adherence to the principle of the historically-situated **subject,** thus rejecting the doctrine of 'impersonality' which characterised the work of many male postmodern novelists. And in *A Poetics of Postmodernism*, Linda Hutcheon argues that, in the context of postmodernism's move to rethink margins and borders, the 'ex-centric' perspective – whether in terms of class, race or **gender** – takes on a new significance as a result of the implied recognition that our culture is not really as homogeneous as we imagine.

POSTSTRUCTURALISM Exemplified in the work of such theorists as Michel **Foucault** and Jacques **Derrida**, poststructuralism focuses on the ways in which texts are bound up in systems of power which legitimate the subject of representation. In various ways they attempt to deconstruct these legitimating systems in an attempt to find the gaps and paradoxes within them; a project which is of obvious concern to women. It could be argued, indeed, that feminism is inherently poststructuralist in its orientation, challenging as it does the dominant **patriarchal ideology** – the social system against which it works in perpetual reaction, and which it seeks constantly to transform. For feminist theorists, such as Julia **Kristeva,** who have drawn on poststructuralist approaches in their own work, 'woman' becomes an ideological construction, a place in **discourse**, rather than a sexual **identity**. Other feminists, such as Camille **Paglia**, are openly suspicious of poststructuralist theory, which she dismisses as 'rigid foreign ideology' which has overrun the humanities. Naomi **Wolf**, Rene **Denfeld** and Christina Hoff Somers also represent a **postfeminist** position which regards theoretical feminism as alienating all but a minority of highly-educated women, and which takes feminism out of the real world of social and political interaction.

POTTER, SALLY: FILM DIRECTOR (1949–) During the 1970s and 1980s Sally Potter was a controversial figure in British independent cinema, making films that incorporated theoretical and formalist concerns alongside narrative invention. Her short film *Thriller* (1979) deconstructs the sexual intrigue of opera through a rereading of *La Bohème*. This was followed by her feature debut, *The Gold Diggers* (1983). *Orlando* (1992) marked a move into more mainstream cinema, whilst continuing past concerns, in a free reading of Virginia **Woolf**'s historical fantasia. Produced by her own company, Adventure Pictures, she also co-wrote the score. Potter has also worked in television; on, for instance, *Women in Soviet Cinema* (1988), and run her own **dance** ensemble, the Limited Dance Company. Her film *The Tango Lesson*

(1997) mixes all the characteristics of her complex artistic concerns, mixing reality and fiction, music and dance, in a reflection on life and the tango.

PSYCHOANALYSIS Phyllis **Chesler**'s groundbreaking work with women patients in New York in the early 1970s argued that psychoanalysis regards sickness as a normative characteristic of **femininity**. Men's fear of women, Dorothy **Dinnerstein** went on to argue in *The Mermaid and the Minotaur* (1976), is determined psychoanalytically by women's domination of child care. While initially **second wave feminists** such as Kate **Millett** and Shulamith **Firestone** claimed that the definitions and practices of psychoanalysis were innately **sexist**, Juliet **Mitchell** and others reevaluated **Freud**'s work to argue that his account of the instability of the 'feminine' has radical potential. Feminist **object-relations** theorists – Nancy **Chodorow**, for example – have transferred attention from Freud's Oedipal theories by studying women's and men's early sex-role socialisation in relation to mothers. The **French feminists** Julia **Kristeva**, Hélène **Cixous** and Luce **Irigaray** call these psychical components of pre-Oedipal existence the '**semiotic**', because they relate to **language**. The use of psychoanalytical theories in a feminist context has spread across the disciplines, including literary theory, art criticism and media and film studies.

Q

QUALITATIVE RESEARCH Research that draws its conclusions from findings or data that are not gathered via statistical or quantifiable methods. Qualitative techniques include small-scale in-depth interviewing, participant observation and group interviews. In-depth interviewing is one of the most popular methods in **feminist** research. For example, Janice Radway's investigation into readers of American **romance** novels involved recording open-ended interviews and conversations with forty-four female subjects. These were then transcribed and analysed by Radway who then drew conclusions regarding the complex ways women use and relate to popular romance. Many researchers, including Radway, do not use only one type of data, but combine qualitative with quantitative methods. Joke Hermes (1993) incorporated survey results into her research on magazines as well as employing group discussions and in-depth interviews.

QUEER THEORY A term reappropriated by certain gay and lesbian theorists as a means of breaking down the binary opposition of heterosexual and homosexual; as in 'queering the pitch'. There is not, however, a consensus on the usefulness or definition of queer theory: some gay and lesbian critics regard it as a de-sexualising of sexuality politics – 'queer' may be applied to or adopted by anyone who does not engage in strictly 'vanilla' forms of heterosexual practice, so that it becomes an umbrella term including virtually anyone, thus tending to ignore the physical, verbal and social abuse often faced by 'out' lesbians and gay men. Other critics and theorists, such as Alan Sinfield, work with queer theory as a means of investigating the instability of all sexualities. In North America writers such as Judith **Butler** and Eve Kosofsky Sedgwick have taken the insights of feminism, lesbian and gay politics and **postmodernism** and produced complex accounts of sexuality and **gender** identity in late western capitalist culture. In effect, queer theory represents the effect of **poststructuralism** on feminism and sexuality politics, breaking down all **essentialist** notions of gender and sexual **identity** and replacing them with identities that are contingent on cultural and social negotiation.

R

RACISM *Webster's Dictionary* defines racism as 'the assumption that the characteristics and abilities of an individual are determined by race and that one race is biologically superior to another'. The term 'race' can be categorised by its imprecision and malleability, as it has been variously confused with issues of ethnicity, physical typology, genetics, lineage and nationality. However, the context of racism usually assumes a binary dialectic between the race which has access to the centre and is thus designated the authority of presence, and the subservient race, categorised as **'Other'** in relation to the 'Sovereign Self' of the former. One of the discursive mechanisms of racist **discourse** is what Edward Said describes as **'essentialist** universalism'; a form of essentialist **stereotyping** in which the Other is constructed in order to seem *naturally* inferior – unchanging and unchangeable. This is often done on the dual axes of race and **gender**. Thus the civilised vitality of the Aryan, for example, is contrasted with the **feminine** inscrutability and emotive volatility of the 'othered' race. Racism follows a parallel trajectory to **phallocentrism**, in that it silences the 'Other' and assumes the prerogative to speak for, inscribe and discursively construct that Other in order to consolidate and perpetuate a Sovereign Self. **Feminism** itself, however, is not immune to accusations of racism – **third world feminists** frequently critique the domination of western feminist attitudes and theory on that basis.

RADICAL FEMINISM   A frequent theme of this branch of feminism is the effect of the **patriarchal** system on the **oppression** of women. Unlike women's liberationists, radicals believe that male power is at the root of the social construction of **gender**. They do not believe that this system can be reformed. It must be eradicated, not only at a legal and political level, but at a social and social and cultural level too. Activists such as Ti-Grace **Atkinson** in *Amazon Odyssey* (1974) suggest that **liberal feminism** is 'worse than useless' and that confrontation through a 'declaration of war' against men and society is the only successful way forward. Gender, as a biological as well as cultural concept, is viewed as a constraint especially for women. Kate **Millett**'s *Sexual Politics* (1970) argues that biology is used as a defence for the **ideological** domination of men over women. Radical proposals against sex inequality have ranged from a call for an **androgynous** culture, to a replacing of male **culture** with female culture. Reproduction and motherhood have been taken up by such as Shulamith **Firestone** in *The Dialectic of Sex* (1972). She states that the

302

elimination of sexual roles can only be achieved by eradicating the fixed role women and men play in reproduction. **Contraception**, sterilisation and **abortion** (also since then, artificial insemination) all help to diminish the biological and thus the power differentiation between sexes. These confrontational forms of **feminist** thought have attracted much publicity, not always faithful or favourable. Thus, radical **activism** is often viewed as a main focus of the recent **backlash** against feminism.

RAPE In *Anticlimax: A Feminist Perspective on the Sexual Revolution* (1990), Sheila **Jeffreys** observes that early theories of sexuality, such as those advanced by interwar 'sexologists' such as Edward Carpenter and Havelock Ellis, contained 'no understanding that men and women existed in a power relationship and that male and female sexuality was constructed through material relations of power and powerlessness'. It was not until the **second wave** of feminism that the relationship between sex and power began to be addressed. In 1971, the American philosopher Susan **Griffin** published an article entitled 'Rape: the All-American Crime', which argued that there was an exceedingly fine line dividing the 'average dominant heterosexual' from the habitual rapist, since the pattern of male dominance and female submission could be found in all male-female sexual relationships. That sex has nothing to do with female **pleasure** and everything to do with male power is the view upon which all **feminist** analysis of rape is founded. In *Against Our Will: Men, Women and Rape* (1975),

Susan **Brownmiller** asserts that rape is a crime which affects all women, since it is the unspoken threat which curtails all female activity; thus rape is a cornerstone of **patriarchal** control. Andrea **Dworkin**, in publications like *Pornography* (1981), creates a direct link between rape and **pornography**. Not only does much hard-core pornography depict real acts of rape, but pornography's portrayal of women as 'whores' affects all men's view of all women. Black and **third world feminists** have, however, criticised the views of Brownmiller, Dworkin and others for inadequately addressing the racial aspects of rape. For example, in *Women, Race and Class* (1981) Angela **Davis** critiques cultural depictions of black men as rapists and of black women as victims. Some **postfeminists**, such as Katie **Roiphe** in *The Morning After: Sex, Fear and Feminism* (1992), have contentiously argued that the feminist attempt to combat rape has gone too far, reaching the point where women view themselves as potential victims in every sexual scenario.

RELIGIOUS FUNDAMENTALISM The term 'fundamentalism' is derived from a series of pamphlets called *The Fundamentals: A Testimony to the Truth*, published before the outbreak of the First World War. It was applied to a movement within North American Protestantism. This movement was probably a reaction to developments in the academic study of Christian theology and the Bible in western Europe and North America during the eighteenth and nineteenth centuries. Increasingly Christian theologians were saying that the biblical text needed to be studied in the same way as other kinds of literature, taking into account such factors as the historical context in which it was written. In other words, it could not be taken absolutely as the inerrant or transparent word of God. In addition, developments in liberal Protestant theology, exemplified, for example, in the work of Adolf von Harnack in Germany at the end of the nineteenth century, tried to show the teaching of Jesus in a humane and enlightened sense that would harmonise, particularly, with the cultural values of Protestant Europe at the time. So-called fundamentalists in the United States were opposed to both these tendencies and defined a number of 'fundamental' doctrines such as the literal infallibility of the Bible, the virgin birth of Christ, the efficacy of Christ's death as a remedy for human sin, the resurrection of the body and the second coming of Christ.

More generally, the term 'fundamentalism' is applied to the strong reaffirmation of traditional doctrines and forms of authority within any religious group. In some cases, the term has acquired political overtones. It was applied, for example, to the opponents of the Shah of Iran and their religious and political leader, the Ayatullah Khumayni. In this case, the autocratic secular state of the Shah was contrasted unfavourably with the Islamic state in which the overriding authority was that of Allah. So-called 'fundamentalists' appear to share a suspicion of modernism in all its critical diversity and moral fragmentation. There is a tendency therefore to stress not simply theological or religious traditions but also traditional and usually **patriarchal** patterns of **domestic** authority and social order.

REPRODUCTIVE TECHNOLOGIES Inclusive term which describes a range of scientific interventions within the sphere of reproduction, from the common practices of amniocentesis and **contraception**, as well as the more complex techniques developed to combat infertility, such as in vitro fertilisation (IVF), intracytoplasmic sperm injection (ICSI) and gamete intra-Fallopian transfer (GIFT). Much **radical feminist** argument put forward in the early seventies was generally celebratory of technological intervention in the reproductive process, the most famous example being Shulamith **Firestone**'s claim in *The Dialectic of Sex* (1970) that women's emancipation depended on technological developments that would free them from the biological necessity to bear children. However, Firestone's argument is now portrayed as somewhat naive compared to the flood of influential **feminist** critiques of **technology** that have appeared since then, which voice concerns that reproductive technology, created and controlled by male scientists and serving **patriarchal** interests, **objectifies** and controls women. For example, the American philosopher Susan **Griffin**, in her book *Woman and Nature* (1984), make feminism and science completely antithetical terms. However, lesbian feminists often express a different opinion, regarding reproductive technology as enabling lesbians to become mothers (see Elizabeth Sourbut, 'Gynogenesis: A Lesbian Appropriation of Reproductive Technologies', 1996). The question of who controls such technologies, and in whose interests they are employed, remains, however, an issue of pressing concern.

RE-VISION In her 1971 essay, 'When We Dead Awaken: Writing as Re-Vision', American poet and critic Adrienne **Rich** stated that 'Re-vision – the act of looking back, of seeing with fresh eyes, of entering an old text from a new critical direction – is for women more than a chapter in cultural history: it is an act of survival.' This notion of re-vision, in Rich's terms, primarily referred to literature but may be applied to a whole range of **feminist** scholarship which reinterprets statutory history and/or rediscovers social and cultural pasts which have been forgotten or erased. To some extent this term is dependent on a notion of the past as a retrievable 'truth', but it also engages with the idea of history and writing as a dialectic in which many versions coexist; as Rich argued, re-vision is not about trying 'to pass on a tradition but to break its hold over us'.

RICH, ADRIENNE: POET AND THEORIST (1929–) Born in Baltimore, Maryland, Adrienne Rich gained recognition with her first volume of poetry, A *Change of World* (1951), which won the Yale Younger Poets Award. A Guggenheim Fellowship followed in 1952. In spite of marriage and the birth of three children, Rich continued to teach and write poetry, and also became increasingly politically active in anti-Vietnam protests. However, as she recorded in the **autobiographical** sections of *Of Woman Born: Motherhood as Experience and Institution* (1976), she experienced considerable tension in balancing the demands of her role as wife and mother with her creative life. Following the death of her husband in 1970, Rich became increasingly identified with the **feminist** movement, and began to publish **feminist** theory as well as poetry. Her essays collected in *On Lies, Secrets and Silence* (1979) range from pieces of literary analysis to calls for a feminist pedagogical practice. Of particular importance is her essay 'When We Dead Awaken: Writing as **Re-Vision**', in which she argues for the necessity of 'entering . . . old text[s] from a new critical direction ... not to pass on a tradition but to break its hold over us'. Her influential essay, '**Compulsory Heterosexuality** and Lesbian Existence', was published in 1980, in which she expanded the concept of lesbianism beyond its sexual definition to include female friendship and collective action. As well as her considerable contribution to lesbian theory, Rich has also emerged as a spokesperson for **Jewish feminism**, in 1990 helping to found *Bridges: A Journal for Jewish Feminists and Our Friends*. The central concern in all her work is to give voice to hitherto **silenced** areas of women's **culture**, and her tendency to mingle the personal with the analytical allows the contradictions and uncertainties inherent in such an agenda to be expressed.

RICHARDSON, DOROTHY: NOVELIST (1873–1957) Richardson is one of the foremost British modernist novelists, whose work has often been overshadowed by that of her contemporaries, Virginia **Woolf** and James Joyce. Yet her novel sequence *Pilgrimage* (1915–38) contains innovations every bit as radical as those of *To the Lighthouse* or *Ulysses*.

It consists of twelve individual volumes: *Pointed Roofs* (1915), *Backwater* (1916), *Honeycomb* (1917), *Interim* (1919), *The Tunnel* (1919), *Deadlock* (1921), *Revolving Lights* (1923), *The Trap* (1925), *Oberland* (1927), *Dawn's Left Hand* (1931), *Clear Horizon* (1935) and *Dimple Hill* (1938). *March Moonlight* was added to the second collected edition of 1967.

The sequence is focalised through the consciousness of Miriam Henderson, and reflects Richardson's desire to 'produce a **feminine** equivalent of the current **masculine** realism'. Hence the text has frequent recourse to pioneering stream-of-consciousness techniques. Miriam's relationship with Hypo G. Wilson reflects Richardson's involvement with H. G. Wells in 1906, an affair which resulted in a miscarriage.

RIOT GRRRLS Although various versions of the story are in circulation, the origins of the Riot Grrrl movement appear to lie around the beginning of the 1990s in Olympia, Washington. Members of the all-girl band Bikini Kill coined the term when they created a feminist 'zine' entitled *Riot Grrrl*, and this combination of rock music and fanzines have become the twin preoccupations around which the Riot Grrl phenomenon as a whole revolves. The movement's originators wanted to challenge male domination of the grunge and punk rock scene, and were clearly influenced by **feminist** activist politics. However, no clear Riot Grrrl agenda as such has ever been developed: young women are drawn to the movement through a mutual interest in a particular kind of music and look, and it has taken the form of an assortment of loosely connected groups (or chapters) which cooperate collectively very little, thus promoting an individualistic form of feminism which tends to eschew political **activism**. Although the term itself has been used extensively by the media to label just about any aggressive all-girl band, and has become virtually synonymous with the publicity-loving lead singer of Hole, Courtney **Love**, Riot Grrrls themselves resist conforming to a public image, seeing mainstream attention as detracting from their underground credibility.

ROIPHE, KATIE: WRITER (1968–) Roiphe shot to instant notoriety when her first book, *The Morning After: Sex, Fear and Feminism* was published in 1993, in which she argued that a particular form of **victim feminism** was overrunning American campuses. Half memoir, half cultural analysis, Roiphe's text examines the student culture at Princeton University and claims that **feminist** activism such as Take Back the Night marches and date-rape pamphlets lead women to see themselves at permanent risk of sexual violation. She argues that this climate of paranoia is reinforced by women's studies classes promoting a **politically correct** agenda that cloaks rigid dogmatism in theoretical jargon. Rather than stimulating academic debate, feminist theory works to stifle any dissenting points of view, thus replacing complex issue with a simplistic 'party line'. A particular target for Roiphe is Catherine **MacKinnon**, portrayed as a 'fire and brimstone . . . Puritan preacher' who disseminates a '*Star Wars*' brand of feminism in which 'there is black and white, lots of moralism . . . but all ambiguity is lost'.

On its publication, *The Morning After* was criticised by many on its publication for precisely the same kind of sweeping rhetoric that Roiphe condemns in others: her easy dismissal of rape statistics came under particular scrutiny. Her second book was published in 1997. Entitled *Last Night in Paradise: Sex and Morals at the Century's End*, it is a study of how the sexual behaviour of young Americans has been altered by the advent of AIDS.

ROMANCE The term 'romance' covers a considerably wide genre – ranging from the short stories found in **women's magazines** to the most infamous of all, the Mills and Boon novel – all of which portray the idyllic world of heterosexual love. Mary **Wollstonecraft** criticised the romance novel as conditioning women to accept **patriarchal** authority, yet they retain an undeniable appeal. The hero and heroine are classically **stereotyped**, the outcome inevitable, yet they are a success in the eyes of the thousands of women who read them. The heroine tends to be **objectified** by being portrayed through the eyes of the hero and, by thus placing the woman in the position of being viewed, the novel ensures she is not aware of her sexual potential. Patriarchal society has traditionally demanded that women should be sexually innocent until they find the right man, which they will inevitably marry. Stereotypical romance novels also do little to challenge the belief that women could be stronger than men, who are portrayed in positions of authority and are physically strong.

Feminist critics of the mass-produced romance have concentrated on analysing the reasons for its enduring popularity. In *Reading the Romance* (1984), Janet Radway breaks the narrative down into various stages of plot development in order to address the question of why women read romances in such large numbers. Tania **Modleski,** in *Loving with a Vengeance* (1982), argues that the persistent theme of male brutality being transformed by love is indicative of the **ideological** conflicts women encounter when living under patriarchy.

RUSS, JOANNA: SCIENCE FICTION WRITER AND LITERARY CRITIC (1937–) Russ is known for her **radical** lesbian stance, which permeates both her fiction and non-fiction work. Her best-known novel is *The Female Man*, published in 1975, which combines speculative **science fiction** with **postmodernist** narrative strategies in order to examine the splits engendered in the female psyche under **patriarchy**. It also taps into the **utopian** mode in its ironic portrayal of an all-female society, Whileaway, which the novel constructs as both desirable and compromised. The provocative polemicism of *The Female Man*, which is full of angry diatribes against patriarchy, is evident in all of Russ's writing, most notably in *How To Suppress Women's*

Writing (1983), which examines the strategies, ranging from censorship to ridicule, whereby women are discouraged from writing novels. Russ has also contributed substantially to science fiction criticism, and her essays are collected in *Magic Mommas, Trembling Sisters, Puritans and Perverts: Feminist Essays* and *To Write Like a Woman: Essays in Feminism and Science Fiction* (1995). She regards science fiction as an effective vehicle through which to express feminist critique, categorising it as 'realism disguised as **fantasy**'. In 1987 she began to suffer from the effects of Chronic Fatigue Syndrome, and left her teaching post at the University of Washington in Seattle, although she continues to write. Her most recent publication is *What Are We Fighting For?: Sex, Race, Class and the Future of Feminism* (1998), which seeks to defend feminism against the critiques of the so-called '**postfeminists**'.

RUSSELL, DORA: WRITER, JOURNALIST, EDUCATOR, POLITICAL ACTIVIST AND PEACE CAMPAIGNER (1894–1986) Dora Russell gained a First at Cambridge and in the 1920s travelled to Russia (witnessing the Third International Congress) and China with the philosopher Bertrand Russell, whom she later (and reluctantly) married. In 1923 she went to court to defend the publication of illustrated birth control literature, co-founding the Workers' Birth Control Group to provide information and clinics for working-class women the following year. She believed in free love, criticised **marriage** and in her first book *Hypatia* (1925) argued for women's rights to citizenship, **education** and sexual **pleasure**. In 1927 she started a progressive school based on democratic socialist principles, documented in *The Tamarisk Tree 2*, the sequel to her 1975 autobiography. She was a **pacifist** campaigner from the First World War onwards and took the Woman's Caravan for Peace into Eastern Europe in the 1950s. Some of her prolific writing on humanist and women's issues is collected in the *Dora Russell Reader* (1983).

S

Sappho: Poet (7th–6th century BC) Little is known for certain about the life of Sappho, the Greek lyric poet from the isle of Lesbos. Her poetry survives in fragments. Nevertheless she is an iconic figure, particularly amongst **feminists**, who valorise her erotic love poetry addressed to women.

The *Hymn to Aphrodite* is a plea to the goddess to help Sappho seduce a young girl. Written in the metre named after her, the Sapphic strophes are full of longing. Other fragments include a poem for a girl called Lydia, and a description of the beautiful woman Anactoria. In a narrative poem about Hector and Andromache, Sappho successfully combines the lyric with the epic.

The controversy about the precise nature of Sappho's sexuality has divided commentators: Denys Page was firmly convinced of her lesbianism, whilst Maurice Bowra thought otherwise. Whatever the case, her achievements have inspired many female writers, including Katherine Philips, Anne Killigrew and Aphra Behn.

Schreiner, Olive: Socialist Feminist (1855–1920) Schreiner was born in the Cape Colony of South Africa. Her parents were missionaries, and Schreiner rebelled against their view of Christianity, becoming a fervent freethinker. She came to Britain in 1881, having already begun three novels: *Undine, The Story of An African Farm* and *From Man to Man. The Story of An African Farm* was the first to be published, in 1883, and was the means by which Schreiner came to meet Eleanor Marx, with whom she remained firm friends until Marx's suicide in 1898, and the sexologist Havelock Ellis, with whom she enjoyed a close, but platonic, association. Schreiner published her work of **feminist** analysis, *Women and Labour*, in 1911, in which she argued that women's increasing involvement in the running of society would radically change the entire way in which that society is constructed. Her ideas anticipate many of the views which would be expressed by feminists of the **second wave** fifty years or so later, in particular, that sexual exploitation was the root cause of women's **oppression**, and that **marriage** was little more than legalised prostitution. *Woman and Labour* influenced a generation of **first wave** feminist thinkers, such as Vera **Brittain** and Winifred **Holtby**.

Science Fiction The term 'science fiction' was coined in the mid-nineteenth century, but was 'reinvented' and given wider currency in the late 1920s by the American magazine editor Hugo Gernsback, who popularised the stories deriving from, predominantly, H.G. Wells and Jules Verne. To Gernsback, a science fiction story was one intermingled with scientific speculation and prophetic vision. A product of and response to an era of rapid scientific and **technological** development, science fiction has often been concerned with the promotion of new ways of seeing. Though its popularity may result from the withdrawal of much modern mainstream fiction from traditional forms of storytelling, its concerns as speculative, defamiliarising literature sets it apart from the conventions of classic realism. Science fiction represents a radically different viewpoint from which to ask the question 'What does it mean to be human?' In the hands of **feminist** writers, science fiction can become a way of deconstructing **gender** relationships and roles, and of envisaging new possibilities for women. Feminist science fiction thus always implies the here and now of its production. It does not ignore history, but reviews, reimagines, rewrites and reinterprets it.

SECOND WAVE FEMINISM The term 'second wave' was coined by Marsha Lear, and refers to the increase in **feminist** activity which occurred in America, Britain and Europe from the late sixties onwards. In America, second wave feminism arose out of the **civil rights** and anti-war movements in which women, disillusioned with their second-class status even in the **activist** environment of student politics, began to band together to contend against discrimination. The tactics employed by second wave feminists varied, from highly-publicised activism, such as the protest against

the Miss America **beauty contest** in 1968, to the establishment of small **consciousness-raising** groups. However, it was obvious early on that the movement was not a unified one, with differences emerging between black feminism, **lesbian feminism**, **liberal feminism** and **socialist feminism**. Second wave feminism in Britain was similarly multiple in focus, although it was based more strongly in working-**class** socialism, as demonstrated by the strike of women workers at the Ford car plant for equal pay in 1968.

The slogan 'the personal is political' sums up the way in which second wave feminism did not just strive to extend the range of social opportunities open to women, but also, through intervention within the spheres of reproduction, sexuality and cultural representation, to change their domestic and private lives. Second wave feminism did not just make an impact upon western societies, but has also continued to inspire the struggle for women's rights across the world.

SEMIOLOGY Semiology, a term taken from the work of the French linguist Ferdinand de Saussure, is the system of interpreting signs, and its focus of inquiry is **cultural** meanings. Saussure distinguished between the signifier (the sound or mark which makes a word) and the signified (the concept the word represents), and argued that the relationship between the two was fixed by cultural convention rather than by any intrinsic link. A leading exponent of semiology is Roland Barthes, whose work *Mythologies* (1957) analysed all kinds of artefacts of popular culture, from **adverts** for soap powder to wrestling matches, in order to uncover the **ideological** mechanisms at work in the dissemination of such meanings. Following Barthes, semiology is used by **feminists** to expose the hidden mechanisms of **oppression** in a wide range of cultural products, such as advertising, film, art and literature.

SEMIOTIC In *Revolution in Poetic Language* (1974), Julia **Kristeva** uses the term 'semiotic' to describe the pre-Oedipal stage of a child's development, when it does not differentiate between itself and its mother. The child is thus tied to the rhythms, sensations and pulsations of the maternal body, and it is its gradual ordering of these phenomena which form the base upon which it will eventually develop a system of signification. When the child is initiated into the **symbolic order** and **language** the semiotic is repressed, but never entirely forgotten. Kristeva theorises that meaning originates in the interplay between semiotic and symbolic, whereby one modality regulates the other. The energies of the semiotic allow for a creative use of language which produces new meanings; but without the ordering abilities of the symbolic, it becomes mere 'psychotic' babbling. The semiotic mode is particularly to the fore in poetic language, where it is manifested in rhythm, syntactic irregularities and linguistic distortions such as metaphor and metonymy. However, although the semiotic is identified with the maternal body, it is not a privileged form of female **discourse**; on the contrary, Kristeva argues that the semiotic is equally accessible to both men and women. In fact, the writers she most often cites as particularly creative exponents of the semiotic impulse, such as Mallarmé and James Joyce, are male.

SENECA FALLS CONVENTION In 1848, two Quaker anti-slavery **activists**, Lucretia Mott and Elizabeth Cady **Stanton**, organised the first Women's Rights convention in the US. 250 people (including 40 men) gathered at the Wesleyan Chapel in Seneca Falls, New York. Many of the members of the American women's movement began as abolitionists; anti-slavery was one of the few public platforms available to women at the time. Many, too, saw connections between slavery and their own **oppression**. As one attender, Angelina Grimke, had written in 1836: 'the investigation of the rights of slaves has led me to a better understanding of my own'. Stanton drew up a declaration of sentiments and all resolutions on **equal rights** were passed unanimously, apart from the call for women's suffrage, which barely passed and was seen as very radical indeed. The following year the convention moved to Philadelphia and met annually until the outbreak of the Civil War in 1861.

SEX–GENDER SYSTEM Defined by Gayle Rubin in her essay 'The Traffic in Women' (1975) as 'that set of arrangements by which the biological raw material of human sex and procreation is shaped by human intervention'. Rubin distinguishes between biological sex, which is natural, and **gender**, which is **culturally** constructed, and argues that women are conditioned into assuming '**feminine**' identities which transform them into objects of exchange between men.

Judith **Butler** has developed Rubin's ideas in *Gender Trouble* (1990), although in her analysis, the concept of gender loses much of the negative connotations it accrues in Rubin's essay. Instead of being the axiomatic means of women's enslavement, gender in Butler's discussion is allowed a certain amount of free play; since 'when the constructed status of gender is theorized as radically independent of sex, gender itself has the potential to become a free-floating artifice, with the consequence that *man* and *masculine* might just as easily signify a female body as a male one, and *woman* and *feminine* a male body as easily as a female one'. Butler goes on to examine the means by which these 'free-floating' attributes of gender are regulated in order to produce an intelligible gender identity; a **discourse** which legitimates some sex/gender formulations, but renders others 'developmental failures or logical impossibilities'. Nevertheless, ruptures in the continuity between sex and gender contain the potential 'to open up . . . rival and subversive matrices of gender disorder'.

SEXISM Term which describes the male assumption of authority over women. Feminism argues that sexism appears in a **patriarchal** society at every level, affecting women's access to jobs and **education**, their appearance and behaviour at home and in the workplace, and both their public and private relationships. **Feminists** have located sexism as being perpetuated not only in materialist practices,

but also more subtly through the ways women are portrayed in the **media** – for example, sociologists studying the representation of women in **sport** comment on how emphasis is placed on their appearance and their family relationships, rather than on their actual physical accomplishments, thus suggesting that their traditional '**feminine**' role is more important. Feminist linguists such as Deborah Cameron and Dale **Spender** have also explored how sexism appears in **language**, which routinely belittles or excludes women. Hence, the focus of **women's studies** as a whole is the identification and deconstruction of sexist practices in every area of society.

SEXUAL HARASSMENT Deliberate or repeated sexual behaviour that makes the recipient feel they are unjustifiably viewed as a sexual object, sexual harassment was made illegal in the US 1964 Civil Rights Act and in the UK 1975 Sex Discrimination Act. Covers physical and verbal behaviour – from 'friendly' pats to **rape** and other sexual abuse, from suggestive or belittling remarks to unwanted demands for sex. In 1991, a US Court ruled that the victim's perspective was that from which hostile work environments should be judged, thus recognising predominant issues of male power and aggression. In October Professor Anita Hill accused Clarence Thomas, President Bush's nominee for the US Supreme Court, of sexual harassment. Appellant and defendant were both black; Hill was not believed and Thomas was nominated. Subsequently several prominent American **feminists**, such as Susan

Faludi in *Backlash* (1992) and Naomi Wolf in *Fire With Fire* (1993) have cited the Anita Hill case as a watershed event for feminism, energising the entire debate about men's sexual victimisation of women. Reaction to the Senate verdict included *Sexual Harassment* (Sumrall and Taylor, eds., 1992), accounts by women of all ages and backgrounds of their own experiences.

SEXUAL POLITICS Term coined by the American feminist Kate **Millett** in her book of the same name, published in 1969. *Sexual Politics* was a key text of early **second wave feminism**, in which Millett argued that all relationships between men and women are based on power, and that 'unless the clinging to male supremacy as a birthright is finally forgone, all systems of **oppression** will continue to function'. However, Millett argues that sexual politics is hard to combat because it is concealed within a **patriarchal** system by being constructed as a 'natural' range of phenomena rooted in biological difference. Therefore, women who wish to overthrow patriarchy must deconstruct the entire **sex-gender system**.

SHELLEY, MARY: WRITER (1797–1851) Mary Shelley was the daughter of the leading reformer and radical philosopher William Godwin and Mary **Wollstonecraft**, famed as the author of *A Vindication of the Rights of Woman*, who died soon after giving birth to her. At the age of sixteen, Mary met the poet Percy Bysshe Shelley, and eloped with him to Switzerland, an event which inspired her first publication, *A History of a Six Week's Tour* (1817). Mary gave premature birth to a daughter in 1815, who lived only a few weeks, but bore a son, William, the following year. It was also in 1816 that Mary went with her husband, stepsister, the poet Byron and Byron's physician Dr Polidori to Geneva. It was a holiday that was to inspire her first and greatest novel, for Mary later related how late-night discussions and ghost-story competitions fired her imagination, with the result that she immediately began work on *Frankenstein; or The Modern Prometheus*, published in 1818. The book is both a continuation of the eighteenth-century vogue for Gothic horror novels and also an innovative work in its introduction of a synthetic human character as one of the narrative's two main protagonists. It is for this reason that *Frankenstein* has been credited as one of the finest early works of **science fiction**, a novel which is still evoked as a warning to all scientific overreachers.

Mary's third child, Clara, was born in 1817, but died in Venice in 1818, followed by the death of William in 1819. This tragedy and her own ill health threw her into a depression, partly lifted by the birth of another son in 1819, but compounded by Shelley's drowning in 1822. She supported her surviving son by writing five more novels and some twenty-five short tales. She also prefaced and annotated Shelley's work, which resulted in a four-volume edition of his *Poetical Works*, published in 1839.

SHERMAN, CINDY: ARTIST AND PHOTOGRAPHER (1954–) Cindy Sherman came to prominence at the end of the 1970s with her now famous

313

series of sixty-nine *Untitled Film Stills*. In these small-format black and white photographs, Sherman impersonated female characters from 1950s Hollywood 'B' movies and *film noir*. As simultaneously photographer and model/actress, Sherman in many scenarios features an anonymous but uncannily familiar blonde actress in different roles: glamorous starlet, drunken floozy, voluptuous housewife, sexy secretary. As viewers, we seem to have seen these images before: we are asked to watch again as an array of solitary heroines act out the popular – and often contradictory – clichés of post-war American **femininity**. Sherman has subsequently produced more than ten cycles of photographic work in which she explores the myriad ways in which women, the body and sexuality have been represented. She addresses the stereotypes of historical portraiture and Surrealist photography as well as the image-making of more contemporary mass media. In all of this work, Sherman uses the illusionism of photography to confront powerful fantasies, desires and fears. Widely represented in major international exhibitions during the 1980s and 90s, Sherman's work has at the same time become the subject of much **feminist** art historical writing and debate.

SHOWALTER, ELAINE: LITERARY CRITIC AND CULTURAL THEORIST (1941–) Now Chair of the Department of English at Princeton University, Elaine Showalter made her name with the publication of *A Literature of Their Own* in 1977, which argued that the work of women writers had been systematically excluded from a male-dominated **literary canon**, and that feminist critics must work to retrieve this history of female literary endeavour. Showalter herself divided female literary history into three phases: 'feminine' (1840–80), when women writers *imitated* men; 'feminist' (1880–1920), when writers made political *protests* in their writing; and 'female' (1920–present), when women's writing has become preoccupied with *self-discovery*. In 'Towards a Feminist Poetics' (1979), Showalter coined the term '**gyno-criticism**' to describe the practice whereby the 'psychodynamics of female creativity' can be explored and recorded. Both this essay and *A Literature of One's Own* have become key texts in the establishment of **feminist** literary criticism as a distinct discipline within the academy, illustrating both the potential and limitations of the **Anglo-American** school of feminist thought. Showalter has been criticised – most famously by Toril **Moi** in *Sexual/Textual Politics* (1985) – for her humanist perspective which assumes that 'authentic' experience can be unproblematically retrieved from a text, and for her suspicion of what she terms 'male critical theory'; an argument she pursued in another important essay, 'Feminist Criticism in the Wilderness' (1981).

In *The Female Malady: Women, Madness and English Culture 1830-1980* (1987), Showalter moved further into the area of cultural history in order to examine the traditional association of women with **hysteria**, a project which has continued with the controversial *Hystories: Hysterical Epidemics and Modern Culture*

(1997). Its argument that we are on the verge of 'a hysterical plague', and its classification of Gulf War syndrome, chronic fatigue syndrome and satanic sexual abuse as 'hysterical' events, was not universally well-received. Although Showalter was arguing that hysterical symptoms should be treated seriously, as they represent internal and cultural conflicts which must be attended to, many misread her as dismissing such phenomena as purely imaginary.

Showalter remains a dedicated populariser of academic ideas, as likely to write articles for **women's magazines** as learned journals.

SILENCE In her book *The Feminist Critique of Language* (1990), the linguist Deborah Cameron defines the cultural silencing of women as 'an absence of female voices and concerns from high **culture**'. As feminist linguists such as Cameron point out, women can be silenced by straightforward prohibition – for example, the traditional censorship of women's speech in religious and political contexts – but they can also be silenced through the ridicule of their utterances as meaningless chatter or gossip. The outcome of rendering women inaudible within culture, as Dale **Spender** claims, is that women 'have been unable to pass on a tradition of women's meanings of the world' (*Man Made Language*, 1980).

It is this situation that much **feminist** literary criticism seeks to address. Publications like Tillie **Olsen's** *Silences* (1980), Joanna **Russ's** *How to Suppress Women's Writing* (1984), or Dale Spender's *The Writing or the Sex?* (1989) look at the censoring

mechanisms whereby women's writing is discouraged or suppressed, thus depriving women of a sense of literary tradition, while Elaine **Showalter's** *A Literature of Their Own* (1979) and Spender's *Mothers of the Novel* (1986) seek to delineate that tradition through the recovery of the work of forgotten writers.

While the project of critics like Showalter, Spender, Olsen and Russ seek to break the taboo on women's silence by bringing their voices into culture, the work of feminist theorists such as Julia **Kristeva**, Luce **Irigaray** and Hélène **Cixous** attempts to formulate a female discourse – or *écriture féminine* – which is founded in the dynamics of the body, and thus fundamentally different from the discourse of men. In her essay 'The Laugh of the Medusa' (1976) Cixous maintains that 'woman's *seizing* the occasion to *speak*' will bring about 'her shattering entry into history, which has always been based *on her suppression*'.

SISTERHOOD A concept central to the women's movement, which places stress on female solidarity and co-operation. The notion of sisterhood conveys the implicit assumption that all women have certain areas of experience in common on which a sense of identification can be founded. In 1970 the **radical feminist** Robin Morgan edited a book entitled *Sisterhood is Powerful*, which articulated the strength that can be wielded by women working in concert. The idea of sisterhood also asserts that relationships which do not include men are as, or more, important, than those that do: a concept which is central to Adrienne **Rich**'s essay '**Compulsory Heterosexuality** and Lesbian Existence' (1980), which argues that 'woman identification' is suppressed by a heterosexist **patriarchy**: 'The denial of reality and visibility to women's passion for women, women's choice of women as allies, life companions and community . . . have meant an incalculable loss to the power of all women *to change the social relations of the sexes, to liberate ourselves and each other.*'

Indeed, some feminists, such as the radical lesbian feminist Charlotte Bunch, argue that heterosexuality precludes sisterhood, since 'the very essence, definition and nature of heterosexuality is men first' ('Lesbians in Revolt', 1986). Others reverse the equation: for example, Mary **Daly** argues that friendship must precede any sexual expression of love, for 'it is impossible to be female-identified lovers without being friends and sisters' (*Gyn/Ecology*, 1978). At its most extreme, the concept of sisterhood merges into that of separatism. Mary Daly maintains that sisterhood and separatism are intrinsically linked, while Charlotte Bunch promotes the notion of 'separate spheres', whereby women operate within their own distinct set of institutions.

Soap Opera The term came from 1930s serial dramas on North American radio which were sponsored by soap powder companies and specifically aimed at a female listener. While still culturally regarded as offering lower forms of production and viewing experience than that provided by 'quality' series such as *Casualty* or *Inspector Morse*, soap opera has been a locus of academic debate about popular culture for over twenty years. In the early eighties the British Film Institute produced dossiers, teaching aids and collections of essays regarding popular television, most notably on *Coronation Street*, setting a precedent and providing valuable resources for further study. These accounts examined soaps within the context of popular television rather than judging them as 'good' or 'bad' broadcasting. Richard Dyer, Christine Geraghty, Charlotte Brunsdon and Tania **Modleski** have all produced research which remains essential reading on the subject. Much of the academic 'reclamation' of soap opera has been fuelled by feminist **re-visions** which also examine the **romance** and melodrama as fictions which are particularly consumed by women. Debate tends to centre on the perceived **feminine** characteristics of the form – its lack of closure, for example – the representation of strong women and how various audiences engage with it.

Socialist Feminism This branch of **feminist** thought has grown from **Marxist, radical** and **psychoanalytic** forms. Marxist and psychoanalytical thought suffers from the fact that Marx and **Freud** both tended to ignore the issue of **gender** in their work, with the result that their feminist proponents find themselves separated from the main aims of Marxist and Freudian thought. In *Women's Estate* (1971), Juliet **Mitchell** attempts to synthesise these main branches of feminism under the unifying notion of gender, arguing that the **oppression** of women is rooted in the fact that we live in a **class** society. Women's status and function in private as well as public domains must change if they are to achieve full liberation. Alison Jaggar, in *Feminist Politics and Human Nature* (1983), posited 'alienation' as a concept which would provide a unifying theoretical framework for feminism. Using the 'spirit' rather than the 'letter' of Marxist thought, Jaggar takes the notion of work as a dehumanising activity (distancing the worker from the product of their labour) and connects it to a woman's existence at home, as well as work. Jaggar organises alienation under three headings: sexuality, motherhood and intellectuality. Cultural values and beliefs, which are dominated by male concerns, influence all three spheres. For example, when a woman may say she controls her personal appearance for herself, she is more often than not influenced by dominant beliefs concerning beauty, and thus alienated from that appearance. In the continuing feminist debate between unity and diversity, it is argued that socialist feminism offers the strongest possibility of a unitary theory, as it attempts to include racial, ethnic and individual differences within its rubric.

SONTAG, SUSAN: ESSAYIST, NOVELIST AND CULTURAL CRITIC (1933–) Born in New York, and educated at Chicago and Harvard, Susan Sontag is one of America's leading intellectual voices. Her early marriage to social psychologist Philip Rieff was over by the end of the 1950s, following which she published several articles in *Partisan Review* and *The New York Review of Books*, later collected in *Against Interpretation* (1964). Amongst the topics discussed are French writers Nathalie Sarraute and Jean Genet, and the significance of film in relation to other art forms. The most famous essay is 'Notes on "Camp"', a penetrating study of a certain kind of kitsch irony which she saw as crucial to the sensibility of the 1960s.

Other non-fiction works include *Styles of Radical Will* (1969), the Barthes-influenced *On Photography* (1977), *Illness as Metaphor* (1978), *Under the Sign of Saturn* (1980) and *AIDS and Its Metaphors* (1989). Each of these engages perceptively with issues of both elite and mass **culture**.

Sontag's novels *The Benefactor* (1963) and *Death Kit* (1967), and her short story collection *I, etcetera* (1968), are fascinated with the world of dreams and the hidden self, and develop themes from Kafka and the existentialists.

SPARE RIB British **feminist** magazine founded in 1972 by a group which included Rosie Boycott, Rozsika **Parker** and Marsha Rowe. *Spare Rib* occupied a clear space in opposition to the mainstream, and actually became more, rather than less, radical during its twenty-one years of publication. Owned by various collectives over this period, it became totally unfunded after the abolition of the left-wing Greater London Council. Editorial production, design and administration, what appeared and how it was represented was always informed by political commitment. Even after major redesigns, it retained its mixture of serious articles, reviews and cartoons.

Its radical journalism and commitment to the **women's liberation** movement influenced a far greater number of women than its circulation figures might suggest. It did, however, maintain a circulation of around 25,000 copies per month until it ceased to publish in 1993.

SPECTATORSHIP Feminism's interest in how film and television representations create gendered viewing positions for their spectators begins with Laura **Mulvey**'s work in the early 1970s. Drawing on **psychoanalytic** theory, Mulvey argued that in film the woman is the one looked at, not the one who looks. The viewing position for most mainstream cinema is male, structured around mechanisms of voyeurism and fetishism. Her analysis of 'spectatorship' is therefore of the viewing positions implied, imagined or constructed by the text rather than the responses of actual audiences. The **pleasures** offered by film, she argues, are pleasures provided only for the male spectator. Women are objects, not subjects, of the **gaze**, their bodies eroticised and often fragmented. Female spectators then have two principal options: either to assume a **masculine** viewing position by identifying with the hero, or to assume a passive or masochistic position by identifying with a female character. In the 1980s theorists like Mary Ann Doane and Tania **Modleski** analysed the pleasures offered to the female spectator by '**feminine** genres' like the 'woman's film' or the **soap opera**, concluding that these **genres** offer masochistic fantasies in which the active woman is usually punished, though they also offer the

pleasures of transgression and rebellion. More recently, attention has shifted to the ways in which actual female audiences do or do not take up these viewing positions, with writers like Jackie Stacey arguing that spectators 'negotiate' the meaning of film and television texts, rather than passively accepting the positions offered.

SPENCE, JO: PHOTOGRAPHER (1943–1992) Co-founder of Camerawork and the Photography Workshop, who funded Spence's first collection, *Photography/Politics: One* (1979), and subsequently consolidated her position as one of the leading figures in British photography. Her career covered a variety of photographic styles and subject matter, but she is noted for the visual representation of her experience of breast cancer. During the early 1980s, Spence and Rosy Martin developed 'photo therapy', drawing upon approaches from co-counselling, psychodrama and a technique called 'reframing'. The resulting work included the touring exhibition, *The Picture of Health?* (1983), which emphasises the inhuman and infantilising treatment of cancer patients, and *Silent Health: Women, Health and Representation* (1990). Memory and biography have also been important elements in Jo Spence's work, as showing in *Family Snaps* (1991) which she co-edited with Patricia Holland. In 1995 a retrospective collection of Spence's finest photographs and essays was drawn together, called *Cultural Sniping*.

SPENDER, DALE: LINGUIST AND CRITIC (1943–) Australian **feminist** Dale Spender was educated at the

Universities of Sydney, New South Wales, and New England. She first came to prominence in 1980, with the publication of *Man Made Language*, which argues that **language** structures the way in which we perceive reality. Spender argues that, because language is **patriarchal**, conveying a male picture of the world, women are linguistically marginalised, their female experience remaining unencoded and hence unrecorded. It is a problem that even the most articulate feminist must face, which means that the history of women's writing is one of solitary struggle with meaning. It was an argument that Spender explored further in *Mothers of the Novel* (1986), which traces a hidden history of female **novel-writing**, and examines the strategies used to suppress the products of female authorship. *The Writing or the Sex?* (1989) similarly looks at the means by which women's writing is censored, a situation Spender herself has attempted to remedy in her anthologies of both Australian and British women writers. She is also a dedicated recorder of the history of the feminist movement, the author of *Women of Ideas* (1982), *For the Record: The Making and Meaning of Feminist Knowledge* (1985), and editor of *Feminist Theorists: Three Centuries of Women's Intellectual Traditions* (1983). Recently, however, Spender's focus has shifted slightly: *Nattering on the Net: Women, Power and Cyberspace* (1995) urges women to see network **technology** as a means by which new avenues of female communication can be opened.

SPICE GIRLS The Spice Girls – Sporty, Baby, Posh, Ginger and Scary

– signed a deal with Virgin Records in 1995, and released their first big single, 'Wannabe' in 1996. From the beginning, they were problematic icons. While the assertiveness of the song's lyrics indicated for some that feminism had entered the mainstream, for others the Spice Girls were just another group of bimbos cleverly marketed on the strength of their sex appeal. They caused additional controversy when they voiced political beliefs, claiming that they were 'true Thatcherites', and that Margaret Thatcher 'was the first Spice Girl, the pioneer of our ideology – **Girl Power**'.

Even feminism's 'big names' have intervened in the Spice Girl debate. Camille **Paglia** and Kathy **Acker** have proclaimed admiration, while Germaine **Greer** dismisses them as 'anodyne'. Now, however, their fortunes as a group are in decline. In an attempt to live up to their 'girl power' image, they sacked their manager Simon Fuller and appointed Ginger Spice (Geri Halliwell) as his replacement. But Geri left the group in 1998 amidst rumours of an imminent break-up. Although this has not yet happened, only time will tell whether the Spice Girls and their Girl Power philosophy will prove to be anything more than a passing **fashion** statement.

SPINSTER This term, which refers to an unmarried woman, has a chequered history. Originally it was used simply to indicate marital status; however, it became increasingly pejorative, and has now declined into obsolescence. It was derived from the economic truism that any woman who did not marry (and had no other

319

means of financial support) had no option but to keep herself by working in the 'spinning house'. The **class** distinctions evident in the term's origins acquired greater significance over time, with derision being heaped mainly upon middle-class women.

By the early Victorian era, **patriarchal ideology** had successfully confined middle-class women to the **domestic** sphere; hence, those who did not marry had to remain in the parental home. By the end of the nineteenth century, however, unmarried women began to be seen as parasitic, financial burdens, who had failed to fulfil their feminine duties, and by 1911 unmarried women were labelled 'surplus'.

The pioneering **'New Women'** broadened educational and occupational opportunities for the middle classes, but it was the aftermath of the First World War that allowed the unmarried woman to reclaim her respectability. Equality feminists gradually eroded the residual stigma associated with spinsterhood until **marriage** became an option rather than an obligation.

SPIVAK, GAYATRI CHAKRAVORTY: CRITIC AND CULTURAL THEORIST (1941–) Gayatri Chakravorty Spivak's theoretical orientation is protean, ranging from Marxism through feminism and deconstructivism, to **postcolonialism**. This has led to accusations of 'methodological eclecticism' and inconsistency. However, her method can best be seen as an attempt to combine deconstructivist criticism and Marxist analysis in order to highlight the discursive constitution of the **subaltern** (sexed) subject, drawing attention to the material forces underlying this subject constitution.

Spivak has made significant contributions to the **feminist** debate due to her critiques of the 'benevolence' of various western intellectuals who attempt to act as interlocutors for the marginalised in what she sees as an act of appropriation. She criticises what she perceives to be the **phallocentrism** of theorists such as **Foucault**, Deleuze and **Derrida**, but equally disavows areas of western feminism as patronising and misguided. This is most evident in two essays, 'French Feminism in an International Frame' (1981) and 'Displacement and the Discourse of Woman' (1983).

Spivak's contention that 'there is no place from where the subaltern (sexed) subject can speak' exposes the oppressive nature of both colonialism and **patriarchy**. Moreover, she is critical of **essentialist** views of women, preferring to highlight the cultural and discursive construction of female **subjectivity**. While little is sacrosanct in her work, she has remained resolute in exposing the problems of **othering** and marginality in an attempt to empower **third world** women by speaking *to* and not *for* them.

SPORT Sports sociologists have traced the origins of modern competitive sport back to the nineteenth-century preoccupation with social Darwinism, which spawned a cult of athleticism amongst upper and middle-class males. In Britain, for example, sport was regarded as an essential part of the education of empire-builders, teaching such masculine virtues as determination and self-control, as well as enhancing the physical attributes of manliness, such as strength and muscularity. It is not therefore surprising that women are second-class citizens in the sporting environment which, as many **feminist** sport sociologists observe, is organised by men to serve male interests. For example, the founder of the modern Olympics, Baron Pierre de Coubertin, viewed women's sport as against the 'laws of nature' and 'the most unaesthetic sight human eyes could contemplate'.

Female participation in sports thus poses an implicit threat to the masculine assumptions enshrined within the sporting code, a threat which, as sports feminists frequently argue, is dealt with either by representing the sportswoman herself as masculine, and thus deviant, or by exaggerating her **femininity**. In *Sporting Females* (1994) Jennifer Hargreaves observes how sport is **gendered**, with aesthetic and expressive sports, such as gymnastics and ice-dancing regarded as being acceptable for women, and the power sports, such as football, rugby and weightlifting construed as innately male. Sports sociologists have also observed how the body of the acceptably 'feminine' sportswoman tends to be sexualised for mass consumption (a practice on the increase in light of the increasingly close alliance between sport, fashion and commerce); while those who lie too far outside the dominant feminine paradigm, such as **bodybuilders**, still tend to be extensively critiqued for being 'unnatural'. Lesbianism is an accusation often levelled at sporting

women, and lesbian sportswomen who publicly 'come out' (such as, most famously, the Czech tennis player Martina Navratilova) can face considerable problems in the gaining of sponsorship and favourable press coverage.

Also at issue in sports feminism is the question of women's equal participation, at both the competitive and economic level. For example, the American tennis player Billie Jean King led a boycott in 1970 to protest against the difference in prize money between men and women on the pro tennis circuit. Although she was successful in gaining equal prize money for women at the U.S. Open, the prestigious Wimbledon tennis tournament in Britain is, to date, still refusing to treat women tennis players as men's equals when it comes to rewards.

SPRINKLE, ANNIE: PERFORMANCE ARTIST (1954–) A former prostitute and star of pornographic films, Annie Sprinkle's career as a performance artist began in the late 1980s. Her highly controversial work *Post Porn Modernist* comprised a collage of overtly erotic performances, many focusing on her earlier years in the sex industry. The show has toured internationally, provoking widespread debate both within and outside of **feminist** circles. In this performance work, as in all other aspects of her practice, Sprinkle has continually tested the boundaries between **pornography** and art, using her own body as the vehicle. Her photographic work has been published in *Penthouse* and other pornographic magazines, whilst at the same time being exhibited in international art galleries. In addition, she has written, directed and starred in her own erotic films and videos. Advocating as it does the liberation and empowerment of women, while at the same time employing explicitly sexual or obscene material, Sprinkle's work has proved difficult to analyse from a feminist perspective. In confronting the fraught issue of pornography, she continually challenges feminist criticism and debate. More recently, Sprinkle has advocated a dual notion of female **orgasm**, both physical and spiritual, and has been exploring Tantric sex rituals in a series of all-women workshops.

STANTON, ELIZABETH CADY: ABOLITIONIST AND WOMEN'S RIGHTS ACTIVIST (1815–1902) Stanton was the pre-eminent political theorist of women's rights in nineteenth-century America. She drew parallels between black slavery and women's oppression, asserting that: 'The negro's skin and the woman's sex are *prima facie* evidence that they were intended to be subjected to the white Anglo-Saxon man.' Dedicated to fighting male economic, cultural and intellectual privilege, she agitated for women's reproductive self-determination, sexual freedom and divorce law liberalisation. She helped organise the first American women's rights conference in 1848 and with Susan B. **Anthony** led the campaign for women's suffrage for the next fifty years. Hostile to forms of Christian moralism, she wrote *The Women's Bible* (1898), a hugely popular and irreverent account of Christianity from a **feminist** perspective. Too radical for many of her contemporaries, her stock rose when she was rediscovered by a new generation of feminists in the late 1960s.

STEIN, GERTRUDE: MODERNIST WRITER (1874–1946) Gertrude Stein was born in the United States, the child of Jewish-Bavarian immigrants. She studied psychology at university, a training that influenced both the form and content of her subsequent writing. Another important influence was the artistic milieu of Paris, where she lived for some years: the paintings of such artists as Cézanne, Matisse, and Picasso inspired much of her early work, such as *Three Lives* (1990) and *Tender Buttons* (1914). Stein is also remembered for her sexuality. Much of her writing is explicitly lesbian, the best-known of which is *The Autobiography of Alice B. Toklas* (1932). She also wrote poems in which she attempted to devise a discourse of lesbian eroticism.

STEINEM, GLORIA: AMERICAN FEMINIST AND WRITER (1934–) Gloria Steinem was born in Toledo, Ohio, and travelled with her parents until she was twelve. Only when they divorced in 1945 did she begin to attend school on a regular basis. She graduated from Smith College in Massachusetts in 1956, and began working as a freelance journalist in India and New York. Steinem came to public attention in 1963 when she published an article in *Esquire* describing her experience of working as a Playboy bunny. It was a stunt that summarises her **feminist** agenda, which combines **radicalism** with a desire to bring feminism into the mainstream. Steinem's glamorous image has always belied the media caricature of a feminist as an ugly, bitter woman unable to get a man, and she has never been above using her appearance to get an audience. As an activist, Steinem has helped to found such organisations as the National Woman's Political Caucus, the Women's Action Alliance and the Coalition of Labour Union Women, and is also heavily involved in the pro-choice movement. She founded the feminist magazine *Ms.* in 1972, and her publications include *Feminist Family Values* (1996); a biography of Marilyn Monroe, *Marilyn: Norma Jeane* (1996); and *Moving Beyond Words* (1995). A collection of her journalism, *Outrageous Acts and Everyday Rebellions*, was reissued in 1995.

STEREOTYPING A term taken from printing which denotes something fixed and lacking in originality. In common usage the stereotype can be seen as an **ideological** discursive strategy which demarcates an us/them binary which functions to reinforce the dominant **discourse**. For example, **patriarchy** often operates at the level of the stereotype in order to categorise the roles and characteristics of women which are viewed as *essentially* different to those of men. Within this dichotomous opposition the **feminine** is categorised as inferior, while the **masculine** is valorised. The stereotyped ideal woman is nurturant wife, mother or muse constructed through the scopic gaze of the male. Conversely, female sexuality is conceptualised as terrifying, insatiable and predatory.

Patriarchy constructs and defines what is prototypically feminine, repeatable and unchanging, and then encourages women to identify with these stereotypical representations. Thus, stereotyping is part of an ideological process which allows women to be **interpellated** by patriarchal ideology.

SUBALTERN Term coined by the Indian postcolonialist theorist Gayatri Chakravorty **Spivak** to describe the colonised **subject**. Whereas some sectors of colonised societies co-operate with the authorities, thus gaining an identity within the coloniser's view of the **third world**, the subaltern subject remains on the periphery, constructed half in and half out of the colonialist paradigm. The female subaltern subject is even more marginalised, for, says Spivak in 'Can the Subaltern Speak' (1993), 'If, in the context of colonial production, the subaltern has no history, and cannot speak, the subaltern as female is even more deeply in shadow.' The western **feminist** must 'unlearn female privilege' if she is to speak of the female subaltern subject.

SUBJECTIVITY The traditional conception of the subject is virtually synonymous with the notion of self or ego as an autonomous and self-actuating agent capable of valid self-knowledge. Liberal humanism views the subject as endowed with the power of reason, and thus a conscious and unified self possessing a unique core of **identity**. Later theorists have challenged this notion of the self-determining subject.

The notion of subjectivity results

from a **postmodern** rejection of these models of the subject. The conscious individualism of previous models is replaced with notions of the subject, not as the originator of meaning, but as a function of **discourse** – a recipient site of meaning rather than the source. Agency and the capacity for rational self-determination are seen as illusory products of the subjects' discursive position, as the subject is viewed as fissured and constantly 'in process'.

Feminist theorists have posited the notion of an alienated female subjectivity as the female is determined socially, linguistically and biologically by **patriarchy**, through entrance into the **symbolic order** and recognition of the primacy of the phallus. Thus, female subjectivity is occasioned by lack of the biological penis which gives her entry to the **Law of the Father** represented by the symbolic phallus. Woman is therefore positioned oppositionally within discourse, identified by her **difference**.

SUFFRAGETTES Although women have fought for the vote all over the world, the term 'suffragette', which was coined in 1906, is peculiarly British. In 1897 Millicent Garrett **Fawcett** founded the National Union of Women's Suffrage Societies, which was followed in 1903 by the Women's Social and Political Union formed by Emmeline **Pankhurst**. This organised the first women's march to lobby Parliament in 1906. The suffragettes were at their most active from 1906 until the outbreak of the First World War, but from the start the leadership was split between a belief in a peaceful, 'ladylike' behaviour, and the need for more active protest, especially when Asquith became Prime Minister in 1908, and opposed the women's vote. While Millicent Fawcett led the more restrained branch, the Pankhursts – Emmeline and her two daughters, Sylvia and Christabel – were associated with the militants, who smashed windows, launched arson attacks and other forms of vandalism, and were prepared to go on hunger-strike after they were arrested. The suffragettes became increasingly frustrated at the lack of progress achieved by conventional approaches, and it is difficult to say how the suffrage campaign would have ended had not war broken out in 1914. The 1918 Representation of the People Act gave the vote to women over thirty; full suffrage for women over twenty-one followed in 1928. Although the suffragettes were not directly responsible for achieving the vote, their campaign undoubtedly intensified the pressure on Parliament to act.

SYMBOLIC ORDER In **psychoanalysis**, the term derives from the work of Jacques **Lacan**. For Lacan the entry into the symbolic order is the entry of the child into **culture** itself, into **language**; it is the moment the child takes up its place as a subject. For **feminists**, the symbolic order is **patriarchy**. The pre-symbolic realm is where the child has a blissful, dyadic relationship with its mother, called the **Imaginary** in Lacan's work. Julia **Kristeva** calls the pre-symbolic the '**semiotic**'. For Kristeva, this is the pre-linguistic realm associated with the mother's body. Once we enter the symbolic order we still can feel the effects of the semiotic through rhythm and word play in writing. For a number of **French feminists**, the pre-symbolic is the source of *écriture féminine*, a style of feminine **discourse** in tune with the female body that draws upon that which is repressed on entry into the symbolic order.

T

TAYLOR MILL, HARRIET: FEMINIST WRITER (1807–1858) Best known as the much-idolised wife of John Stuart **Mill,** but also a **feminist** author in her own right, Harriet married John Taylor, a Radical Unitarian wholesale druggist, when she was eighteen. The marriage was not a happy one, and was further destabilised when in 1830 Harriet Taylor met John Stuart Mill. Their mutual attraction was so strong that although they avoided sexual indiscretion, they spent increasing amounts of time together. When Taylor died in 1849, they waited for two years before finally marrying. A strong influence on Mill's feminism, Harriet Taylor herself wrote significant contributions to the feminist debate, the best known of which is an article in the *Westminster Review*, 'The Enfranchisement of Women', published anonymously. In many ways it anticipates Mill's arguments in *The Subjection of Women* by insisting: 'The real question is, whether it is right and expedient that one-half of the human race should pass through life in a state of forced subordination to the other half.' Arguing that women should be categorised as more than mothers, Taylor concluded: 'What is wanted for women is equal rights, equal admission to all social privileges; not a position apart, a sort of sentimental priesthood.' After her death from tuberculosis in 1858, Mill

dedicated himself to further publicising what he claimed were her ideas. She is extensively eulogised in his *Autobiography* (1873), and was an intellectual influence on several of his other works, including his *Principles of Political Economy* (1848) and *On Liberty* (1859).

TECHNOLOGY The feminist engagement with technology has always been problematic. In her book *Feminism and the Technological Fix* (1994), Carol A. Stabile claims that feminist reactions to technology fall into two main camps. Feminists influenced by **essentialist** or ecological views tend to be *technophobic*, identifying technology as working to further female separation from **nature**. Fundamentally **patriarchal** in its orientation, technology replaces the notion of working in harmony with the environment with a **masculinist** principle of domination and control. What Stabile terms *technomania* argues precisely the opposite: that technology offers **utopian** possibilities for women, containing the potential to liberate them from the straitjacket of **gender** identity. In 1970 the American feminist Shulamith **Firestone** published *The Dialectic of Sex*, which eagerly anticipated a future in which technological advances would free women from the burden of childbearing – more recently, Donna

Haraway has offered us the hybrid figure of the **cyborg**, representative of a world in which no one can escape the imprint of technology. However, Haraway's cyborg is also representative of a **postmodern** concern with technology which, while it rejects essentialist visions of a world free from its operations, also acknowledges that it is bound up in a system of social processes and power relations. But as theorists such as Haraway, Sadie **Plant** and Evelyn Fox Keller argue, this makes feminist engagement with technology more, not less, urgent.

TEXTILES 'Textiles' derives from the Latin, *texere*, meaning 'to weave', but in its contemporary forms (and following Roland Barthes's observation on text and textiles in *The Pleasure of the Text*, 1975) it has come to signify a wide range of material speculations, conceptual propositions and **semiotic** readings. Textiles are part of everyday life and are imbued with a complex set of histories. As such, textiles have encompassed ideas of function, decoration, religious and social activities, colonialism and trade, **gender** and politics. Contemporary textile practices also challenge the false dichotomies of fine art and craft and may be situated within an expanded field of visual arts references. The scholarly and critical writing which accompanies its interpretation draws upon many other discourses, including those from **psychoanalysis**, feminism, anthropology and **queer theory**, and its reception is permeated by critiques of institutions.

THIRD WAVE A term which describes a resurgence of interest in feminist **activism** on the part of young women who wish to differentiate themselves from the **postfeminist** label. Third wave feminism is characterised by a desire to redress economic and racial inequality as well as 'women's issues'. Groups identified with the movement include the Women's Action Coalition and Third Wave, both formed in 1992. However, third wave feminism has yet to attain the widespread publicity and enthusiastic support enjoyed by **second wave feminism** at its height, and has been viewed with scepticism by many as merely a short-lived fashion rather than a genuine indication that women have reached the next stage in the **feminist** struggle.

THIRD WORLD FEMINISM Third world feminism poses a challenge to the dominance assumed by western **feminists** in the general development of feminist thought, which often tends to ignore the specific experiences of ethnic groups located outside the western cultural perspective. Feminists such as Gayatri **Spivak**, Chandra Talpade Mohanty and Chela Sandoval critique western feminist theorists for presuming to intervene in cultural issues that have nothing to do with them: in 'Under Western Eyes' (1991), for example, Chandra Talpade Mohanty attacks the reductive way in which the 'average third world woman' is represented in feminist discourse. While western women are portrayed 'as educated, as modern, as having control over their own bodies and sexualities, and the freedom to make their own decisions', she argues that the average third world woman is portrayed as leading 'an essentially truncated life based on her **feminine** gender (read: sexually constrained) and her being "third world" (read: ignorant, poor, uneducated, tradition-bound, **family**-orientated, victimized, etc.)'. Gayatri Chakravorty Spivak's conception of the '**subaltern**' theorises the process by which non-western women are 'spoken for' in first world writing, which renders them the mute, passive (and implicitly grateful) recipients of western ideas, and which often ignores strategies evolved by third world women themselves to contend against their own **oppression**. Third world women speaking from both within and without western **culture** destabilise the notion of a seamlessly unified global feminism, yet it may make possible the evolution of a specific and localised feminist practice which nevertheless seeks to establish overlapping areas of purpose which span cultural boundaries: what Chandra Talpade Mohanty terms an 'imagined community' of women.

TICKNER, LISA: CULTURAL HISTORIAN Lisa Tickner has written extensively on aspects of **feminist** visual art practice, both contemporary and historical. In 1978 she published a challenging article in the first volume of *Art History*, the new journal of the Association of Art Historians. The article itself as well as the correspondence it provoked have subsequently been reproduced in a number of anthologies, this in turn archiving Tickner's work as a significant contribution to feminist art historical critique. Titled 'The Body Politic', Tickner's article surveyed recent trends in the exploration of sexuality and the female body by women artists. She both described and illustrated work that attempted to produce a new kind of body art: one which recognised that living in a female body is different from looking at it, as a man. In other words, she was concerned with women's art that challenged many existing cultural taboos, especially those around fertility and sexuality. From a more historical point of view, Tickner's research into women's image-making has included an important study of the British **suffrage** campaign between 1907 and 1914 (*The Spectacle of Women*, 1987).

TRANSSEXUALISM Transsexualism – the changing of **gender** through surgical and chemical intervention – has become a much-disputed subject within **feminist** debate. The transsexual can certainly be regarded as the perfect symbol of technological **postmodernity** in which gender is rendered fluid and multiple, thus bringing new geometries of **desire** into play. In 'The Empire Strikes Back: A Posttransexual Manifesto', Sandy Stone, herself a male-to-female transsexual, argues precisely this point; that 'the disruptions of the old patterns of desires that the multiple dissonances of the transsexual body imply produce not an irreducible alterity but a myriad of alterities . . . physicalities of constantly shifting figure and ground that exceed the frame of any possible representation'. However, the male-to-female transformation is one that many feminists find problematic. In *Gender Trouble* (1990), Judith **Butler** speaks of male-to-female transsexuality as 'disavowed homosexuality', an attempt to 'displace and conceal . . . [a] preheterosexual history in favour of one that consecrates a seamless hetero-sexuality'. What many feminists find disturbing about male-to-female sexual transformations is that they incarnate extremely traditional, not to say **essentialist**, notions of **femininity**. In *Anticlimax* (1990) Sheila **Jeffreys** argues that 'transexual males want to become their image of what women should be, not a liberated or feminist version'. The feminist/transsexual debate took a contentious turn in Britain in 1997, when Germaine **Greer** resigned her post as Special Lecturer at the all-female Newnham College, Cambridge, on the appoint-ment of a Fellow who had formerly been male. Greer has since made her point of view perfectly clear in *The Whole Woman* (1999), in which she compares the transsexual to the **rapist**, 'forc[ing] his way into the few private spaces women may enjoy'.

TRUTH, SOJOURNER: ABOLITIONIST AND EVANGELIST (1797–1883). Truth was a New York-born former slave, named Isabella Baunfree. Truth grew up speaking Dutch as her first language, and then English. In 1826 Truth was to sue in the New York courts for the return of one of her thirteen children, Peter, who had been illegally sold away to Alabama. After succeeding in having Peter returned she escaped from slavery. In 1843, after a religious experience she named herself Sojourner Truth. Know-ledgeable about the bible despite never learning to read or write, Truth began travelling as an abolitionist speaker, becoming famous for her 1851 speech at the Women's Rights Convention held in Akron, Ohio. Six feet tall and wearing a white turban, she addressed the white audience in a thunderous voice: 'Look at my arm! I have ploughed, and planted, and gathered into barns, and no man could head me! And a'nt I a woman?' Truth was one of the first women (black or white) to challenge the white ministers' denouncement of women's rights. At one of the earliest **feminist** conventions Truth, unlike many white feminists, challenged **racism** and **sexism** and **class** division, concerns that are still addressed by contem-porary **African-American feminists**.

TUBMAN, HARRIETT: ABOLITIONIST, SPY AND ARMY SCOUT (1821–1913) Tubman escaped brutal slavery in Maryland in 1849. Known affection-ately as 'Moses', in nineteen trips back to the slave states she was responsible for leading around 300 slaves to freedom, including her parents, two of her children and a sister. In the South there was a 40,000-dollar price on her head, yet no one ever betrayed her. At the outbreak of the Civil War in 1861, her local knowledge made her invaluable to the Union army and she became an army scout, spy and nurse. She led many Union soldiers from the South to freedom and in 1863 in a raid on a Confederate supply dump, became the only woman in American history, black or white, to lead troops into battle. After the war she set up The Home for Indigent and Aged Negroes, financing it through sales of her auto-biography and speaking tours.

UNCONSCIOUS A fundamental concept in Freudian **psychoanalysis**. For **Freud**, many human actions are inexplicable without recourse to the idea that we often act but are unaware of the reasons why. The reasons are repressed: only in response to analysis (Freud's famous 'talking cure' as one patient called it) does their motivation become clear. The unconscious for Freud is that which is forbidden and repressed from consciousness. His explanation of why certain thoughts and **desires** are repressed is the theory of **psychoanalysis** itself. Access to the unconscious is through the analysis of dreams and slips of the tongue, in other words when the unconscious ruptures conscious thought. For a number of **feminists**, various forms of cultural production – writing, art, film and music – can tap into the unconscious ways that disrupt the rational and largely **patriarchal**, **gendered** self and subject its certainties to interrogation.

UTOPIA Sir Thomas More's *Utopia* (1516) introduced into the English language the word 'utopian', a pun on 'eutopia' ('a better place') and 'outopia' ('no place'). Utopias are products of the moral rather than the literary sense, and as political or social commentary they contain a strongly didactic element. In *Dreaming the Impossible* (1986), Tom Moylan distinguishes between the 'literary utopia', which works to reinforce the dominant **ideology**, and the 'critical utopia', which he defines as 'a neutral space in which opposition can be articulated and revived'.

There has always been a fruitful interplay between **feminist** writers and theorists: when Shulamith **Firestone** complained in 1970 that there was 'no feminist utopian literature yet in existence', she had not foreseen the influential role feminist theory was to play in the formulation of a pile of feminist utopias published throughout the 1970s – including Ursula Le Guin's *The Dispossessed* (1974), Joanna **Russ**'s *The Female Man* (1975), Marge Piercy's *Woman on the Edge of Time* (1976) and Sally Miller Gearhart's *The Wanderground* (1979) – all of which, in one way or another, used the utopian mode as a vehicle for feminist social critique. Nor is the transmission of ideas all one way: the **postmodern** theorist Donna **Haraway**, for example, consciously presents her writing as working from within the utopian tradition, as concerned with visualising the future as with analysing the here and now.

VICTIM FEMINISM Term used by Naomi **Wolf**, Katie **Roiphe** and others to describe a form of feminism which defines women as the helpless victims of **patriarchal** violence. In *The Morning After* (1992), a study of students' attitudes towards sex and feminism at Princeton University, Roiphe argues that feminism engenders a victim culture whereby women expect men to assault them in sexual situations, and in which they gain status by proclaiming themselves to be victims. In *Fire With Fire* (1993) Naomi Wolf attempts to tread the middle ground with regard to this issue. Like Roiphe, she claims that **second wave** feminists such as Andrea **Dworkin**, Catherine **MacKinnon** and Adrienne **Rich** are guilty of focusing 'on female victimization at the expense of social agency'. Yet she also criticises Roiphe for 'doing something slick and dangerous with the notion of victimization', ignoring the fact that sex crime is a real and dangerous phenomenon. Wolf herself draws a distinction between the necessity of recognising that women are victimised within a male-dominated society, and the building of what she terms 'a cult of the victim' which 'redefine[s] victim status itself as a source of strength and identity'.

VIRGIN MARY The earliest reference to the mother of Jesus is in Paul's letter to the Galatians 4:4 (c 57 CE). But there are surprisingly few references to Mary in the New Testament and some of these seem intended to distance Jesus from her rather than to accord her any particular honour (see Mark 3:34–35). A presumption of Mary's virginal intactness, however, has acquired great weight, especially in the light of Augustinian teaching that the human taint of sin is passed on to every new generation via sexual intercourse. Within the Roman Catholic Church the perpetual virginity of Mary, in conception, as well as in giving birth, was affirmed at the Council of Chalcedon (451 CE) and she was given the title Aeiparthenos (ever-virgin). This was confirmed as a dogma – a mandatory belief for Roman Catholics – at the first Lateran Council (649 CE). Two further dogmas, the Immaculate Conception and the Assumption, celebrate Mary's peculiar status in this respect. The doctrine of the Immaculate Conception proclaims Mary to have been born without sin. As she was born without sin so she was also free from the consequences of sin which included the pain and suffering of childbirth and the corruption of the grave. The Virgin's Assumption asserts that Mary was taken up body and soul into the glory of heaven. In the Eastern Churches, the Virgin's

Dormition is a similar teaching but suggests rather that the Virgin's body is taken up to rest until the last day whilst her soul remains in the presence of God. In both cases however, her body is preserved from any physical decay and this is directly linked to her conception and status as virgin.

Ideas about Mary's virginity play upon the profound ambiguities of Christian teaching about sexuality and material existence. Whilst they can be directly related to incarnational theology which celebrates the material world and the human body as the creation of God and the sphere of his creative Word, they also reflect dualistic, body-hating elements which have been evident within Christianity since at least the era of Gnostic philosophy which flourished in the first and second centuries CE. Modern **feminist** commentators have drawn attention to the sense in which popular traditions about Mary appear to preserve some pre-Christian **goddess** traditions and function, within a highly **patriarchal** religious structure, as the surviving remnant of the feminine divine. By inveighing against Marian traditions as idolatrous, Reformation theologians and Church leaders reduced, still further, the sig-nificance of women and the feminine within the Christian Church.

VISUAL PLEASURE This term is irrevocably linked to Laura **Mulvey** and her article 'Visual **Pleasure** and Narrative Cinema' (1975). Mulvey proposed that narrative cinema is predicated on the 'male **gaze**', a controlling and determining look which fixes 'The image of woman as (passive) raw material for the (active) gaze of man' through the pleasures of scopophilia: 'pleasure in looking at another person as an erotic object'. Following the psychoanalytic models of Sigmund **Freud** and Jacques **Lacan**, she argued that traditional film-making acts to subordinate women, thereby asserting the authority of the male **symbolic order**. This pivotal work was reconsidered by Mulvey in 'Afterthoughts on "Visual Pleasure and Narrative Cinema" . . . '(1981) and has been challenged by other **feminist** work in film studies. Lorraine Gamman and Margaret Marshment's collection, *The Female Gaze: Women as Viewers of Popular Culture* (1988), was a direct response to Mulvey, examining the potential for female **spectatorship**.

W

WALKER, ALICE: NOVELIST, POET, ESSAYIST AND ACTIVIST (1944–)
Walker was born in rural Georgia, the eighth child of poor sharecroppers. While heavily involved in the **civil rights** movement, she began to write poetry and fiction about the various strategies of capitulation and resistance used by black women in a **racist, patriarchal** culture. She coined the word 'womanism' to describe a kind of feminism that took note of the special difficulties facing black women. Some critics were disturbed by her shocking portrayal of the brutalisation of black women by black men. This led to charges of complicity with the racist **stereotype** of the sexually violent black male. Her first novel, *The Third Life of Grange Copeland* (1970), describes the appalling brutality of generations of the Copeland menfolk. While *Meridian* (1976) was a well-regarded novel of the civil rights movement, Walker became world-famous with the publication of the prizewinning *The Color Purple* (1982), the story of the separation and final reunion of Celie and her sister Nettie. The novel brought an intensification of the earlier criticisms of her male characters. While these men are frequently cruel in their treatment of women, Walker attempts to understand the source of their brutality and they are offered (but do not always take) their chances

for redemption. Other novels by Walker are the historical narrative *The Temple of My Familiar* (1989); *Possessing the Secret of Joy* (1992) concerning **clitoridectomy**, or female circumcision; and *By the Light of My Father's Smile* (1998), which explores the links between spirituality and sexuality. Walker has also made a significant contribution to literary criticism: *In Search of Our Mother's Gardens: Womanist Prose* (1983) did for black women writers what Elaine **Showalter**'s *A Literature of Their Own* achieved for white female novelists, retrieving them from a history of neglect and dismissal.

WALTER, NATASHA: JOURNALIST AND WRITER (1967–) Natasha Walter has written for *Vogue*, the *Independent* and the *Guardian*, and published her first book, *The New Feminism*, in 1998. Both the tone and the content of *The New Feminism*, as well as the marketing of its good-looking and articulate author, quickly instated Walter as the British counterpart of Naomi **Wolf**. Like Wolf, Walter insists that feminism must pause to appreciate the considerable gains it has made for women since the institution of the **second wave**. She argues that feminism has penetrated most bastions of power, and now operates from the inside, 'throwing up **feminist** breakthroughs in different and diverse

333

places'. Not surprisingly, therefore, Walter's work has attracted the same kind of criticism as Wolf's has done – she has been labelled part of the backlash, a **postfeminist** who doesn't now see any need for feminism. However, while calling for feminism to interfere less with aspects of women's private lives, such as **fashion** and sexuality, *The New Feminism* also asserts the necessity for continuing 'concrete political, social and economic reforms' on behalf of women. Nevertheless, the book's innate bias is encapsulated in Walter's epilogue, in which she appreciates the freedom of being able to sit alone in a London cafe, wearing a trouser-suit and paying for her coffee 'with my own money, that I earn from my own work'. While undeniably appealing, this self-portrait of a young, professional and single woman is indicative of the **liberal** philosophy of self-empowerment which informs her argument. Walter's most recent publication is a collection of essays entitled *On the Move: Feminism for a New Generation* (1999).

WARNER, MARINA: NOVELIST AND CULTURAL HISTORIAN (1946–) From the time of editing *Isis* (1967) to her role as Visiting Professor, Queen Mary & Westfield College, University of London, Marina Warner has been recognised in virtually every field of literature. Her fiction includes Booker shortlisted and Commonwealth Writer's Prize (Eurasia) winner *The Lost Father* (1987), *Indigo, or Mapping the Waters* (1992) and short stories such as *Wonder Tales: Six French Stories of Enchantment* (1996). Her non-fiction is equally well known, including *Monuments and Maidens:*

the Allegory of the Female Form (1985), *Joan of Arc: the Image of Female Heroism* (1981) and *Alone of All Her Sex: Myth and Cult of the Virgin Mary* (1985). She is arguably best known for her two books on folklore and fairytale, *From the Beast to the Blonde: On Fairy Tales and their Tellers* (1994), and *No Go the Bogeyman: Scaring, Lulling and Making Mock* (1998). In the latter she examines the ways in which we give voice to our fears in order to master them. She has also written essays and introductions, books and stories for children, opera libretti and film scripts. In 1994, she delivered the Reith Lectures for the BBC, published as *Managing Monsters: Six Myths of Our Time*.

WEST, REBECCA: JOURNALIST AND WRITER (1892–1983) Rebecca West was the pseudonym for Cicily Isabel Fairfield, and was a name she appropriated from a character in Ibsen's play *Romersholm*. She began her career as a regular contributor to the **feminist** weekly *The Freewoman*, which brought her to the attention of the writer H.G. Wells, with whom she had a ten-year relationship. Although West famously proclaimed in her essay 'Mr Chesterton in Hysterics' (1913) that 'I myself have never been able to find out what Feminism is; I only know that people call me a Feminist whenever I express sentiments that differentiate me from a doormat or a prostitute', her journalism, essays and book reviews all reveal a decidedly feminist point of view. Her first book, a study of the American writer Henry James, published in 1916, is an early work of feminist literary criticism, in which she condemns James for portraying women only as 'failed sexual beings'. West is now remembered primarily as a writer of fiction – she wrote eleven novels between 1918 and 1986 (the final two were published post-humously) – but her real interest came to lay in charting the political and social turmoil of Europe during and following the years of the Second World War. Her record of her travels in Yugoslavia, *Black Lamb and Grey Falcon*, were published in 1942, and her coverage of the Nuremberg war crime trials for the *New Yorker* was the inspiration for *The Meaning of Treason* (1947).

WILD ZONE Feminists have long argued that because our society and language are both **androcentric**, women have been relegated to the margins and forced to speak and write in modes that are not their own. In her essay 'Feminist Criticism in the Wilderness' (1981), the American literary scholar Elaine **Showalter** draws on the work of the cultural anthropologist Edward Ardner to formulate the concept of the 'wild zone'; a conceptual space into which fall those areas of female experience which do not lie within the bound-aries of the dominant cultural paradigm. Showalter argues that some feminist critics, such as the **French feminists**, focus exclusively on the wild zone in order to make it 'the theoretic base of women's **difference**'. Hence, it corresponds to the Kristevan notion of the **semiotic**, or **Cixous**'s 'feminine' language. Although she is not explicit on the matter, Showalter appears to be somewhat suspicious of this, claiming

that, while the **utopian** elements in women's writing constitute an attempt to imagine the wild zone, it is not a place one *can* reach, except in **fantasy**. In reality, she asserts, women are writing from two literary traditions simultaneously: a mainstream male-dominated one and a hidden, muted tradition of female endeavour. What Showalter terms 'gynocentric' criti-cism would focus on both the muted *and* the mainstream aspects of the female literary tradition.

WILLIAMSON, JUDITH: JOURNALIST, FILM-MAKER, LECTURER IN CULTURAL STUDIES (1954–) Williamson's first book, *Decoding Advertisements* (1978), is still required reading for those wishing to understand how **advertising** works, particularly in relation to women as consumers and subjects. It began life as a graduate project at the University of California but its roots lay in her own early inability to reconcile the attraction she felt to 'feminised' **culture**, via ads and **women's magazines**, with her growing political consciousness. It draws upon the fields of psychology, semiotics, structuralism, art history and **feminist** theory to describe and analyse advertising as an **ideological** form. Williamson also pointed out the strategies of some advertisers in the seventies of appropriating and subverting certain images and ideas from 'Women's Lib' in order to serve their own **sexist** purposes. *Consuming Passions* (1986), a collection of essays and articles, focuses on aspects of popular culture, bringing a feminist perspective to bear on the wider issues of representation and sexual politics they evoke.

WILSON, ELIZABETH: WRITER, EDITOR, JOURNALIST, BROADCASTER, PROFESSOR OF SOCIAL STUDIES (1936–) The ideas expounded in Elizabeth Wilson's work have always been grounded in a personal search for meaning and **identity**, as well as her involvement in psychiatric social work, gay rights **activism** and **feminist** socialism. Her first book, *Women in the Welfare State* (1977), was followed by *Only Halfway to Paradise* (1980), a study of women in post-war Britain. Further works included an autobiography, *Mirror Writing* (1982), and she co-edited *Pornography and Feminism: the Case against Censorship* (1991). She explored the nature of women's experience in the urban environment in *Hallucinations: Life in the Post-Modern City* (1988) and *The Sphinx in the City* (1991), and the role played by **fashion** in the contemporary world in *Adorned in Dreams* (1985). A lifelong interest in style and dress also informs contributions to *Chic Thrills: A Fashion Reader* (1992) and the book of the BBC series *Through the Looking Glass*, co-written with Lou Taylor.

WITCH Midwives, women healers and 'wise women' were respected figures in so-called 'primitive' societies. In medieval Europe midwives had developed a sophisticated natural pharmacy of herbal medicines. However, as the practice of medicine became more institutionalised, women were systematically excluded. The *Malleaus Maleficarum*, a witch-hunter's guide of 1486, states that 'if a woman dare to cure without having studied, she is a witch and must die'. As women were not allowed to study medicine until towards the end of the nineteenth century, this was nothing more than an outright prohibition. An official strategy of persecution against witchcraft began in the sixteenth century, with any woman classified as deviant becoming vulnerable to torture and death. In *Gyn/Ecology*, Mary **Daly** speaks of this period as an 'atrocity' that aimed to 'purify' society of women who lived outside **patriarchal** control, such as **spinsters** and widows. In a modern context, however, the term has lost much of its sinister associations. The practice of 'wicca', a religion which claims to uphold the principle of female power, is accepted, and in the area of **feminist** theory, too, the witch has become a heroic figure of female revolt, as in Hélène **Cixous**'s and Catherine Clément's essay 'The Guilty One', in which the 'sorceress . . . converts the unlivable space of a stifling Christianity'.

WITTIG, MONIQUE: NOVELIST AND THEORIST (1935–) Wittig is the author of *Les Guérillères* (1969), *Lesbian Peoples: Material for a Dictionary* (1976), and *The Lesbian Body* (1886), **postmodernist** works which use experimental narrative strategies in order to formulate systems of signification through which a lesbian **subjectivity** can be expressed: in *Les Guérillères*, for example, Wittig tries to eliminate the **masculine** pronoun *il*, and to make the **feminine** form, *elle*, universal. In *The Straight Mind* (1992), Wittig argues for a materialist approach to women's **oppression**, which, she says, 'shows that what we take for the cause or origin of oppression is in fact only the mark imposed by the oppressor: the "myth of woman", plus its material effects and manifestations in the appropriated consciousness and bodies of women'. What 'woman' signifies in materialist terms must therefore be deconstructed, a task for which Wittig argues the lesbian subject is perfectly situated, since 'Lesbian is the only concept I know of which is beyond the categories of sex . . . , because the designated subject (lesbian) is not a woman, either economically, politically or **ideologically**. For what makes a woman is specific social relation to a man . . . a relation which lesbians escape by refusing to become or stay heterosexual.' For Wittig, therefore, lesbian subjectivity functions as a **utopian** strategy available to every woman, signifying the possibility of escaping **patriarchal** control on both the material and the ideological level.

WOLF, NAOMI: AMERICAN FEMINIST WRITER (1962–) Wolf's first book, *The Beauty Myth* (1990), opens with a conundrum: while women have gained immeasurably since the **feminist** movement of the late sixties onwards, paradoxically they have lost personally in relation to their bodies. In the public domain women have a voice, more rights, more power and more money than ever before. However, in the private domain women are pressurised to look like cadavers, their bodies shaped by a **patriarchal** agenda set by the media and **fashion** industry. Ironically, increasing numbers of women are suffering from **eating disorders** to conform to an etiolated, prepubescent image, while the largest growth in **cosmetic surgery** is breast enhancement. Wolf argues that this is 'the **beauty myth**', the cultural wing of a **backlash** against the rights women have secured. In her second book *Fire With Fire* (1993) Wolf controversially claims that it is women themselves who determine their political status and they need to replace the earlier **'victim' feminism** with what she calls 'power feminism'. Women need to adopt men's tactics and fight 'fire with fire' to gain political and economic power. The semi-autobiographical *Promiscuities* (1997) discusses women's sexuality within a patriarchal society.

WOLFF, JANET: SOCIOLOGIST Writing extensively on the sociology of **modernist** and **postmodernist** culture, Janet Wolff's work has influenced **feminist** thinking in different fields of research and practice, including art history, literature, photography and film. An underlying premise of her work is that **culture** does more than simply reflect existing social assumptions about **gender**. On the contrary, **cultural** practices at any given moment actively shape or constitute gender identities and social divisions. Thus, from a feminist perspective, art and writing can become legitimate arenas of cultural contestation and critique. In her much-cited 1990 publication *Feminine Sentences: Essays on Women and Culture*, Wolff developed her arguments across an impressive range of topics, from the nineteenth-century culture of separate spheres, to contemporary feminist politics of the body. Formerly Director of the Centre for Cultural Studies at the University of Leeds, Janet Wolff now lectures and teaches in the United States.

WOLLSTONECRAFT, MARY: FEMINIST THEORIST (1759–97) Often seen as the founder of modern feminism, Mary Wollstonecraft experienced an unsettled and unhappy childhood, and grew up needing to support herself financially. She tried most of the avenues then open to an educated middle-**class** woman: being a lady's companion, setting up a school, and working as a governess. At the same time, however, she was meeting radical theorists and publishing her first pamphlet, *Thoughts on the Education of Daughters* (1787), as well as her first novel, *Mary, A Fiction* (1788). Her *Original Stories from Real Life* (1788) were subsequently illustrated by William Blake. In 1791 she responded to Burke's *Reflections on the Revolution in France* (1790) with *A Vindication of the Rights of Men*, followed in 1792 by her *Vindication of the Rights of Woman*, which aimed largely at strengthening the moral and mental outlook of middle-class women.

Wollstonecraft was particularly keen to improve women's **education**, and to show them that 'elegance is inferior to virtue'. She wanted to stamp out all kinds of affectation, which she felt contemporary practices and conventions encouraged in women, to the exclusion of physical resilience and common sense. 'It is time to effect a revolution on female manners,' Wollstonecraft argued in the *Vindication*, '– time to restore them to their lost dignity – and make them, as part of the human species, labour by reforming themselves to reform the world.' The *Vindication* does not, as one might expect, suggest any major restructuring of women's roles in society: on the contrary, it assumes that most women will still want to be wives and mothers. Wollstonecraft's aims was to make them better citizens, which would then increase their chances of influencing society to their own and their children's good. Although it would be inaccurate to see the *Vindication* as the first **feminist** treatise, it has acquired that reputation through its author's fame and its own historical emergence during the time of the French Revolution. The *Vindication* remained out of print for much of the nineteenth century, but now occupies a key place in the evolution of modern feminism.

WOMEN ARTISTS SLIDE LIBRARY (WOMEN'S ART LIBRARY) During 1976 a group formed to establish a slide library of art by women where all were welcome to submit slides of their work. By 1981 the centre was formally established in London, and in addition to functioning as an archive for both contemporary and historical work, it also organised other events. These included the Women and Art Education conference in October 1982 and the exhibition 'Women and Textiles – Their Lives and Their Work' in November 1983. After changes of both name and location, the organisation is still in existence. It contains an extensive collection of 35mm slides, documentation, books, catalogues and archives on the work of women artists past and present, national and international. It also publishes *Make*, formerly known as *Women's Art Magazine*, and before that as the *Women Artists Slide Library Journal*.

Women's Art Library, Fulham

Place, Bishops Avenue, London SE6 6EW. http://www.womensart.org.uk

WOMEN'S LIBERATION The term first seems to have been used in 1969, although the idea was implicit in the identification of women as 'slaves' made by Mary Astell in 1700; later Sojourner **Truth** spoke of the inequality between black men and women, despite Negro emancipation in 1867. A century later white and black women were still seen as subordinate in the radical political movements against the Vietnam War and for the liberation of black people; it became apparent that women were going to have to liberate themselves. In 1969 the New York Radical **Feminists** announced an ongoing confrontation with men, recognising that the 'liberation of women' would not be welcomed without a struggle. In the same year the first manifesto of Women's Liberation was drawn up by the Redstockings (NY), and in the UK Bristol Women's Liberation was set up. Three years earlier Juliet **Mitchell** had written of the 'need for liberation', followed by other influential voices like that of Sheila Rowbotham. In 1970 the first National Women's Liberation conference was held in Ruskin College, Oxford. Subsequently the term was shortened to 'Women's Lib' by male-dominated **media** intent on trivialisation and mockery – it is still largely used in a derogatory manner.

WOMEN'S MAGAZINES The subject of countless discussions, articles, books and theses. Some **feminists** see magazines as reinforcing an **oppressive ideology**, in which unacceptable notions of sex, **class** and **racism** are promulgated, a form of 'opium' which breeds false consciousness and encourages unhealthy escapist fantasies and guilt over shortcomings in body image and **domestic** skills. Others, particularly cultural historians like Janice Winship, have focused on the **pleasure** they produce, as well as the problems they raise, identifying closely with the individual reader who participates in a 'female world' with the magazine as friend, confidante and adviser. In Britain, *The Lady's Magazine* (1770–1874) was followed by others reflecting Victorian preoccupations with domesticity and gendered labour. At the beginning of the 20th century editors initiated the chatty, 'cosy' relationship with readers particularly significant in the Second World War, when magazines like *Housewife* supported women now often in sole charge; informed citizenship was high on the agenda. Elements of this survived in high-circulation weeklies like *Woman* and *Woman's Own*, alongside fashion and fiction, until the introduction of titles like *Bella* and *Best* from Germany in the 1980s. American imports included *Good Housekeeping* (1922) and *Cosmopolitan* (1972): *Spare Rib* was launched in 1972 to provide an anti-capitalist feminist alternative for UK women.

WOMEN'S STUDIES Women's studies began to be developed in the academy from the 1960s onwards. The first British women's studies course was taught by Juliet **Mitchell** at the Anti-University in 1968–9, and the first full women's studies programme was launched at San Diego State University in 1970. The focus of women's studies is interdisciplinary, stretching across both the humanities and the sciences, and it seeks not only to bring a **feminist** academic perspective into existing university structures, but also to reform the curriculum in order to better reflect women's concerns and interests. In an essay written in the early years of women's studies, 'Toward a Woman-Centered University' (1975), Adrienne **Rich** argues that the **androcentric** nature of the university itself must change before women's studies can be seen as anything more than a 'fad', quite separate from the 'real', male-centred curriculum. She goes on to assert that women's studies should be taught in personal, anti-hierarchical style to allow women to 'discover and explore . . . [their] root connection with *all women*'. Other feminists are suspicious of keeping women's studies out on a pedagogical limb, and argue for more integrationist strategies, which include the use of the broader term '**gender studies**'.

WOOLF, VIRGINIA: AUTHOR (1882–1941) A distinguished British novelist and literary critic, part of the literary circle known as the Bloomsbury Group. Woolf began her career by writing reviews for the *Times Literary Supplement*. Along with the political journalist Leonard Woolf, whom she married in 1912, she founded the Hogarth Press in 1917. A principal exponent of **modernism**, Woolf's novels explores the limitations of conventional narrative, and attempt to formulate a form of female self-expression. It was not until the publication of *Jacob's Room* in 1922

that Woolf felt herself to be a true novelist: 'There's no doubt in my mind that I have found out how to begin (at 40) to say something in my own voice.' Other books include *Mrs Dalloway* (1925), *To the Lighthouse* (1927), *The Waves* (1931), *The Year* (1937) and *Between the Acts* (1941). Woolf was also an important **feminist** critic, formulating a modernist manifesto in 'Mr Bennett and Mrs Brown' (1923), and author of the classic text *A Room of One's Own* (1929), in which she explores the cultural and economic constraints that have hampered female creativity. One of her best-known proclamations included the need for a woman to have £500 and 'a room of one's own' if she is to write. Woolf's other significant work of feminist polemic is *Three Guineas* (1938), in which she attempted to define a distinctively female **identity** which would transcend boundaries of nationality and political alignments: 'As a woman I have no country. As a woman I want no country. As a woman my country is the whole world.' Recurring bouts of mental illness that had haunted Woolf since childhood resulted in her suicide by drowning in the River Ouse in March 1941.

WORKING-CLASS FEMINISM In the 1970s, a rise in the percentage of women over 25 in the workplace, and a similar rise in trade union membership and involvement in strike action paralleled the general feminisation of labour in the workplace as a whole. The movement evolved mainly from the activities of **feminists** in the trade unions working to obtain equal rights for women against the very real barriers erected by employers against female applicants and workers. In contrast to university-based feminism, working-class feminism is based in the workplace and the home, and is thus focused on more limited, but practical, goals. Equal pay, training, wider career choices, improved childcare and moves to contest sexual harassment are fundamental issues, and draw attention to the fact that women no longer simply work up to the point of **marriage** or giving birth. Although the **ideology** of working-class feminism is rooted in **socialist** and **radical** feminist thought, its attachment to the everyday practicalities of a working woman's life draws attention to class differences within the feminist movement. Sheila Rowbotham's work, such as *Women's Consciousness, Man's World* (1973) and *Dreams and Dilemma* (1983) explore the double oppression of working women, both at work and in the home. Working-class women have much less access to good jobs, health-care and **education** than middle-class women. Thus, this branch of feminism not only encourages feminist thought to confront the practical as well as the ideological issues of women's **oppression**; it also helps to highlight the diverse experiences of women with regard to ethnicity and **class**.

WURTZEL, ELIZABETH: WRITER (1967–) Elizabeth Wurtzel graduated from Harvard, and immediately embarked on a successful journalistic career. Her first book, the autobiographical *Prozac Nation*, was published in 1996, which records a history of depression, drug abuse and failed suicide attempts. More than a personal story, it sets its author up as the voice of a struggling and alienated generation of women, unsure of the benefits, if any, that feminism has brought them. Wurtzel followed this up with *Bitch: In Praise of Difficult Women* (1998), which asks the question: why is it that modern women want to be bad? The old idea of **feminine** virtue has thoroughly fallen from grace, and now putting out one's sexual energy for public consumption no longer makes you a bimbo – it makes you smart. Wurtzel aligns herself with the problematic feminism of other young women of her generation, such as Katie **Roiphe** and Rene **Denfeld**, in focusing on what she perceives to be the failures of feminism. Like them, she is also an astute manipulator of her own media image, evinced by the fact that glamorous photographs of her adorn the covers of both her books, with the result that she has gained an audience as much on the basis of how she looks as on what she says.

Y

YOUNG, IRIS MARION: PHILOSOPHER
(1949–) Professor of Public and International Affairs at the University of Pittsburgh, Young has published *Throwing Like a Girl* (1990), *Justice and the Politics of Difference* (1990), *Intersecting Voices: Dilemmas of Gender, Political Philosophy and Policy* (1997), and numerous articles, as well as editing collections of essays in **feminist** philosophy. After her earlier writings on embodiment, Young formulates an alternative to the liberal theory of distributive justice. While the liberal conception of rights assumes a conception of the public which excludes people not culturally identified with white European male norms, Young's theory resists the suppression of **difference**. She also rejects feminist theories of embodiment which retain an ideal of a shared **subjectivity** and unified desires over the basic opaqueness and asymmetry of subjects and their desires. Young exhibits a distinctive passion for the **postmodern** that finds the desire for community among the members of radical organisations dangerous. Young's vision of the good society is the differentiated, culturally plural network of contemporary urban life.

YOUTH CULTURE The **fashions**, music, language and behaviour of young people have constituted an object of academic study and media debate since the advent of wealthy teenagers in western nations after WWII. Academic studies tended to focus on young men. Much of the groundbreaking work in this field has emerged from the Centre for Contemporary Cultural Studies at the University of Birmingham. The scrutiny of punks, mods and rockers by writers such as Dick Hebdige in the 1970s made the terms 'youth **culture**' and 'subculture' virtually interchangeable. In the 1980s feminist writers such as Angela McRobbie challenged the definition of 'youth culture' as a public practice and brought the private rituals of young women and girls into the debate. The boundaries of youth culture, particularly as a commercial market, continue to expand down through secondary and primary school and up through young professionals entering their late twenties and early thirties, also known as 'middle youth'.

INDEX

343